Public History

Public History: A Textbook of Practice is a guide to the many challenges historians face while teaching, learning, and practicing public history. Historians can play a dynamic and essential role in contributing to public understanding of the past, and those who work in historic preservation, in museums and archives, in government agencies, as consultants, as oral historians, or who manage crowdsourcing projects need very specific skills. This book links theory and practice and provides students and practitioners with the tools to do public history in a wide range of settings. The text engages throughout with key issues such as public participation, digital tools and media, and the internationalization of public history.

Part I focuses on public history sources, and offers an overview of the creation, collection, management, and preservation of public history materials (archives, material culture, oral materials, or digital sources). Chapters cover sites and institutions such as archival repositories and museums, historic buildings and structures, and different practices such as collection management, preservation (archives, objects, sounds, moving images, buildings, sites, and landscape), oral history, and genealogy. Part II deals with the different ways in which public historians can produce historical narratives through different media (including exhibitions, film, writing, and digital tools). Part III explores the challenges and ethical issues that public historians encounter when working with different communities and institutions. Either in public history methods courses or as a resource for practicing public historians, this book lays the groundwork for making meaningful connections between historical sources and popular audiences.

Thomas Cauvin is Assistant Professor of History at the University of Louisiana, Lafayette.

Public History
A Textbook of Practice

Thomas Cauvin

NEW YORK AND LONDON

First published 2016
by Routledge
711 Third Avenue, New York, NY 10017

and by Routledge
2 Park Square, Milton Park, Abingdon, Oxon, OX14 4RN

Routledge is an imprint of the Taylor & Francis Group, an informa business

Library of Congress Cataloging in Publication Data
Names: Cauvin, Thomas, author.Title: Public history : a textbook of practice /
Thomas Cauvin.Description: New York : Routledge, 2016.Identifiers: LCCN
2015039262| ISBN 9780765645906 (hbk) | ISBN 9780765645913 (pbk) |
ISBN 9781315718255 (ebk)Subjects: LCSH: Public history--Textbooks. |
Public history. | Public historians.Classification: LCC D16.163 .C38 2016 |
DDC 907.2--dc23LC record available at http://lccn.loc.gov/2015039262

ISBN: 978-0-7656-4590-6 (hbk)
ISBN: 978-0-7656-4591-3 (pbk)
ISBN: 978-1-315-71825-5 (ebk)

Typeset in Goudy by
Servis Filmsetting Ltd, Stockport, Cheshire

To Sophie – forever my love, forever my inspiration.
To Angelo and Eirinn – forever in my heart. I live for you in all I do.

Contents

Figures

Foreword

When I was in graduate school, more decades ago than I am willing to admit, there was no textbook in the field of public history. In truth there was no field of public history as far as I knew at the time, but there was a field called "historical administration" – and I took one of the early graduate courses under that rubric. Over the decades that have followed, public history has emerged and flourished, and I have become a public historian. The field now boasts strong professional organizations in many nations, a new and growing international organization, an impressive body of literature addressing both theory and practice, scholarly journals, and an ever-growing array of undergraduate and graduate programs. Yet while there have been numerous efforts to address curriculum and training, pedagogical literature has been confined largely to volumes of collected essays, leaving unmet too long the need for a textbook, a single coherent volume that pulls together the theory and practice of this very complex field. Which gets us to this volume, taken on by a fearless and knowledgeable young public historian. Indeed Thomas Cauvin is the right person at the right time – a public historian who represents where the field is going rather than where it's been. While the field is still dominated by American practitioners and too many of us from the first generations, the future embraces differences in perspective and practice internationally and across generations, recognizing that one size does not really fit our dynamic field. Of French nationality, with a Ph.D. from the European University Institute in Florence, Italy, and a dissertation on Irish national museums, Thomas embodies the capacious field we see growing by leaps and bounds. While public history endured decades of denigration as an alternative career for those who couldn't make it in a tight job market, it is today a field eagerly pursued by young scholars such as Thomas who are attracted to its richness and complexity, the opportunity to engage with new audiences in ways that could not be predicted only a generation ago. As we flourish, textbooks such as this are critical, laying out the field, its complexities, and the career possibilities for the generations ahead. When Thomas told me he was writing this, I thought it was genius – he's the perfect author for a textbook for the future, for a field constantly changing and evolving, a field that will be shaped in ways I cannot imagine but Thomas and his contemporaries can.

Jim Gardner
The National Archives (U.S.)

Acknowledgments

I thank my family, my wife and children, for their love and support. I am a better person, and my book is a better book, because of them. I thank my parents, Marie-Claude and Guy Cauvin, for believing in me and for always encouraging me to pursue my dreams. And I thank my grandfather, Jacques Saillard, for his wisdom and truth.

I also thank my friends and colleagues from the Department of History, Geography, and Philosophy at the University of Louisiana at Lafayette. These past two years would have been harsher without the friendly and stimulating environment they provided.

My name only on the front cover hides a reality; I could not have authored this book without the feedback, comments, and advice of so many people. I must acknowledge two special people who were there from the beginning. The first one is the late Jannelle Warren-Findley, a wonderful friend and a great scholar. I truly can say that without her, this book probably would never have been written. Jann should have been in charge of this book, but unfortunately due to illness, she did not have the strength to begin such a project. Upon her recommendation, the publisher contacted me to write this book. Jann believed in me, and for that, I will always be grateful. Also at the beginning was Serge Noiret, who introduced me to the debates and practices in public history. For that also, I will always be grateful.

I also thank Jim Gardner for helping me for many years, and for accepting my invitation to write this book's foreword. I also thank – and apologize for the additional work I gave them – my friends and colleagues who read (sometimes several times) the 13 chapters of this book. I salute the following book reviewers for devoting their time and effort:

Serge Noiret (European University Institute), Jim Gardner (National Archives and Records Administration), Tammy Gordon (North Carolina State University), Rebecca Conard (Middle Tennessee State University), Chuck Arning (National Park Service), Jean-Pierre Morin (Aboriginal Affairs and Northern Development Canada), Arnita Jones (American University), Anna Adamek (Canada Science And Technology Museum), John Troutman (University of Louisiana at Lafayette), Michael Martin (Center for Louisiana Studies, University of Louisiana at Lafayette), Mark Tebeau (Arizona State University), David Dean (Carleton University), Jerome De Groot (Manchester University), Melissa Bingmann (West Virginia University), Alix Green (University of Central Lancashire), Ciaran O'Neill (Trinity College Dublin), Claire Hayward (Kingston University), Sheila Brennan (George Mason University, Center for History and New Media), Steven Lubar (Brown University), Jeff D. Corrigan (State Historical Society of Missouri), Constance B. Schulz (University of South Carolina), Paul Knevel (University of Amsterdam), Cathy Stanton (Tufts University), Courtney Ann Neaveill (Free University Berlin), Hope Shannon (Loyola University Chicago), and Ruth Foote (University of Louisiana at Lafayette).

I also thank all of those who have helped me in my quest for information, images, and materials: Bob Karachuk (Association for Documentary Editing), Liz Ševčenko (Columbia University), Philip Cantelon (Historical Research Associates), Simon Prince (Canterbury Christ Church University), Robert Townsend (American Academy of Arts & Sciences), John Dichtl (American Association for State and Local History), Sheila Brennan and Sharon Leon (George Mason University, Center for History and New Media), Tom Dawson (University of St Andrews), Dan Kerr (American University), Jean-Pierre Morin (Aboriginal Affairs and Northern Development Canada), Li Na (Chongqing University), Christian Fontenot (University of Louisiana at Lafayette), Jon Hunner (New Mexico State University), Anna Adamek (Canada Science and Technology Museum), Michelle Moon (Peabody Essex Museum), Cathy Stanton (Tufts University), Randy Bergstrom (University of California at Santa Barbara), Stephanie Rowe (National Council on Public History), Morgen Young (Alder, LLC), Natalie Zemon-Davis (University of Toronto), Tim Causer (University College London), Sharon Macdonald (University of York), Eric Scott (Levine Museum of the New South), Martina Christmeier (Dokumentationszentrum Reichsparteitagsgelände), Ramses Delafontaine (Ghent University), Rebecca Onion (Slate. com), Jean-Sebastien Cluzel (Université Paris-Sorbonne), William Thomas, Patrick Jones, and Jacob K. Friefeld (University of Nebraska-Lincoln), Suzanne Campbell (Angelo State University), Sheilley Bernstein (Brooklyn Museum), Michael Wagenen (Georgia Southern University), Marianne Martin (Colonial Williamsburg), Marie-Pierre Besnard (Université de Caen), Mark Carnes (Reacting to the Past), Mark Souther (Cleveland State University), and Troy Reeves (UW-Madison Archives).

And for making this book a reality, I thank Steven Drummond (M.E. Sharpe Publishing), Kimberly Guinta, and Margo Irvin and Dan Finaldi (Routledge).

Abbreviations

AAM	American Alliance of Museums
AASLH	American Association for State and Local History
ACH	Association for Computers in the Humanities
ACHP	Advisory Council on Historic Preservation
ACPH	Australian Council of Professional Historians
ADE	Association for Documentary Editing
ADHO	Alliance of Digital Humanities Associations
AHA	American Historical Association
AHRC	Arts and Humanities Research Council
AIC	American Institute for Conservation of Historic and Artistic Works
ALLC	Association for Literary and Linguistic Computing
BBC	British Broadcasting Corporation
B.C.E.	Before Common Era
CAD	Computer-Assisted Design
C.E.	Common Era
CERCLA	Comprehensive Environmental Response, Compensation and Liability Act
CHNM	Center for History and New Media
CHS	Certified Historic Structure
CLAGS	Center for Lesbian and Gay Studies
CLG	Certified Local Governments
CRM	Cultural Resource Management
CW	Colonial Williamsburg
CWM	Canadian War Museum
DDA	Downtown Development Authorities
DDE	Digital Documentary Edition
EAD	Encoded Archival Description
EHPS	European Historical Primary Sources
GIS	Geographic Information Systems
GPMP	Guantánamo Public Memory Project
HABS	Historic American Buildings Survey
HAER	Historic American Engineering Record
HSR	Historic Structure Report
HTML	HyperText Markup Language
HTR	Healing Through Remembering
ICOMOS	International Council on Monuments and Sites
IDA	International Documentary Association

IDTR	Institute for Dark Tourism Research
IFLA	International Federation of Landscape Architects
IFPH	International Federation for Public History
IRB	Institutional Review Boards
LGBT	Lesbian, Gay, Bisexual, and Transgender
NAGARA	National Association of Government Archives and Records Administrators
NAGPRA	Native American Graves Protection and Repatriation Act
NAPC	National Alliance of Preservation Commissions
NARA	National Archives and Records Administration
NASA	National Aeronautics and Space Administration
NCPH	National Council of Public History
NCPTT	National Center for Preservation Training and Technology
NHL	National Historic Landmarks
NHPA	National Historic Preservation Act
NHPC	National Historical Publications Commission
NHWM	National Women History Museum
NMAH	National Museum of American History
NMAI	National Museum of the American Indian
NPS	National Park Service
NRHP	National Register of Historic Places
NTHP	National Trust for Historic Preservation
OAH	Organization of American Historians
OCLC	Online Computer Library Center
OHA	Oral History Association
PWD	Papers of War Department
RDM	Rich Digital Master
RITC	Rehabilitation Investment Tax Credit
RTTP	Reacting To The Past
SAA	Society of American Archivists
SARA	Superfunds Amendments and Reauthorization
SCAPE	Scottish Coastal Archaeology and the Problem of Erosion
SHFG	Society for History in the Federal Government
SHPO	State Historic Preservation Officer
TDR	Trusted Digital Repository
TEI	Text Encoding Initiative
THATCamp	Technology and the Humanities Camp
TRCC	Truth and Reconciliation Commission of Canada
UNESCO	United Nations Educational, Scientific and Cultural Organization
URL	Uniform Resource Locator
USHMM	United States Holocaust Memorial Museum
USIP	United States Institute for Peace
VHSI	Visual History Summer Institute
XML	Extensible Markup Language

Introduction
Historians' Public Roles and Practices

The past is a very popular topic of discussion. Marks of popular interest take various shapes, such as visits to museums and historic sites, historical books, magazines, websites, movies and documentaries, festivals, commemorations, genealogy, and many other fields. In 1998, Robert Rosenzweig and David Thelen conducted a survey on the presence of the past in American everyday life (1998). One reason for the popular interest in the past has been, according to them, that people turn to the past "as a way of grappling with profound questions about how to live" (1998, 18). The past can help us interpret who we are and why we do things. We use the past to shape our identities, but for other purposes as well, such as, for instance, a source of entertainment. The past has been one of the main sources of games (e.g., *Trivial Pursuit*) and television quiz shows (e.g., *Jeopardy*; *Are You Smarter than a Fifth Grader?*). Given this popular interest in the past, one might assume that the public widely acknowledges the authority and expertise of historians.

Actually, the situation is quite different. For instance, in a post on the 2013 commemoration of the March on Washington and Martin Luther King's speech in August 1963, Jason Steinhauer regretted "the absence of any historians, public or academic, from the day's list of speakers" (2013). Steinhauer makes a powerful argument and distinguishes between the numerous and vibrant examples of public "remembrances" and the absence of historical reflection. People may be interested in the past, but they do not necessarily trust professionally trained historians.

The misunderstanding comes from the distinction between history – as an interpretation of the past based on critical analysis of primary sources – and the past as built on multiple sources such as oral traditions, popular culture, and commemorations that fulfill diverse social and political needs. Rosenzweig and Thelen argued that people "preferred constructing their own versions of the past to digesting those prepared by others" (1998, 178). Certainly, historians serve a role in teaching and training students, but their role outside the classroom seems more limited. Historians may be seen – and more importantly may see themselves – as experts, but we must face the truth that representations and interpretations of the past in public often come from non-historians.[1] For instance, millions of people study their family history through genealogy software and websites with which historians do not collaborate. The point here is not to discuss the historical validity of these activities, but to argue that historians may be completely absent from the most popular representations of the past. Why is this so and why should we be concerned?

The absence of historians from public debates and public representations of the past is purposefully overstated – a large number of historians have public activities – but it remains true that their number is not proportional to public interest in the past. This discrepancy raises questions not only about the role of historians in our societies, but also about the sort of history we have been proposing to our audiences. The limited links between trained historians and the public partly come from historians themselves. Since the 19th century, some professional historians have seen themselves as entirely devoted to the discipline, working merely for the sake of history. On the one hand, this devotion allowed the creation of more professional practices and organizations. On the other hand, this isolation from popular audiences – with internal peer-reviewed systems, academic conferences, and academic journal publications – meant a limited presence in public debates. Although this isolation was, at first, mostly seen as providing a safe place to search for objectivity, it has increasingly become the symbol of historians' limited impact and contribution to our modern societies (Wiener 2004).

This textbook aims first to re-assert the need for history – and historians. People should not forget that the past is reached through sources and interpretation. In the *Introduction to Public History* that she edited in 1986, Barbara Howe reminded us that "the validity of any history rests upon the historian's ability to evaluate evidence from the past and to put it in a comprehensible narrative" (Howe and Kemp 1986, 1). Critical analysis and contextualization of sources distinguish history narratives from mere opinions. Because representations and interpretations of the past are public and popular does not mean that they should be devoid of historical understanding. This is particularly important in a context in which, thanks to the spread of new media, information is, today more than ever, easily – and without intermediaries – available to the public.

This textbook also aims to show how historians can participate in public understanding of the past. Historians have a role to play, but this role comes with a set of obligations. Historians should accept that they do not work for the sake of history only, to advance historical research, but also for and with others. As public historian Patricia Mooney-Melvin puts it, "All historians should remember that they are citizens as well as scholars and they possess some responsibility to the larger civic community" (2006, 17). Through an introduction to public history practice, the textbook contributes to the re-assessment of the traditional role for historians as well as their relations with the multitude of actors involved in the production of historical narratives.

The Role of Historian: A Short History

An introduction to public history must primarily deal with the changing definitions of the historian's role. While the public history movement in the United States emerged during the 1970s, historians' public role and activity are much older. Historian Ronald Grele – who has written several studies on the links between oral and public history – rightly points out that "from its earliest times, the study of history has been a public act, although different historians at different times have had different publics" (1981, 41). It is, therefore, important to explore the history of historians' role in the public space.

Professional Historians

The Rise of Scientific History in the Late 19th and Early 20th Centuries

Although Herodotus in Ancient Greece can be considered the father of historical methodology, scientific and professional history did not emerge in Europe until the second half of the 19th century (Porciani and Lutz 2010). Rigor and scientific methodology were first introduced in Germany. As Peter Novick wrote in his history of the American historical profession, "the United States remained (in the 1880s) a net importer of ideas" (1988, 21). The first honorary member of the American Historical Association (AHA), Leopold von Ranke was an inspirational model for 19th century American historians. The German historian was, with other French scholars like Charles Victor Langlois and Charles Seignobos, at the origin of a new quest for objectivity and professional methodology.

The search for historical objectivity and professional methodology relied on historicism, primary sources, and factual analysis. Historicism relies on historical awareness, in other words, on the faculty to comprehend the difference between the present and the past. Professional history also resulted from a "scientific" methodology to recover facts and avoid opinions. Langlois and Seignobos argued, in their *Introduction aux études historiques*, that "historical construction has ... to be performed with an incoherent mass of minute facts, with detailed knowledge reduced as it were to a powder" (Novick 1988, 37). Professional history was utterly fact-oriented. Historians' subjectivity had to be suppressed.

Primary sources emerged as the foundational elements of the new scientific history. The need to focus on primary documents had two direct consequences. In order to access and use primary sources, historians became increasingly interested in preservation. New professional historians encouraged – and sometimes participated in – the creation of local, state, and national archives. The other consequence was the need for appropriate training. Critical analysis of sources was necessary to determine the reliability of the document. Most American research universities adopted the German model of the seminar in the late 19th century. Universities introduced students to techniques for "ferreting out and verifying the historical fact; palaeography, numismatics, epigraphy, sphragistics, and many more" (Novick 1988, 23).[2]

The rise of scientific history also induced the professionalization and institutionalization of the discipline. Previously part of the American Social Sciences Association (ASSA), historians could then join the AHA. Founded in 1884, the AHA became the symbol of the institutionalization of history in the United States. Robert Townsend explains in his history of the history profession in the United States that the number of historians employed in academia increased by 10 percent every year from 1885 to 1910 (2013, 14). The new professional academic historian – holding a PhD, teaching in universities, and writing factual history – became dominant in the late 19th and early 20th centuries. Academic historians were the model of the new professional history, and the adoption of scientific practices had important consequences for the relations between historians and their audiences.

Historians in Ivory Towers

The concept of the "ivory tower" was developed in the 19th century and referred to a supposedly "disconnected world of intellectuals" (Suny 2012). Associated with a pejorative description of academic elites, the term ivory tower implies that academic scholars – among them historians – have lost sight of popular audiences. It is true that some aspects of the professionalization of history have affected the relationship between historians and their audiences. Historians' capacity to communicate with each other, with other scholars, and ultimately with public audiences was affected by the specialization of the discipline. The amount of work – under the common joke, a scientific historian must be ready to cross oceans to check a comma in an archive – requested by the new scientific methodology triggered specialization. As Townsend writes, from the late 1930s, "the various professions of history set off on distinct trajectories – firming up their own networks and identities in increasing isolation from each other, while embarking on separate processes of specialization and technical refinement of their own." He concludes that "after 1940 it is hard to find anyone actively trying to articulate a common vision of the historical enterprise that embraced all areas of work in the discipline" (Townsend 2013, 181). The process of specialization in sub-fields had an impact on the overall process of historical production.

By the early 20th century, academic historians published their PhD as original pieces of history. Historical journals became crucial actors of dissemination. French historians Gabriel Monod and Gustave Fagniez created the *Revue Historique* (*Historical Review*) in 1876. The *American Historical Review* was founded in 1895 and was soon associated with the AHA. Academic audiences became the natural audience for professional historians. In order to convince their peers, professional historians also adopted a very specific writing style.

Two prerequisites of any scientific knowledge were, first, that scholars must prove their assertions, and second, that readers must be able to build upon the published results. Professional history writing, therefore, resulted in the multiplication of footnotes as evidence and sources. In addition to the format, the contents changed as well. A benchmark of scientific history was to suppress any subjective and partisan comment. Scientific history was based on facts. As a result, academic historians' writing tended to be extremely factual, sophisticated, and dry. Professional historians celebrated the factual historical narrative as the "instrument of liberation from the suffocating temperature and humidity of overarching systems" (Novick 1988, 43). The high specialization of the research topics, the peer-review systems, and the fact-based writing style contributed to the creation and development of a gap between professional historians and popular audiences.

The gap between professional historians and popular audiences has recently been the subject of public discussion. In a recent article, Jonathan Zimmerman, Professor of History at New York University, invited historians to come out of the ivory tower. He wrote "Historians, The Public Needs You! But you need the public, too. Don't turn away from it, as so many of us have been taught to do. The job you save may be your student's. Or your own" (2014). To some extent, this call results from the previously mentioned professionalization of history. However, Zimmerman's vibrant call forgets that many other historians, with non-academic jobs, have had a public role in the 20th century.

Diversity of Public Profiles

The emerging gap between some professional historians and popular non-academic audiences in the late 19th and early 20th centuries had many exceptions. Thinking that historians have acquired public roles only recently is misleading. The concept of the ivory tower is itself somehow overstated. In a recent blog post on the historical relations between the AHA and public historians, Robert Townsend demonstrates the long history of bridges between professional historians and non-academic audiences (2015). He explains that "even some of the more traditional academics, such as J. Franklin Jameson at Chicago and Lucy Salmon at Vassar, were actively promoting documentary editing, historical societies, and other activities now widely recognized as public history" (Townsend 2015). Townsend demonstrates that the isolation of professional historians in ivory towers was actually much more complex. For instance, he shows that the disconnection between professional historians and public institutions also came from the fact that the latter – such as archives and historical societies – developed new professional practices and standards "in ways that even the most attentive scholars found difficult to track or understand." As a result, "the academics were increasingly shut out of conversations that were growing esoteric in their own ways" (Townsend 2015).

Another misconception is the idea that historians' public practices only developed in the last three or four decades. Chris Hilliard notes in his history of public history in New Zealand that there has been a "prehistory of public history," in other words, something we now call public history but that was simply called history before (2001). Likewise Ian Tyrrell underlines about the United States, "scholars tend to see public history as something new" but "the roots run much deeper ... historians have long addressed public issues" (2005, 154). In her article on the pragmatic roots of public history, Rebecca Conard usefully reminds us of the pioneer historians in public activities. Those historians belonged to two main fields: local history and government policy (Conard 2015).

Local Historians

One main common point between historians working outside academic circles before the 1970s was their interest in local history and local institutions. Ronald Grele explains that "prior to the emergence of public history, it was the local history movement which offered the most thoroughgoing alternative to the historical work done in the academy" (1981, 43). The local history movement partly developed in opposition to the academic institutionalization of history. While some academic historians lost track of popular audiences, local – academic or not – historians remained connected with local actors.

The creation of the American Association for State and Local History (AASLH) in 1940 was symbolic of the strength of local history. Local historians working in archives and historical societies greatly increased in number in the 1920s and 1930s. The creation of archives – and archival jobs for historians – was part of a wider growth of historically-related institutions.[3] The number of historical societies recognized by the AHA increased from 215 in 1905 to 375 in 1916 (Townsend 2013, 49). Archives and historical societies symbolized the rise of local history and the growing possibilities for historians to find jobs outside academia – as archivists, documentary editors, and curators in historical societies – in relation with popular audiences.[4]

Government, Military Historians, and the Concept of Applied History

In her book on Benjamin Schambaugh and the roots of public history, Rebecca Conard demonstrates how historical figures such as J. Franklin Jameson (at the Carnegie Institution of Washington), Herbert Friedenwald (at the Library of Congress), and Benjamin Schambaugh (at the State Historical Society of Iowa) embodied the utilitarian aspect of history and saw "the value of using history to explain contemporary issues, to make history relevant to the present" (2002, 10). This trend materialized in what Schambaugh called "applied history." He stated in 1909: "I do not know that the phrase 'Applied History' is one that has thus far been employed by students of history and politics ... But I believe that the time has come when it can be used with both propriety and profit" (Conard 2002, 33).[5] Schambaugh linked history with political applications and public policy. It was actually representative of some historians' involvement in policymaking in North America and Europe before World War II.

The links between historians and politics are very old.[6] Historians have worked for or advised various governmental agencies for generations. The U.S. Department of Agriculture established a history office in 1916. Likewise, Samuel B. Harding from Indiana University was hired to work for the Committee on Public Information during World War I. Along with the rise of federal political power in the 1930s, historians' involvement in the federal government became particularly visible during the New Deal. The U.S. government was looking for expertise to stimulate the economy in every field. This gave birth to governmental interest in historic preservation and the management of National Parks. Created in 1916, the National Park Service (NPS) obtained full responsibility for national historic sites, parks, and memorials in 1933. This resulted in an unprecedented need for trained historians who had to locate, identify, evaluate, and research possible historic sites. The creation of the National Trust for Historic Preservation in 1949 and the National Historic Preservation Act in 1966 provided for an Advisory Council on Historic Preservation to coordinate state, local, and federal effort (Jones 1999, 23). Although the links between historians and the federal government tended to decrease after the 1960s, they never disappeared, as attested by the creation of the Society for History in the Federal Government in 1979. This involvement in policymaking was not specific to the United States. In the United Kingdom, government departments created historical sections and programs of official histories right after World War II (Beck 2006).

Likewise, many historians have worked within military organizations. In the United States, Maj. Gen. Henry W. Halleck – commander of the Union Army – initiated a project to collect and publish Civil War military records in 1863 (Reuss 1986, 294). As Rebecca Conard explains, World War I transformed isolated military history initiatives "into a more serious effort to document various aspects of the war as it was taking place" (2002, 149–150). In the United Kingdom, historian Alix Green demonstrates how official war histories were the foundation for the British experiment in history in government (2015b).

Historians under Contract

Another aspect of applied history was, according to Schambaugh, about historians working under contract. The emergence of historians in the private sector took place during World War II. For instance, in 1943 Firestone hired a historian (William D. Overman) to preserve and archive the papers of Harvey Firestone and his sons. Professionally staffed archives in corporate sectors developed in the 1950s with historians working for Coca-Cola, Bank of America, Texaco, Ford Motor Company, and many others (Conard 2002, 161).

In addition to corporate archives, wealthy sponsors also contributed to the creation of historic places. In 1929, Henry Ford opened a museum in Dearborn, Michigan, "celebrating the triumphs of industrial capitalism" as well as "Greenfield Village, an outdoor assemblage of restored historic buildings replete with Americana celebrating the folkways that industrial capitalism was erasing." Similarly, in the 1930s John D. Rockefeller Jr. "invested nearly $80 million in restoring, researching, and reconstructing buildings in Williamsburg, Virginia, to re-create a tidied-up version of the village as it appeared circa 1790" (Conard 2002, 161). Those sites proposed new opportunities for historians to work outside academia.

By the 1960s, academic historians working in universities were, therefore, only one category of historians, although they dominated historical organizations. Many historians were working outside of academia in archives, historical societies, national parks, museums, federal government agencies, or in corporate societies. Historians working outside academia had their own associations organized by fields. In addition to the AHA, the American Association of Museums (AAM), the Society of American Archivists (SAA), and the AASLH were created in 1906, 1936, and 1940 respectively. These activities did not go unnoticed within academic circles. Some universities established training programs that focused on specialized historical practices. For instance, the history department at the American University in Washington, DC created a program in archival administration in 1939 (Conard 2002, 163). However, there was no agreed-upon common denominator for historians working outside the academy. As Arnita Jones highlights in an article on the history of public history:

> there were few opportunities to discuss how these efforts did or did not fit within the graduate curriculum in history departments or how a younger generation could learn to use historical analysis as an important tool for solving problems outside higher education institutions.
>
> (1999, 24)

It was in this context of a general need to create cohesion among historians working outside universities that the public history movement emerged.

The Emergence of a Public History Movement

Local History, Social Engagement, and Activism

Local and public history practices shared common roots (Kyvig and Marty 2010; Kammen 1987). For most of the 20th century, public practices of history mostly came from local history. Both public and local history practices felt the consequence of the new professional history in the late 19th century. In his history of American historiography, Ian Tyrrell demonstrates that, as a consequence of the rise of scientific history, academic historians have gradually attempted to link local events to the production of national history (2005, 208). While national history became increasingly important for academic historians, local historians, according to academic standards, became associated with amateurism. For most of the 20th century, local history remained in the field of the public practice of history and accordingly disconnected from academic works. Due to its connection with non-academic audiences, public history practices have had privileged relations with local history.

New approaches and new fields emerged in history and other social sciences in the 1950s and 1960s. Minority rights and discrimination issues had an impact on some historians. The development of black history and feminist history shed light on the links between historians and contemporary activism. In other words, history could be used to address injustice.[7] More generally, the rise of social history in the 1960s played a major role in the redefinition of the purposes and practices of historians. The Annales School in France was symbolic of a move from political to social and later cultural history.

One of the main consequences of the rise of social history was a new interest in ordinary people. Oral history was perhaps the most symbolic example of the interest in ordinary people. Studs Terkel in the United States and Alessandro Portelli and Luisa Passerini in Italy brought to light the experiences of people historians had ignored. In the 1960s, the new interest in ordinary people, and the move away from the elite-oriented national history, encouraged the development of both local and public practices. This focus on the local was adopted by the Micro-History movement in Europe. Micro-historians reduced the scale of their research to local contexts, communities, families, and other networks. As a consequence of this new interest in local history and ordinary people, historians' interest in oral history rose. In the 1980s, Alessandro Portelli analyzed collective memories through oral testimonies gathered in the community of steelworkers in Terni, Italy (1985). Oral history provided a way to study, convey, and work with local audiences and is now a well-developed field of history (Sheftel and Zembrzycki 2013). The bottom-up interpretation resulted in new investigation and the creation of new primary sources for historians and public historians. Oral history is symbolic of the way historians have adopted a micro-history approach to local pasts. In this context of re-evaluation of the relations between local, national, and international frameworks, the public history movement emerged.

Until recently, the term public history was unfamiliar in Britain (Boniface 1995). It does not mean that historians did not have any public activities. Instead of public history, British historians have preferred using terms like heritage or people's history. Comparing historical practice in the United States and Britain, Ian Tyrrell stresses that "the British tradition facilitated popular and working class recording of their own historical experiences and involved important contributions to this process by trade unions, workers' education, and local history groups" (2005, 157). The creation of the History Workshop movement by Raphael Samuel at Ruskin College (Oxford, England) in 1967 symbolized this British tradition. The History Workshop movement was a process of democratization of history through participation-led seminars that involved large non-academic audiences (History Workshop Online 2012). Some other experimental projects developed in Europe. For example, in 1969, students and teachers from the University of Leuven (Belgium) organized "Clio 70," which aimed to spread historical narratives outside schools to broad audiences through new media (Zelis 2013, 157). As a result, the group created the Fonderie (Museum of Industry and Labor for the Brussels Region) in 1980.

In the United States, the New Left and its attacks on the alliances between historians and the federal government contributed to a new focus on ordinary people in the 1960s. The New Left's main criticism was not about the use and application of history by policy-makers, but rather about the fact that "historians had become prisoners of a very political and conservative view of the world" (Tyrrell 2005, 246). The New Left supported activism in favor of feminism, civil rights, African American culture, and trade unions.

Historians' new interest in people's history coincided with a general increase in public access to culture and education. Types of audiences changed after World War II. Better-educated citizens, the rise of the middle class, and increased vacation time encouraged access to and consumption of historical production. The development of transportation facilities and road networks and the increasing number of cars helped the public access historic sites and historical institutions. For instance, visitors to national parks in the United States increased from 6 million in 1942 to 33 million in 1950, to 72 million in 1960 (Meringolo 2012, 164). The economic and social context brought about new opportunities for historians to work outside the academy.

This was particularly important due to a job crisis in American universities. Alongside the 1970s economic crisis, the shortage of tenure-track jobs led many doctoral programs to decrease the number of students. There were too many historians for too few jobs in universities. By 1977, the crisis had reached such a level that major historical institutions established programs and committees to search for new answers – and hopefully new opportunities – for historians. The National Coordinating Committee for the Promotion of History was set up in 1977. Focusing on career issues, the Committee worked at building bridges between universities and the non-academic world. Public history practice came to be seen as one solution.

The Public History Movement in the United States

Some programs opened in the United States during the 1970s to offer new specific training. For instance, Auburn University opened an Archival Training program in 1972, and Middle-Tennessee State University opened a Historic Preservation program in 1973. However, those programs provided neither history nor public history training. Although historians' public practices were not new and not specific to the United States – Raphael Samuel had been operating the History Workshop for almost a decade – the rise of the public history movement challenged the overall definition and conception of doing history in public. Thinking back to the origins of the movement, Barbara Howe was convinced that "something happened thereafter that created a new way for us to identify ourselves" (Howe and Kemp 1986, 9).

There is now quite a large amount of literature on the rise of the public history movement (Johnson 1999; Jones 1999). The term "public history" was first coined at the University of California at Santa Barbara (UCSB) by Robert Kelley in 1975 (Schulz 2006, 31). University professor, consultant, and expert witness for the state on matters related to water rights, Kelley was symbolic of the attempts to link academic and non-academic historians. With the help of G. Wesley Johnson, Kelley applied for a grant from the Rockefeller Foundation to build a program that would encourage the links between history and policy (Meringolo 2012, xvii). He perceived the program as, first of all, targeting positions in government offices and public policy. In order to do so, he explained that:

> the best method was to begin training small groups of graduate students in public history skills, imbuing them with the idea of a public rather than an academic career, and sending them out, one by one, to demonstrate their value by their work.
>
> (Conard 2002, 164)

The first graduate program in public history opened in 1976 at UCSB. In addition to the first university program, Wesley Johnson received a grant from the Arizona Humanities Council to organize the first of several conferences about public history (Johnson 1999, 168–169). The conferences organized between 1978 and 1980 led to the creation of the National Council on Public History (NCPH), which would become the main association for public historians in the United States. Wesley also used the Rockefeller Foundation grant as well as a National Endowment for the Humanities to publish the first edition of *The Public Historian* in 1978, a journal entirely devoted to public history. By the early 1980s, the public history movement had new university programs, a brand new organization, an annual conference, and a journal.

The objectives of the public history movement were threefold. First, it intended to provide historians working outside the academy a forum to discuss the specificity of their activities. This purpose partly explains the lack of a strict definition for public history that initially served to gather a broad range of practitioners. The movement also aimed at offering university training for history students who wished to work outside the academy. Finally, the movement pressed for the recognition of the status of public historian (Howe and Kemp 1986, 9).

The movement rapidly spread to the United States and beyond. Canada, Australia, and New Zealand were the first countries outside the United States where the public history movement developed. For instance, as early as 1983, the fifth annual meeting of the NCPH was held in Waterloo, Canada. In September 1982, the Erasmus University in Rotterdam, in collaboration with the British Social Science Research Council, organized a conference on Applied Historical Studies (Knevel 2009). In 1992, the Australian Professional Historians' Association launched the *Public History Review* that would become, with *The Public Historian*, one of the two main journals in the field.

After the 1982 conference in Rotterdam, Wesley Johnson undertook a tour of Europe to explain public history and to evaluate the connection with existing history programs. Johnson noticed the Istituto per la Scienza dell' Amministrazione Pubblica in Italy that was directed by historians to train practicing public servants for administrative responsibilities. Likewise, the Istituto Storico della Resistenza di Reggio Emilia (Institute for the History of the Resistance in Emilia), founded in 1965, has participated in multiple public projects. In spite of evidence of public practices, no specific training about public history emerged in Europe.

Public History: Approaches and Definitions

Defining Public History: A Difficult Task

From its creation in the 1970s, the movement in the United States went through intense debates and criticisms regarding the definition of public history. As Ludmilla Jordanova acknowledges in her book on historical practices, "we should concede from the outset that 'public' is a difficult term" (2000, 141). The definitions of the term "public" have varied in time and place. For more than three decades, conferences and forums about public history have attempted to provide a clear and shared definition of the terms. Making the definitions even more complex, the translation of the term "public history" does not always make sense. For example, in France the term *histoire publique* could oppose a supposedly "private history" and might be rather associated with the study of the public space and public institutions.

It might help to go back to the origins of the terms. When he invented the term in the mid-1970s, Robert Kelley defined public history as history practiced outside the classroom. He explained that "public history refers to the employment of historians and historical method outside of academia" (1978, 16). At first, the public history movement was considered as a process to gather people who were not working in the academy but were nonetheless doing history. The historians who first presented themselves as public historians adopted a defensive, and anxious, tone (Conard 2002, 172). Kelley, Johnson, and other historians at the origins of the movement defined public history in opposition to what they perceived as a traditional academic and isolated history that ignored the public. They made clear they were historians, although not working in the academy. Public history was loosely gathering practitioners in many different fields who were defined by what they were not, namely working merely in the academy. We should not forget that one purpose of the movement was to give a common identity to historians who were working outside the academy and who did not have official status in the overall historical enterprise. The loose definition resulted from a focus on the common aspect shared by those practitioners. In other words, public history was practiced, but not easily defined. Proposing a strict definition of public history might have been initially counter-productive.

Another drawback of the initial definition of public history as being history practiced outside the classroom resulted in a too strict division between public and academic historians. The differentiation between academic and public historians had some sense in the

1970s when the latter were in need of a common identity. However, in spite of specific public history practices, the opposition between academic and public historians may not be the best approach to the field. The frontier between academic and public historians is permeable. First, public historians are not second-rate historians. In order to explain "How Public History (is) Different From 'Regular' History," the website of the NCPH states that "in terms of intellectual approach, the theory and methodology of public history remain firmly in the discipline of history, and all good public history rests on sound scholarship" (NCPH 2015). Doing public history requires as much methodology as any other kind of historical practice. Second, when can one consider that a historian becomes a public historian? Should any historian having a weblog or being interviewed on television be considered a public historian? Likewise, how many historians live in an ivory tower, whose works are read by academics only? Joyce Appleby wonders whether we (historians) should not all become public historians (1997).

This last point is developed by Alix Green in her post on what she calls "academic citizens" (2015a, 2015b). She points out that "the act of definition is problematic, however, for more important reasons than semantics." She argues that any definition "sets 'public history' apart from 'history' in way that has never applied to other specializations, such as social, economic, Black or women's history" (2015a, 2015b). By defining public history in opposition – it is not practiced in university classrooms – to academic history, public historians always have to re-assert their professional standards and practices. Like Appleby in 1997, Green proposes to redefine the concept of academy and academic practices. She states that "as historians, we are connected and have responsibilities to many people: to our colleagues; to our students; to our networks and audiences, now increasingly global" (2015a, 2015b). Public history is, in this case, a reminder (some historians might have forgotten) to historians – who may or may not have jobs in university and research centers – that they have, as citizens of broad communities, duties toward many different actors.

While all historians may be, at one point or another, in contact with large and non-academic audiences, that does not mean that doing history in public does not require specific skills, approaches, and practices. We may all become public historians, but it requires training and an awareness of the challenges we can face while working in and for the public.

Historians and Popular Non-Academic Audiences

A recent trend among public historians is to stop focusing on what public history is and rather explain what public historians do. It helps shift from asking what public history is, to what public history wants, and therefore helps consider the various contexts in which historians practiced public history. Public history has at its core a consideration for popular non-academic audiences. Kelley encouraged "the employment of historians and historical method outside of academia" (1978, 16). Jordanova agrees, and writes that "public history is popular history – it is seen or read by large numbers of people and has mostly been designated for a mass audience" (2000, 141).

The survey undertaken by Robert Townsend and John Dichtl in 2008 (Figure I.1) shows a variety of hosting agencies and institutions for public historians. The breadth of the field "outside of academia" explains why we can find public historians in public sites such as museums, historical societies, governmental agencies, archives, libraries, historic buildings, newspapers, or park services. We may read, hear, and see them on television, in movies, on the radio, on the Internet and in every new medium. Public history does not imply a single public audience, however. One critical challenge for public historians is to be aware and to

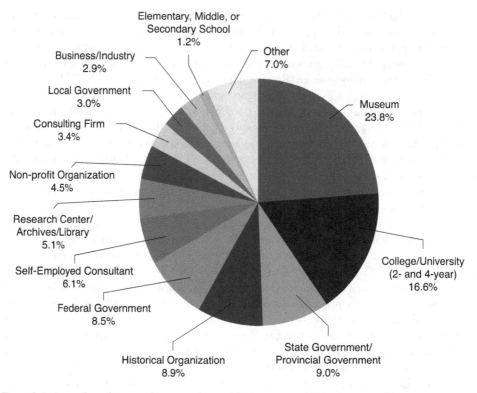

Elementary, Middle, or
Secondary School
1.2%

Business/Industry
2.9%

Local Government
3.0%

Consulting Firm
3.4%

Non-profit Organization
4.5%

Research Center/
Archives/Library
5.1%

Self-Employed Consultant
6.1%

Federal Government
8.5%

Other
7.0%

Museum
23.8%

College/University
(2- and 4-year)
16.6%

State Government/
Provincial Government
9.0%

Historical Organization
8.9%

Figure I.1 Area of employment for responding public historians, 2008. Courtesy of American
Historical Association/Robert Townsend.

take into account the variety of audiences they have to deal with. As public historian Nick
Sacco writes:

> public historians are teaching and communicating with audiences – just like academic
> teachers – but they frequently work with people of all ages, many of whom are not
> enrolled in a school and who do not engage in historical thinking on a daily basis.
>
> (2013)

Different audiences result in different knowledge, different interests, different interrogations, and different ways to learn.

Public or Applied History? The Uses of the Past

Coming from the debated definitions of the term "public," historians have been arguing
about the impact of working with a variety of non-academic audiences. Historians who,
for instance, design exhibits for museums may have to deal with a broad range of visitor
profiles such as families, school trips, tourists, scholars, military groups, and so on. But what
about historians who work in and for specific communities, in government agencies, or
private companies? Novick argues that, instead of public, most of what is done under the
name public history is in fact "private history," either in the service of political agencies,
private companies, or organizations with particular agendas (1988, 513). It is true that

some historians work with non-academic but very limited and particular audiences. Those historical practices position history as a service used by different audiences.

In *Introduction to Public History*, Barbara Howe regrets that "traditional historians have rarely confronted the issue of utility, they have dismissed it from their vocabulary as irrelevant or commercial" (Howe and Kemp 1986, 14). Public historians put great emphasis on the ways in which the public uses the past. The concept of usability is at the core of public history. This concept is not new and was supported in the early 20th century through applied history.

Applied history refers to the history applied to present issues, interrogations, audiences, actors, and policies. It is, therefore, problem-solving oriented. History can be applied to specific projects in which historians work as consultants for various clients and agencies. The purpose is then not necessarily to touch a public as broad as possible, but rather to apply historical methodology to the production of narratives for a corporate demand and/or more specific audiences.

We touch here upon the controversial activities of historians as entrepreneurs. The corporate use of history was one reason why Peter Novick is highly critical toward public history. He defines public history as seeking "to legitimize historical work designed for the purposes of particularist current constituencies." This definition of public history contrasts with the "noble dream" of what he presents as "the universalist ethos of scholarship" (Novick 1988, 471–472, 510). There is even greater criticism of historians working for private companies, such as Historical Research Associates and The History Group Inc. Novick wonders whether consultants, under the pressure of their clients, focus merely on the historical records that "support the case they were making, and did their best to sweep under the rug or trivialize discrepant findings" (1988, 514). This criticism reflects the argument that historians working outside the academy are subject to pressure and censorship from the different stakeholders or clients they are working with/for.

Conversely, in an article on historian-entrepreneurs, Shelley Bookspan regrets that the links between history and entrepreneurship "generally remains unexplored." She argues for "history as a platform on which to build new businesses" because "it has been far likelier for non-historians to create history-based enterprises, or even history-based industries" (2006, 67). Dutch corporate historian Ries Roowaan explains how history can contribute to any corporation's development (2009). What is more, arguing – as Novick does – that historians working in an academic environment are insulated from outside pressure is debatable. It is true that public historians collaborate with many different stakeholders whose roles challenge the omnipotent control that historians working in universities and research centers may think they have on their research. But although less direct than for consulting historians, for instance, pressure on academic historians exists through tenure requirements, peer assessment, private universities that want to increase their market, and public/private funding requests.

Historians are well aware that history can be used – and sometimes distorted – for many different purposes. Through the heritage industry, history has become a precious tool for marketing. Some historians have faced the impact of consumer culture through theme parks, leisure, and entertainment. While historians look for accurate representations of the past, other actors such as marketing departments may first and foremost want to attract visitors. The tension – noted by Mike Wallace in his book on American museums – is between historians' interest in educating audiences and the commercial interest in providing leisure (1996). For instance, in 1994 the Disney Corporation proposed to open a "Disney's America" in Virginia with a raft ride through "Native America," a "Civil War village," and a recreated factory town with a high speed ride called the "Industrial Revolution" (Glassberg 2001, 14). Although the project was ultimately rejected by local officials, it raised questions about the use of the past to sell experiences to visitors.

Debates relate to the relations between past and present. Critics of the use of the past fear that the present dictates historical interpretation of the past. Public historians should not be naive and must consider this risk. Nevertheless, the distance put by some historians between the past and present may also be seen as naive. History is not the past; it is a present interpretation, no matter what historians believe. A more interesting position is to accept the present construction of history while encouraging audiences to think of the past as a period different from the present. By doing so, this complex relationship between past and present allows both historicism – the awareness of the otherness of the past – and public uses of the past for present-day purposes.

What is certain is that the past has and will be used by different for-profit companies. However, it does not mean that historians should remain in ivory towers instead. In the early 1980s, while reviewing public history and its possible development in France, Henry Rousso – who was not convinced by the public history approach – evoked the choice every historian had to make – either the historian is interested in the possible application of his/her work and takes it into consideration in his/her research, or he/she leaves any application and uses of his/her work to "men of action" (Rousso 1984, 107). Historical works are used anyway; the question is whether historians want to participate in the discussions about how their work is used. Public historians should develop coherent relationships between the academy, historical research, (new) media, and the different uses of the past to contribute to better representations of the past. The relations between historians and their partners are at the core of many controversies in public history. It is necessary to explore if, why, and how historians can share authority.

Working "With" Audiences: Public Historians and Shared Authority

Public history is based on collaboration. This is also why Bookspan compares historians to entrepreneurs. "Public historians like entrepreneurs, must be collaborators … So for example, a public historian curating a museum exhibit must collaborate with designers, donors, other historians, board of directors, interpreters, and audiences" (2006, 67). And collaboration is sometimes not an easy process, especially for historians whose training may not have encouraged collaboration. Historians are usually trained to choose individually their own topics, methodology, sources; they usually control the schedule of production.

Collaboration is not limited to other scholars and other professionals. More radical is the collaboration with non-academic audiences. Public history is, indeed, not only working for but also with non-academic audiences. In 1990, oral historian Michael Frisch presented a new concept that would be very important for the conceptualization of the relations between historians and audiences. He argued that history was based on "shared authority" (Frisch 1990). Shared authority relates to the democratization of the knowledge-building process. In other words, audiences are never passively consuming knowledge produced by expert historians. Many public historians would today accept that public history is not doing history for the general public but with them. The participatory construction of history results in a major redefinition of the role and authority of historians. Historians cannot see themselves as missionaries who bring truth to non-academic audiences, but they should be prepared to collaborate, and to share authority. Shared authority comes from the conviction that historians do not own history, but that it is rather a sort of public domain. As we will see through the different chapters of this textbook, public collaboration influences every step of the construction of historical narratives and representations, from the collection and construction of sources, through the presentation and storytelling, to the various uses of the past.

Collaboration and shared authority create new challenges for historians. Writing about the concept of shared authority, oral historian Linda Shopes acknowledges that "collaborative work is personally and intellectually demanding, requiring an ability – even the courage – to deal with people and situations that can be difficult" (2003, 37). Historians in contact with audiences may have to deal with public emotions regarding sensitive issues, and may also have to deal with their own emotions, for example while receiving uncomfortable and offensive comments. While historians who communicate mostly by journals, books, and academic conference may very well avoid direct emotions and out-of-control situations, public historians hardly can. A mortal sin for professional historians, emotions have returned to the foreground through public history practice (Tyson 2013).

Emotions actually belong to broader interrogation about the consequences of public practice to the role of historians. Public historians must be ready to share authority. Debates no longer focus on the need to share authority, but rather on the extent to which it could be done. Public historian Jim Gardner argues that the concept of "radical trust" is one of the crucial current challenges for public historians. According to him, "looking to the public for content and direction" has become the next step in public history, and forces public historians to "giving up control ... in other words, radical trusts means letting the public (via communities) determine the future of public history" (2010, 53). What he argues is that shared authority is not synonymous with relativism – the sense that one interpretation or vision of the past is just about as acceptable as another. The challenge for public historians is to both share authority and defend historical analysis of the past as mediator or as "communicator" as Jason Steinhauer recently advocated (2015).

History, Memory, and Audiences

In the last three decades, public history has been a vibrant subject of discussion among historians, academic or not. One major reason was a new interest among historians and other academics in memory and memory studies. The development of oral history participated in a broader discussion about the links between memory and history. Memory studies – and the focus on memory – has made the public history approach more palatable to academic scholars.

During the 1980s, many works were published in Europe and in the United States about the concept of memory and its use for historians (Nora 1996; Lowenthal 1985; Connerton 1989). These publications took place in a broad context of public anniversaries and commemorations such as the Bicentenary of the French Revolution in 1989. Commemorations were perfect occasions for historians to enhance their public roles. In order to do so, historians increasingly had to take a position regarding the use and study of memories. The development of public history and memory studies was not only simultaneous, but it was based on common interrogations and practices.

A watershed in memory studies was the shift from individual to collective – or group – memories evoked by Maurice Halbwachs in the 1920s (1925). Collective memories became a social object that could be studied by scholars. For example, French historian Henry Rousso studied how the memories of World War II – and in particular the French collaboration with the Nazis – changed after 1945 (1991). Historians were very careful to distinguish between memory – the topic of their research – and history. David Lowenthal opposes historians who "while realizing that the past can never be retrieved unaltered ... still strive for impartial, checkable accuracy, minimizing bias as inescapable but deplorable" and those – he does not call them historians – who "see bias and error as normal and necessary" (1997, 32). In other words, history would tend to objectivity, while memory would be subjective. Memory was defined as present-oriented, composed of emotions, non-universal since supported by social groups, and therefore constantly changing. Memory was seen by historians as the opposite to the scientific, professional, and academic history. Some of these arguments were similarly used to criticize historians' public practices.

Public historians are more careful and consider that memory is not a form of blindness while history is about objective "truth" (Noiret 2011, 9). The strict opposition between memory and history is not convincing. Public history is a very good example of how history and memory influence each other. The scholarship on memory offers a new way to think about public history as well. In 1996 and 1997, David Glassberg led a discussion in *The Public Historian* about the links between public history and memory (1996). As Robert Archibald points out in this discussion, "the new memory research is especially important because it is audience-focused and recognizes that examining how humans receive information and construct memory is critical to our work" (1997, 64). The different uses and interpretations of the past by the public are not something historians are usually trained for – since professional history avoids personal involvement – but it is crucial for public historians who intend to understand how audiences make "sense of history," or as Glassberg puts it, as evidence of the intersection of the intimate and the historical (2001, 6). Individual and collective memories can be part of the public history production. For example, it is very important for public historians involved in historic preservation to ask local residents during public meetings what they think of and what their experience of the site under consideration has been.[8] Public memories of sites may help discover divergence between popular and official memories and interpretations of the past.

The public involvement in the various steps of public history raises new questions about the role of historians. In line with the works on memory studies, public historians are now aware of the fact that interpretation differs according to audiences. Historians no longer doubt that they cannot fully control how historical narratives are interpreted and used by audiences. Individuals and groups not only interpret the past differently, but they also use it according to their personal needs and experiences. Since memories and interpretations of the past may vary from individual to individual, it is necessary to discuss Carl Becker's famous phrase – everyone his own historian – and the possible consequence of historical relativism in which every interpretation is equally valid.

Without denying the right of free speech, historians must strive against relativist interpretations of the past. As Jim Gardner rightly points out in an article about "Radical Trust," we should not confuse knowledge and opinion (2010, 54). This is especially relevant in the context of the democratization of expression issued from the rise of the Internet. It is increasingly possible to express one's views through personal blogs, websites, comments, and social networks. Although the process of democratization is necessary, public interpretations of the past seem to be more and more associated with personal memories that do not always support critical study of the past. Gardner was right when he juxtaposed opinion and knowledge. The rise of public memories should not hide the fact that interpreting the past is never an easy process. This is where historians and, more precisely in engaging communities, public historians can play a role by providing critical analysis of sources and helping people to set individual and group memories in the broader context of interpretation. Situating oneself in relation to audiences and their interpretation of the past has become one of the most difficult tasks for public historians. The civic and public role of historians is not to hide behind the myth of equal validity for personal interpretations of the past. There is a gap between the need to foster participatory construction of public history and the absence of any critical interpretation of the past.

Institutionalization and Internationalization of Public History

The strict distinction between academic historians and public historians faces a different reality. Numerous historians have been both academic and public historians. Robert Kelley himself had an academic position at UCSB. Other founding members of the public history movement had academic positions too.[9] The Organization of American Historians (OAH) as well as the AHA include and encourage public history. Every year, their conferences give voice to public historians and public history projects. Every few years, the OAH and the NCPH share their annual conferences. Instead of making clear-cut distinctions between academic and public historians, it might be more valid to stop seeing public history as a separate track and to see public history as a central component of what all historians could do.

The reconsideration of the opposition is also due to the rise of public history programs within universities. The roots of the public history movement lay in universities. Public historians with academic positions have been extremely visible and powerful in the rise of the public history movement. In Britain, Raphael Samuel created the History Workshop at Ruskin College, Oxford, which is one of the highest ranked academic places in Europe. Although many historians had worked outside universities for decades, the historians who were at the origins of the movement had positions in the academy. It seemed as if North American universities discovered in the 1970s and 1980s that history could be produced and used outside of the classroom.

There is a growing academic interest in public history training. More and more history departments propose courses.[10] Originally located in North America, public history programs are now present worldwide. The NCPH's *Guide to Public History Programs* listed 220 university programs around the world in 2013.[11] Among others, public history centers have been created in South Africa, Ireland, Germany, China, and Brazil. Today, *history@work* – a blog sponsored by the NCPH to serve as an online "commons" – includes an international section. *The Public Historian* journal has "International Consultants" on its board of editors. Those examples encapsulate the increasing attention paid to what is done outside the United States. The growing discussion on international issues not only raises questions about the definition of public history, it also forces us to consider the extent to which the emergence of new centers has affected public practices and contributed to the creation of international public history networks and practices.

Nevertheless, the disagreements and dissimilar definitions of "public history" make difficult – but not impossible – international discussion and projects. In a review of public history in Britain, Priscilla Boniface underlines that the British remain unfamiliar with the term public history and stresses the "difficulty in the UK in understanding exactly the meaning of the American term" (1995, 23). In 2013, when experienced North American public historians participated in a seminar at Chongqing University (China), intense discussions focused on the concept of public history and its meaning in China. Other historians have reacted to what they perceive as the North American model of public history. For instance, public history in Australia developed "partly as a critique of the US public history movement." In an article on what public history is, Jill Liddington argues that "involved in city-planning, courtroom, community battles, and other public commitment, Australian public historians have been much more radical in their criticism of university historians luxuriating in their tenure-induced languor" (2002, 86). Besides, more than in the United States, public history in Australia, New Zealand, and Canada has focused on battles for ethnic minorities, especially regarding native populations.[12]

Another approach has been proposed in France. During his tour of Europe, Wesley Johnson visited France and noticed the "lack of opportunities outside of the state-dominated employment system for historians, curators, and archivists" (1984, 91). Public practice in France has been closely associated with public service. In France, as for many other countries, state-sponsored projects have been at the origins of public practices. Likewise, federal government initiatives participated heavily in the development of public practices in Canada. Projects such as the Museum of Civilization or the Canadian Museum of Science and Technology came from former Prime Minister Pierre Trudeau's wish to enhance pride in national Canadian culture to compete with the French Canadian independence movement (Dick 2009, 8). State-sponsored history has also become a major field in New Zealand where the War History branch of the Department of Internal Affairs is home to the massive official history series of New Zealand's involvement in World War II (Dalley 2012, 77).

The rise of state-sponsored public history in some countries has fostered suspicion regarding the uses of history. The links between public history and the private sector have certainly been the subject of the most aggressive criticisms toward the field in Europe. For instance, in 2005 three French historians founded the Comité de Vigilance face aux Usages Publics de l'Histoire (Watchdog Committee Against the Public Uses of History) to distinguish between history, memories, and their political uses.[13] The Committee's Manifesto made a clear distinction between academic history and public memories; the uses of the past being part of the latter.

In spite of the disagreement on the definitions and approaches of public history, some historians have created international structures and networks.[14] An international committee was formed within the NCPH during the mid-1990s to assess the need for, and how to start, an international discussion on the public practice of history (Warren-Findley 1998, 11). Likewise, the International Federation for Public History was created in 2010 "to bring together international public historians, to promote the development of a growing worldwide network of practitioners, and to foster national public history programs and associations" (Noiret 2014). The first and second International Symposia of Public History were organized in 2012 and 2014 in Brazil based on the Rede Brasileira de História Pública (Brazilian Network of Public History) (Almeida and Rovai 2011). The symposia and other international conferences demonstrate that, in spite of sometimes-dissimilar definitions of public history, historians can discuss and explore across national contexts the skills and practices – like oral history, digital media, historic preservation, advising – used to communicate with non-academic and popular audiences. The internationalization of media – best exemplified by the development of the Internet – gives historians new opportunities to work for and with international audiences (Noiret and Cauvin 2016).[15]

A Textbook of Practice

Why a Textbook on Public History?

As previously mentioned, the public role of historians is not new. However, the rise of public history movements since the 1970s has contributed to better preparing historians to face work in public, for and with various partners. Training is necessary because public historians are engaged in collaboration and may face situations barely covered in traditional history training. Doing public history is not a simple shift of the communication framework. Doing public history requires particular skills and has consequences for the overall production of historical narratives. Historians are not born but become public historians.

Public History: A Textbook of Practice covers the many challenges historians face while teaching, learning, and practicing public history. The broad and debated definitions of public history result in the existence of several sub-fields. Although they may overlap, each one of these sub-fields raises specific challenges for historians. Historians who work in historic preservation, in museums and archives, in government agencies, as consultants, as oral historians, or who manage crowdsourcing projects, need very specific skills. This textbook provides an introduction for most of the sub-fields and can be used by graduate and undergraduate programs in public history. Because public history is an approach that any history course can adopt, the textbook can help instructors enrich the conception and practice of history training at large. This textbook can also allow public historians to learn about alternative practices and media – film and documentary, virtual reconstruction, blogs and websites – to produce history. Public practitioners are usually so submerged by the amount of work to be undertaken for their projects that they lack the time to reflect on issues at stake in their practice. The textbook can help such practitioners further develop the links between theory and practice.

An immense amount of literature is available for anyone interested in the different fields such as archives, museums, historic preservation, oral history, digital history, documentary editions, and so on, and it is extremely difficult for public historians and instructors to cover the many different fields. What is more, fields and practices such as archives and collections management often lack discussion of the role of history and historians. For instance, there have long been programs in historic preservation, oral history, archival management, museum studies, and public policy, but some of those programs may have no historical training at all. This may result in students in historic preservation or public policy, for instance, considering themselves as more closely aligned with architecture, urban planning, and legislation. Instead of merely providing introductions to the different practices of public history, the textbook explores what historians can bring to the related fields and how the public practices and applications affect historical methodology.

Historians have, since the 1980s, used some important collective resources on public history. Public history journals such as *The Public Historian* and the *Public History Review*, blogs – *Public History Commons* from North America, *Public History Weekly* from Europe, and other related journals – *Rethinking History*, the *Journal of Historical Review*, or *History & Memory* – have participated in intense discussions on the field. A few collections of essays provided rich overviews of public history as well. Barbara Howe and Emory Kemp edited *Public History: An Introduction* in 1986. Even though it is now partially outdated – especially regarding new technology – this collection is one of the most exhaustive works. More recently, Jim Gardner and Peter LaPaglia, Paul Ashton, Hilda Kean, and Paul Martin edited similar introductions to the field (Gardner and LaPaglia 2006; Ashton and Kean 2009; Kean and Martin 2013).[16] The only example of a single-author public history textbook is, so far, *Public History: A Practical Guide* published by Faye Sayer in the UK (2015).

Students as well as public history practitioners must be aware of the need for self-reflectivity, and should address the tensions between theory and practice in the field. In his overview of public history practice in Europe and North America, French historian Henry Rousso argued that "pragmatism is not a French quality (or impairment)" (1984, 114).[17] He implied that American scholars are – perhaps too eagerly – more driven by practice than the theory of public history. Before any application of public history, French historians would need, according to Rousso, more theoretical debates about the pros and cons of developing the field. Rousso was right to some extent. In the United States, Rebecca Conard considers practice as "where one begins to understand what sets public history apart" (2006, 11). However, public history has increasingly been self-reflective. Introductory courses on public history need to provide both an overview of the multiple public practices and theoretical discussions on the field. Instructors need to balance theoretical readings and applications outside the classroom through public history projects, internships, and collaboration with non-academic stakeholders.[18] Self-reflectivity is not limited to the application of theory to practice, but reflects examples when practice can inform theory as well. It is not uncommon for instructors in public history training programs to ask students to write final papers discussing how their projects and other practical experiences could help re-assess public history theoretical works they have previously read. This assignment embodies how public history is designed on constant dialogue between theory and practice, or as Katharine Corbett and Howard Miller argue in their article on shared inquiry, on "reflective practice" and "reflection-in-action" (2006, 18).

From Practice to Practices

The textbook is divided into three parts that reflect the different steps in public history. Every chapter offers an introduction to the history, debates, practices, necessary skills, and literature relevant to comprehend the field and collaborate with the various possible partners. Instead of having specific chapters about them, key issues such as public participation, digital tools and media, and internationalization of public history are discussed in every chapter. For instance, the use of digital tools affects the management of collections and cultural resources, documentary editing, or oral history sources, public writing (through blog and websites), exhibit design, and preservation (through virtual reconstruction).

Since historians may work for and with a variety of actors, flexibility is often one of their key qualities. Due to the great variety of sources, sites, and collaboration, public historians are often confronted with unforeseen situations. Shelley Bookspan notices that more traditional historians show "discomfort with uncertainty, a reluctance to deviate from a chosen path … there is a kind of safety working with the confines of the past," but she underlines that "uncertainty is a desirable ally" (2006, 37). Flexibility and adaptation are certainly two of the main qualities of public historians. And in order to be flexible, public historians must be "polyglot." While knowing different languages may become more and more important for public historians due to the internationalization of the field and audiences, the term "polyglot" also refers here more to the variety of technical languages.

Doing history in public requires historians to be able to communicate with the many different partners involved in the project. History for popular non-academic audiences may require, for instance, the use of reader-friendly writing styles (Chapter 4). Various other types of collaboration invite public historians to know the basics of technical languages to work with exhibit designers, architects, computer scientists, marketing officers, film directors, policymakers, or lawyers. The use and impact of new techniques and skills are developed throughout the first part of the textbook.

Part I focuses on public history sources, and offers an overview of the creation, collection, management, and preservation of public history materials (archives, material culture, oral materials, or digital sources). Chapters cover sites and institutions such as archival repositories and museums, historic buildings and structures, and different practices such as collection management, preservation (archives, objects, sounds, moving images, buildings, sites, and landscape), oral history, and genealogy.

Part II deals with the different ways in which public historians can produce historical narratives through different media (exhibitions, movies, writing, digital tools, and so on). As public historian Philip Scarpino explains, "all historians conduct research; all historians analyze and interpret what they find; and all historians communicate their findings to others." However, the difference for public historians is "found in the area of communication, in the audiences with whom we communicate, and in the methods that we use to communicate our scholarship to those audiences" (Sacco 2013). The media to produce and convey historical representations of the past are key elements in public history. Chapters of this textbook cover different media such as writing (Chapter 4), editing (Chapter 5), exhibiting and interpreting (Chapter 6), radio and audio-visual production (Chapter 7), as well as digital public history (Chapter 8).

Technology has been a key component of the links between historians and their audiences and partners. Ian Tyrrell rightly explains that "at each new development, new technologies raised anxieties about the role of academics and popular history making" (2005, 251). It is even truer about the consequence of the latest technological advance. The rise of the Internet and the digital tools has been revolutionary for some public historians. Through the Web 2.0 and participatory process, historians have been increasingly able to engage with audiences. Web 2.0 is a perfect embodiment of shared authority in public history, and raises questions about the role and practice of historians.

Finally, it is important to evaluate the consequences of collaborative practice on the historian's role. Throughout Part III, chapters focus on issues such as teaching, shared authority, civic engagement and social justice, consulting, and public history ethics. Although every historian must deal with ethics and self-reflectivity, public history raises specific issues coming from the multiple collaborations public historians are committed to. In one of the first issues of *The Public Historian*, Robert McKenzie asked how historians could "maintain objectivity without the traditional protection of distance from the subject under study?" (1979, 4). Codes and debates about ethics cannot prevent historians from being wrong, but can prevent them from being unethical.

Notes

1 See for instance public debates about the historical adaptation of Lincoln's life by Steven Spielberg in 2012.
2 For example, Herbert Baxter Adams played a major role in the development of modern and scientific research practices at Johns Hopkins University (Townsend 2013, 13).
3 Three percent of AHA members were already working in archives in 1900 and the U.S. National Archives were created in 1934 (Townsend 2013, 39).
4 One major and constant popular use of archives is for the purpose of genealogical practices.
5 Similar arguments in history's public purpose could be found in Europe too, for instance, John Robert Seeley (1834–1895) in Britain (Tosh 2014).
6 See Chapter 13.
7 See Chapter 12.
8 See Chapter 2.
9 Ernest May at Harvard, Joel Tarr at Carnegie Mellon, Noel Stowe at Arizona State University, Anna Nelson, then at George Washington University, Barbara Howe at West Virginia, Patricia Mooney-Melvin at the University of Arkansas, or Dick Kirkendall at Indiana University.
10 Although it does not mean that those history departments prepare historians to work in the public

environment. Courses and programs are sometimes merely created to limit the decrease of history major in universities. See Chapter 10.

11 Although non-exhaustive, the list demonstrates the extreme predominance of English-speaking countries. Of the programs, 193 were located in the United States, 8 in Great Britain, 7 in Canada, 5 in Australia, 2 in Ireland, 1 in India, 1 in China, 1 in Belgium, 1 in Holland, and 1 in Germany. However, the list was not exhaustive, other programs exist in South Africa, Switzerland, and Germany, for instance.

12 See Chapter 12.

13 See Chapter 13.

14 See for instance the international examples of international collaboration for exhibit design in Chapter 6, as well as the International Sites of Conscience in Chapter 12.

15 See Chapter 8.

16 Gardner and LaPaglia's first edition was published in 1999.

17 The author translated from French to English.

18 See Chapter 10.

Bibliography

Achenbaum, W. Andrew. "Public History's Past, Present, and Prospects." *The American Historical Review*, 92/5 (December 1987): 1162–1174.

Almeida, Juniele R. and Rovai, Marta G.O., eds. *Introdução à História Pública*, São Paulo: Letra e Voz, 2011.

Appleby, Joyce. "Should We All Become Public Historians?" *Perspectives on History* (March 1997), www.historians.org/publications-and-directories/perspectives-on-history/march-1997/should-we-all-become-public-historians (accessed May 2, 2014).

Archibald, Robert R. "Memory and the Process of Public History." *The Public Historian*, 19/2 (Spring 1997): 61–64.

Ashton, Paul and Kean, Hilda. *People and Their Pasts: Public History Today*, London: Palgrave Macmillan, 2009.

Beck, Peter. *Using History, Making British Policy: The Treasury and the Foreign Office, 1950–76*, Basingstoke: Palgrave Macmillan, 2006.

Boniface, Priscilla. "History and the Public in the UK." *The Public Historian*, 17/2 (Spring 1995): 21–37.

Bookspan, Shelley. "Something Ventured, Many Things Gained: Reflections on Being a Historian-Entrepreneur." *The Public Historian*, 28/1 (Winter 2006): 67–74.

Conard, Rebecca. *Benjamin Shambaugh and the Intellectual Foundations of Public History*, Iowa City: University of Iowa Press, 2002.

Conard, Rebecca. "Public History as Reflective Practice: An Introduction." *The Public Historian*, 28/1 (Winter 2006): 9–13.

Conard, Rebecca. "The Pragmatic Roots of Public History Education in the United States." *The Public Historian*, 37/1 (February 2015): 105–120.

Connerton, Paul. *How Societies Remember*, Cambridge: Cambridge University Press, 1989.

Corbett, Katharine T. and Miller, Howard S. "A Shared Inquiry into Shared Inquiry." *The Public Historian*, 28/1 (Winter 2006): 15–38.

Dalley, Bronwyn. "Shades of Grey: Public History and Government in New Zealand." In *Public History and Heritage Today*, edited by Paul Ashton and Hilda Kean, London: Palgrave Macmillan, 2012, 74–91.

Dick, Lyle. "Public History in Canada: An Introduction." *The Public Historian*, 31/1 (Winter 2009): 7–14.

Evans, Jennifer "What is Public History." Public History Resource Center, 2000, www.publichistory.org/what_is/definition.html (accessed September 12, 2015).

Fishel, Leslie and Hayes, Rutherford B. "Public History and the Academy." In *Public History: An Introduction*, edited by Barbara Howe and Emory L. Kemp, Malabar: Robert E. Krieger Publishing Company, 1986, 8–20.

Frisch, Michael. *A Shared Authority: Essays on the Craft and Meaning of Oral and Public History*, Albany: State of New York University Press, 1990.

Gardner, James B. "Trust, Risk and Public History: A View from the United States." *Public History Review*, 17 (December 2010): 52–61.

Gardner, James, ed. *The Oxford Handbook of Public History*, Oxford: Oxford University Press, forthcoming 2016.

Gardner, James B. and LaPaglia, Peter. *The Public History: Essays From the Field*, Malabar: Krieger Press, 2006.

Glassberg, David. "Public History and the Study of Memory." *The Public Historian*, 18 (Spring 1996): 7–23.

Glassberg, David. *Sense of History: The Place of the Past in American Life*, Amherst: University of Massachusetts Press, 2001.

Green, Alix. "Back to the Future? Public History and the New Academic Citizen." *Public History Weekly*, 3/7 (March 5, 2015a), DOI: dx.doi.org/10.1515/phw-2015-3590 (accessed September 3, 2015).

Green, Alix. "History as Expertise and the Influence of Political Culture on Advice for Policy Since Fulton." *Contemporary British History*, 29/1 (2015b): 27–50.

Green, Howard. "A Critique of the Professional Public History Movement." *Radical History Review*, 25 (1981): 164–171.

Grele, Ronald J. "Whose Public? Whose History? What is the Goal of a Public Historian?" *The Public Historian*, 3 (1981): 40–48.

Halbwachs, Maurice. *Les Cadres sociaux de la mémoire*, Paris: F. Alcan, 1925.

Hayes, Kathryn, Ross, Jesikah Maria, and Middleton, Beth Rose. *Making Collaborative History. The Restore/Restory Project, Art of Regional Change: Project Report*, University of California Davis, May 2012, http://artofregionalchange.ucdavis.edu/files/2010/11/ARC_Report_FINAL.pdf (accessed September 13, 2014).

Hilliard, Chris. "A Prehistory of Public History: Monuments, Explanations and Promotions, 1900–1970." In *Going Public: The Changing Face of New Zealand History*, edited by Bronwyn Dalley and Jock Phillips, Auckland: Auckland University Press, 2001, 30–52.

History Workshop Online. "History of History Workshop." *HWJ*, November 22, 2012, www.historyworkshop.org.uk/the-history-of-history-workshop/ (accessed September 12, 2015).

Howe, Barbara. "Perspective on an Anniversary." *The Public Historian*, 1/3 (Summer 1999): 9–14.

Howe, Barbara and Kemp, Emory L., eds. *Public History: An Introduction*, Malabar: Robert E. Krieger Publishing Company, 1986.

Johnson, G. Wesley. "An American Impression of Public History in Europe." *The Public Historian*, 6/4 (Fall 1984): 87–97.

Johnson, G. Wesley. "*The Origins of the Public Historian* and the National Council on Public History." *The Public Historian*, 21/3 (Summer 1999): 167–179.

Jones, Arnita. "Public History Now and Then." *The Public Historian*, 21/3 (Summer 1999): 21–28.

Jordanova, Ludmilla. *History in Practice*, London and New York: Oxford University Press, 2000.

Kammen, Carol. *On Doing Local History: Reflections on What Local Historians DO, Why, and What It Means*, Nashville: The American Association for State and Local History, 1987.

Karamanski, Theodore J., ed. *Ethics and Public History: An Anthology*, Malabar: Robert E. Krieger Publishing, 1990.

Kean, Hilda and Martin, Paul, eds. *The Public History Reader*, London and New York: Routledge, 2013.

Kelley, Robert. "Public History: Its Origins, Nature, and Prospects." *The Public Historian*, 1 (Fall 1978): 16–28.

Knevel, Paul. "Public History: The European Reception of an American Idea?" *Levend Erfgoed. Vakblad voor public folklore & public history*, 6/2 (2009): 4–8.

Kyvig, David E. and Marty, Myron A. *Nearby History: Exploring the Past Around You*, Lanham: AltaMira Press, 2010.

Langlois, Charles V. and Seignobos, Charles. *Introduction aux études historiques*, Paris: Librairie Hachette, 1898.

Liddington, Jill. "What is Public History? Publics and Their Pasts, Meanings and Practices." *Oral History*, 30/1 (Spring 2002): 83–93.

Lowenthal, David. *The Past is a Foreign Country*, Cambridge: Cambridge University Press, 1985.

Lowenthal, David. "History and Memory." *The Public Historian*, 19/2 (Spring 1997): 31–39.

McKenzie, Robert. "Letter to the Editor." *The Public Historian*, 1/3 (Spring 1979): 4–5.

Meringolo, Denise. *Museums, Monuments, and National Parks: Toward a New Genealogy of Public History*, Amherst and Boston: University of Massachusetts, 2012.

Mooney-Melvin, Patricia. "Professional Historians and the Challenge of Redefinition." In *The Public History: Essays From the Field*, edited by James B. Gardner and Peter Lapaglia, Malabar: Krieger Press, 2006, 5–21.

National Council on Public History. "What is Public History?" NCPH website, undated, http://ncph. org/cms/what-is-public-history/ (accessed September 15, 2015).

Noiret, Serge. "La 'Public History': una Disciplina Fantasma?" *Memoria e Ricerca*, 37/2 (2011): 9–35, www.academia.edu/881804/La_Public_History_una_disciplina_fantasma_Public_History_a_ Ghost_Discipline_ (accessed September 12, 2015).

Noiret, Serge. "Internationalizing Public History." *Public History Weekly*, 2/34 (2014), http:// public-history-weekly.oldenbourg-verlag.de/2-2014-34/internationalizing-public-history/ (accessed September 15, 2015).

Noiret, Serge and Cauvin, Thomas. "Internationalization of Public History." In *The Oxford Handbook of Public History*, edited by James B. Gardner, Oxford: Oxford University Press, forthcoming 2016.

Nora, Pierre, ed. *Les lieux de mémoire*, vols I, II, III, Paris: Gallimard, 1984–1989.

Nora, Pierre. *Realms of Memory: Rethinking the French Past*, vol. I, New York: Columbia University Press, 1996.

Novick, Peter. *That Noble Dream: The "Objectivity Question" and the American Historical Profession*, Cambridge: Cambridge University Press, 1988.

Porciani, Ilaria and Lutz, Raphael, eds. *Atlas of European Historiography: The Making of a Profession 1800–2005*, Basingstoke: Palgrave Macmillan, 2010.

Portelli, Alessandro. *Biografia di una Città: Storia e Racconto: Terni 1830–1985*, Torino: Einaudi, 1985.

Reuss, Martin. "Federal Historians: Ethics and Responsibility in the Bureaucracy." *The Public Historian*, 8/1 (Winter 1986): 13–20.

Riopel, Marc. "Réflexions sur l'application de l'histoire." *RHAF*, 57/1 (Summer 2003): 5–21.

Roowaan, Ries. *A Business Case for Business History: How Companies Can Profit from their Past?* Amsterdam: Uitgeverij Boom, 2009.

Rosenzweig, Roy and Thelen, David. *The Presence of the Past: Popular Uses of History in American Life*, New York: Columbia University Press, 1998.

Rousso, Henry. "L'histoire appliquée ou les historiens thaumaturges." *Vingtième Siècle*, 1/1 (1984): 105–122.

Rousso, Henry. *The Vichy Syndrome: History and Memory in France since 1944*, Cambridge, MA: Harvard University Press, 1991.

Sacco, Nick. "Challenges in Explaining Public History to My Friends and Family." *Exploring the Past*, December 21, 2013, https://pastexplore.wordpress.com/2013/12/21/challenges-in-explaining-public-history-to-my-friends-and-family/ (accessed September 13, 2015).

Sayer, Faye. *Public History: A Practical Guide*, London: Bloomsbury, 2015.

Schulz, Constance B. "Becoming a Public Historian." In *Public History: Essays from the Field*, edited by James B. Gardner and Peter LaPaglia, Malabar: Krieger Press, 2006, 23–40.

Sheftel, Anna and Zembrzycki, Stacey, eds. *Oral History Off the Record: Toward an Ethnography of Practice*, Basingstoke: Palgrave Macmillan, 2013.

Shopes, Linda. "Commentary: Sharing Authority." *The Oral History Review*, 30/1 (Winter–Spring 2003): 103–110.

Steinhauer, Jason. "Missing the History from the Historic March on Washington Commemoration."

Public History Commons, September 4, 2013, http://publichistorycommons.org/march-on-washing ton-commemoration/ (accessed September 12, 2015).

Steinhauer, Jason. "Introducing History Communicators." *Public History Commons*, January 29, 2015, http://publichistorycommons.org/introducing-history-communicators/ (accessed September 15, 2015).

Suny, Ronald. "What Ivory Tower?" *Eisenberg Institute for Historical Studies, News and Events* (Winter 2012), www.lsa.umich.edu/UMICH/eihs/Home/News/Newsletter/W12_newsletter.pdf (accessed September 26, 2015).

Tosh, John. "Public History, Civic Engagement and the Historical Profession in Britain." *History*, 99/335 (2014): 191–202.

Townsend, Robert. *History's Babel: Scholarship, Professionalization, and the Historical Enterprise in the United States, 1880–1940*, Chicago: University of Chicago Press, 2013.

Townsend, Robert. "The AHA on the Path to Public History." *Public History Commons*, March 9, 2015, http://publichistorycommons.org/the-aha-on-the-path-to-public-history/ (accessed September 13, 2015).

Tyrrell, Ian. *Historians in Public: The Practice of American History, 1890–1970*, Chicago: University of Chicago Press, 2005.

Tyson, Amy. *The Wages of History: Emotional Labor on Public History's Front Lines*, Amherst and Boston: University of Massachusetts Press, 2013.

Wallace, Mike. *Mickey Mouse History and Other Essays on American Memory*, Philadelphia: Temple University Press, 1996.

Warren-Findley, Jannelle. "The Globalizing of Public History: A Personal Journey." *The Public Historian*, 20/4 (Autumn 1998): 11–20.

Wiener, John. *Historians in Trouble: Plagiarism, Fraud, and Politics in the Ivory Tower*, New York: New Press, 2004.

Zelis, Guy. "Vers une Histoire Publique." *Le Débat*, 177/5 (2013): 153–162.

Zimmerman, Jonathan. "Calling All Professional Historians – 'Come Out of the Ivory Tower'." *Newsworks*, March 11, 2014, www.newsworks.org/index.php/local/thats-history/65450-calling-professional-historians-out-of-the-ivory-tower (accessed September 25, 2015).

Part I

Collecting, Managing, and Preserving the Past

Public History and Sources

Like all historians, public historians rely on traces from the past to construct narratives. Issued from the 19th century professionalization of history, the historian's job mostly consists in the search, the analysis, and the interpretations of primary sources. Solid grounding in research methodology is essential for successful, productive careers. Public history university programs provide intensive research seminars and ask for original historical production. Nevertheless, it is also true that public history has specific relations with resources from the past. Whereas academic historians search for and analyze primary sources to write articles, dissertations, or books, public historians may be in charge of other duties such as creating, collecting, managing, editing, curating, preserving, and diffusing materials from the past.

The public use and application of history force historians to reconsider the definition and collect of primary sources. Although academic historians mostly interpret archives, public historians must be ready to participate in the collection and management of primary materials. Some archival training and cultural resources management skills may be required to do public history. Public historians must know how to select sources for their authenticity, reliability, accuracy, and usefulness. For instance, the production of oral history sources is much more than the simple recording of voice. The collection and archiving of oral resources imply some specific training.

Public history has engendered a redefinition of what historians have considered as archives in the 20th century. Doing history outside the classroom means that public historians have had to work on different sites of history production. Public historians may need fieldwork skills, such as those of folklorists and archaeologists. Some public historians deal with landscapes, battlefields, buildings, and other terrains, and may need rudimentary skills in locating, extracting, and cataloguing objects. The relations between sources and public historians do not stop after the collection or interpretation but include duties for the management and preservation of materials. Cultural resources management and historic preservation are therefore very important skills for public historians. New tasks for historians are composed of saving historic sites, adapting them to new – sometimes conflicting – purposes, reviving historic neighborhoods, reconstructing lost spaces. This section will therefore provide examples of collection management for archives and museums, family history and genealogy, historic preservation, oral history production, and digital management of primary sources.

In addition to new relations to primary sources, the public history movement has also redefined the links between historians and audiences. Public historians should not see themselves as modern missionaries providing truth to their audiences. Instead, the public should be part of the various steps of the historical production. In other words, public historians should collaborate with non-academic audiences in the history production. This collaboration with audiences in the history production implies new practices for historians. Collaboration should not be limited to the final steps but should be part of the initial collection and management of primary sources as well. The public dimension of the historian's job is perfectly visible through the access of historical materials. One major duty for public historians is to facilitate public access to the sources. While digital and open access approach is a perfect example, other formats – museum collection, oral history archives, historic buildings, and so on – should be considered as well. Public historians should be familiar with various approaches and have rudimentary skills for collecting, preserving, managing, and publishing the past.

1 Collection Management
Archives, Manuscripts, and Museums

This chapter introduces the main principles, methodologies, and practices developed and applied to create, manage, and preserve archival and museum collections. The selection, management, and preservation of items with enduring value drive the role of archival, manuscript, and museum collections. In order to appreciate the complexity of collection management, historians need to better understand what archivists, curators, registrars, and other collection staff do (Dearstyne 1986, 6). Historians need to situate the different actors and their role in specific collection management processes (Malaro 1998, 3–22). Historians must explore the various steps of collection management, be aware of the legal issues and responsibilities, and the profession's codes of ethics (O'Toole and Cox 2006). The following chapter outlines the various steps of collection management – planning and acquisitions, appraisal and examination, accessioning, recording, and preservation. However, the format (mostly three-dimensional objects for museums, papers and electronic records for archives and manuscript collections) and management of the collections vary according to the agency. Thus the chapter also distinguishes between the specific archival and museum collection practices.

Archives, Manuscripts, and Museum Collections

Archives and Manuscript Collections

The professions of archivists and historians took different paths in the first part of the 20th century. In the United States, following the creation of the National Archives in 1934, archivists broke away from the American Historical Association (AHA) and, in 1936, created their own professional association, the Society of American Archivists (SAA). As the professions grew apart, the historians and archivists began to develop their own vocabulary that affects our contemporary understanding of the term *archives*. The term has three possible meanings. First *archives* may be construed as materials, the tangible sources of historical data: objects, and visual and textual documents. Understood as *materials*, the archives are defined as "the non-current records of individuals, groups, institutions, and governments that contain information of enduring value" (SAA undated a). Next, *archives* are the repository or storage location that holds the collections. Finally, *archives* are the agencies that take care of collections (Hunter 2004, 2).

Since archives are linked to specific institutions, therefore archivists often collaborate with current record managers. Generally, in large organizations that maintain historic and operational records, archivists collaborate with record managers responsible for vast quantities of current records, most of which will never become archives. In this context, archivists only assume custodianship over a small percentage of records that have long-term value. However, in small institutions, archivists may have to deal with both current records and archives (Tryon 2006, 58–60).

Another distinction must be made between two sorts of repositories: archives and manuscript collections. Strictly speaking, archives are maintained by their creators (government, corporation, church, etc.) while manuscript collections are held by institutions other than the original creators and custodians, such as universities, libraries, historical societies, and private research centers (Miller 1986, 37). It means that manuscript repositories often manage private and family papers. Manuscript repositories have papers while archives have records, but both may contain letters, diaries, ledgers, receipts, sound recordings, pictures, and born-digital objects that make collection management increasingly difficult. Archival repositories – composed of both archives and manuscripts – are as diverse as the institutions and people they serve. In the United States, the National Archives and Records Administration (NARA), the National Association of Government Archives and Records Administrators (NAGARA), the Manuscript Division of the Library of Congress, and the 15 Presidential Libraries and Museums hold very large archival collections (Fawcett 2006; Montgomery 2003).

Museum Collections

Public museums emerged in the 19th century and have now become one of the main components of public history. In Figure 1.1, one curator is cataloguing items in his laboratory at the United States National Museum in 1886. The term laboratory refers to the activities of curators who analyze items. Like archival repositories, museums create, manage, and preserve memories (Crane 2005). The definition of museums remains a difficult question though (Dillenburg 2011). The American Association of Museums (AAM) defines the museum as "an organized and permanent non-profit institution, essentially educational or aesthetic in purpose, with professional staff, which owns and utilizes tangible objects, cares for them, and exhibits them to the public on some regular schedule" (Genoways and Ireland 2003, 4). The main attributes of museums and/or collections vary in scope and format but are typically composed of objects.

According to the Institute of Museum and Library Services, there are 35,000 active museums in the United States (Institute of Museum and Library Services 2014a).[1] Most of them are defined by their approach (science, history, arts) and by the objects they collect. While many museums are defined by their collections, a growing number of institutions define themselves through the ideas/themes they promote, such as the Museum of Tolerance in Los Angeles. In 2014, history museums represented 7.5 percent of all museums, while art museums represented 4.5 percent, and historical societies, historic preservation, historic houses and sites represented 48 percent (Institute of Museum and Library Services 2014a, 2014b). History museums cover a vast range from outdoor agricultural museums to county historical societies, to city museums, to national specialized museums (Woodhouse 2006, 189). By far, small historical museums are the most prevalent across the United States (Dolan 1986, 241). Local historical museums are often concerned with the history of ordinary people, events, and happenings within a definable geographic boundary (Simmons 2006). They tell the history of families and communities through photographs, documents, artifacts, and regional memorabilia (Dolan 1986, 242).

Due to their exhibitions and public access, museums are natural sites of public history. However, the public role of museums has changed since the 19th century (Skramstad

Figure 1.1 Curator in his laboratory, Smithsonian Museum, Arts and Industries Building, 1886. Courtesy of the Smithsonian Institution Archives.

1999). In the 19th century, public museums often played a role in the construction of identity, especially national identity (Kaplan 1994). Museums were sometimes designed as weapons to promote nationalistic representations of the past (Cauvin 2011). Museums were conceived as influencing visitors. However, this approach has changed since the debates of the 1970s about the function and nature of museums. The field of museum studies also began to change with the arrival of new authors such as Eilean Hooper-Greenhill (Hooper-Greenhill 1992). This shift in the field, a movement called New Museology, was critical of the elitist approach and function of museums (Vergo 1989; Macdonald 2006; Mason 2006; Carbonell 2004; Macdonald and Fyfe 1996).

The democratization of museums aimed to transform museums from repositories to public forums. Museums work not only for, but more and more with, their public. Museums shifted from temples housing relics to forums of discussion (Clifford 1997). Rather than the collection, it is the visitor who is now at the center of the museum policy (Anderson 2004). This trend is crucial, as the new focus on audiences provides public historians with new opportunities to foster public engagement with collections.

Introduction to Collection Management

The Selection Process: Planning, Acquisition, and Examination

In principle, collection managers might seek to document and preserve the records of the broadest possible range of individuals, socio-economic groups, governance, and corporate entities in society. However, archives and museums cannot save everything, and collecting practices are therefore based on selection. Even for archives that only deal with their institution's records, they typically only preserve 2 percent of records (Tryon 2006, 58). The selection is based on the value attributed to the document according to various criteria as outlined by the collection planning guidelines. Creating a collection planning guideline is a crucial initial step. Repositories are usually defined by a mission statement that stresses the purpose, scope, and use of the collection (American Association of Museums 1989; George and Sherrell-Leo 2004; Lord and Lord 2002).

It is necessary to think in the long-term to determine what collections will be pertinent in the future. The mission statement varies according to the type of repository. In order to create a mission statement, archivists working with a specific agency, such as a corporation, must take into consideration its specific needs and expectations. In other repositories, such as museums or manuscript collections, the mission statement is intended more for the public, and creates a collection policy that reflects that aim. The mission statement serves as a roadmap for strategic planning and collection planning to fulfill the needs of the given institution (Genoways and Ireland 2003, 75–91).

Once the mission statement and collecting policy have been determined, collection managers can launch the acquisition process. Acquisition is the process of legally obtaining records, manuscripts, or objects and supplementary data for a repository through gifts, purchases, exchanges, transfers, and field collecting (Reibel 1997, 32–43). Part of the acquisition process results from the item's appraisal. The appraisal is the process of deciding whether or not materials have enduring research value and should therefore be retained (SAA undated b). To appraise the value of an item, collection managers must know what they should look for when accessing materials. Different models exist according to the format – papers and manuscripts, objects, images, sound, or born-digital items (Reibel 1997, 78–84). In Figure 1.1, the curator had received a box of seven mammal teeth – on the right part of the table – sent by Thomas J. Newland for inspection from Sulphur Valley, A.T. (Arizona Territory) and was proceeding to their appraisal.

In terms of historical value, public historians are well equipped to understand the records, manuscripts, and objects in their historical context and assess whether an item should be preserved. Historians should determine the intrinsic value of the item, in other words, the value deriving from the originality and uniqueness of the document. Value may also derive from links between an item and other documents – its specificity, its representation of a cultural context (Hunter 2004, 51–56). However, the value highly depends on the mission statement, which ultimately varies from repository to repository. Any change in the archival and museum collection's role and function affects the acquisition process.

Throughout acquisition, collection managers should not forget to document the donors and provenance (when and where it was obtained) of the item. Collection managers may interview the donor and ask for supplementary information, especially concerning the use/function of an item. In theory, it is also possible to ask for oral testimonies from users to complement the history of the collected items. Those details may, in the end, help further collect records about the document or eventually be integrated into a display (testimonies of donors on how the item was used, for instance).

While it is essential to know what to collect, it is also important to understand what cannot/should not be collected. Before accepting items, collection managers need to study title and ownership, to avoid stolen items, material improperly excavated and illegally removed from archaeological or paleontological sites, and specimen taken in violation of state, national, or international laws (Genoways and Ireland 2003, 177). An acquisition policy is needed to assert that the repository will not violate any local, state, federal, or international laws, treaties, conventions, or regulations. Historians must take into account copyright protection, the Endangered Species Act, the Archaeological Resources Protection Act, the Native American Graves Protection and Repatriation Act, the 1970 UNESCO Convention, and other legal issues (Malaro 1998). Managers may have to refuse donations for legal reasons, or because the historical value attributed to the item does not justify its preservation, or because the repository does not have the resources such as storage facilities to assure its long-term preservation (Grant 2010).

Recording Collections: Accessioning, Arrangement, and Description

Accessioning and Arranging

Once collection managers have selected and examined items to be preserved, their work continues as they access, arrange, and describe the items according to various standards. Accessioning immediately follows the selection of items. It is the process by which the repository takes physical and legal custody of the items and documents their transfer (Pearce-Moses 2005). The process of establishing custody and control over an accession enables the items to be made available for use (Roe 2005, 45–56). Accessioning varies according to the type of repository – archives, manuscript or museum collections. Since they deal with institutional records, the process of accessioning for agency and corporate archives is straightforward. Due to the multiple donors, other types of collections such as museums must pay more attention to the legal framework of the accession.[2] After the accessioning process takes place, collection managers have to sort items according to an agreed-upon structure (Buck and Gilmore 1998). Archival managers must then follow strict standards.[3]

Description and Metadata

Archives and museums must be able to describe their holdings for uses. Description is the creation of an accurate representation of the material by the process of capturing, collating, analyzing, and organizing information that serves to identify material and to explain the context of their production (SAA 2013, xvi). This is an important task that contributes to public access. The amount of description and level of detail depends on the importance of the material, the resources of the repository, and access requirements of the users. A description may consist of a multilevel structure that begins with an account of the entire material and proceeds through increasingly more detailed descriptions of the parts of the material (Hunter 2004, 131–157). Within a given body of materials, the repository may choose to describe some parts at a greater level of detail than others. A single item may be described in detail, whether or not it is part of a larger body of material (SAA 2013, xvii). Description focuses on the main elements of the document, its identity (name, title, date, etc.), its contents and structure, and how it was acquired.

The description relies heavily on metadata. Metadata are data about data; they describe attributes of items and give them meaning, context, and organization. Metadata creation is one of the core activities of collecting institutions. Metadata creation is just as important as the care, preservation, display, and dissemination of collections. Adequate planning and resources must be devoted to this ongoing, mission-critical activity. A specialist of digital record management, Anne J. Gilliland provides a rich introduction to metadata and their use in collection management (2008). Metadata have a long history in the practice of cataloguing items, but new kinds of metadata emerged with the rise of digital technology.

The types and functions of metadata can be classified into three, sometimes overlapping, broad categories: descriptive, structural, and administrative. Descriptive metadata describe and identify information resources; they include bibliographic attributes such as title and author, and identifiers such as URL. Structural metadata facilitate navigation and presentation of electronic resources; they include table of contents, index, or tags. Administrative metadata facilitate short-term and long-term management and processing of digital collections; they include details about the resolution, bit depth, copyrights, and license (Cornell University Library undated a). To the three aforementioned categories of metadata, Gilliland adds preservation, and applies metadata that help collection management to be more accurate (2008).

Metadata create contextual information for the use of archival materials, and therefore are fundamental to link primary sources and the public. Public historians should use metadata to increase the public accessibility to archival materials. Metadata also help to foster interoperability by creating standards of description that can be shared by many archival repositories. For instance, *Cataloging Cultural Objects* helps to create sharable metadata and to build best practices for museums, digital libraries, and archives (Baca et al. 2006). Metadata can also make it possible to search across multiple collections or to create virtual collections from materials that are distributed across several repositories – but only if the descriptive metadata records are the same or can be mapped across all the collections (Gilliland 2008).

Description and metadata must follow standards to foster consistency between repositories. However, there is no single standard that can match the requirement of the different archival repositories. Standards vary according to practice and to the format of the item. Archives and museums may therefore differ in their standards. In order to choose between standards – MARC 21, EAD, Dublin Core, etc. – the collection manager must know the basis of recording (Society of American Archivists 2013, xxi).

The SAA published an exhaustive guide called *Describing Archives: A Content Standard*, which is the U.S. implementation of international standards that provides information about every step of the process (2013, 7–83). It provides information about descriptive systems such as MARC 21, Encoded Archival Description (EAD), and Encoded Archival Context (EAC) (SAA 2013). MARC is a family of metadata standards for representing library resources. It is based on the mechanism by which computers exchange, use, and interpret bibliographic information.[4] Although chiefly used by libraries to describe bibliographic material (books or periodicals), it is sometimes used to describe non-book material (e.g., images) or archival collections. EAD provides a standard for encoding descriptions. It adopts a multilevel approach to description, providing information about a collection as a whole and then breaking it down into groups, series, and individual items (Library of Congress undated b).

When dealing with objects, collection managers can use *Cataloging Cultural Objects* (Baca et al. 2006). Repositories dealing with objects often prefer other standards such as Dublin Core, VRA Core or Categories for the Description of Works of Art (CDWA). Dublin Core standards – part of a larger set of metadata specifications maintained by the Dublin Core Metadata Initiative (DCMI) – is a set of 15 properties to describe items (Dublin Core Metadata Initiative undated). The VRA Core is a metadata standard for the description of works of visual culture as well as the images that document them (Library of Congress 2014). CDWA describes information about works of art, architecture, artifacts, groups and collections of works, and related images (Baca and Harpring 2014). Other metadata standards focus on the types of metadata (technical, preservation, structural, users) but implemented less frequently. Software such as Pastperfect or Emu (Electronic Museum management system) are other collection management systems that help collection managers keep a consistent description standard.

Preserving Collections

Treatment and Conservation

Preserving collections not only deals with conservation, but includes the maintenance, treatment, and digitization of materials. Actors in charge of the preservation must be able to examine the physical composition of every format of document, and identify the possible threat of deterioration. In addition to the documents, the environment in which they are conserved must be taken into consideration (Archives and Public History Digital undated). Among the different techniques, digital preservation is increasingly important for collection managers. The goal of digital preservation is to maintain the ability to display, retrieve, and use digital collections in the face of rapidly changing technological and organizational infrastructures and elements. Preservation varies from repository to repository, but also from item to item. It is, therefore, a complex task to establish general preservation policies.

Treatment is a major issue for preservation. It is the deliberate alteration of the chemical and/or physical aspects of an item in order to prolong its existence. Treatment can consist of the stabilization of the deterioration or its restoration that intends to return the item to a previous state. More often, preservation deals with preventive care in which the deterioration is reduced by the implementation of procedures such as the appropriate environmental conditions or an emergency plan. Archivists and curators should know the basic rules regarding the storage environment (Thomson 1986). In particular, issues such as light, humidity, and air pollution are major factors in the deterioration and preservation of items (Padfield 1996; Michalski 1994, 6–8). Chris Caple's – a specialist in artifact conservation – guide on conservation provides the basics for the different issues of storage and environment (Caple 2000). Likewise, Conservation Online and the American Institute for Conservation of Historic and Artistic Works (AIC) provide resources for different materials and sorts of items.

Preservation and Digitization

Digital technology has deeply changed preservation policy. Digitization or digital imaging can be defined as "electronic snapshots taken of a scene or scanned from documents, such as photographs, manuscripts, printed texts, and artwork" (Cornell University Library undated b). A digital copy can be made of written documents as well as images, moving images, and sound. The digital image is made of a grid of dots or pixels that assign a color. Digitizing collections, therefore, create digital objects that archivists and curators must be capable of handling. Digitization has multiple advantages for collection management, in particular when preserving fragile items. Digitization can help collection managers to protect and preserve originals while making a digitized copy not only available, but more easily accessible. Rich Digital Master (RDM) image file – or archival image – contains all of the significant information about the represented source. Creating a high-quality RDM helps protect a vulnerable original since users can use the RDM instead of the primary document (Cornell University Library undated c). Digitizing objects also allows repositories to store a larger amount of documents. A good example is the Digital Public Library of America. It had seven million items in early 2014, from more than 1,300 institutions that hold manuscripts, photographs, maps, moving images, and sound.

In order to digitize collections, managers must know the basic terms and technologies such as bit depth, resolution, and compression technology, to name a few (Cohen and Rosenzweig 2005). Digital image capture must take into consideration the technical processes involved while converting from analogue to digital representation as well as the attributes of the source documents themselves: physical size and presentation, level of detail, tonal range, and presence of colors. Cornell Library's Digital Imaging Tutorial provides a very useful explanation of the different components of the digitization, the file formats, and the overall digitization chain (Cornell University Library undated c, undated d, undated e). Historians can then choose the material – scanners (flat-bed, 3D), camera – according to the format of the document (SAA undated c; BCR 2008). Although the technology is more complex, digitization also applies to objects. For instance, the Smithsonian Museum has launched a vast campaign of 3D scanning technology (Smithsonian undated).

Public historians and collection managers must be aware of the limits and challenges of digital preservation. First of all, due to the size of digital files, digitization may be accompanied by compression that reduces file size for storage, processing, and transmission. Compression alters the set of binary code from an uncompressed image through complex algorithms. Compression can be lossless or lossy. Lossless schemes shorten the binary code without changing any information, so that a compressed file can be decompressed to its original identical format. Other compression models – like JPEG for image – are lossy (Cornell University Library undated f). They utilize a means for averaging or discarding the least significant information, based on an understanding of visual perception (Cornell University Library undated b). Because the file cannot be decompressed to its original form, lossy models go against the principle of preservation itself.

Deaccessioning

Collection management is not a linear process but must be seen as a cycle. Managers should constantly re-appraise their collections and sometimes accept deaccessioning (Malaro 1998, 216–239). Deaccessioning is "the process by which an archives, museum, or library permanently removes accessioned materials (i.e., collections, series, record groups) from its holdings" (SAA 2012a, 3). As the SAA's guideline on Reappraisal and Deaccessioning asserts, "since the 1980s, the archival profession has more readily come to acknowledge reappraisal and deaccessioning as parts of good collections management practices" but these practices "remain controversial and not fully accepted by the profession" (SAA 2012b). Repositories cannot preserve everything, and with the increasing number of subjects and formats of items collected, deaccessioning may become more and more relevant. A clear process must be established before deciding to deaccession items, to avoid endangering the integrity of the collection and the reputation of the repository.

The process of deaccessioning must be well documented and must follow legal considerations established during the acquisition contract (SAA 2012a, 6–7). The repository should make sure that it holds the title to legally deaccession the item (Genoways and Ireland 2003, 192). Although limited to archives, the SAA's Guideline for Reappraisal and Deaccessioning provides a step-by-step procedure, a checklist, templates, and a bibliography that can help any collection managers (2012a, 8–34; American Alliance of Museums 2012). Deaccessioning should only be used to improve the quality and integrity of the collection. The process must be systematic and not limited to one part of the collection. It must be transparent and collaborative. It may involve other institutions and communities who may take advantage of the collections. Preferably items should be offered to other collections, and transferred rather than sold or destroyed. In some particular cases, deaccessioning may help the return of collections to their communities (Malaro 1998, 234–238). Exchanging deaccessioned items can also reinforce collaboration and create more appropriate collections to match the repository's mission statement.

Challenges in Archival Collection Management

Although collection management processes for archives, manuscripts, and museum collections share many similarities, they also differ on very specific terms and steps. This is the reason why the two following parts focus on the specific challenges in archival and museum collections.

Selection Process in Archival Repositories

The examination of historical papers and other written archival documents to be preserved follows the traditional historical methodology on primary sources. The format and contents of the documents must be analyzed and set into their historical context. Archivists should examine how the document connects to people, how it reflects the values of its historical context, and how its meaning changed over time (Gurian 2004). In other words, archivists must determine to what extent the document enriches the general knowledge of the period (Smithsonian Education undated).

Furthermore, it is necessary to distinguish between archives that preserve their institution's records, and other repositories that deal with several different agencies and donors. Much more than managers of museum collections, archivists benefit from professional standards to assess the value of objects. The value of items falls into two broad categories: primary values for the originating agency, and secondary values for other agencies and private users (Schellenberg 1956). The primary value of an item derives from its links with the institution that produced it. The mission statement in institutional and corporate archives greatly results from internal needs. Items can be used for operating, administrative, legal, and fiscal issues about the producing institution. For corporate archives, collection managers should consider how companies could use the records to improve their public relations and to promote new products as well. The specificity, functioning, and future needs of the institution – for instance federal government, private company – greatly affect the selection process. The value of the record is directly linked to the institution's policy, history, and uses.[5] Archives that deal directly with institutional records must therefore have strong links with other internal actors. This is especially true for corporate archive management that requires collaboration with the different departments within the company to uniformly represent the work of the institution (Eulenberg 1984).

The type of user who accesses the evidence determines the secondary value of the item. The profile of the users is as varied as repositories themselves. The users include – but are obviously not limited to – researchers, genealogist, journalists, attorneys, ethnic minorities, and other community groups. For example, Native Americans may use archival records to establish legal claims to land and privileges guaranteed by federal and state governments. Users may need the item as a piece of evidence (evidential value) on the organization and functioning of the body that produced it. Users can also look for information (informational value) on persons, groups, communities, institutions, issues, and conditions with which the originating actors had been dealing (Schellenberg 1956). Thanks to their understanding of the public uses of the past, public historians can help collection managers understand the many possible uses of an item.

Born-Digital Archives: New Specific Items

Every aspect of collection management has been affected by digital technology. This led to the establishment of digital curating and digital archiving (Cunningham 2008). Born-digital archives result from this digital innovation and raise new challenges for archivists. Born-digital archives are archives that have been created in a digital format (University of Virginia Library undated). Emails, websites, digital photography, digital videos, and other digital formats have become primary sources that may have to be collected. Born-digital items pose a great challenge to collection managers. First, the life expectancy of those sources is usually very brief. In their guide on digital history, members of the Center for History and New Media (CHNM) Daniel Cohen and Roy Rosenzweig discuss the fragility of digital materials, while explaining why and how to preserve them (2005). The quantitative aspect is problematic too. For example, how should historians approach and participate in the preservation of the 40 million emails produced by Bill Clinton's administration?

Various projects have been trying to archive sources from the Internet. Among them is the Internet Archive that, since 1996, has attempted to archive the web. The Wayback Machine indexes billions of webpages that go back to the 1990s (Wayback Machine undated). Digital archivists have to be innovative in collecting new formats. For instance, in addition to audiobooks, audio recording, and videos, the Internet Archive has the largest collection of historical software in the world, which can be crucial in documenting the history of computer technology (Internet Archive Software Collection undated). In order to collect, manage, and preserve born-digital documents, a broader and deeper understanding of their specificity must be developed, and this understanding must be incorporated into the training of new archival professionals, professional development programs, and continuing education (University of Virginia Library undated).

The examination of born-digital objects may, at first, seem problematic. The main challenge in the appraisal and examination of born-digital objects is their authenticity. The rise of the Internet has both resulted in a multiplication of digital sources and a loss of identification. It may, for instance, be difficult to identify the author of a digital photograph in a web collection. Based on traditional analysis of primary sources and on the specificity of the format, archivists and librarians have worked on a methodology to examine the authenticity of born-digital sources. Berkeley Library provides useful guides to study the authenticity of digital sources (UC Berkeley 2012). The criteria of examination do not change, but when examining born-digital sources it is the subject that is different. For instance, regarding websites, archivists should examine URL, webmasters, successive updates, and uses of sources.[6] The map of hyperlinks within the website also helps to situate the object in digital networks. Using web analysis tools – such as Google Analytics or Alexa – can also clarify the website traffic and users.

Arrangement in Archival Repositories

Although every repository is confronted with the process of arranging items in their collection, there are numerous standards in place that help guide archivists through the process.

Two main principles that guide the process of arrangement: the principle of provenance and the principle of original order. The principle of provenance means that the records that were created, assembled, accumulated, and/or maintained by an organization or individual must be represented and arranged in a similar order, distinct from other records. This principle requires the items to be sorted by creator, and not by topic. The principle of order means that the issuing institution, group, or persons of origin arranged materials. Those records must be kept together (i.e., identified as belonging to the same aggregation) in their original order, if such order exists or has been maintained (Muller et al. 2002, 19). Together, these principles form the basis of archival arrangement (SAA 2013, xvi).

Born-digital materials can have multiple arrangements (or rather, multiple arrangements can be represented), such as the original order of the files as they were received or a different order – for instance chronological – applied by the archivist. The most crucial factor is the stabilization of the born-digital object. The format and structure of the item must not change according to the display tool. So it is extremely important for managers to understand the file environment such as software and file format, and to keep it consistent for the sake of preservation.

Arrangement also requires archivists to identify sub-groups of materials within the documents when the original ordering established by the creators is unknown (Holmes 1964). This process creates hierarchical groupings of materials, with each step in the hierarchy described as a level. Archivists have usually worked with levels such as – from broader to specific – collections, record group, series, file, and item (SAA 2013, xvii). Series and files should be arranged according to some logical patterns that reflect the interrelationships among documents (Schellenberg 1956). The final step in the arrangement process consists of shelving and boxing items. Normally, non-loose items can be shelved according to the aforementioned hierarchy of levels. Loose items are boxed, in other words, put into archival containers.

The Specific Management of Museum Collections

Selection Process

The specificity of the museum collection management derives almost entirely from both the multiple donors and origins of artifacts, as well as a focus on objects. Unlike archives that deal with a limited number of donors, manuscript and museum collections usually have to evaluate a broader range of possible acquisition. Thus, collection managers have to design a broader and more complex mission statement, which is still attainable. Collection planning begins with an intellectual framework that states the rationale for the collections, long-term preservation, and use of the material (Gardner and Merritt 2004, 5). The mission statement and collecting policy should not be too restrictive in designing collection areas, it should underline the preservation and interpretation objectives, and identify the target audience (Gardner and Merritt 2004, 7, 11–27). A collections plan must provide information about the discipline, geography, time period, groups, culture, and types of items the institution intends to collect (AAM 2008). When a large number of donors exist, the selection process may become more problematic. In order to fill gaps in their collections, managers may, for instance, have to establish surveys of potential donors to solicit them for gifts or purchases (Ham 2006). The managers have to clearly decide what areas they are willing and able to document.

Selection also depends on the changing historical value attributed to items. For instance, appraising the value of historical objects has changed since the 19th century (Conn 2010, 20–21). Items are today less likely to be collected for their monetary value, but rather for their capacity to embody interpretations of the past (Pearce 1993). Today, in other words, objects are increasingly acquired for their relevance to historical interpretation rather than for their material value. In the past, museum history collections mostly focused on the expensive, unusual, fine, or emotionally meaningful artifacts. Today, more and more history museums collect and preserve the ordinary objects, representative of everyday life (Woodhouse 2006, 190).

Examination of Material Culture

Historians are less accustomed to the examination of material culture than the analysis of written sources. They may, therefore, be less equipped for the process of examination in museum collections. Historians may follow different methodologies applied to the examination of material culture. One of the methods applied frequently to the examination of material culture is a model proposed by McClung Fleming (1974). Fleming suggested that to understand an object, researchers first describe five *properties* of an artifact: history, materials, construction, design, and function. Once they understand the properties, material culture researchers proceed to conduct four *operations* on these properties: identification, evaluation, cultural analysis, and interpretation.

The properties, history, materials, construction, design, and function allow the researchers to describe the object. In examining the history of the object, we need to question who made the document, when, and where was it created. The materials category helps us to determine what the object is made of, and what role each material plays in the object. The construction unravels techniques employed to make the object. The design deals with the structure, style, and form of the object. Finally, the function provides information about its uses and the audience of the object. The four operations that researchers conduct on the objects, identification, evaluation, cultural analysis, and interpretation, allow material culture historians to understand the object and place it within a broader context. The identification deals with the authentication of the object. The evaluation assigns the item to a category of artifacts, and during evaluation the object is compared to other items either similar or very different to the artifact in question. The cultural analysis details the relations between the object and its contemporary culture; it offers information on the society that made and consumed the artifact, and the context in which it was created and used. Finally, the interpretation provides the meaning and significance of the object throughout its life as assigned by its creators and various users (Kyvig and Marty 2000, 149–153).

Examination is never a simple description. Determining the properties and operations requires research and reading on specific aspects of material culture. In the end, examination creates intrinsic data about the object in order to provide a better appraisal of its value and to determine proper preservation. Collected data will also be useful for creating records about objects. In order to better undertake examination, historians can use the lists of questions and tutorials provided by different museums and organizations (Smithsonian Education undated).

Accessioning Items from a Variety of Donors

Once again, the relationship with donors (or other sources of acquisition) must be considered (Malaro 1998, 65–206). This is particularly important for repositories that are –

unlike archives – not associated with particular institutions. The variety of donors forces museums – and to some extent manuscript collections – to apply strict rules of accession. Accessioning includes a very important legal process. Legal control over the document is officially transferred through a contract from the former owner to an archive or a museum. This contract can be undertaken through a purchase agreement, a letter, a will, a deposit agreement, or a deed of gift agreement (Hunter 2004, 102). The accession policy also ensures that information on the acquirement of the item (from its former owner) is preserved in the repository. The policy should require that donors have acquired and possessed the items both legally and ethically. For instance, the repository must make sure the object was not stolen or that the original site was not damaged when the object was found and acquired. The contract stipulates the name of the donor, the recipient, the date, the material, the transfer of rights, and the eventual restriction of use and access (Buck and Gilmore 1998). Repositories should ensure that donors understand the policies and processes associated with accessioning sufficiently so that they can participate effectively in the process, providing necessary information and guidance relevant to the item (University of Virginia Library undated, 18).

Items added to the collection need to be assigned accession numbers (Reibel 1997, 44–57). The accession record is the acquiring institution's legal record of the transfer of possession of an item. All documents pertaining to an object or group of objects need to have accession numbers placed on them. There is no general guide to the numbering system for accessions since every institution may adopt a preferred classification, but the agreed system should be acknowledged in the collection management policy (Genoways and Ireland 2003, 180). Generally, an accession number is a two-part number corresponding to the year in which the item was acquired and the chronological number of accessions within that year, for instance 2010/31 stands for the 31st item collected in 2010. The number of items in a lot may also be included, 2010/31/1 being the first item of the lot.

What Can Public Historians Bring to Collection Management?

Relationships between academic historians and archivists/curators have often suffered from tension regarding the ultimate uses of collections. The differing educational backgrounds of academic historians and the archivists/curators partly explains the gap between collection managers and users. On the one hand, since the rise of professional and scientific history in the late 19th century, the analysis of archives and other primary sources has been the central activity of historians. The extreme specialization of academic historians in terms of research resulted in their involvement in the process of historical interpretation. Academic historians rarely participate in the creation and management of collections and merely see the value of archives as repositories of useful historical primary sources. On the other hand, archivists and curators are mandated to care for and preserve collections (Buchanan 2011). Curators and archivists, often defined by their respective institutions as managers, require skills in budgeting and project management rather than historical knowledge. In his article on the links between historians and archival procedures, Tom Nesmith shows how archivists moved from an acknowledged historical background in the early 20th century to a later rejection of historical knowledge as a key component of an archivist's expertise and professional identity (2004, 1).

It is of paramount importance that public historians re-connect collection management with the history profession. Public historians strive to participate in a larger process of doing history, from selections and acquisition of historical collections to the multitude of presentations of history through media, collaborative projects, exhibitions, and advocacy. Public historians are also needed because of the changing practices in collection repositories that increasingly search for public engagement. This can be achieved through the design of contemporary historical collections as well as through public access and participation in collection management.

The Design of Historical Collections

Historians can assist managers in developing a better historical understanding of their collections. Historians can provide details about the establishment of the collections – who started them, when, and why (University of North Carolina Library 2012). Historians can also be of great help in identifying missing and underrepresented historical areas/ periods in the collections. Anthropologist Michel-Rolph Trouillot brilliantly explains how silences in historiography arise first from collecting and archiving policies that have ignored certain areas of the past (1995; Cook and Schwartz 2002). Collection managers are powerful actors in determining what societies do and do not remember from their past.

Since historians are aware of the broad spectrum of potential uses of a document in historical research, they are also well equipped to appraise the historical value of items. Scholarship cannot be the only criterion in determining how useful an item is. Although every appraisal is somewhat subjective, public historians are arguably best trained to foresee how researchers in the future may apply an archival document to their inquiries. This is particularly useful for contemporary collecting issues. Archives and museums increasingly document contemporary societies (Cox 1986, 40). This belongs to the general shift in collection management that puts users at the center of the process. Contemporary collecting helps connect users with familiar items. However, contemporary collecting is a challenge for collection managers who have to decide what aspect of present-day history is worth saving (Rhys 2001). At the crossroads between historical interpretation and the public uses of the past, public historians are well equipped to identify collections that both appeal to visitors and possess historical value.

Historians have also participated in the creation of historically driven repositories. These repositories focus on a historical theme, site, event, individual, or period. The collecting principle differs from traditional repositories. Items do not necessarily have the same provenance. Cohen and Rosenzweig stress that instead of a shared provenance these website producers create their own virtual collections, often mixing published and unpublished materials in ways that "official" archives avoid (2005). One of the earliest and most famous examples was the Valley of the Shadow project. Developed in the early 1990s by the University of Virginia's Institute for Advanced Technology in the Humanities, the project compared the experience of two communities on either side of the Mason–Dixon Line during the Civil War. The project has gathered a massive number of documents about the two communities before, during, and after the Civil War, including photographs, newspaper articles, letters, census records, and Geographic Information Systems (GIS) maps. As Cohen and Rosenzweig argue, the site offers (at the very least) an implicit interpretation of these materials rather than taking the hands-off approach of most archives, and this blurring between archive and historical argument perhaps makes Valley of the Shadow and similar sites more like edited collections of documents rather than a traditional archive (2005).

Public Historians and the Tension Between Use (Access) and Storage (Restriction)

The balance between use and storage or between access and restriction has been a crucial issue in collection management. The profile of public historians working in collection management can trigger a debate about conflicting objectives. Historians may first encounter a personal tension between their historical expertise and their management of a collection. Historians working in archival and museum repositories should be aware of possible conflicts of interest. They can only undertake personal research that has been approved by their employers. Besides, historians should not own private collections in areas covered by the institutions, at the risk of being unethical. Clear policies and standards should be established to avoid conflicts of interest (American Association of Museums 2009). Likewise, archivists and curators may encounter sensitive materials and may have access to restricted information – that other researchers would not – and should never reveal privileged information.

What is more, public historians should balance public access with restriction. On the one hand, public historians should aim at increasing public access to the collection. For example, the SAA adopted a Code of Ethics for Archivists in 1980 – revised in 1992 and 2005 – that explains "archivists discourage reasonable restrictions on access or use." On the other hand, public historians must participate in the preservation of the items and sometimes restrict their access. The Code of Ethics adds that archivists "may accept as a condition of acquisition clearly stated restrictions of limited duration" (SAA 1980, 414). Public historians should contribute to the discussion on the balance between use/access and storage/preservation.

Public historians must understand the ethics and condition to access. Historians can access many different resources regarding ethics in museums, archives and libraries (Institute of Museum Ethics undated; American Alliance of Museums undated; Edson 1997; American Association of Museums 2000; American Institute for Conservation 1994; International Council on Museums undated; Benedict 2003; SAA undated d; International Council on Archives 1996; Danielson 2010; Mix 2013). Restrictions to access collections may come from two main issues: the item itself, or the contract agreed upon during its acquisition. Regarding the item, collection managers must make sure that public access would not deteriorate its state. Managers must recognize that the balance between preservation and use of collection objects is delicate, and must discourage uses of the collection that may unnecessarily hasten the degradation or deterioration of any object (American Association of Museums 2009). Some objects, such as human remains, sacred objects, and funerary objects, are particularly sensitive. Collection managers should consult with descendant communities regarding handling, storing, and exhibiting materials with consideration and respect for cultural traditions (American Association of Museums 2009). When dealing with Native American collections, managers must ensure that they comply with the Native American Graves Protection and Repatriation Act (NAGPRA) (Richman and Forsyth 2004, 165–251). Institutions must undertake inventories and may have to access demands of repatriation of Native American objects.[7]

The second main reason to limit access to collections derives from the legal framework of the attribution, such as copyrights, privacy laws, freedom of information, and repatriation, in order to better identify the limits to public access (Genoways and Ireland 2003, 291–313). Navigating legal issues is one of the many challenges faced by historians working with collection management (Behrnd-Klodt 2008). Legal issues may deal with access for visitors with disabilities, repatriation, liability, or rights and copyrights. Collection managers must respect the conditions of access agreed upon during the acquisition. Confidentiality and copyrights are of paramount importance for access, loans, and exhibitions of materials. Sometimes, conditions of access are not clear, so that managers "must balance the sometimes conflicting rights of donors, records creators, researchers, and 'third parties' affected by archival disclosure" (Jimerson 2006, 88–89). Indeed, confidentiality is not restricted to donors but needs to be extended to third parties who appear in the records and who may want to be protected from disclosure. Their consideration of the various uses of the past may equip public historians with a solid understanding of what public access could offer to both the repository and the different users. Obviously, use and preservation, or access and restriction, are not mutually exclusive. Digital technology can, however, help public historians reach compromises.

Maintain Public Access to the Collection

While understanding the need for preservation and the possible legal restriction, public historians may contribute to increased public access to the collection. In order to do so, public historians can use multiple digital tools (Theimer 2011). Websites can give public access to indexes and lists of materials or to digital copies of the collections. Social networks can also foster public interest in primary sources (James 2009). Through the processes of digitization, repositories can make their collections available online. Online collections can be accessed from anywhere in the world. For instance, in 1997 the French National Library developed the Gallica project that provides online access to their digital collections. Likewise, many archives of newspapers are available online. ProQuest has created a Digital Vault Initiative and today provides one of the largest digital archival collections, including the *New York Times*, *Wall Street Journal*, and *Washington Post*. Digital access is not limited to written documents. For instance, the Smithsonian Museum has 3D-scanned the life masks of Abraham Lincoln, and made them available online for downloading and printing on a standard 3D printer (Lohr 2014). It is therefore critical for public historians in collection management to have digital skills in order to foster public access.

Public historians should not only create but also maintain public access. Indeed, one challenging issue is about the durability and accessibility of the collections. Due to fast-changing technology, digital-born objects have a short life expectancy. The obsolescence of digital technology is the major problem in storage and preservation of born-digital archives. Data stored on floppy disks is a good example of this challenge. This format was completely replaced by CD-ROM, DVD and flash drive, thus making access to data stored on a floppy disk a difficult and sometimes tricky ordeal. Ideally, a repository needs to acquire every kind of hardware to transfer the data to be stored and preserved (Digital Preservation Management undated). Although extremely expensive, acquiring hardware might still be feasible, however the software issue is even more problematic.

Some files created by specific software may not be readable by other software and may therefore be lost. One current famous example is Adobe's Portable Document Format (pdf) that can only be read through Acrobat reader. Preservation practice should make sure digital items can always be read in the future, and favors open-source software in which source code is openly available. Digital public historians have a role to play in making sure digital archives can be accessed. For instance, the Open Archives Initiative develops and promotes interoperability standards that aim to facilitate the efficient dissemination of content.

In order to assure access to digital items, repositories may have to act on their collections. They can refresh their collections, which involves copying content from one storage medium to another (for example from CD-ROMs to DVD). Repositories can also migrate data. Migrating is the process of transferring digital information from one hardware and software setting to another or from one computer generation to subsequent generations. The update is not only about the media but also takes into consideration the environment in which the data were originally created. Technology preservation is the act of preserving the technical environment that runs the system, including operating systems, original application software, and media drives (Digital Preservation Management undated). When the technical environment needed to view and use data is recreated, the process is called emulation. This is achieved by maintaining information about the hardware and software requirements so that the system can be re-engineered (Cornell University Library undated a). The relevance of the digital environment explains why the Internet Archives' process of archiving software is so important. We need to preserve software in order to preserve data. All those operations contribute to creating a trusted digital repository (TDR). A TDR must "provide reliable, long-term access to managed digital resources to its designated community, now and in the future" (Research Library Group 2002, 5). Since 2002, several reports have been published about TDR (Digital Preservation Management undated). They help digital collection managers to design sustainable projects, and ensure future access.

Collaboration and Public Participation

The number of online repositories has exploded in the last ten years. It is more and more necessary for repositories to collaborate in order to create large online platforms that direct users and provide access to collections. For instance, the Digital Public Library of America brings together the riches of America's libraries, archives, and museums, and makes them freely available to the world. The Library of Congress took part in the American Memory project for public domain image resources from various institutions. Other portals are more specific to historical primary sources. The European Historical Primary Sources (EHPS) was created in 2009 at the European University Institute (Italy). It provides an index of digital repositories that contain and give access to primary sources for the history of Europe. Because of their knowledge of historical context and the various uses of primary sources, digital public historians can be of great help to archival repositories by creating those online public platforms that help users find documents.

Public historians can also foster public interaction, a shift explained by Stephen Weil in his book *Making Museums Matter*, wherein he stresses that museums change from being about something to being for somebody (2002). Users are becoming increasingly important in the selection of objects and archives (Pugh 2005). Figure 1.2 shows the interaction between a member of the local community, a historian, and a graduate student. The scene takes place during a history harvest project in 2010. History harvest collects artifacts gathered from communities. Initially designed by the history department at the University of Nebraska-Lincoln, harvests now take place across the United States. History harvest is a collaborative, team-oriented, student-centered, and community-based project. In the picture, the member of the community brings an artifact and explains its (hi)stories to the student and historian. The member of the community is not a traditional donor – in this case, the artifact is not collected but is digitally captured and then shared in a free web-based archive – but an actor of the historical understanding of the past. The stories are recorded and help provide a meaning to the artifact and more broadly of the past. The popular involvement also helps challenge the supremacy of traditional elite sources and gives students experience in public history practice.

To consider all of the possible future uses of a given item would be an overwhelming and

Figure 1.2 University of Nebraska-Lincoln history professor, William G. Thomas III (second on the right), and graduate student, Robert Voss (right), discuss contributed objects with a community member at the 2010 History Harvest. Courtesy of History Harvest/University of Nebraska-Lincoln.

almost impossible task for archivists and curators; therefore, it may be useful to open the selection process to the public. Cooperative or open-collecting helps curators and archivists to better decide what to collect. Archivists, curators, researchers but also community members "determine the aspects of the society that need documenting, identify institutions that may have records shedding light on these aspects, and work with those institutions to preserve and even create records, if necessary" (Hunter 2004, 99). Public historians should be inventive and offer opportunities to the public to participate in selecting what is worth preserving – and therefore remembering – about the past. This public selection could be done through public meetings, surveys, or through digital repositories where historians could consider public discussion to decide the value of an item. For instance, the National Museum of African American History and Culture has been asking people to participate in deciding what should be collected. This helps collection managers to deal with the polysemic aspects of documents whose meaning may differ according to users. Working with the public can also allow repositories to "actively document those whose voices have been overlooked or marginalized" (SAA 2011). Public engagement might contribute to limiting historical silences in collections.

Through digital public collections, public historians have to deal with the changing role of collection managers and discuss how the public engagement affects the whole collection process (Hollowak 2009). Some repositories are now entirely digital. Some museums – called virtual museums – have an exclusively online presence. The Internet has become the most diverse, and the largest, repository of historical primary sources in the world. Digital public historians have created user-generated digital collections based on audience participation. What is specific is that the users create the contents. The public downloads digital items and enriches the database/collection. For instance, the September 11 Digital

Archives project "contains more than 150,000 digital objects, including more than 40,000 personal stories and 15,000 digital images" (Brennan and Kelly 2009).

A similar digital repository was created after hurricanes Katrina and Rita in November 2005 in Louisiana. Sheila Brennan and Mills Kelly, the creators of the Hurricane Archives, explain: "we demonstrate how you can create a digital archive and encourage public participation without losing the integrity of evidence collected or compromising the privacy of a contributor" (Brennan and Kelly 2009). Figure 1.3 is a screenshot of the current Hurricane Digital Memory Bank website that aims at "Collecting and Preserving the Stories of Katrina and Rita." As seen on the screenshot, individuals can upload first-hand accounts through pictures, online stories, oral histories, videos, or maps. The digital format and the simplicity of the uploading system made possible the collection of items right after the event occurred. The project gives voice to those who have been directly affected by the hurricanes. The digital format allows a variety of archival formats directly uploaded by members of communities. Due to the relocation of so many people, the geolocation of items also allows to better contextualize the digital archives. The role of public historians is to help redesign a model of relations between collection managers and the public. Collection managers have to decide the extent to which they wish to open their collections to the public, not just for passive use, but also for collaboration.

Public historians and collection managers may opt for open access to the repository. An open repository makes all information available to users, including previously hidden metadata. Opening data to users and peer institutions has the potential to increase collaborative activities. Public historians can help the public participate in the creation of metadata (Getty Foundation undated). With new digital technology, tagging of items by different users can help repositories to enrich the metadata of their collections. The challenge for collection managers is to open the collection while preserving the status of the documents and tracing participation. One way is to allow users to comment on – but not alter – documents. Archival repositories and museums can employ Web 2.0 and new media to increase participation in their collections. Collection managers have used photo-sharing sites as an

Figure 1.3 Screenshot of the Hurricane Digital Memory Bank, "Collecting and Preserving the Stories of Katrina and Rita," http://hurricanearchive.org/, September 2015. Courtesy of the Hurricane Digital Memory Bank.

outreach tool, making digital images of collection materials available to the public. Tools like Flickr or Pinterest allow the sharing of digitized primary sources with the public, and to ask for descriptive metadata – or tags – from users. They can also engage repositories in dialogue with users about the collections (The Interactive Archivist undated). The Oregon State University Archives has used Flickr to engage users with its photograph collection (Edmunson-Morton 2009). Tags and social bookmarking can help public interaction. Through tags, users can create links between items and between collections.

To conclude, public historians have a lot to contribute to the collection management process. Public historians are not only familiar with the historical context and the analysis of sources, but also the public and academic uses of the past; as such, they can greatly contribute to the enrichment of collection management. Through their training, they acquire skills necessary to identify material that carries historical significance and is crucial in understanding and interpreting the past for the public. The reflective aspect of public history – especially on shared authority – can also bring new approaches to the complex balance between preservation and use of the past. In order to put the relations between sources and public at the center of every practice of collection management, public historians have to be familiar with the different ethics and professional standards, but they also need to explore the different tools (in particular digital technology) to create a space and/ or platform for interaction.

Students of public history who wish to seek employment in collection management fields should contact and cooperate with librarians, archivists, and curators from local institutions. They can also take advantage of the numerous online resources on collection management, such as blogs, forums, as well as associations, journals, and other networks.[8] Public historians may benefit from exploring how collection management is taught in archival and museum studies programs.[9] Also, the National Park Service provides a very useful online museum handbook that details the practices for collections and records (NPS undated). Likewise, the University of North Carolina established an Archival Processing Toolbox that details the different steps of archival management such as processing, arranging, describing, and preserving material (University of North Carolina Library 2012).

Notes

1 Regarding the relevance of museums in public space, some argue that attendance has dropped since the 1970s, and that there are possibly too many and above all too much alike institutions to explain a possible end of history museums (Carson 2008, 13–16). Others, more optimistic, speak of a second golden age for museums (Conn 2010, 1). The Institute of Museum and Library Services (IMLS) announced that there are 35,144 museums in the United States, more than double the agency's working estimate of 17,500 from the 1990s.
2 See below the specificity of accessioning for archives and museum collections.
3 See below the part on archives.
4 MARC became USMARC in the 1980s and MARC 21 in the late 1990s (Library of Congress undated a).
5 For instance, corporate archives may take into consideration the value of an item for future internal policy uses.
6 The Wayback Machine (Internet Archive) is very useful here to examine the various updates.
7 For more details on NAGPRA and Repatriation, see Chapter 12.
8 Organizations and resources about museums, see the American Alliance of Museums (AAM) www.aam-us.org/; The Institute of Museum and Library Services www.imls.gov/; the American Association for State and Local History (AASLH) http://about.aaslh.org/home/; the International Council of Museums http://icom.museum/; International Association of Museums of History www. aimh.org; the Museum Computer Network www.mcn.edu; The Smithsonian Center for Learning

and Digital Access (SCLDA)'s list of journals http://museumstudies.si.edu/Header2.html (their website also provides a rich list of reading and online resources). For a bibliography on museum, see also http://museumstudies.si.edu/ICOM-ICTOP/sources.htm; organizations and resources about archives: see the Society of American Archivists (SAA) www2.archivists.org/; the International Council of Archives www.ica.org/; International Council on Archives www.Ica.org; National Association of Government Archives and Records Administrators www.nagara.org; Mid-Atlantic Regional Archives Conference www.marac.info; Archivists Round Table of Metropolitan New York www.nycarchivists.org; National Archives and Records Administration www.archives.gov; New York State Archives www.archives.nysed.gov; New York City Department of Records www.nyc.gov/html/records/home.html. See also the American Archivist online http://archivists.meta-press.com/content/120809

9 For an introduction to museums studies, see the museum studies at Leicester www.futurelearn.com/courses/museum (accessed September 13, 2015).

Bibliography

Alivizatou, Marilena. "Intangible Heritage and Erasure: Rethinking Cultural Preservation and Contemporary Museum Practice." *International Journal of Cultural Property*, 18/1 (2011): 37–60.

American Alliance of Museums. *Standards and Best Practices for Museums*, undated, www.aam-us.org/resources/ethics-standards-and-best-practices/standards (accessed July 25, 2015).

American Alliance of Museums. "Deaccessioning Activity." 2012, www.aam-us.org/docs/continuum/deaccessioning-activity.pdf?sfvrsn=2 (accessed July 25, 2015).

American Association of Museums. *Organizing Your Museum: The Essentials*, Washington, DC: American Association of Museums, 1989.

American Association of Museums. *A Code of Ethics for Museums*, Washington, DC: AAM, 2000.

American Association of Museums. *National Standards and Best Practices for U.S. Museums*, Washington, DC: AAM, 2008.

American Association of Museums. *A Code of Ethics for Curators*, Washington, DC: AAM, 2009, www.aam-us.org/docs/continuum/curcomethics.pdf?sfvrsn=0 (accessed July 25, 2015).

American Institute for Conservation. *Code of Ethics and Guidelines of Practice*, 1994, www.nps.gov/training/tel/Guides/HPS1022_AIC_Code_of_Ethics.pdf (accessed July 25, 2015).

Anderson, Gail. *Reinventing the Museum: Historical and Contemporary Perspectives on the Paradigm Shift*, Lanham: AltaMira Press, 2004.

Archives and Public History Digital. *Introduction to Preservation and Reformatting*, undated, http://aphdigital.org/courses/introduction-to-preservation-and-reformatting/ (accessed July 25, 2015).

Baca, Murtha, ed. *Introduction to Metadata*, Los Angeles: Getty Publications, 2008, www.getty.edu/research/publications/electronic_publications/intrometadata/index.html (accessed July 25, 2015).

Baca, Murtha and Harpring, Patricia, eds. *Categories for the Description of Works of Art*, Los Angeles: Getty Trust Association, 2014, www.getty.edu/research/publications/electronic_publications/cdwa/ (accessed July 25, 2015).

Baca, Murtha, Harpring, Patricia, Lanzi, Elisa, McRae, Linda, and Whiteside, Ann. *Cataloguing Cultural Objects: A Guide to Describing Cultural Works and Their Images*, Chicago: ALA Editions, 2006, http://cco.vrafoundation.org/index.php/toolkit/cco_pdf_version/ (accessed July 25, 2015).

BCR. *BCR's CDP Digital Imaging Best Practices Version 2.0*, June 2008, http://mwdl.org/docs/digital-imaging-bp_2.0.pdf (accessed July 25, 2015).

Behrnd-Klodt, Menzi. *Navigating Legal Issues in Archives*, Washington, DC: Society of American Archivists, 2008.

Benedict, Karen. *Ethics and the Archival Profession: Introduction and Case Studies*, Chicago: Society of American Archivists, 2003.

Boles, Frank. *Selecting and Appraising Archives and Manuscripts*, Chicago: Society of American Archivists, 2005.

Brennan, Sheila A. and Kelly, Mills. "Why Collecting History Online is Web 1.5." 2009, http://chnm.gmu.edu/essays-on-history-new-media/essays/?essayid=47 (accessed July 25, 2015).

Buchanan, Alexandrina. "Strangely Unfamiliar: Idea of the Archive from Outside the Discipline." In *The Future of Archives and Recordkeeping: A Reader*, edited by Jenny Hill, London: Facet Publishing, 2011, 37–62.

Buck, Rebecca A. and Gilmore, Jean Allman. *New Museum Registration Methods*, Washington, DC: American Association of Museums, 1998.

Caple, Chris. *Conservation Skills: Judgement, Method and Decision Making*, London and New York: Routledge, 2000.

Caple, Chris, ed. *Preventive Conservation in Museums*, London and New York: Routledge, 2011.

Carbonell, Bettina Messias, ed. *Museum Studies: An Anthology of Contexts*, Malden, MA: Blackwell Publishing, 2004.

Carson, Cary. "The End of History Museums: What's Plan B?" *The Public Historian*, 30/4 (November 2008): 9–27.

Cauvin, Thomas. "Quando è in gioco la Public History: musei, storici e riconciliazione politica nella Repubblica d'Irlanda." *Memoria e Ricerca*, 37 (2011): 53–71. English translation, "When Public History is at Stake: Museum, Historians and Political Reconciliation in the Republic of Ireland," www.fondazionecasadiOriani.it/modules.php?name=MR&op=body&id=550 (accessed July 25, 2015).

Clifford, James. "Museums as Contact Zones." In *Routes: Travel and Translation in the Late Twentieth Century*, edited by James Clifford, Cambridge, MA: Harvard University Press, 1997, 188–219.

Cohen, Daniel and Rosenzweig, Roy. *Digital History: A Guide to Gathering, Preserving, and Presenting the Past on the Web*, Philadelphia: University of Pennsylvania Press, 2005.

Conn, Steven. *Do Museums Still Need Objects?* Philadelphia: University of Pennsylvania Press, 2010.

Cook, Terry and Schwartz, Joan. "Archives, Records, and Power: The Making of Modern Memory." *Archival Science*, 2 (2002): 1–19.

Cornell University Library. *Moving Theory into Practice: Digital Imaging Tutorial*, undated a, www.library.cornell.edu/preservation/tutorial/metadata/metadata-01.html (accessed July 25, 2015).

Cornell University Library. *Introduction*, undated b, www.library.cornell.edu/preservation/tutorial/intro/intro-01.html (accessed July 25, 2015).

Cornell University Library. *Conversion*, undated c, www.library.cornell.edu/preservation/tutorial/conversion/conversion-01.html (accessed July 25, 2015).

Cornell University Library. *Presentation Table*, undated d, www.library.cornell.edu/preservation/tutorial/presentation/table7-1.html (accessed July 25, 2015).

Cornell University Library. *Technical Infrastructure*, undated e, www.library.cornell.edu/preservation/tutorial/technical/technicalA-01.html (accessed July 25, 2015).

Cornell University Library. *Compression Techniques*, undated f, www.library.cornell.edu/preservation/tutorial/presentation/table7-3.html (accessed July 25, 2015).

Cox, Richard J. "Archivists and Public Historians in the United States." *The Public Historian*, 8/3 (Summer 1986): 29–45.

Crane, Susan. "The Conundrum of Ephemerality: Time, Memory and Museum." In *The Blackwell Companion to Museum Studies*, edited by Sharon MacDonald, New York and Oxford: Blackwell Publishers, 2005, 98–109.

Cunningham, Adrian. "Digital Curation/Digital Archiving: A View from the National Archives of Australia." *American Archivist* (Fall/Winter 2008): 530–543.

Danielson, Elena S. *The Ethical Archivist*, Chicago: Society of American Archivists, 2010.

Dearstyne, Bruce W. "Archives and Public History: Issues, Problems, and Prospects: An Introduction." *The Public Historian*, 8/3 (Summer 1986): 6–9.

Desnoyers, Megan Floyd. "Personal Papers." In *Managing Archives and Archival Institutions*, edited by James Gregry Bradsher, Chicago: University of Chicago Press, 1991, 78–91.

Diamond, Judy. *Practical Evaluation Guide: Tools for Museums and Other Informal Educational Settings*, Walnut Creek: AltaMira Press, 1999.

Digital Preservation Management. *Obsolescence: Hardware and Media*, undated, http://dpworkshop. org/dpm-eng/oldmedia/obsolescence2.html and *Digital Preservation Strategy*, undated, http:// dpworkshop.org/dpm-eng/terminology/strategies.html (accessed July 25, 2015).

Dillenburg, Eugene. "What, If Anything, Is a Museum?" *Exhibitionist* (Spring 2011): 8–13, http://name-aam.org/uploads/downloadables/EXH.spg_11/5%20EXH_spg11_What,%20if%20Anything,%20 Is%20a%20Museum__Dillenburg.pdf (accessed July 25, 2015).

Dolan, Douglas C. "The Historian in the Local Historical Museum." In *Public History: an Introduction*, edited by Barbara Howe and Emory L. Kemp, Malabar: Robert E. Krieger Publishing Company, 1986, 241–250.

Dublin Core Metadata Initiative. Undated, http://dublincore.org/documents/dcmi-terms/ (accessed July 25, 2015).

Duncan, Carol. "From the Princely Gallery to the Public Art Museum: The Louvre Museum and the National Gallery." In *Representing the Nation: A Reader*, edited by David Boswell and Jessica Evans, London: Routledge, 1999, 304–331.

Edmunson-Morton, Tiah. "Talking and Tagging: Using CONTENTdm and Flickr in the Oregon State University Archives." *The Interactive Archivist*, June 19, 2009, http://interactivearchivist. archivists.org/case-studies/flickr-at-osu/ (accessed July 25, 2015).

Edson, Gary. *Museum Ethics*, London: Routledge, 1997.

Eulenberg, Julia Niebuhr. "The Corporate Archives: Management Tool and Historical Resource." *The Public Historian*, 6/1 (Winter 1984): 20–37.

Fawcett, Sharon K. "Presidential Libraries: A View from the Center." *The Public Historian*, 28/3 (Summer 2006): 13–36.

Flinn, Andrew. "The Impact of Independent and Community Archives on Professional Archival Thinking and Practice." In *The Future of Archives and Recordkeeping: A Reader*, edited by Jennie Hill, London: Facet Publishing, 2011, 145–169.

Gardner, James B. and Merritt, Elizabeth E. *The AAM Guide to Collections Planning*, Washington, DC: American Association of Museums, 2004.

Genoways Hugh H. and Ireland, Lynne M. *Museum Administration: An Introduction*, Walnut Creek: AltaMira Press, 2003.

George, Jerry and Sherrell-Leo, Cindy. *Starting Right: A Basic Guide to Museum Planning*, Walnut Creek: AltaMira Press, 2004.

Getty Foundation. *Practical Principles for Metadata Creation and Maintenance*, undated, www.getty. edu/research/publications/electronic_publications/intrometadata/principles.html (accessed July 25, 2015).

Gilliland, Anne J. "Setting the Stage." In *Introduction to Metadata*, edited by Murtha Baca, Los Angeles: Getty Publications, 2008, www.getty.edu/research/publications/electronic_publications/ intrometadata/setting.html (accessed July 25, 2015).

Grant, Daniel. "How to Say 'No Thanks' to Donors." *Wall Street Journal*, May 19, 2010, http:// online.wsj.com/article/SB10001424052702304222504575173803616852666.html (accessed July 25, 2015).

Gurian, Elaine Heumann. "What is the Object of this Exercise? A Meandering Exploration of the Many Meanings of Objects in Museums." In *Reinventing the Museum: Historical and Contemporary Perspectives on the Paradigm Shift*, edited by Gail Anderson, Lanham: AltaMira Press, 2004, 269–283.

Ham, Debra N. "Manuscript Curators and Specialists." In *Public History: Essays from the Field*, edited by James Gardner and Peter LaPaglia, Malabar: Krieger Publishing Company, 2006, 178–185.

Ham, Gerald. *Selecting and Appraising Archives and Manuscripts*, Chicago: SAA, 1993.

Hill, Jenny. *The Future of Archives and Recordkeeping: A Reader*, London: Facet Publishing, 2011.

Hollowak, Thomas L. "Baltimore '68: Riots and Rebirth – The Building of a Digital Collection." *The Public Historian*, 31/4 (Fall 2009): 37–40.

Holmes, Oliver. "Archival Arrangement – Five Different Operations at Five Different Levels." *The American Archivist*, 27/1 (January 1964): 21–41, www.archives.gov/research/alic/reference/archives-resources/archival-arrangement.html#note (accessed July 25, 2015).

Hooper-Greenhill, Eilean. *Museums and the Shaping of Knowledge*, London: Routledge, 1992.

Hunter, Gregory S. *Developing and Maintaining Practical Archives: A How-To-Do-It Manual*, New York: Neal-Schuman Publishers, 2004.

Institute of Museum Ethics. *Links to Resources*, undated, http://museumethics.org/links-to-resources/ (accessed July 25, 2015).

Institute of Museum and Library Services. "Government Doubles Official Estimate: There Are 35,000 Active Museums in the U.S." IMLS website, May 19, 2014a, www.imls.gov/government_doubles_official_estimate.aspx (accessed July 25, 2015).

Institute of Museum and Library Services. "Museum Universe Data File." 2014b, www.imls.gov/assets/1/AssetManager/MUDF_TypeDist_2014q3.pdf (accessed July 25, 2015).

The Interactive Archivist. *Photo-Sharing Sites*, undated, http://interactivearchivist.archivists.org/technologies/photo-sharing-sites/ (accessed July 25, 2015).

International Council on Archives. *Code of Ethics*, 1996, www.ica.org/5555/reference-documents/ica-code-of-ethics.html (accessed July 25, 2015).

International Council on Museums. *Code of Ethics*, undated, http://icom.museum/professional-standards/code-of-ethics/preamble/L/0/ (accessed July 25, 2015).

Internet Archive Software Collection. Undated, https://archive.org/details/software/v2 (accessed July 25, 2015).

James, Russell D. "Using Facebook to Create Community: The SAA Group Experience." *The Internet Archivist*, May 18, 2009, http://interactivearchivist.archivists.org/case-studies/facebook-saa-group/ (accessed July 25, 2015).

Jimerson, Randall C. "Ethical Concerns for Archivists." *The Public Historian*, 28/1 (Winter 2006): 87–92.

Jones, Arnita A. and Cantelon, Philip L., eds. *Corporate Archives and History: Making the Past Work*, Malabar: Krieger Publisher, 1993.

Kaplan, Flora E.S., ed. *Museums and the Making of "Ourselves": The Role of Objects in National Identity*, London: Leicester University Press, 1994.

Kelly, Linda. "How Web 2.0 is Changing the Nature of Museum Work." *Curator: The Museum Journal*, 53/4 (October 2010): 405–410.

Kyvig, David E. and Marty, Myron A. *Nearby History: Exploring the Past Around You*, Walnut Creek: AltaMira Press, 2000.

Lane, Victoria and Hill, Jennie. "Where Do We Come From? What Are We? Where Are We Going? Situating the Archive and Archivists." In *The Future of Archives and Recordkeeping*, edited by Jennie Hill, London: Facet Publishing, 2011, 3–23.

Library of Congress. *MARC Standards*, undated a, www.loc.gov/marc/ (accessed July 25, 2015).

Library of Congress. *Encoded Archival Standards*, undated b, www.loc.gov/ead/ (accessed July 25, 2015).

Library of Congress. *VRA Core 4.0 Introduction*, October 28, 2014, www.loc.gov/standards/vracore/VRA_Core4_Intro.pdf (accessed July 25, 2015).

Lohr, Steve. "Museums Morph Digitally: The Met and Other Museums Adapt to the Digital Age." *The New York Times*, October 23, 2014.

Lord, Barry and Lord, Gail Dexter. *The Manual of Museum Planning*, Walnut Creek: AltaMira Press, 2002.

McClung Fleming, E. "Artifact Study: A Proposed Model." *Winterthur Portfolio*, 9 (1974): 153–173.

Macdonald, Sharon. "Expanding Museum Studies: An Introduction." In *A Companion to Museum Studies*, edited by Sharon Macdonald, Oxford: Blackwell, 2006, 1–12.

Macdonald, Sharon and Fyfe, Gordon, eds. *Theorizing Museums: Representing Identity and Diversity in a Changing World*, Oxford: Blackwell, 1996.

Malaro, Marie C. *A Legal Primer on Managing Museum Collections*, Washington, DC: Smithsonian Books, 1998.

Mason, Rhiannon. "Cultural Theory and Museum Studies." In *A Companion to Museum Studies*, edited by Sharon Macdonald, Oxford: Blackwell, 2006, 17–32.

Michalski, Stefan. "Relative Humidity and Temperature Guidelines: What's Happening?" *CCI Newsletter*, 14 (September 1994).

Miller, Frederic. "Archives and Historical Manuscripts." In *Public History: An Introduction*, edited by Barbara Howe and Emory L. Kemp, Malabar: Robert E. Krieger Publishing Company, 1986, 36–56.

Mix, Lisa, ed. *SAA Sampler: Law and Ethics*, Chicago: Society of American Archivists, 2013.

Montgomery, Bruce P. "Presidential Materials: Politics and the Presidential Records Act." *American Archivist* (Spring/Summer 2003): 102–138.

Muller, Samuel, Feith, J.A., and Fruin, R. *Manual for the Arrangement and Description of Archives*, Chicago: Society of American Archivists, 2002.

National Park Service. *Museum Handbook*, undated, www.nps.gov/museum/publications/handbook.html (accessed July 25, 2015).

Nesmith, Tom. "What's History Got to Do with It? Reconsidering the Place of Historical Knowledge in Archival Work." *Archivaria*, 57 (Spring 2004): 1–27.

O'Toole, James M. and Cox, Richard J. *Understanding Archives and Manuscripts*, Chicago: Society of American Archivists, 2006.

Padfield, Timothy. *The Effect of Light on Museum Objects*, 1996, www.padfield.org/tim/cfys/fading/light_i.php (accessed July 25, 2015).

Pearce, Susan. *Museums, Objects, and Collections*, Washington, DC: Smithsonian Press, 1993.

Pearce-Moses, Richard, ed. *A Glossary of Archival and Records Terminology*, Chicago: The Society of American Archivists, 2005, www2.archivists.org/glossary (accessed July 25, 2015).

Pugh, Mary Jo. "Identifying Uses and Users of Archives." In *Providing Reference Services for Archives and Manuscripts*, edited by Mary Jo Pugh, Chicago: Society of American Archivists, 2005, 33–73.

Rectanus, Mark W. "Globalization: Incorporating the Museum." In *A Companion to Museum Studies*, edited by Sharon Macdonald, Oxford: Blackwell, 2006, 381–397.

Reibel, Daniel B. *Registration Methods for Small Museum*, Lanham: AltaMira Press, 1997.

Research Library Group. *Trusted Digital Repositories: Attributes and Responsibilities. An RLG-OCLC Report*, Mountain View, 2002, www.oclc.org/content/dam/research/activities/trustedrep/repositories.pdf?urlm=161690 (accessed July 25, 2015).

Rhys, Owain. *Contemporary Collecting: Theory and Practice*, Edinburgh: Museums Etc, 2001.

Richman, Jennifer R. and Forsyth, Marion P., eds. *Legal Perspectives on Cultural Resources*, Lanham: AltaMira Press, 2004.

Ritzenthaler, Mary Lynn. *Preserving Archives and Manuscripts*, SAA Archival Fundamentals Series, Chicago: Society of American Archivists, 2010.

Roe, Kathleen M. *Arranging and Describing Archives and Manuscripts*, Chicago: Society of American Archivists, 2005.

Rosenzweig, Roy "Scarcity or Abundance? Preserving the Past in a Digital Age." *American Historical Review* (June 2002), https://chnm.gmu.edu/digitalhistory/links/pdf/introduction/0.6b.pdf (accessed July 25, 2015).

Schellenberg, Theodore R. "The Appraisal of Modern Records." *Bulletins of the National Archives*, 8 (October 1956), www.archives.gov/research/alic/reference/archives-resources/appraisal-of-records.html (accessed July 25, 2015).

Shapiro, Michael S., Miller, Brett, and Steiner, Christine, eds. *A Museum Guide to Copyright and Trademark*, Washington, DC: American Association of Museums, 1999.

Simmons, John E. *Things Great and Small: Collections Management Policies*, Washington, DC: American Association of Museums, 2006.

Skramstad, Harold. "An Agenda for American Museums in the Twenty First Century." *Daedalus*, 128/3 (1999): 109–128.

Smithsonian. *X3D*, undated, http://3d.si.edu/ (accessed July 25, 2015).

Smithsonian Education. *Artifacts Analysis*, undated, www.smithsonianeducation.org/educators/lesson_plans/idealabs/artifacts_analysis.html and http://www.smithsonianeducation.org/idealabs/ap/artifacts/index.htm (accessed July 25, 2015).

Society of American Archivists. *So You Want to Be an Archivist: An Overview of the Archives Profession*, undated a, www2.archivists.org/profession (accessed July 25, 2015).

Society of American Archivists. *A Glossary of Archival and Records Terminology*, undated b, www2. archivists.org/glossary (accessed July 25, 2015).

Society of American Archivists. *External Digitization Standards*, undated c, www2.archivists.org/standards/external/123 (accessed July 25, 2015).

Society of American Archivists. *Ethics, Values, and Legal Affairs*, undated d, www2.archivists.org/ standards/code-of-ethics-for-archivists and www.archivists.org/governance/handbook/app_ethics. asp (accessed July 25, 2015).

Society of American Archivists. "A Code of Ethics for Archivists." *The American Archivist* (Summer 1980): 414–418.

Society of American Archivists. *SAA Core Values Statement and Code of Ethics*, Washington, DC: SAA, 2011.

Society of American Archivists. *Guidelines for Reappraisal and Deaccessioning*, Washington, DC: SAA, 2012a,www2.archivists.org/sites/all/files/GuidelinesForReappraisalAndDeaccessioning-May2012. pdf (accessed July 25, 2015).

Society of American Archivists. *Guidelines for Reappraisal and Deaccessioning*, May 2012b, www2. archivists.org/groups/technical-subcommittee-on-guidelines-for-reappraisal-and-deaccessioning- ts-grd/guidelines-for-reappraisal-and-deaccession (accessed July 25, 2015).

Society of American Archivists. *Describing Archives: A Content Standard*, Washington, DC: SAA, 2013, http://files.archivists.org/pubs/DACS2E-2013.pdf (accessed July 25, 2015).

Theimer, Kate. "Interactivity, Flexibility and Transparency: Social Media and Archives 2.0." In *The Future of Archives and Recordkeeping: A Reader*, edited by Jenny Hill, London: Facet Publishing, 2011, 123–144.

Thomson, Garry. *The Museum Environment*, London: Butterworths, 1986.

Trouillot, Michel-Rolph. *Silencing the Past: Power and the Production of History*, Boston: Beacon Press, 1995.

Tryon, Roy H. "Archivists and Records Managers." In *Public History: Essays from the Field*, edited by James Gardner and Peter LaPaglia, Malabar: Krieger Publishing Company, 2006, 57–74.

UC Berkeley. *Evaluating Web Pages: Techniques to Apply & Questions to Ask*, 2012, www.lib.berkeley. edu/TeachingLib/Guides/Internet/Evaluate.html (accessed July 25, 2015).

University of North Carolina Library. *Archival Processing. How to Proceed: Preparing to Process*, 2012, www2.lib.unc.edu/wikis/archproc/index.php/How_to_Proceed:_Preparing_to_Process#Prelimi nary_Research_and_Survey (accessed July 25, 2015).

University of Virginia Library. *Digital Curation Service: AIMS White Paper*, Glossary, Bibliography, Digital Community, undated, http://dcs.library.virginia.edu/aims/white-paper/ (accessed July 25, 2015).

Vergo, Peter, ed. *The New Museology*, Chicago: University of Chicago Press, 1989.

Wayback Machine. Undated, https://archive.org/ (accessed July 25, 2015).

Weil, Stephen E. *Making Museums Matter*, Washington, DC: Smithsonian Institution Press, 2002.

Weldon, Edward. "Archives and the Practice of Public History." *The Public Historian*, 4/3 (Summer 1982): 49–58.

Woodhouse, Anne. "Museum Curators." In *Public History: Essays from the Field*, edited by James Gardner and Peter LaPaglia, Malabar: Krieger Publishing Company, 2006, 187–202.

2 Historic Preservation

Preserving the Past: Definitions, Purposes, and Debates

Cultural Resource Management, Historic Preservation, and Public History

As Thomas King points out in the *Companion to Cultural Resource Management*, there is no agreement on a definition of Cultural Resource Management (CRM) (2011a, 1). One definition is to see CRM as an interdisciplinary field that deals with the research, administration, conservation, preservation, and stewardship of historic sites, properties, and material culture. The term is often associated with federal programs such as the National Park Service (NPS) whose Cultural Resources Programs has produced the CRM journal. CRM is a vast field that includes – but is not limited to – historic preservation.

Historic preservation aims at preserving the past for future generations. The historic preservation movement has its origin in the opposition to the demolition and disappearance of artifacts, buildings, and memories that have historical relevance. Preserving the past was, in the United States, first seen as "an antidote to modernism, seeking evidence of simpler times in an idealized agricultural folk culture or an adventurous and virtuous colonial experience" (Meringolo 2012, 161). This nostalgic approach to the past explains why historic preservation was born as a grassroots movement.

For a long time, the architectural and aesthetic components were the main issues in historic preservation. Still today, part of environment, design, or architecture departments, some historic preservation programs mostly focus on architecture, technology, laws, and administration without providing any specific historical skills. Likewise, a recent report examines the practice and presentation of American history in the NPS (Whisnant et al. 2011). The report highlights the NPS's lack of investment in history work – through lack of funding as well as lack of adequate training. In particular, the authors note how historians' work, research, interpretation, and dialogue with the public is undervalued (Whisnant et al. 2011, 68). However, preserving the past does not only intend to preserve the structure, but also the history that took place on the site. As historians help finding arguments to preserve sites and structures in an historical context, history provides a perspective beyond just the built environment (Howe 1986, 111–112). It appears therefore all the more important for public historians to bring historical interpretation to historic preservation projects. Historians must know how to approach, study, and preserve sites/structures in order to be involved in historic preservation projects.

The links between CRM, historic preservation, and public history are tenuous (Padgett 1978). Historians involved in historic preservation can work for governmental and state agencies, can be employed by consulting firms, or work as independent historians (Lee

2006, 129). They may also work in universities and collaborate in historic preservation projects. The links between historic preservation and public history are threefold: the relevance of place, the role played by communities and interdisciplinary partners, and the different uses of the past.

Preserving historic sites and structures relates to the character of public spaces (Irwin 2003, xv). As David Glassberg argues, "a sense of history and a sense of place are inextricably intertwined; we attach histories to places, and the environmental value we attach to a place comes largely through the historical associations we have with it" (2001, 8). Public history contributes to preserving and giving meanings to place. As trained historians with an emphasis in the unique methodology of studying place, they are able to provide the historical context needed to convey significance and develop a research methodology that includes a wide variety of sources including property titles, wills, photographs, and archival material.

Historic preservation is also based on public participation. Increased accessibility means that members of the public should be able to participate in the process without resorting to the cost of hiring a professional historian (Lee 2006, 131). In his list of objectives for historic preservation, Kirk Irwin asserts that it "provides a means for people to participate in the making of the physical environment" and that it "is a means by which communities may define the character of public space" (2003, xx). Public historians should be intermediaries with communities (Kaufman 2004). As historic preservation has the ability to add new sites, new aspects of the past, and to challenge the stories already told, it is important to foster cultural diversity through this process (Spenneman 2006).

The links between sites, individuals, and communities have been at the center of the historic preservation. Public participation has become a key component of historic preservation. One important skill for historians getting involved in preservation is the ability to facilitate public dialogue and civic engagement. The inability to connect with local actors who are the critical stakeholders from which we need insight may result in project failures. In order to be effective, preservationists and historians must be prepared to present oral testimony before review boards, planning commissions, and local governing boards or speak before community groups and professional peer groups (Lee 2006, 131). Historians must use vocabulary acceptable to technical experts and yet understandable and meaningful to the general public (Lee 2006, 133). They should be prepared to stand up in public meetings to argue about the significance of historic places. For instance, opponents may question the balance of individual rights with the rights of the community – especially when private properties have to obey ordinances – or argue that the federal government cannot legislate on aesthetics based on the principle that beauty depends on the viewer (Irwin 2003, xv). In any case, historians must translate dry and factual information into a compelling narrative as to why a property should receive formal recognition (Lee 2006, 132).

The third major link between historic preservation and public history relates to the uses of the past. Historians may have to undertake research at the request of and on the terms of others (Lee 2006, 134). Historians who work in historic preservation must deal with clients who may provide the topic for research, the schedule of work, and the purpose of the preservation. Historic preservation is therefore at the core of public history activities. While historic preservation practitioners may want to assure the viability of their projects, this principle of viability is open to discussion. First, the preservation of the past can be undertaken for different reasons that affect the definition of viability. Historic preservation can be undertaken to save objects/structures/sites; to revitalize old downtown areas; to encourage cultural tourism; or to increase the value of properties and neighborhoods. In any case, historians have to be aware of the future uses of their work. Second, the benefit of historic preservation cannot always be quantitatively evaluated. A major purpose of historic preservation is about educating the community about the significance of their sites and places. The viability of a project can also derive from the contribution to public awareness of their heritage.[1]

Historic Preservation Practices

There is a long history of debates regarding the definition of preservation. Some – like Viollet-le-Duc (France, 19th century) – have argued that structures could be restored not necessarily as they originally were, but how they should have been; others – like John Ruskin (England, 19th century) – thought that structures should not be restored and should remain untouched (Tyler et al. 2009, 18–24). Stabilization/preservation, restoration, reconstruction, and rehabilitation all belong to historic preservation. They are defined as official categories by the U.S. Secretary of Interior's Standards (NPS undated a). But they all result both from divergent interpretations of the field, and from different considerations of the future uses of the site/structure.

Stabilization/preservation consists of the maintenance of a property without significant alteration to protect against further damage. It accepts the successive changes – acknowledged as part of its history – which the building went through (NPS undated a). A famous example is Seattle's Pike Place Market, which is has been continuously operating since its establishment in 1907 (Tyler et al. 2009, 192–193). Restoration refers to the process of returning a building to its condition at a specific time period, often but not always to its original condition (NPS undated a). Restoration may be justified when some relevant portions of the structure have been lost or in specific cases where its relevance comes from a specific time period.[2] Any project of restoration needs to decide on a specific date/period to which the site/structure must be restored. Any addition past this date may be documented and then removed. Reconstruction applies when a site/structure that no longer exists needs to be rebuilt for contextual reasons (NPS undated a). For instance, at the beginning of the Colonial Williamsburg (CW) project, Governor's Place had been destroyed and was no longer part of the site.[3] The relevance of the place was considered important enough to justify its reconstruction. Any reconstruction is, however, controversial, and must be based on accurate documents, descriptions, drawing, as well as strong public outreach. Apart from few exceptions, the NPS is reluctant to rebuild demolished structures.[4]

Because of its flexibility, rehabilitation is perhaps the main practice in historic preservation. It preserves aspects that convey the structure's historical, cultural, or architectural values while making compatible reuse of the property possible (Tyler et al. 2009, 197). This is why rehabilitation is often associated with the term reuse or adaptive-use (NPS undated a). While exteriors often hardly change, the interiors of structures are assigned new uses. Through the concept of adaptive use, alterations are allowed that would enable buildings to continue to the economic vitality of a community (Tyler et al. 2009, 54). A good example is the rehabilitation of Union Station, in St Louis (Missouri), which was transformed after it was no longer needed for trains in the 1980s. The station building was adapted to new uses, including shops, restaurants, and a hotel (Tyler et al. 2009, 198). It should be noted that moving a structure is not considered as an official part of the historic preservation categories in the United States. Impending demolition may be the only acceptable justification for relocating a structure from its original location. For instance the impact of climate change – flooding for instance – may force the relocation of buildings. However, in most cases, relocation prevents nomination to the National Register of Historic Places.

Historic preservation practice also differs according to countries and cultures. The term historic preservation itself is debated. In the United Kingdom and more broadly in Europe, the term heritage and heritage conservation is preferred (Graham et al. 2000). Based on the relations between people and place, heritage and historic preservation may have different approaches and result in different practices. For instance, the Chinese do not consider the preservation of physical structures as critical (Tyler et al. 2009, 24). As David Lowenthal explains, "the Chinese disdain the past's purely physical traces. Old works must perish for new ones to take their place ... preserving objects and building reduces creation to commodity; it demeans both object and owner" (Lowenthal 1992, 162). In his book on *The Future of the Past*, Alexander Stille writes a complete chapter on what he defines as the Chinese "Culture of the Copy" (2003, 40–70).

In Japan, the preservation of a structure may come through its destruction and its reconstruction on an adjacent site, matching the previous site and structure in every way. For instance, Figure 2.1 shows a Buddhist temple near Nara – ancient imperial capital – in Japan. Two pagodas were originally constructed in the 8th century but one was destroyed in the 16th century. The pagoda on the picture was reconstructed in 1981 on the model of the other pagoda that had been preserved (Cluzel 2007). The Japanese consider each structure not a replication of the original but a recreation of it (Tyler et al. 2009, 25). Although the destruction and reconstruction of a site may be debated, the Western trope must not prevent us from seeing the advantage of alternative approaches. For instance, a major asset of the Japanese approach is to transmit historical practice through preservation. In order to reconstruct structures, actors of preservation must be able to reproduce the techniques used to design the original site. Historic preservation in Japan therefore contributes to the preservation of technologies and techniques as well.

Actors and History of Historic Preservation: Grassroots and Official Programs

Historians need to know who is who in historic preservation and know the actors they may have to work with (Howe 1986; Heffern 2014). At its inception in the 19th century, the U.S. historic preservation movement was based on grassroots activism. Preservation began with small groups working on the conservation of historic buildings. An early example of preservation was the purchase of Independence Hall – threatened by demolition – by the city of Philadelphia in 1816, although it was not until the 1850s that the preservation movement started to come to the forefront. In its first phase, a form of patriotism "to protect and elevate to national significance the icons of a predominantly white, Anglo-Saxon American past" supported historic preservation (Meringolo 2012, 160). The early examples of historic preservation focused on homes of the Founding Fathers and successive U.S. presidents. Historic preservation initially created "shrines to historic personages" for national pride (Murtagh 2006, 16). The Mount Vernon Ladies' Association, led by Ann Pamela Cunningham, formed in 1853, aimed at saving the former home of George Washington in Mount Vernon (Barthel 1996, 19). This association became a model and marked the first successful national preservation organization.

Led by John D. Rockefeller and Henry Ford, a new form of historic preservation emerged in the early 20th century in the United States to create historical parks. In 1926, John D. Rockefeller established CW and began one of the most extensive investments in historic preservation of its time (Tyler et al. 2009, 36–37). CW aimed at the restoration of an entire 18th century town, houses, dependencies, public buildings, streets, and landscapes. The project also inspired the construction of Greenfield Village by Henry Ford. Established in

Figure 2.1 Pagoda of a Buddhist temple in Nara (Japan), 2002. Dating back to the 8th century C.E., the pagoda was destroyed in 1528 and reconstructed in 1981. Courtesy of Jean-Sebastien Cluzel.

Dearborn, Michigan, Greenfield Village was a mixture of structures dedicated to American invention, such as Edison's workshop. Buildings were all relocated to Dearborn (Tyler et al. 2009, 37–38).

CW and Greenfield Village helped to shift the preservation movement from individual house museums or structures to the development of larger historic districts (Stipe 2003, 6). Several years after CW and Greenfield Village, Charleston, South Carolina established the "Old and Historic District" in 1931. The idea that the "character of an area is derived from its entirety, or the sum of its parts, rather than from the character of its individual buildings" was a radical step in historic preservation. Charleston also turned out to be one of the earliest experiments in municipal historic preservation ordinances and historic commissions that New Orleans, Savannah, Georgia, and Annapolis quickly adopted (Stipe 2003, 7).

The process of the state's maintenance of historic sites originated in England. John Lubbock was a Member of the British Parliament as well as a fervent supporter of a national heritage policy to protect historic sites and monuments in the late 19th century. His work led to the Ancient Monuments Protection Act in 1882 and to the creation of the National Trust for Places of Historic Interest or Natural Beauty in 1894. The beginning of heritage conservation in England was, unlike in the United States where it derives from popular involvement, due to a political act. The Australian and U.S. state programs for historic preservation modeled themselves after the English National Trust (Barthel 1989, 88–95). In the United States, the first federal historic preservation legislation surfaced in the early twentieth century. Passed in 1906, the Antiquities Act was written with the growing problem of site looting and illegal trade of artifacts in mind. Specifically the law prevented any "unlicensed excavation, removal or injury of historic or prehistoric ruin or monument or object of antiquity situated on lands owned or controlled by the federal government" (Murtagh 2006, 39). The Act was a gateway to more specific legislation that offered increasing strength to historic preservation. In particular, the Act has proven to be a significant tool allowing U.S. presidents to bypass Congress to create and protect nationally significant sites.

Inspired by the Antiquities Act, many federal structures were created. The U.S. Department of the Interior established the National Park Service in 1916, responsible for creating and managing national parks as well as historic monuments and objects (Barthel 1996, 21).[5] Federal involvement in historic preservation increased during the New Deal. President Roosevelt, in 1933, transferred all federal parks, battlefields, monuments, and cemeteries to the administration of the NPS, giving the NPS authority for historic preservation and interpretation on a federal level.[6] The NPS is the mother institution that hosts many relevant actors such as the Historic American Buildings Survey (HABS), the National Heritage Areas (NHA), and the National Center for Preservation Training and Technology (NCPTT) (Murtagh 2006, 42).[7]

The United States founded the National Trust for Historic Preservation (NTHP) in 1949. More state and local oriented than the NPS, the NTHP is a private organization chartered by the U.S. Congress. It was the "most notable development that kept the preservation movement on track" with "increased reliance on private-sector funds disbursed through non-profit organizations" (Hurley 2010, 17). In its charter, the National Trust was empowered to own historic properties, provide leadership and support for preservation, and advocate for federal and state preservation policies. This was the first step that led to listing historic structures. It was continued by the National Historic Preservation Act (NHPA), signed into law in 1966 (Advisory Council on Historic Preservation 2000). It was a watershed for historic preservation and has been the most far-reaching preservation legislation enacted in the United States (Morton 1992). The Act first authorizes the Secretary of the Interior to expand and maintain a National Register of Historic Places (NRHP), an inventory of sites, buildings, structures, objects, and districts significant to American history, architecture, culture, or archaeology that the Secretary of the Interior finds to be of local, statewide, or national significance (Murtagh 2006, 51). National Register criteria are the basis of historic preservation policy nationwide. Listing in the Register qualifies a property for federal grants, loans, and tax incentives. Through the development of the National Register, the NPS was able to craft the various criteria, which would be taken into account to define significance and worthiness.[8]

In addition to federal funding for preservation activities, the NHPA created the Advisory Council on Historic Preservation (ACHP). The primary goals of the ACHP are to contribute to policy on national preservation issues, and to comment on historic properties that are affected by federal funds. For instance, the ACHP settles disputes over federal legal provisions for historic and archaeological sites. Importantly, it deals with Section 106.[9] Section 106, named after Section 106 of the NHPA, has become the centerpiece of federal protection for historic properties. Section 106 requires government agencies to evaluate the impact of all government-funded construction projects (Advisory Council on Historic Preservation undated).

The local level of historic preservation includes three main categories of actors: State Historic Preservation Officers, Certified Local Governments, and Local Preservation Commissions. Shortly after the passage of NHPA, the Secretary of the Interior decentralized new responsibilities. To do that, the Secretary requested each state government appoint a "State Liaison Officer" (Tyler et al. 2009, 55–58). Later named "State Historic Preservation Officer" (SHPO), the officer acts as the leading preservation official in each state, (s)he initiates and approves national register nominations, and oversees the Section 106 review process (Murtagh 2006, 56). Whether it is guiding citizens through the process of listing important historic resources or neighborhoods on the NRHP, or considering the impact of large projects on historic landscapes or archeological sites, the SHPO is the major partner in preservation projects (Stipe 2003, 83). Many advocacy groups are not part of state or federal programs but greatly contribute to historic preservation. One famous example is the non-profit Indiana Landmarks that was created in the 1960s, and that is now involved in many different historic preservation projects.

Amendments to the NHPA in the 1980s created Certified Local Governments (CLG). An NPS program, the CLG gives municipalities the option of strengthening local historic preservation activities through exclusive funding incentives and enhanced technical assistance. CLGs help SHPO with Section 106 reviews, National Register nominations, and allowed municipal governments to expand their outreach through federal and state preservation networks. Likewise, local preservation commissions (also named architectural review board, historic preservation commission, or Local Historical Commission) identify sites and properties to be preserved. They are created through the adoption of a local preservation ordinance. The local preservation commission is the governmental agency that approves or denies changes to designated historic properties that are privately owned. Local commissions are supported by the National Alliance of Preservation Commissions (NAPC), which serves as a "national voice," and also offers education, advocacy, and training.

Last but not least, public historians can foster public participation in the various steps of historic preservation. For instance, many projects now start with public meetings in which members of the community can not only provide knowledge about the sites and places, but also help design applications. Public historians can help organize what is called "charrette." Over the course of several days, all interested actors of historic preservation projects publicly meet to agree on a plan and objectives. Unlike more traditional processes in which historic preservation plans and projects are merely presented as final products to the public, charrettes are participatory processes that give space for multiple visions, interpretations, and benefits (National Charrette Institute undated).

Finding and Describing Historical Resources

One challenge is the variety of sites and buildings that may be preserved. Historic preservation has multiple layers. The decision-making criteria to preserve a site can be different for local community actors and for broader application to national programs. Disagreement may also arise as to how the site will be used in the future. Donna Harris thus proposes, in *New Solutions for House Museums*, different examples of how historic houses can be used through historic preservation (co-stewardship agreement, long or short-term leases, sale, donation to government entity) (2007). Experts from various disciplines have different perspectives and often fail to reach a consensus about what should be preserved. In historic preservation, historians may collaborate with architects, geographers, anthropologists, folk-lorists, city managers, lawyers, tourism officers, and consultants for private companies. It is also crucial to acknowledge and support cultural diversity. For a long time, historic preserva-tion focused on the "legacy of wealth and power." In doing so, it contributed to silencing the memories of minorities. Not preserving sites and structures related to minorities contributes to forgetting their part in local and national histories. Historians must pay attention to the "ghosts" in urban landscapes (Ladd 1998). As Hayden wrote, "Today, debates about the built environment, history, and culture take place in much more contested terrain of race, gender, and class, set against long term economic and environmental problem" (1995, 6).

Historic Houses

Historians can take part in many different projects about buildings and structures. Very often, historic preservation is undertaken for individual buildings. Historic houses have certainly retained most attention in historic preservation since Mount Vernon (Harris 2007; Durel and Durel 2007). The NTHP defines historic house museums as "a museum whose structure itself is of historical or architectural significance and whose interpretation relates primarily to the building's architecture, furnishings and history" (Murtagh 2006, 63). However, preservation of historic houses increasingly encompasses broader geographical and historical context to provide richer understanding of the house's environment (Harris 2007). Historic houses require historical interpretation and allow for the conservation and display of material culture (Donnelly 2002). Historians can therefore help set the building into larger historical contexts.

   The concept of the house museum came about as an "answer to the question of how to keep buildings important to American history" (Murtagh 2006, 64). House museums can both communicate a sense of place and environment, and propose representation of larger architectural and historical trends. They can be located in the urban landscape – Chateau Ramezay in Montreal (Canada) or Isaac Bell House Newport, Rhode Island – or in more rural areas like Oak Alley Plantation in Louisiana. The NPS and the American Association for State and Local History provide various resources to understand and proceed with the preservation of historic houses. The Historic House Trust also provides support and resources.

Urban and Industrial Sites

A majority of historic houses are part of urban landscapes (Hayden 1995). Some studies detail historic preservation projects in large cities (DeJean 2014; Ladd 1998). Among examples of historic preservation of urban sites, industrial structures have received increas-ing attention. The preservation of these structures has benefited from what has been called industrial archaeology. It is a field of study concerned with the investigation, surveying, recording and, in some cases, the preservation of industrial monuments (Kemp 1986, 175). The Grand Hornu (an early 19th century mining complex in Belgium) developed as one of the first sites of industrial archaeology in Europe. A World Heritage site since 2012, the site is also a museum of archaeological industry. In the United States, the discipline first emerged at the Smithsonian Institution in Washington, DC, and formed the Society for Industrial Archaeology (Kemp 1986, 177). As for archaeology, the inventory of the industrial site is of major importance. Industrial archaeology is also associated with engineering to preserve railroads, bridges, canals, and other structures linked with industrial sites. In the United States, the Historic American Engineering Record (HAER) was established in 1969 to record the technology and engineering involved those structures. In addition to the inventory of the site, historians can work on the classification and taxonomy of the various structures (Kemp 1986, 180). The classification and taxonomy is essential to evaluate the integrity and the historical significance of the structure to decide whether the structure is unique or merely one of thousands of other examples.

The historic preservation of the urban landscape is particularly challenging due to the fast-changing economic, social, and cultural composition of urban areas. For example, in 1970, 75 percent of the residents of New York City were white, in 1990 this reduced to 38 percent (Hayden 1995, 6). Any public participation in historic preservation must therefore take into consideration not only the changing structure but also the changing community partners. Ethnic minorities should be represented through preservation. Too often, minorities are underrepresented and are sometimes "invisible" (Hayden 1995, 82–97). This leaves many neighborhoods and ordinary dwellings and their stories off the preservation process. These ordinary dwellings, such as the tenements preserved in the Lower Eastside Tenement Museum in New York City, tell a compelling story of life in the city and how various immigrant groups managed to survive and grow. The Tenement Museum highlights the cultural diversity of migrants whose stories have been associated with the Lower East Side. Through such innovative strategies as employed by the Lower Eastside Tenement Museum, the concept of historic preservation can be an active participant in the rediscovery of urban cultural diversity in downtown urban environments.

Landscape and Parks: (Re-)Source and Preservation

Historic preservation and CRM are linked to space. Within the NPS, CRM complements natural resources. It is important for historians to consider the surroundings of the different sites to understand the complex relations between the object of study and its context. Historians need to interpret the landscape as an object of study (Glassberg 2004). The NPS includes the preservation of rural historic landscapes.[10] For instance, in addition to the architecture design of its house, the Bingham Homestead rural historic landscape has had a long association with farming and ranching in the Pleasant Valley. Farmsteads and their surrounding planted fields have become the object of historic preservation (Conard 2004, 14). Historians need to understand the forces that have shaped rural properties, interpret their historical importance, and plan for their protection (McClelland et al. 1999). Historians can help provide the historic context and background information on the rural property "with important historic trends or themes, such as dairy farming or cattle grazing, indicating whether the property is unique or representative of its time and place" (McClelland et al. 1999).

Landscape – and particularly the cultural landscape – has become a new source of interpretation (Longstreth 2008).[11] For instance, a survey of the cultural landscape shows the nature and extent of change over time, such as the impact of farming on the natural environment (Kyvig and Marty 2010, 165). Cultural landscape is the association between the physical components and human activities (Riesenweber 2008). Cultural landscape is now entirely part of historic preservation (Alanen and Melnick 2000).[12] As Rebecca Conard argues, it is necessary to reconcile the built and the natural environment, physical and human components of landscapes (Conard 2004, 7; Sacco 2015). Landscape and environment have been at the core of the NPS in the United States since its founding (Hosmer and Verne 1994). Absent at the beginning, historians became part of the NPS during the New Deal when historical projects were seen as a tool for economic development.

A crucial element to understand the preservation of landscape has been the new interest in environment and sustainability. The multiple threats to the environment have contributed to the desire for its preservation. The NPS promotes the specific category of historic landscape that, among other criteria, has significance as a design or work of art, has a historical association with a significant person, trend, event, etc. (Keller and Keller undated). The landscape investigation consists of obtaining information, identifying the type of historic landscape, highlighting the characteristic features, evaluating the historic significance, and evaluating the integrity (Keller and Keller undated). In addition to providing guidelines, the NPS's *Guidelines for the Treatment of Cultural Landscapes* recommend that historians working on the preservation of historic landscapes should know about landscape architecture, cultural geography, horticulture, gardening, and planning (NPS 1992). The NPS lists the different styles of historic landscapes that can be preserved (Keller and Keller undated). Among them, historic gardens play a significant role and exemplify the difficult task of preserving landscapes. The challenge is due to constant and fast changes that landscapes undergo. Geographic tools – especially to map the absences – appear particularly useful for historic preservation (Hunter 2011, 102).

In 1982 the International Council on Monuments and Sites (ICOMOS) and the International Federation of Landscape Architects (IFLA) published the Florence Charter about historic gardens. The Charter noted the fact that "The constituents are perishable and renewable," which implies "balance between change and preservation" (Irwin 2003, 247). As a living monument, a historic garden has specific rules, for instance "Whether or not it is associated with a building in which case it is an inseparable complement, the historic garden cannot be isolated from its own particular environment." The garden should always be considered as a whole, so that historians should not act only on certain parts of the garden (Irwin 2003, 247–251). Regarding historic landscapes, historians cannot always rely on visual descriptions, making the preservation/restoration a difficult task (Keller and Keller undated). Historians can help preservationists navigate the different types of primary sources to collect information about the sites. Preserving historic gardens can, as the Cleveland Cultural Gardens show, enable historians to develop tours and other public history events.

Sites of Death

Death, violence, and wars are major topics for historians, as they are for historic preservation. Scholars are more and more interested in what they have defined as "dark tourism." The Institute for Dark Tourism Research (IDTR; University of Central Lancashire) defines dark tourism as "the act of travel and visitation to sites, attractions and exhibitions that have real or recreated death, suffering or the seemingly macabre as a main theme" (IDTR undated). Battlefields have, for instance, received a lot of attention (Gettysburg, Waterloo, Gallipoli). The preservation of battlefields has greatly been associated with national identity. The NPS stresses that "Our nation achieved independence through the trial of battle, and military action often determined the very boundaries of this country" (Andrus 1992). A recent review of the NRHP reveals that 35 percent of the 236 battlefields listed in the

National Register deal with the Civil War (Andrus 1992). Other eras, such as the period 1866 to 1900, which covers the major period of the Indian Wars in the trans-Mississippi West, have not been as much represented. The preservation of these underrepresented battlefield sites can provide a great opportunity to engage the communities and their stories. The development and preservation of these battlefield sites can act as a catalyst in closing the gap in the historical narratives.

The idea of preserving an entire battlefield emerged when the U.S. Congress established the Chickamauga-Chattanooga National Military Park in 1890 (Andrus 1992). One initial question relates to the location of battlefields (Farrell 2011, 299). They are often small, forgotten places that are hard to locate (Farrell 2011, 301). Archaeology and site inventory techniques are particularly useful here. The methodology is very similar to the preservation of historic landscapes. Natural features, land uses, vegetation, and historic building types also define many battlefields (Andrus 1992). The threats to rural landscapes – changing land uses, highway construction, loss of vegetation, alterations to natural features, loss and replacement of historic buildings are also occurring on many battlefields. One should not forget that battles also affected the landscape, and this impact should be part of any preservation package as well (Andrus 1992; Farrell 2011). Finally, battlefields are oftentimes memorial sites associated with mourning, pride, and/or glory. The sacred component associated with battlefields can make them particularly controversial sites.

Other sites such as prisons have recently received attention. There are more than one hundred prison museums worldwide. The Eastern State Penitentiary and Alcatraz Island (United States) interpret and preserve the lives of inmates. In Ireland, the preservation of Kilmainham Gaol started in the 1950s. The prison was the site where Irish Republican prisoners were sent by the English authorities during the Anglo-Irish wars (Zuelow 2004). Likewise, sites of torture during dictatorship in Latin American countries – like the Estadio Nacional, a soccer stadium in Chile that was used as a prison under the 1973–1990 dictatorship – have recently been part of preservation processes. One particular challenge in this case is to preserve a building without bringing its aesthetic to the foreground.[13]

Graves, cemeteries, and other types of burial places require unique approaches in their preservation. Interest in cemetery preservation stems from a growing emphasis on the history of ordinary individuals, grassroots movements, and cultural landscapes. At the same time, the maintenance and preservation of burial places is increasingly threatened through neglect, ignorance, and vandalism. Cemeteries, because they are sacred places, can be problematic in historic preservation (Burg 2008). The historic preservation of small places can encounter opposition (National Register Eligibility of National Cemeteries 2011). Families of the interred often view graves and cemeteries as sacred and inviolable places opposed to the public aspect of preservation. Due to a sense of reverence and devout sentiment that can overshadow objective evaluation, cemeteries and graves are among those properties that are usually not considered eligible for inclusion in the NRHP unless they meet special requirements. The preservation of graves and cemeteries could have greater emphasis as it may give access to voices previously forgotten or unheard, but certainly requires engaging the affected community.

The concern of Native Americans about the preservation of burial remains and objects of their ancestors resulted in the Native American Graves Protection and Repatriation Act of 1990. It sets out the rights of Indian Tribes and Native Hawaiian organizations regarding human remains, funerary and sacred objects, and other culturally significant objects for which they can demonstrate lineal descent or cultural affiliation. The NPS provides guidelines about burial customs, types, and evaluation (Walton Potter and Boland 1992).

The National Register Criteria for Evaluation include considerations by which burial places may be eligible for inclusion in the National Register.[14]

Public Archaeology

Archaeology is the study of the past through material remains, but it encompasses many different fields (McGimsey 2003). For example, archaeology can be about the distant or more recent past (Moratto 2011; King 2011a, 2011b). Archaeology of the recent past considers various items such as buildings and structures, sites, districts, and objects (Parker 1985). Archaeological remains can also be underwater. In addition to shipwrecks, there are many other types of sites that are submerged (Langley 2011). The techniques to assess a site are very important for archaeologists (Hardesty and Little 2009). The relevance of the site for archaeologists (such as the size and distribution of camps, villages, towns, and special places) has helped preservationists and historians to better evaluate their projects (Little et al. 2000). The archaeological use of maps and photographs to find site boundaries is particularly useful in historic preservation. An archaeological investigation can produce more information about a particular historic property than more traditional studies. For additional information on the use of archaeological techniques for historic preservation, readers can use the numerous collections of essays or the Secretary of the Interior's *Standards for Archaeological Documentation* provided by the NPS (Sebastian and Lipe 2010; Merriman 2004; NPS undated e).

Public archaeology is not new; it already informed the 1906 Antiquities Act (Jameson 2004). However, the field has recently received more attention, including on an international scale (Schadla-Hall 1999).[15] The *Online Journal in Public Archaeology* gives details about the field and the various debates in Europe.[16] Public archaeology may have different meanings (Moshenska 2010). In this chapter, the focus is on how archaeologists have lifted the veil on their practice to produce more inclusive projects of preservation (Merriman 2004). Archaeologists work more and more often with communities, descendants, and other popular actors (Moyer and Gadsby 2014). For example, public archaeology has been very useful to foster public engagement with historic slave quarters. Excavation of slave sites at the Hermitage plantation was undertaken with public participation. Discussion between visitors and archaeologists on site, examination of artifacts, and some participation were encouraged (McKee and Thomas 1998). Likewise, public excavations of different archaeological sites in Montpellier (Virginia) have helped local community members to participate in the rediscovery of local forgotten heritage.

There is a need for a community-based archaeology (Derry and Malloy 2003). In *Beyond Preservation*, Hurley dedicates a chapter to historic preservation in St Louis (Missouri) and explains how a community group used public archaeology to investigate and preserve a site. Named the Old North St. Louis Restoration Group (ONSTLRG), the group used public archaeology to carry out excavations in search of historic artifacts about the neighborhood (Hurley 2010, 83–86). Likewise, the Hampden Community Archaeology Project (HCAP) involves the community of Hampden (close to Baltimore). HCAP hosted public workshops to address community questions about the historic landscape, economy, women and children in the past, textile work, and race. Students assisted with excavations while members of the public were invited to site tours and "dig days" (Moyer and Gadsby 2014). In the UK, *Time Team* (a television program on archaeology) ran a national "Big Dig" in 2003 in which members of the public were encouraged to excavate test pits (De Groot 2008, 66). For instance, Figure 2.2 shows a project of Scottish Coastal Archaeology and the Problem of

Figure 2.2 Members of the community excavating on the island of Sanday, Orkney (Scotland), 2015. The site is a Bronze Age Burnt Mound that was exposed on the beach during a storm. Courtesy of Tom Dawson/SCAPE.

Erosion (SCAPE). Winner of two British Archaeological Awards in 2014, SCAPE is based at the University of St Andrews. SCAPE used public archaeology to save threatened sites in Scotland. In the image, members of the local community, with the help of historians and archaeologists, excavate the remains of a Bronze Age site exposed on a beach after a storm. Public archaeology creates links between the members of the community and their past (Pearson and Ramilisonina 2004).

Finally, digital tools can foster the public component of archaeology (McDavid 2004; Richardson 2013). Public archaeologists use digital technology and social media to better engage their audiences.[17] Digital technology can make archaeology – and more broadly historic preservation – come alive through geographic data and visual representation (Little et al. 2000, ch. VII). Augmented reality can provide new kinds of public access for archaeological sites.[18] In Florence (Italy), the public can now access archaeological sites through smartphone applications. Based on a PhD research thesis, some images have been reconstructed and are provided on the app (Izi Travel undated). Some archaeologists even call for a webarchaeology.[19]

Historic Preservation and Sustainability

Since the adoption of the UNESCO Convention in 1972, the international community has embraced the concept of "sustainable development." When a property inscribed on the World Heritage List is threatened by serious and specific dangers, the Committee considers placing it on the List of World Heritage in Danger to foster active policy.[20] In the United States, historic preservation and public history at large have increasingly – especially since the publication of Martin Melosi and Phillip Scarpino's *Public History and the Environment* – focused on the environment through the concept of sustainability (Glaser 2013). In 1987, the international Bruntland Commission defined sustainable development as "meeting the needs of the present without compromising the ability of the future generations to meet their own needs" (Glaser 2013). The 2014 annual National Council on Public History conference was about sustainable public history. Topics such as Public History and Climate Change emerged in the last few years (Glaser 2012).

The impact of our changing climate should not be underestimated. However, the preservation community has been late in realizing the tremendous negative impact climate change will have on policy, nomination criteria, etc. Climate change requires adapting historic preservation policy to better fight the risk of losing sites. For instance, with increased flood threats and higher sea levels, it may be unavoidable to move buildings at the risk of destruction. Does it mean that such buildings may no longer be classified as NRHP sites, or should we start adapting criteria that fully allow the preservation of endangered sites? A panel at the 2015 Massachusetts Historic Preservation Conference thus discussed "how can preparedness reduce potential damage to historic buildings and areas, collections, and landscapes – from both gradual changes and sudden disasters?" (Massachusetts Historic Preservation Conference 2015).

In his article on coastal erosion in Scotland, Tom Dawson gives concrete examples of the links between historic preservation and environmental issues. In Scotland, the SCAPE Trust and the University of St Andrews have been working with the public to update previous surveys and to nominate and undertake practical projects at locally valued sites (Dawson 2014, 31). The links between heritage and sustainability have engaged the public in the preservation of "their" landscape. In Figure 2.3, members of the local community near

Figure 2.3 Community survey of coastal erosion as part of the Scotland's Coastal Heritage at Risk Project (SCHARP). River Clyde, near Glasgow (Scotland), 2015. Courtesy of Tom Dawson/SCAPE.

Glasgow (Scotland) participate in the study and measure the impact of coastal erosion on the landscape and its preservation. It also contributes to the public awareness of the impact of global warming on cultural heritage. In their new project, Scotland's Coastal Heritage at Risk Project (SCHARP), Tom Dawson and his team created an app for mobile devices to both obtain and record information on archaeology and coastal erosion (Dawson 2015). The project provides an atmosphere of shared knowledge as the local communities along the Scottish coast become citizen-archaeologists, chronicling the changes brought about by a changing climate upon their community.

Traditionally the value of a structure is measured through its historical, cultural, or architectural significance. Environmental significance has become part of the overall consideration for a more sustainable future (Merlino 2014). For instance, the National Trust for Historic Preservation has asked to recognize preservation's key role in supporting and advancing the values of sustainability. The Trust provides a list of arguments (energy savings, material recycling, and high density urban planning) (Merlino 2014). Likewise, demolition costs energy, so that preservation may very well be the greenest solution (Merlino 2014, 71).[21]

Evaluation of Sites and Structures: Preliminary Preservation Research

The process of historic preservation starts with the evaluation of the site or structure. Preservationists and historians must decide if the site/structure should and could be preserved. It is therefore necessary to explore the physical remains. Historians should learn how to "read" a site and/or building (Kuranda 2011; Hardesty and Little 2009). The history of architecture is very important in the area of historic preservation. Public historians should know about the main architectural styles such as the European styles (colonial, Georgian, Federal), the Classical styles (Greek Revival, Beaux-Arts Classicism), the Romantic styles (Gothic Revival, Second Empire, Colonial Revival, Tudor), and 20th century styles (Tyler et al. 2009, 63–101). Guides and guidelines are very useful (Poppeliers and Chambers 2003). Historians should be able to date a structure according to its style. *Preservation Briefs*, published by the NPS's Technical Preservation Services, particularly issues 17 and 35, help identify the visual character and significant features of structures (Nelson 1988). For instance, they should be able to see "ghosts" – signs of former sub-structures – in structures (Howe 1986, 119). It is important that the fieldwork evaluation should not be limited to the immediate structure itself. The preservationists should be mindful of the challenge of dating a structure simply by its "style." Often a change in ownership, even within a family, can promote changes that reflect two or three styles in building, all of which are important in telling the story of the entire building. The narrative of change is an important part of the built landscape and historians can help investigate it. As for any archival materials, the site/structure must be replaced in a broader context. Public archaeology has demonstrated how neighboring sites, buildings, ways of communications must be considered to understand a site.

Fieldwork is not enough to evaluate the possible preservation of a site/structure. Historical research helps preservationists better assess the historical significance of a site/structure (National Register Bulletin 1998). In order to collect information, historians can start by contacting the previous/current owners of the site/structure. In doing so, oral history has been very successful in bringing historical details. Historians have to be inventive to find information about sites. They can consult architectural or construction firms, local municipal departments (for title history or building permits), local libraries and archives, city directories, courts (for wills, deeds, and inventories), read local newspapers, contact community groups, and so on (Kyvig and Marty 2010, 165–180). For instance, deeds record the name of the seller, the buyer, the date of the transaction, and some descriptions of the property that may help trace the change in the structure (Howe 1986, 117). Historians should look particularly for visual descriptions (lithographs, bird's-eye perspectives) and maps of the site. For instance, Sanborn Fire insurance has a very rich collection of maps (published by Sanborn Map Company from the mid-1800s to the present day). In addition, local historical societies can be rich repositories of images, maps, and institutional knowledge that can be invaluable for the researcher. Thanks to their methodological skills, public historians are well equipped to help preservation practitioners present better historically designed projects.

After the initial "reading" of the site/structure and the historical research, historians should get measured drawings and record notes (Burns 2003).[22] In addition to photographs, historians can now rely on 3D scanners in association with Computer-Aided-Design software to collect cloud points and later digitally reconstruct the site/structure.[23] Information collected on site enables historians to help preservationists to write a Historic Structure Report (HSR), a sort of roadmap for later steps in the preservation process.[24] It includes the *Chronology of Development and Use*, which lists the important dates for the site/structure (construction, changes, additions).

Designing a Nomination for Historic Preservation

Process

Designing a nomination is a key activity in historic preservation, and public historians should be able to make a case for historical significance. In the United States, sites and structures can mostly be nominated for the NRHP, and to a lesser extent, as National Historic Landmarks. At an international level, historians usually nominate the site/structure for the UNESCO's World Heritage Site category. A nomination has several assets: it provides the property with some protection against any project initiated by the federal government (Section 106), it provides eligibility for grants, and tax credits, and it attracts popular attention through cultural tourism. The NPS provides a very rich and detailed overview of the nominating process (NPS undated d).

Too often, a process of nomination results from structures threatened with disappearance – through demolition or disrepair. It is usually only at that time that actors in the community become aware of the significance of the structure. Nomination should not wait for such a late stage, and should not be the only solution (Harris 2007). This is why local actors should undertake, and regularly update, surveys and inventories of their built and non-built heritage. Sites and structures should be identified and inventoried so that any historic preservation can apply in appropriate and faster terms.

In the United States, anyone can nominate a property to the NRHP. A local actor – for example the local historical commission, historical society, CLG offices – a state or a national-level program may initiate a designation. Consultants, architectural firms, and university historic preservation programs can also prepare nominations. Designations must be submitted to the SHPO for review. It is rare that designation comes from the owner of the property. However, it is important to include, even partner with, the property owner, for it makes the nomination more viable. Owners – as well as local officials – would receive a notification of the process of designation; if they object to the designation, the structure can only be determined eligible for listing. If the designation is approved by the SHPO, it is then sent to the Secretary of the Interior in Washington, DC with a period of review and comments, and is – in case of favorable decision – officially listed in the National Register. Many resources published by the NPS can help historians prepare a designation.[25]

National Historic Landmarks (NHL) are properties that have national historic significance. They represent a special category of designated historic structures and properties with exceptional value or quality (Tyler et al. 2009, 150). The nominations resemble those for the NRHP. The requested national significance of the structure can be linked to larger theme studies. The themes include, among others, American civil rights, Japanese Americans during World War II, or the American aviation heritage. The nomination can also be part of more special studies – such as the War of 1812 or the Mississippi Delta – that typically focus on a specific topic rather than a broad theme. The NPS provides the full list of themes with detailed explanation, historical context, and recent studies (NPS undated c). The National Park System Advisory Board reviews nominations. If the nomination is successful, the structure is automatically listed in the NRHP as well.[26] Historians can use the leaflet *How to Prepare National Historic Landmark Nominations*, and other publications from the NPS (NPS undated c).

Determining a structure's historical and architectural significance is the major role of the team in charge of the nomination. For a long time, aesthetic and architectural designs were the most important aspects to design and evaluate a nomination. However, history and historical significance have played an increasing important role in the process. Historical skills are greatly valued for the design of a nomination. Historians help preservationists determine whether the structure is unique or merely one of hundreds built at the same time (Howe 1986, 120). In order to do so, historians must be sure to abandon some rules of academic writing. Readers of the nominations would only have a limited time for assessment, so writers cannot develop long explanations. The first paragraph must be straightforward in explaining why this structure needs to be nominated. Writers can use the NPS publication and other guidelines on assessing the nomination process (Van West 1998).

Criteria for Nomination

In order to design a successful nomination, the team must follow certain rules and be sure to apply specific criteria. To guide the selection of properties included in the National Register, the NPS developed Criteria for Evaluation. These criteria are standards by which every property that is nominated to the National Register is judged. The main document provided by the NPS is entitled *How to Apply the National Register Criteria for Evaluation Bulletin?* (Andrus and Shrimpton 2002). It explains how the NPS applies these criteria in evaluating the properties.

One of the new and important challenges for the NRHP is in developing criteria that reflect the impact of our changing climate on historic structures. In many cases, it is a question of resources as to whether a site can be listed on the NRHP, and, more importantly, be saved. Historic structures along the seaboard are in danger of rising sea levels. Those with sufficient resources can be moved or in other ways protected, while other structures, with limited resources, are in danger of being lost forever or at least not being able to meet NRHP criteria, thus losing elements of protection.

Among the various criteria historians must be very careful with two main issues: historical significance and historical integrity. Historical significance is based on historical/cultural importance and architectural value. The structure must be associated with a significant historical aspect. Many factors may increase a historic property's significance. If the property is associated with events that have made a significant contribution to the broad patterns of American history; if it has been associated with the life of a significant person in the American past; if it embodies distinctive features of a type, period, method of construction, or high artistic values, or represents a significant and distinguishable entity whose components may lack individual distinction; or if the property and its site yield, or are likely to yield, important information in history or prehistory (NPS 2002). Historians can help re-evaluate usually underrepresented stories, especially about women and ethnic minorities (Dubrow and Goodman 2002).[27] This then improves the site's chances of a successful nomination. Careful delineation of these components are critical to a successful nomination, as is the developing of a strong narrative. The more aspects historians can demonstrate the better chance the nomination has of being successful.

Integrity is the second key issue in nominating a site/structure. It can be summed up in one short question: How well does the property represent the period or theme for which it is being recognized? This is such an important condition that the National Register has developed a list of seven elements to determine the level of integrity necessary for historic significance: location, design, setting, materials, workmanship, feeling, and association (Andrus and Shrimpton 2002, ch. VII). The NPS's guidelines also explain how to assess each of them (NPS 1995, 45–49).

The designation process is stronger when the property can be placed in a context of larger trends that is often developed through a synthesis of current historical literature. This is why historians should be part of the nominating process. Historians must evaluate what is so specific about the site/structure. Identifying the number and type of similar properties remaining in the region/state helps. Like for NHL, thematic/historic themes are also very important to demonstrate the value of the site/structure. Determining historic themes associated with a property is necessary when evaluating local, regional, statewide, or national significance (Tyler et al. 2009, 144). The NPS encourages evaluating historic properties, districts, and NHLs according to a "thematic framework." There are eight thematic categories.[28] This process belongs to the historical research – often required through the Historic Context Statement – demanded by the NPS. Historians should yet be careful not to restrict the significance of the site to these themes, and should not hesitate to explore underrepresented issues (Dubrow and Goodman 2002). However, history is too often used as description rather than interpretation. The evaluation is based on the notion of significance of material much more than on the historical meaning of the site/structure. To some extent, the NRHP and the NHL are still driven by architectural and structural criteria much more than historical relevance. Public historians can contribute to designing a strong narrative for richer and more successful nominations.

Australia's national heritage list offers more focus on non-material historical representation. The Australian National Heritage criteria include the "place's importance in the course, or pattern, of Australia's natural or cultural history," "the place's potential to yield information that will contribute to an understanding of Australia's natural or cultural history," or "the place's importance as part of Indigenous tradition" (Australian Heritage Council 2009, 5–7). The approach seems more multicultural, with concerns such as a strong or special association with a particular community or cultural group for social, cultural, or spiritual reasons, or importance in exhibiting particular aesthetic characteristics valued by a community or cultural group (Warren-Findley 2001). Besides, the historical significance receives more attention in the Australian case.

Exceptions, Exclusions, and Refusals

There is no official guideline about what kind of sites/structures cannot be nominated for the NRHP or the NHL. However, some criteria help understand the rationale. For instance, structures that have been altered lose historical integrity. Any modern addition to a property would undermine its integrity. Structures still in their original form are favored. Likewise, if moved to a new site, the property would lose parts of its integrity as well. Nominations for reconstructed buildings are discouraged for similar reasons, except in rare cases where the work is based on authentic documents and is an integral part of a larger master plan (Tyler et al. 2009, 148). However, it is still valuable to consider the fact that both criteria for the NRHP and NHL will need to be reviewed in light of the impact of our changing climate.

In terms of age, the 50-year-old rule is commonly accepted as a criterion for historic significance. This remains true although this rule has been lately reconsidered to give room to more modern properties. For example, the 1984 AT&T – now named Sony – Building in New York City is listed in the NRHP. The NPS has published a specific guideline about structures that are less than 50 years old (Sherfy and Luce 1998). This reflects an international trend in preserving more modern structures. Created in Europe in the 1990s, the Documentation and Conservation of Buildings, Sites, and Neighborhoods of the Modern Movement (DOCOMODO) also encourages the preservation of more recent structures.

Religious sites and structures are even more complex. Ordinarily cemeteries, birthplaces, or graves of historical figures, or properties owned by religious institutions or used for religious purposes, are not nominated. They are not accepted because they have little to do with the person's historical importance. Similarly the nomination of statues and commemorative structures is discouraged because they do not represent directly an event or a person. Many exceptions exist though. Such properties will qualify if they are integral parts of historic districts or if they fall within certain categories.[29] Besides, many churches are included on the basis of architectural or national significance. For instance, the Touro Synagogue – the oldest synagogue building in the United States – in Newport (Rhode Island) is part of the NTHP as it is considered the most historically significant Jewish building in the United States. The designation of religious properties may be very controversial due to their sacred characteristics. Though courts have upheld the right of municipalities to make such designations, churches can be among the most vocal and active opponents of historic designation (Tyler et al. 2009, 130).[30]

International Criteria: UNESCO's World Heritage Sites

UNESCO is in charge of the identification, protection, conservation, and presentation of World Heritage Sites since the adoption of the World Heritage Convention in 1972. The Convention foresaw the establishment of a "World Heritage Committee" and a "World Heritage Fund." Both the Committee and the Fund have been in operation since 1976. The list includes cultural, natural, and mixed sites.[31] A large proportion of these sites are in Europe – like the Palace of Versailles or the historic center of Florence – while a few – such as the Cahokia Mounds State or the Monumental Earthworks of Poverty Point – are located in the United States.

Prior to listing the site in the World Heritage List, a country must develop an inventory of possible submissions called the Tentative List (Green 2011, 432). World Heritage Sites must have Outstanding Universal Value. Outstanding Universal Value means cultural and/or natural significance, which is so exceptional as to transcend national boundaries and to be of common importance for present and future generations of all humanity. Unlike the U.S. NRHP, the nation should therefore not be the main prism through which the historical significance of the site/structure should be evaluated. International and transnational criteria are put forward. Monuments such as "architectural works, works of monumental sculpture and painting, elements or structures of an archaeological nature, inscriptions, cave dwellings and combinations of features, which are of Outstanding Universal Value from the point of view of history, art or science" can be listed (Ahmad 2006, 295). To be included on the World Heritage List, sites must be of outstanding universal value and also meet at least one out of ten selection criteria.[32]

When preparing a nomination for a property, a State Party should first identify all of the applicable significant attributes of authenticity. Like for the NRHP, integrity and historical significance are crucial. Examining the conditions of integrity requires assessing the extent to which the property:

(1) includes all elements necessary to express its Outstanding Universal Value;
(2) is of adequate size to ensure the complete representation of the features and processes which convey the property's significance;
(3) suffers from adverse effects of development and/or neglect.[33]

However, the international scope makes their definitions more challenging. The significance of the site may very much be related to local or national representations, values, and cultural heritage. The respect due to different cultures requires that cultural heritage must be considered and judged primarily within the cultural contexts to which it belongs. In other words, the evaluation of nomination must balance between universal values and local cultural heritage. Given the variety of approaches in historic preservation, a challenging issue is, for instance, to evaluate the applications for reconstructed sites in China and Japan. While the concept of reconstructed sites utterly makes sense in Chinese and Japanese historic preservation, UNESCO only accepts reconstruction on the basis of complete and detailed documentation.

Due to their international – and universal – characteristics, the World Heritage Site may also be sources of numerous conflicts between archaeologists, historians, tourism agencies, local or religious peoples, and environmental activists. For instance, Great Zimbabwe is a World Heritage Site about one of the greatest African kingdoms: the Kingdom of Zimbabwe from 1200 to 1450 C.E. Archaeologists discovered lots of information about African civilizations. A tourism destination, the site is also of major religious importance to the Shono people, and to the government who even banned archaeologists for digging sites considered as sacred (Green 2011, 421).

Protection and Preservation Technology: Standards, Styles, and Materials

Legal Protection and Economic Assets

Ways of protection vary according to the status of sites and structures. In addition to the concrete repair/restoration/rehabilitation of a site/structure, protection can also derive from legal and economic approaches. Historic preservation teams may use financial attractiveness (tax incentive), mediation (Section 106 of the NHPA), or legal tools (regulation and ordinances) to preserve structures.

Preservationists must be aware of the legal and economic context of the sites (King 2011c). The law and protection of sites – especially for archaeology and digs – have been the subject of many works (Richman and Forsyth 2004). The protection of privately owned structures is less clear. First of all, it should be clear that – apart from a few exceptions – property owners have the right to do as they wish with their property. The Fifth Amendment to the U.S. Constitution establishes the principle that private property would not be "taken" for public use without fair compensation (Tyler et al. 2009, 121). The government has no authority to guarantee that a privately owned structure would be protected or preserved. The real protective power of historic preservation is found at the local level. Only at the local level can historic properties be regulated and protected through legal ordinances (Tyer et al. 2009, 59–60).

However, the 1978 U.S. Supreme Court decision, *Penn Central Transportation Company (PCTC)* v. *City of New York* marked a landmark in historic preservation in the United States. The case opposed the right of the owner (here PCTC) to develop a property versus the right of a city (here NYC) to review and regulate the development of a designated historic property (Tyler et al. 2009, 123). PCTC had applied to the New York City Landmarks Preservation Commission (LPC) for permission to construct an addition over the listed Grand Central Station building. The permission was denied by the LPC. Confirmed by the U.S. Supreme Court, the denial provided support for towns and cities commission to establish control on historic properties.[34] Most of the protection power lies in historic district commission. Historic district commissioners are given power of approval over exterior modifications, proposed additions, demolition of designated historic structures, and changes within historic districts (Tyler et al. 2009, 132).

Section 106 is the centerpiece of federal protection for historic properties through the requirement for government agencies to evaluate the impact of all government-funded construction projects. Additionally, those agencies must allow time for the NRHP to comment on the project's impact, mitigation, and course of action before the project can proceed (Stipe 2003, 45). It essentially gives the community an opportunity to voice concern about the built or natural heritage environment affected by federally funded projects (Tyler et al. 2009, 51–53). The SHPO manages most of the Section 106 process locally. The ACHP provides a rich list of publications and resources to understand and apply Section 106.

Section 106 is not a guarantee of protection of historic resources though. It is important to understand that Section 106 only applies to projects in which the federal government is involved via funding, project management, or administration. Therefore, Section 106 review applies to NPS facilities, federal building projects, federally funded highways, or state projects partially funded through federal grants. Section 106, in absence of federal funding, does not regulate state, municipal, private, or privately funded actions that threaten historic properties or resources (Stipe 2003, 45). Even for federal projects, Section 106 only requires the agency to complete assessments, consider alternatives, and receive comments from the necessary parties. The agency is not required to implement their 106 findings after cost and feasibility studies are considered. After the process, a memorandum of agreement binds the agency to the agreement and the course of action outlined during the review. Federal funding may be withdrawn but the Section 106 review process does not have the power to stop work even if it will have significant negative impact on a historic property.

Economic development can also drive historic preservation. To be successful, in the private sector, historic preservation must make financial sense in order to attract partners and be economically sustainable (Mason 2005). Private sector or commercial historic preservation projects also provide benefits for communities (Rypkema 2005; Tyler et al. 2009,

237–239). Projects can explore the costs for the different options: preservation/stabilization, restoration, reconstruction, and rehabilitation. Interestingly, preservationists may be aware that the cost of rehabilitation – and therefore reuse – can be significantly less than new construction (Tyler et al. 2009, 240). A recent report from the ACHP lists the different criteria to evaluate the cost and benefits of historic preservation (jobs, property values, heritage tourism, environmental impact, social impact, and downtown revitalization) for the whole community (Advisory Council on Historic Preservation 2011). Being economically viable, the protection of a site/structure would be more attractive and successful.

Preservationists must also know the different options regarding the tax system. The 1976 Tax Reform Act was a watershed in historic preservation. Following two decades of urban demolitions, the Act stated that developers could no longer consider the cost of demolition of historical structures as a deductible business expense. The Act also created a tax incentive program for the rehabilitation of historic structures. It permitted a tax advantage for substantial rehabilitation of historic structures, allowing owners to take greater tax deductions (Tyler et al. 2009, 249). This allowed for more private-sector partners in historic preservation. Old structures could then be seen as financial opportunities for private partners.

The 1978 Tax Act went further by establishing a tax credit program for rehabilitating older buildings. The Rehabilitation Investment Tax Credit (RITC) program allowed developers a 10 percent tax credit for the cost of rehabilitating a historic structure used in a trade or business or held for income-producing purposes (Tyler et al. 2009, 249). Some local preservation ordinances also allow for a reduction in property taxes for designated historic properties. In order to apply for tax credit, the structure must have the Certified Historic Structure (CHS) status attributed by the NPS to prove its historical significance. Other financial advantages such as a "historic easement" – in which the owner retains use of the property, but agrees to relinquish part of the "bundle of rights" in return for favorable tax treatment – or a Transfer of Development Rights, or a Purchase of Development Rights (PDR) are also available (Tyler et al. 2009, 245–248). In order to know more about economic resources, historians can consult Schwartz's report on state tax credits and a variety of other resources (2014).

Preservation Technology

Public historians interested in historic preservation should be familiar with preservation technology. Preservation technology is the set of methods and materials used to protect and conserve historic buildings, sites, and artifacts (Tyler et al. 2009, 189). Since historic buildings are often described in terms of architectural style, it is important for public historians who want to be involved in historic preservation to know the basics of architecture. It is necessary to know about the different materials teams may have to work with.

Among the different approaches – preservation/stabilization, restoration, reconstruction, and rehabilitation – restoration and reconstruction are often the most expensive solutions. As for restoration, the security requirements (electricity, air-conditioning, humidity control, public access – exits, elevators, ramps) and the implication of the Americans with Disabilities Act for historic preservation raise acute challenges (Howe 1986, 115; Tyler et al. 2009, 231–235). Rehabilitation is often the preferred option for preservation, but here again, preservationists and historians must obey some rules. They need to choose between contextual design, matching, or compatible styles. Contextual design emphasizes compatibility for which architects and preservationists must respect the scale, height, setback, materials, and detailing of surrounding older buildings (Tyler et al. 2009, 105). When designing an addition to a historic building or a new building in a historic district, an architect or a designer should carefully consider the question of context. For matching structures, new architecture imitates the old, in the same style, with similar materials and detailing. Some arguments against this solution focus on the public's inability to easily discern the difference between the original and new structures. Finally, a compatible model is the most common approach. In this case, new designs should be sensitive to historic structures and compatible with them in terms of size, scale, color, material, and character (Tyler et al. 2009, 107).

In order to know more about preservation technology, historians can use the NPS's standards and guidelines dealing with the rehabilitation and restoration of historic buildings. The Secretary of the Interior's *Standards for the Treatment of Historic Properties* provide a lot of information about the preservation, restoration, rehabilitation, and reconstruction of historic structures (NPS undated a). The Standards for Rehabilitation – first published in 1979 – present the ten standards that are now commonly accepted practice for preservation design.

Historians should be able to discuss with architects and contractors about the different components of historic structures. They should learn about the form of the building, the proportion issue, mortar and masonry, and building elements (columns, roofs, floors, walls, windows, doors, gutters, fireplaces, etc.) (Irwin 2003, 3–46, 83–86, 96–125, 139–164; NPS undated b) The NPS provides guidelines for materials such as masonry, wood, and metals (Tyler et al. 2009, 221–231; NPS undated b). In addition to technical works, public historians may consult the Association for Preservation Technology International and its bulletin. Historians can also get training from the NPS's Historic Preservation Training Center, or from RESTORE. However, no training will replace work undertaken under a restoration architect, or in a preservation project.

Historic Districts, Revitalization, and Cultural Repair

Unlike more traditional academic historians, public historians are required to be more aware of the public uses of the past. Similarly, they should be aware of the impact and uses of historic preservation for the community. The creation of historic districts and urban historic preservation in general can have tremendous consequences on the life and organization in towns and cities.

Creating Historic Districts

Historic districts may be created for various reasons. They can result from the wish to protect historic properties (Alamo Plaza district in San Antonio), they can serve to control new urban development (Pioneer Square in Seattle), they can help control urban redevelopment (Station Square in Pittsburg), they can contribute to stabilizing property values (lower downtown in Denver), or they can help promote a neighborhood to attract tourism (Lowell, Massachusetts) (Tyler et al. 2009, 156–164). It is clear that history is merely one – with urban planning, tourism, and marketing – use of historic districts.

The creation of a district is first of all the creation of boundaries. The district must unify properties with similar architectural and historical characteristics. This does not mean that the area should be frozen in time. Ideally several historical periods should be represented in the historic district to show change over time and foster cultural and historical diversity (Hamer 1998, 95). For too long, historic preservation has favored white, wealthy, and

Christian heritage while silencing the part played by ethnic minorities in the history of the city, state, and nation. Most cities have a changing history that represents many time periods, and historic districts should represent the full spectrum of a community's past, not simply a selected slice through it at one particular time period (Tyler et al. 2009, 164).

In order to create a historic district, the next step is to set up a historic district commission at the local level. This may come from a citizens' petition to a town/city council. Town and city councils can only create such commissions after receiving governmental permission through enabling legislation or a historic preservation act. Once established, a commission can create a historic district, can identify historic resources, can acquire certain resources for historic preservation, and can assign penalties (Tyler et al. 2009, 168–169). For example, if a property falls into disrepair, the commission may take the initiative and begin action against the owner.

Ordinances are legal documents that historic district commissions can use to enforce historic preservation. They control the exterior alteration and demolition of structures through explicit criteria and standards. Ordinances include due diligence and due process. Due diligence deals with the consistency with which awarding certificates, applications, meetings, minutes and agenda, and notices help and inform owners of historic properties. Due process deals with the legal procedures that are available to all applicants, including the opportunity to address the commission, to object or agree with a ruling, and to appeal a decision by the commission (Tyler et al. 2009, 175). For more information, historians can contact the SHPO and consult the Secretary of Interior's *Standards for the Treatment of Historic Properties*.

Urban Revitalization

The creation of historic districts and historic preservation at large resonate in urban planning. Although the relations between preservation teams and city planners are not always peaceful, they are natural collaborators. For example, the American Planning Association published a report entitled "Preparing a Historic Preservation Plan," which includes ten major components for better relations between city planning and historic preservation (Roddewig and White 1994). A historic preservation plan should be part of a larger city comprehensive plan (Kelly and Becker 2000).

Historic preservation can definitely participate in sustaining the community life (Hurley 2006). A historic preservation plan can both contribute to the preservation of the community history and attract economic partners. When the historic character of an older downtown is preserved, it can become a tourist attraction, enhancing both the local economy and the sense of community pride (Tyler et al. 2009, 278). Historic preservation contributes to saving functional aspects too. It can avoid demolition and the disappearance of older downtowns.

However, the changing demographic repartition in American cities since World War II has affected urban historic preservation. Historians must take into consideration that a large part of the population now lives in suburban areas. The NPS has therefore provided guidelines to undertake historic preservation of those areas (Ames and McClelland 2002). Changes have also affected downtown areas. The Housing Act of 1949 and Urban Renewal Act of 1954 provided funding to purchase and demolish old urban neighbourhoods in disrepair. These acts contributed to the destruction of old city downtowns and, in reaction, to a rising interest in urban historic preservation. For instance, Downtown Development Authorities (DDA) were created in the 1970s to deal with older downtowns.

One particular program designed by the NPS to encourage the revitalization of historic downtowns is entitled the Main Street program. It was established to explore how the rehabilitation of older commercial buildings could be an important part of downtown revitalization efforts (Tyler et al. 2009, 280). Created in 1980, the program assists shopkeepers with tax and grant incentives to rehabilitate buildings, attract new businesses, and promote the Main Street commercial district. It is composed of coalitions of business owners, chambers of commerce, tourism commissions, and municipal government to demonstrate the economic benefits of historic preservation and preservation planning (National Trust for Historic Preservation undated). The purposes of the program are not only historical but also include the organization, the promotion, the design, and the economic restructuring of main streets. Based on eight core principles, the Main Street program has been successful in bringing actors of the community into historic preservation programs (National Main Street Center undated).

It is crucial that urban historic preservation engages with communities. In his work *Beyond Preservation: Using Public History to Revitalize Inner Cities*, Andrew Hurley speaks of the importance of community involvement in urban landscapes, particularly with preserving and revitalizing inner-city areas (2010). Empowering communities is key for historic preservation and cultural diversity. Hurley asserts that "inner-city communities can best turn preserved landscapes into assets by subjecting them to public interpretation at the grass roots" (2010, ix). Stressing the importance of grassroots preservation efforts, Hurley retraces the ubiquitous conundrum of preservation's legacies of gentrification and subsequent displacement (2010, 53). Some historic preservation projects have silenced stories from marginalized parts of the population. Mary Battle shows that "despite Charleston's significant role as the largest North American entry point for the trans-Atlantic slave trade … Tour guides overwhelmingly marginalized or ignored African American history." Besides, in Charleston, "preservation often led to increased costs of living and displacement in low-income neighborhoods predominantly occupied by African Americans" (Battle 2011). Poor African American populations were displaced from downtown Charleston (Weyeneth 2000, 68).

On the surface, the gentrification of a neighborhood is considered a success that results in improved housing, rising property values, beautification of a neighborhood, and blight reversal. Such measures of success, however, are at the cost of displacing a largely poor and minority residential community. It also goes against cultural diversity in old downtown areas. It is up to the preservation community to develop innovative strategies to gentrify a neighborhood without displacing current residents (Stipe 2003, 149). The future of the field is more than saving buildings and reviving economic development. The future includes the preservation of historical and cultural landscapes, scenic byways, and inclusion of minority populations. Creating a sense of place is important to a community's identity, and should inform historic preservation practice.

In *The Power of Place: Urban Landscapes as Public History* Dolores Hayden examines the relationships between urban Los Angeles and its different ethnic groups (Hayden 1995). She defines "the power of place" as "the power of ordinary urban landscapes to nurture citizens' public memory, to encompass shared time in the form of shared territory" (1995, 9). Hayden asserts that this power is still largely unrecognized for many ethnic groups and women in the cities of this country. Hayden's work shows a different approach to tell the history of urban landscapes by focusing on "social and political issues, rather than physical ones" as the bedrock of the history, giving "primary importance to the political and social narratives of the neighborhood, and to the everyday lives of working people" (1995, 235).

Rebecca Amato (City University of New York) therefore asked whether "rather than locating 'neighborhood character' in buildings and parks, might preservationists and public historians consider preservation of people – that is alliances with the organizations fighting displacement – a legitimate aim? And how would this work?" (Amato 2011). In addition to the structure, preservation may therefore have to consider how the process of inventory, repairs, and rehabilitation can better involve local populations through the creation of jobs and through the management of the site itself.

Cultural Repair of Post-Industrial Areas

Cultural repair is a term that Cathy Stanton has used to define historic preservation projects in some post-industrial areas (2012). Post-industrial areas may be composed of "empty factories or warehouses resulting from decentralization, deteriorating inner city infrastructures, and neglected built environment due to population and tax revenue loss" (Innovative Re-Use in the Post-Industrial City undated). Case studies include the steel mill at Bagnoli (Naples, Italy) and the West Georgia Textile Heritage Trail (United States). The concept is not new though. Already in the 1930s, the U.S. government used historic preservation to fight the consequences of the Great Depression. For instance, Hopewell Furnace (Pennsylvania) was transformed into a national park by the federal government's efforts during the 1930s (Stanton 2012, 58). A more recent example has been New England's textile city of Lowell, Massachusetts (Stanton 2006). It was used as an experimental site in creating a new kind of urban national park that would help to reinvent a de-industrialized community for a post-industrial economy (Stanton 2012, 58). The Lowell National Park was created in 1978. Locally driven, the project used historic preservation as a way to adapt the site to the modern economy. Stanton demonstrates that it "paid off in the form of greatly increased property values, many new residents and businesses, continued public and private reinvestment in the city's downtown and an improved reputation in the region and beyond" (Stanton 2012, 66–67)

To conclude, historians should bring historical analysis and contextualization to historic preservation projects. They have specific skills that preservationists cannot always master. Once they know and understand the rules and methodology of historic preservation, public historians can contribute to the engagement with communities. In addition to evaluating the historical significance of the project, public historians can help recognize the value of preserving the physical and cultural heritage for economic and social benefits and give residents a sense of place.

Public historians interested in historic preservation can consult a large number of books. Some present the history of the movement (Murtagh 2006; Stipe 2003; Lee 1992). Handbooks and textbooks can also help historians better understand the issues at stake (Tyler et al. 2009; Irwin 2003). They provide lists of funding, preservation resources, and architectural terms (Tyler et al. 2009, 265–268, 349–355, 360–364). Multiple resources are published or provided by historic preservation agencies as well.[35] In terms of training, courses in heritage conservation and historic preservation deal with the principles and practice of preservation, architectural history, historical archaeology, laws and legislation, building materials, and material culture. It is essential for students to undertake fieldwork to get practical experience. The NPS provides a list of professional qualifications in historic preservation for history, archaeology, architecture, architectural historians, and historic architecture (Secretary of the Interior's Standards and Guidelines undated). The National Council for Preservation Education lists programs in historic preservation (undergraduate,

graduate, certificate), as well as very useful syllabi to teach historic preservation. Training can also be received through digital courses and workshops. The National Center for Preservation Technology and Training provides training videos (for example, mortar and masonry) and podcasts. In his handbook, Irwin provides useful worksheets and checklists (Irwin 2003, 313–342).

Notes

1 The author wants to thank Chuck Arning for his comments on the public component of viability in historic preservation.
2 An example is Frank Lloyd Wright's home in Oak Park, Illinois.
3 For more information about CW, see the following pages.
4 For an example of an NPS reconstruction of a demolished site, see the Manzanar case study. Manzanar War Relocation Center was one of ten camps where Japanese American citizens and resident Japanese aliens were interned during World War II. www.nps.gov/civic/casestudies/manzanar.pdf (accessed August 13, 2015).
5 The NPS is a federal agency. It is the lead agency of the federal government for matters of historic preservation and cultural resources management. The NPS houses the National Register of Historic Places, HABS/HAER, and offices that advise the public on preservation, conservation, and how to fill out government forms.
6 The Roosevelt administration passed the Historic Sites Act of 1935. The act created the first federal list of historic sites worthy of preservation that maintained national significance. The Historic Sites Act gave the Secretary of the Interior, under the jurisdiction of the NPS, the authority to recognize historic and archaeological properties of national significance.
7 HABS resulted in one of the most extensive building surveys in the United States and remains an active program administered by the Library of Congress. One more recent addition to the NPS in the 1980s was the National Heritage Areas (NHA) program. NHA bring cultural and natural interests together to benefit historic preservation, land conservation, heritage tourism, and regional advocacy. Likewise, the National Center for Preservation Training and Technology (NCPTT) was established in 1992. NCPTT promotes training and technology development, methodological experiments, and project assistance. Its mission is to "stimulate the development and application of cutting-edge technologies" to the practice of preservation (Murtagh 2006, 37).
8 See below the criteria for application.
9 See the section on laws and historic preservation.
10 A rural historic landscape is defined as a geographical area that historically has been used by people, or shaped or modified by human activity, occupancy, or intervention, and that possesses a significant concentration, linkage, or continuity of areas of land use, vegetation, buildings and structures, roads and waterways, and natural features (McClelland et al. 1999).
11 Historic sites or landscapes are considered cultural landscapes when they are defined as significant for their association with a historic event, activity, or person, and may include battlefields, historic campgrounds, trails, and farms, but also historic scenes, designed landscape (Tyler et al. 2009, 327).
12 *Landscape Journal, Landscape Architecture* journals. See also the bibliography (although it is quite dated now) provided by the NPS: www.nps.gov/nr/publications/bulletins/nrb18/nrb18_7.htm (accessed May 2, 2015).
13 See Chapter 12, in particular, the section about the Nazi past.
14 To qualify for listing under Criteria A (association with events), B (association with people), or C (design), a cemetery or grave must meet not only the basic criteria, but also the special requirements of Criteria Considerations C or D, relating to graves and cemeteries (Walton Potter and Boland 1992).
15 In Italy, a national Public Archaeology congress was organized in 2012, www.archeopubblica2012.it/ (accessed April 16, 2015).
16 *Online Journal in Public Archaeology*, http://arqueologiapublica.blogspot.com/ (accessed March 29, 2015). See especially vol. 2 for the debates in Public Archaeology.
17 "On-Site Public Interpretation" and "Public Interpretation" (Silberman 2012).
18 See Chapter 9.

19 For instance see the website www.webarchaeology.com/html/Default.htm (accessed August 13, 2015).

20 See the list of world heritage sites in danger, http://whc.unesco.org/en/danger/ (accessed August 14, 2015).

21 The Environmental Protection Agency defines "green building" as "the practice of creating structures and using processes that are environmentally responsible and resource-efficient throughout a building's life-cycle from siting to design, construction, operation, maintenance, renovation and deconstruction." U.S. Environmental Protection Agency, "Green Building," www.epa.gov/greenbuilding/pubs/about.htm (accessed April 28, 2015).

22 HABS provides a rich documentation and guidelines for measurement.

23 See Chapter 9.

24 See *Preservation Brief* No. 43: The Preparation and Use of Historic Structure Reports. For the key steps of the HSR see Tyler et al. (2009, 216–217).

25 See in particular: *How to Apply the National Register Criteria for Evaluation? How to Complete the National Register Registration Form? Guidance on How to Submit a Nomination on Disk*, www.nps.gov/nr/publications/ (accessed June 2, 2015).

26 NHL represent only 3 percent of the structures listed in the NRHP.

27 For a discussion on gender and ethnic minorities representations in public history, see Chapter 12.

28 Peopling places; Creating Social Institutions and Movements; Expressing Cultural Values; Shaping the Political Landscape; Developing the American Economy; Expanding Science and Technology; Transforming the Environment; Changing Role of the United States in the World Community. See National Park Service, *History in the National Park Service: Themes and Concepts*, www.nps.gov/parkhistory/hisnps/NPSThinking/themes_concepts.htm (accessed May 12, 2015).

29 (a) A religious property deriving primary significance from architectural or artistic distinction or historical importance; or (b) A building or structure removed from its original location but which is significant primarily for architectural value, or which is the surviving structure most importantly associated with a historic person or event; or (c) A birthplace or grave of a historical figure of outstanding importance if there is no appropriate site or building directly associated with his productive life; or (d) A cemetery which derives its primary significance from graves of persons of transcendent importance, from age, from distinctive design features, or from association with historic events; or (e) A reconstructed building when accurately executed in a suitable environment and presented in a dignified manner as part of a restoration master plan, and when no other building or structure with the same association has survived; or (f) A property primarily commemorative in intent if design, age, tradition, or symbolic value has invested it with its own exceptional significance; or (g) A property achieving significance within the past 50 years if it is of exceptional importance. These exceptions are described further in NPS's "How To" booklet No. 2, entitled *How to Evaluate and Nominate Potential National Register Properties that Have Achieved Significance Within the Last 50 Years* available from NPS.

30 See Frank Lloyd Wright's Unity Temple, Oak Park, Illinois (Tyler et al. 2009, 130–131).

31 See UNESCO website, http://whc.unesco.org/en/list (accessed August 12, 2015).

32 1) represent a masterpiece of human creative genius; 2) exhibit an important interchange of human values, over a span of time or within a cultural area of the world, on developments in architecture or technology, monumental arts, town-planning or landscape design; 3) bear a unique or at least exceptional testimony to a cultural tradition or to a civilization which is living or which has disappeared; 4) be an outstanding example of a type of building, architectural or technological ensemble or landscape which illustrates (a) significant stage(s) in human history; 5) be an outstanding example of a traditional human settlement, land-use, or sea-use which is representative of a culture (or cultures), or human interaction with the environment especially when it has become vulnerable under the impact of irreversible change; 6) be directly or tangibly associated with events or living traditions, with ideas, or with beliefs, with artistic and literary works of outstanding universal significance; 7) to contain superlative natural phenomena or areas of exceptional natural beauty and aesthetic importance; 8) to be outstanding examples representing major stages of earth's history, including the record of life, significant on-going geological processes in the development of landforms, or significant geomorphic or physiographic features; 9) to be outstanding examples representing significant on-going ecological and biological processes in the evolution and development of terrestrial, fresh water, coastal and marine ecosystems and communities of plants and animals; 10) contain the most important and significant natural habitats

for in-situ conservation of biological diversity, including those containing threatened species of Outstanding Universal Value from the point of view of science or conservation.

33 IUCN, *Conditions of Integrity*, May 2011, whc.unesco.org/document/115532 (accessed May 13, 2015).
34 As some argue, though, the decision did not establish how far a public agency could go in limiting the rights of private owners to develop their properties (Tyler et al. 2009, 126).
35 The Society for Architectural Historians, English Heritage, and the American Cultural resources Association (ACRA) are useful for public historians. *Preservation Action* is a national preservation lobby that coordinates a network of preservationists, community activists, and civic leaders who provide grassroots support for preservation. Journals such as *Preservation Education and Research*, *CRM: The Journal of Heritage Stewardship* and *Preservation* or blogs such as *PreservationNation* can also be very useful, http://blog.preservationnation.org (accessed August 1, 2015).

Bibliography

Advisory Council on Historic Preservation. *Section 106 Regulations Summary*, undated, www.achp. gov/106summary.html (accessed August 13, 2015).

Advisory Council on Historic Preservation. *National Historic Preservation Act of 1966, As amended through 2000*, 2000, www.achp.gov/NHPA.pdf (accessed August 13, 2015).

Advisory Council on Historic Preservation. *Measuring the Economics of Preservation: Recent Findings*, 2011, www.achp.gov/docs/final-popular-report6-7-11.pdf (accessed September 13, 2014).

Ahmad, Yahaya. "The Scope and Definitions of Heritage: From Tangible to Intangible." *International Journal of Heritage Studies*, 12/3 (May 2006): 292–300.

Alanen, Arnold R. and Melnick, Robert. *Preserving Cultural Landscapes in America*, Baltimore: Johns Hopkins University Press, 2000.

Amato, Rebecca. "Developing the East Village." Case Statement for the NCPH Working Group: Public History and Gentrification: A Contentious Relationship, 2011, http://ncph.org/cms/wp-content/uploads/Combined-Gentrification-Statements.pdf (accessed May 13, 2015).

Ames, David L. and McClelland, Linda Flint. *Historic Residential Suburbs: Guidelines for Evaluation and Documentation for the National Register of Historic Places*, Washington, DC: National Park Service, 2002, www.nps.gov/nr/publications/bulletins/suburbs/index.htm (accessed August 13, 2015).

Andrus, Patrick W. *Guidelines for Identifying, Evaluating, and Registering America's Historic Battlefields*, Washington, DC: National Park Service, 1992, www.nps.gov/nr/publications/bulletins/nrb40/ (accessed August 11, 2015).

Andrus, Patrick W. and Shrimpton, Rebecca H. *How to Apply the National Register Criteria for Evaluation Bulletin*, Washington, DC: National Park Services, 2002, www.nps.gov/nr/publications/ bulletins/nrb15/ (accessed August 13, 2015).

Australian Heritage Council. *Guidelines for the Assessment of Places for the National Heritage List*, Canberra: Department of the Environment, Water, Heritage and the Arts, 2009.

Barrett, Brenda and Taylor, Michael. "Three Models for Managing Living Landscapes." *CRM: The Journal of Heritage Stewardship*, 23/1 (2007): 33–36.

Barthel, Diane. "Historic Preservation: A Comparative Analyses." *Sociological Forum*, 4/1 (March 1989): 88–95.

Barthel, Diane. *Historic Preservation: Collective Memory and Historical Identity*, New Brunswick: Rutgers University Press, 1996.

Battle, Mary. "African American History Tours and Gentrification in Charleston, South Carolina." *Case Statement for the NCPH Working Group: Public History and Gentrification: A Contentious Relationship*, 2011, http://ncph.org/cms/wp-content/uploads/Combined-Gentrification-Statements. pdf (accessed May 2, 2015).

Burg, Stephen B. "From Troubled Ground to Common Ground: The Locust Grove African-American Cemetery Restoration Project. A Case Study of Service-Learning and Community History." *The Public Historian*, 30 (Spring 2008): 51–82.

Burns, John, ed. *Recording Historic Structures*, Hoboken: John Wiley & Sons, 2003.

Cluzel, Jean-Sébastien. "Preserve / Restore / Rebuild / Renovate: The Archipelagos of Mystical Thought in Japan and Europe." *Réseau Asie's Editorial*, August 1, 2007, http://www.reseau-asie.com (accessed September 24, 2015).

Conard, Rebecca. "Spading Common Ground: Reconciling the Built and Natural Environments." In *Public History and the Environment*, edited by Martin Melosi and Philip V. Scarpino, Malabar: Krieger Publishing Company, 2004, 3–22.

Dawson, Tom. "A View from Scotland's Coast." *The Public Historian*, 36/3 (August 2014): 31–49.

Dawson, Tom. "Taking the Middle Path to the Coast: How Community Collaboration Can Help Save Threatened Sites." In *The Future of Heritage as Climates Change: Loss, Adaptation and Creativity*, edited by David C. Harvey and Jim Perry, London: Routledge, 2015, 248–269.

De Groot, Jerome. *Consuming History: Historians and Heritage in Contemporary Popular Culture*, London: Routledge, 2008.

DeJean, Joan. *How Paris Became Paris: The Invention of the Modern City*, London: Bloomsbury, 2014.

Derry, Linda and Malloy, Maureen, eds. *Archaeologists and Local Communities: Partners in Exploring the Past*, Washington, DC: Society for American Archaeology, 2003.

Donnelly, Jessica Foy, ed. *Interpreting Historic House Museums*, New York: AltaMira Press, 2002.

Dubrow, Gail Lee and Goodman, Jennifer B. *Restoring Women's History through Historic Preservation*, Baltimore: Johns Hopkins University Press, 2002.

Durel, John and Durel, Anita Nowery. "A Golden Age for Historic Properties." *History News* (Summer 2007): 7–16.

Farrell, Nancy. "Historic Battlefields: Studying and Managing Fields of Conflict." In *A Companion to Cultural Resource Management*, edited by Thomas F. King, Oxford: Wiley-Blackwell, 2011, 298–318.

Glaser, Leah. "Public Historians Take on Climate Change." *History@Work*, April 29, 2012, http://publichistorycommons.org/public-historians-take-on-climate-change/ (accessed August 12, 2015).

Glaser, Leah. "Public History and Sustainability: An Overview and Invitation." *History@Work*, June 7, 2013, http://publichistorycommons.org/public-history-and-sustainability-intro/ (accessed September 12, 2014).

Glaser, Leah. "Identifying Issues of Environmental Sustainability in Public History Practice." *The Public Historian*, 36/3 (August 2014): 10–16.

Glassberg, David. *Sense of History: The Place of the Past in American Life*, Amherst: University of Massachusetts Press, 2001.

Glassberg, David. "Interpreting Landscapes." In *Public History and the Environment*, edited by Martin Melosi and Philip V. Scarpino, Malabar: Krieger Publishing Company, 2004, 23–36.

Graham, Brian, Ashworth, G.J., and Tunbridge, J.E., eds. *A Geography of Heritage: Power, Culture and Economy*, London: Arnold Press, 2000.

Green, Thomas J. "International Variety in Cultural Resource Management." In *A Companion to Cultural Resource Management*, edited by Thomas F. King, Oxford: Wiley-Blackwell, 2011, 420–439.

Hamer, David Allan. *History in Urban Places: The Historic Districts of the United States*, Columbus: Ohio State University Press, 1998.

Hardesty, Donald L. and Little, Barbara J. *Assessing Site Significance: A Guide for Archaeologists and Historians*, second edition, Walnut Creek: AltaMira Press, 2009.

Harris, Donna Ann. *New Solutions for House Museums: Ensuring the Long-Term Preservation of America's Historic Houses*, Lanham: AltaMira Press, 2007.

Hayden, Dolores. *The Power of Place: Urban Landscapes as Public History*, Cambridge, MA: The MIT Press, 1995.

Heffern, Sarah. "A Who's Who of Preservation Organizations." *Preservation Nation Blog*, January 28, 2014, http://blog.preservationnation.org/2014/01/28/10-tuesday-whos-preservation-organizations/#.VczWiudQjRL (accessed August 13, 2015).

Hosmer, Charles B. Jr. and Verne, E. "Chatelain and the Development of the Branch of History of the National Park Service." *The Public Historian*, 16/1 (1994): 25–39.

Howe, Barbara J. "The Historian in Historic Preservation: An Introduction." In *Public History: An Introduction*, edited by Barbara Howe and Emory L. Kemp, Malabar: Robert E. Krieger Publishing Company, 1986, 111–129.

Hunter, William. "Geographies of Cultural Resource Management: Space, Place, and Landscape." In *A Companion to Cultural Resource Management*, edited by Thomas F. King, Oxford: Wiley-Blackwell, 2011, 95–113.

Hurley, Andrew. "Narrating the Urban Waterfront: The Role of Public History in Community Revitalization." *The Public Historian*, 28/4 (Fall 2006): 19–50.

Hurley, Andrew. *Beyond Preservation: Using Public History to Revitalize Inner Cities*, Philadelphia: Temple University Press, 2010.

IDTR. "Frequently Asked Questions." Undated, http://dark-tourism.org.uk/faqs (accessed August 14, 2015).

Innovative Re-Use in the Post-Industrial City. A 2014 NCPH Working Group. "About." Undated, https://postindustrialurbanreuse.wordpress.com/about/ (accessed August 13, 2015).

Irwin, J. Kirk. *Historic Preservation Handbook*, New York: McGraw-Hill, 2003.

Izi Travel. "The Excavations of the Roman Theatre in Florence." Undated, https://izi.travel/en/9fe0-the-excavations-of-the-roman-theatre-in-florence/en (accessed August 13, 2015).

Jameson, John H. Jr., ed. *Presenting Archaeology to the Public: Digging for Truths*, Walnut Creek: AltaMira Press, 1997.

Jameson, John H. Jr. "Public Archaeology in the United States." In *Public Archaeology*, edited by Nick Merriman, London and New York: Routledge, 2004, 21–58.

Kaufman, Ned. "Historic Places and the Diversity Deficit in Heritage Conservation." CRM: *The Journal of Heritage Stewardship*, 1/2 (2004): 68–85.

Keller, J. Timothy and Keller, Genevieve P. *How to Evaluate and Nominate Designed Historic Landscapes*, Washington, DC: National Park Service, www.nps.gov/nr/publications/bulletins/nrb18/ (accessed August 13, 2015).

Kelly, Eric D. and Becker, Barbara. *Community Planning: An Introduction to the Comprehensive Plan*, Washington, DC: Island Press, 2000.

Kemp, Emory L. "A Perspective on Our Industrial Past Through Industrial Archaeology." In *Public History: An Introduction*, edited by Barbara Howe and Emory L. Kemp, Malabar: Robert E. Krieger Publishing Company, 1986, 174–198.

King, Thomas F., ed. *A Companion to Cultural Resource Management*, Oxford: Wiley-Blackwell, 2011a.

King, Thomas F. "Archaeology of the Recent Past." In *A Companion to Cultural Resource Management*, edited by Thomas F. King, Oxford: Wiley-Blackwell, 2011b, 78–94.

King, Thomas F. "Cultural Resource Laws: The Legal Melange." In *A Companion to Cultural Resource Management*, edited by Thomas F. King, Oxford: Wiley-Blackwell, 2011c, 405–419.

Kuranda, Kathryn. "Studying and Evaluating the Build Environment." In *A Companion to Cultural Resource Management*, edited by Thomas F. King, Oxford: Wiley-Blackwell, 2011, 13–28.

Kyvig, David E. and Marty, Myron A. *Nearby History: Exploring the Past Around You*, third edition, Lanham: AltaMira Press, 2010.

Ladd, Brian. *The Ghosts of Berlin: Confronting German History in the Urban Landscape*, Chicago: University of Chicago Press, 1998.

Langer, Adina. "Reflections on Relocating." *History@Work*, December 16, 2014, http://publichistory commons.org/reflections-on-relocating-part-1/ (accessed August 13, 2015).

Langley, Susan B. "Challenges of Maritime Archaeology: In Too Deep." In *A Companion to Cultural Resource Management*, edited by Thomas F. King, Oxford: Wiley-Blackwell, 2011, 223–244.

Lee, Antoinette J., ed. *Past Meets Future: Saving America's Historic Environments*, Washington, DC: The Preservation Press, 1992.

Lee, Antoinette J. "Historic Preservationists and Cultural Resources Managers: Preserving America's Historic Places." In *Public History: Essays from the Field*, edited by James Gardner and Peter LaPaglia, Malabar: Krieger Publishing Company, 2006, 129–139.

Little, Barbara, ed. *Public Benefits of Archaeology*, Gainesville: University Press of Florida, 2002.

Little, Barbara, Seibert, Erika Martin, Townsend, Jan, Sprinkle, John H. Jr., and Knoerl, John. *Guidelines for Evaluating and Registering Archeological Properties Bulletin*, Washington, DC: National Park Service, 2000, www.nps.gov/nr/publications/bulletins/arch/ (accessed August 16, 2015).

Longstreth, Richard, ed. *Cultural Landscapes: Balancing Nature and Heritage in Preservation Practice*, Minneapolis: University of Minnesota Press, 2008.

Lowenthal, David. "A Global Perspective on American Heritage." In *Past Meets Future: Saving America's Historic Environments*, ed. Antoinette J. Lee, Washington, DC: Preservation Press, 1992, 157–163.

McClelland, Linda Flint, Keller, J. Timothy, Keller, Genevieve P., and Melnick, Robert Z. *Guidelines for Evaluating and Documenting Rural Historic Landscapes*, Washington, DC: National Park Service, 1999, www.nps.gov/nr/publications/bulletins/nrb30/ (accessed August 13, 2015).

McDavid, Carol. "Towards a More Democratic Archaeology? The Internet and Public Archaeological Practice." In *Public Archaeology*, edited by Nick Merriman, London: Routledge, 2004, 159–187.

McGimsey, Charles R. "The Four Fields of Archaeology." *American Antiquity*, 68/4 (2003): 611–618.

McKee, Larry and Thomas, Brian W. "Starting a Conversation: The Public Style of Archaeology at the Hermitage." *Southeastern Archaeology*, 17/2 (Winter 1998): 133–139.

Mason, Randall. *Economics and Historic Preservation: A Guide and Review of the Literature*, The Brookings Institution Metropolitan Policy Program, 2005, www.brookings.edu/~/media/research/files/reports/2005/9/metropolitanpolicy-mason/20050926_preservation.pdf (accessed August 13, 2015).

Massachusetts Historic Preservation Conference. "Ready or Not: Preparing for Climate Change." 2015, www.mapreservationconference.org/sessions.html (accessed August 11, 2015).

Meringolo, Denise. *Museums, Monuments, and National Parks: Toward a New Genealogy of Public History*, Amherst and Boston: University of Massachusetts, 2012.

Merlino, Kathryn Rogers. "[Re]Evaluating Significance: The Environmental and Cultural Value in Older and Historic Buildings." *The Public Historian*, 36/3 (August 2014): 70–85.

Merriman, Nick, ed. *Public Archaeology*, London and New York: Routledge, 2004.

Moratto, Michael. "Archaeology of the Distant Past." In *A Companion to Cultural Resource Management*, edited by Thomas F. King, Oxford: Wiley-Blackwell, 2011, 54–77.

Morton, W. Brown III. "Forging New Values in Uncommon Times." In *Past Meets Future: Saving America's Historic Environments*, edited by Antoinette J. Lee, Washington, DC: The Preservation Press, 1992, 37–38.

Moshenska, Gabriel. "What is Public Archaeology?" *Present Pasts*, 1 (2010): 46–48.

Moyer, Teresa and Gadsby, David. "Pulling Back the Layers: Participatory and Community-Based Archeology." *History@Work*, August 1, 2014, http://publichistorycommons.org/participatory-and-community-based-archaeology/#sthash.7snfEpQC.dpuf (accessed January 15, 2015).

Murtagh, William J. *Keeping Time: The History and Theory of Preservation in America*, Hoboken: John Wiley & Sons, Inc., 2006.

National Charrette Institute. *The NCI Charrette System*, undated, www.charretteinstitute.org/charrette.html (accessed August 15, 2015).

National Main Street Center. *The Eight Principles*, undated, www.preservationnation.org/main-street/about-main-street/the-approach/eight-principles.html#.VVIkKGOKuSo (accessed August 15, 2015).

National Park Service. *History in the National Park Service: Themes and Concepts*, undated a, www.nps.gov/parkhistory/hisnps/NPSThinking/themes_concepts.htm (accessed January 29, 2015).

National Park Service. *Illustrated Guidelines for Rehabilitating Historic Buildings*, Washington, DC: National Park Service, undated b, www.nps.gov/tps/standards/rehabilitation/rehab/ (accessed August 16, 2015).

National Park Service. *National Historic Landmark Program: Full List of NHL Theme Studies*, undated c, www.nps.gov/nhl/learn/themestudieslist.htm (accessed August 12, 2015).

National Park Service. *National Register of Historic Places Program: Fundamentals*, undated d, www.nps.gov/nr/national_register_fundamentals.htm (accessed August 15, 2015).

National Park Service. *Secretary of the Interior's Standards for Archeological Documentation*, Washington, DC: National Park Service, undated e, www.nps.gov/history/local-law/arch_stnds_7.htm#guide (accessed August 15, 2015).

National Park Service. *The Secretary of the Interior's Standards for the Treatment of Historic Properties*, undated f, www.nps.gov/tps/standards.htm (accessed August 2, 2015).

National Park Service. *The Secretary of the Interior's Standards for the Treatment of Historic Properties*, Washington, DC: National Park Service, 1992, www.nps.gov/tps/standards/four-treatments/landscape-guidelines/ (accessed August 12, 2015).

National Park Service. "How to Apply the National Register Criteria for Evaluation." *National Register Bulletin*, Washington DC: National Park Service, 1995, www.nps.gov/nr/publications/bulletins/pdfs/nrb15.pdf (accessed January 29, 2015).

National Park Service. "Criteria for Evaluation." *The National Register of Historic Places Brochure*, U.S. Department of the Interior, National Park Service, 2002, www.cr.nps.gov/nr/publications/brochure/ (accessed May 3, 2015).

National Register Bulletin. *Researching a Historic Property*, Washington, DC: The National Park Service, Department of the Interior, 1998.

National Register Eligibility of National Cemeteries. *A Clarification of Policy*, September 8, 2011, www.nps.gov/nr/publications/guidance/Final_Eligibility_of_VA_cemeteries_A_Clarification_of_Policy_rev.doc (accessed August 14, 2015).

National Trust for Historic Preservation. "Welcome to the National Main Street Center, Inc." Undated, www.preservationnation.org/main-street/ (accessed March 31, 2015).

Nelson, Lee H. *Preservation Brief 17: Architectural Character Identifying the Visual Aspects of Historic Buildings as an Aid to Preserving their Character*, Washington, DC: Technical Preservation Services, The National Park Service, Department of the Interior, 1988.

Padgett, William. "Letter to the Editor: Historical Preservation and Significance." *The Public Historian*, 1/1 (1978): 11.

Parker, Patricia L. *Guidelines for Local Surveys: A Basis for Preservation Planning Bulletin*, Washington, DC: National Park Service, 1985, Appendix I (Archaeology), www.nps.gov/nr/publications/bulletins/nrb24/appendix1.htm (accessed June 21, 2015).

Pearson, Mike P. and Ramilisonina. "Public Archaeology and Indigenous Communities." In *Public Archaeology*, edited by Nick Merriman, London and New York: Routledge, 2004, 224–239.

Poppeliers, John C. and Chambers, S. Allen Jr. *What Style Is It? A Guide to American Architecture*, New York: John Wylie & Sons, 2003.

Richardson, Lorna. "A Digital Public Archaeology?" *Papers from the Institute of Archaeology*, University College London, August 30, 2013, http://doi.org/10.5334/pia.431 (accessed August 12, 2015).

Richman, Jennifer R. and Forsyth, Marion P., eds. *Legal Perspectives on Cultural Resources*, Walnut Creek: AltaMira Press, 2004.

Riesenweber, Julie. "Landscape Preservation and Cultural Geography." In *Cultural Landscapes: Balancing Nature and Heritage in Preservation Practice*, edited by Richard Longstreth, Minneapolis: University of Minnesota Press, 2008, 23–34.

Roddewig, Richard and White, Bradford. *Preparing a Historic Preservation Plan, Planning Advisory Service Report 450*, Chicago: American Planning Association, 1994.

Rypkema, Donovan D. *The Ecnomics of Historic Preservation: A Community Leader's Guide*, Washington, DC: National Trust for Historic Preservation, 2005.

Sacco, Nick. "Bridging the Gap Between 'Nature' Sites and 'History' Sites in the National Park Service." *Exploring the Past: Reading, Writing, and Blogging about History*, March 9, 2015, https://pastexplore.wordpress.com/2015/03/09/bridging-the-gap-between-nature-sites-and-history-sites-in-the-national-park-service/ (accessed May 13, 2015).

Schadla-Hall, Tim. "Editorial: Public Archaeology." *European Journal of Archaeology*, 2/2 (1999): 147–158.

Schwartz, Harry K. *State Tax Credits for Historic Preservation: A Policy Report Produced by the National Trust for Historic Preservation*, Washington, DC: National Trust for Historic Preservation, 2014, www.preservationnation.org/take-action/advocacy-center/additional-resources/historic-tax-credit-maps/Chart-July-2014.pdf (accessed March 13, 2015).

Sebastian, Lynne and Lipe, William D., eds. *Archaeology and Cultural Resource Management: Vision for the Future*, Santa Fe: SAR Press, 2010.

Secretary of the Interior's Standards and Guidelines. *Archeology and Historic Preservation*, National Park Service, undated, www.nps.gov/history/local-law/arch_stnds_9.htm (accessed August 2, 2015).

Sherfy, Marcella and Luce, W. Ray. *Guidelines for Evaluating and Nominating Properties that Have Achieved Significance Within the Past Fifty Years*, Washington, DC: National Park Service, 1998, www.nps.gov/nr/publications/bulletins/nrb22/ (accessed August 14, 2015).

Silberman, Neil Asher. *The Oxford Companion to Archaeology*, Oxford: Oxford University Press, 2012.

Spenneman, Dirk H.R. "Gauging Community Values in Historic Preservation." *CRM: The Journal of Heritage Stewardship*, 3/2 (2006): 6–20.

Stanton, Cathy. *The Lowell Experiment: Public History in a Postindustrial City*, Boston: University of Massachusetts Press, 2006.

Stanton, Cathy. "The Past as a Public Good: The U.S. National Park Service and 'Cultural Repair' in Post-Industrial Places." In *Public History and Heritage Today*, edited by Paul Ashton and Hilda Kean, London and New York: Palgrave Macmillan, 2012, 57–73.

Stille, Alexander. *The Future of the Past*, New York: Picador, 2003.

Stipe, Robert E., ed. *A Richer Heritage: Historic Preservation in the Twenty-First Century*, Chapel Hill: University of North Carolina Press, 2003.

Tyler, Noman, Ligibel, Ted J., and Tyler, Ilene R. *Historic Preservation: An Introduction to Its History, Principles, and Practice*, second edition, New York and London: Norton & Company, 2009.

UNESCO. *Convention Concerning the Protection of the World Cultural and Natural Heritage*, http://whc.unesco.org/en/about/ (accessed March 28, 2015).

Van West, Carroll. "Assessing Significance and Integrity in the National Register Process: Questions of Race, Class, and Gender." In *Preservation of What, for Whom?*, edited by Michael Tomlan, Ithaca: The National Council for Preservation Education, 1998, 109–116.

Walton Potter, Elisabeth and Boland, Beth M. *Guidelines for Evaluating and Registering Cemeteries and Burial Places Bulletin*, Washington, DC: National Park Service, 1992, www.nps.gov/nr/publications/bulletins/nrb41/ (accessed August 1, 2015).

Warren-Findley, Jannelle. *Human Heritage Management in New Zealand in the Year 2000 and Beyond*, Wellington: The Ian Axford New Zealand Fellowship in Public Policy, 2001.

Weyeneth, Robert R. *Historic Preservation for a Living City: Historic Charleston Foundation 1947–1997*, Columbia: University of South Carolina Press, 2000.

Whistnant, Anne Mitchell, Miller, Marla B., Nash, Gary B., and Thelen, David. *Imperiled Promise: The State of History in the National Park Service*, OAH, 2011, www.oah.org/programs/the-oah-national-park-service-collaboration/imperiled-promise-the-state-of-history-in-the-national-park-service/ (accessed August 1, 2015).

Zuelow, Eric. "Enshrining Ireland's Nationalist History Inside Prison Walls: The Restoration of Kilmainham Jail." *Eire-Ireland*, 39 (Fall/Winter 2004): 180–201.

3 Collecting and Preserving People's Stories
Oral History, Family History, and Everyday Life

Since the 1960s, various currents in historiography – social history, history from below, people's history, or bottom-up history – have moved from the study of elites to a focus on ordinary people (Thompson 1966; Zinn 1980). This focus on ordinary people has had two main consequences for public history practices. First, the lives of ordinary people have become sources for (public) historians. Family and everyday life are now among the different historical sources of (public) history projects. However, more associated with popular and amateur history, the everyday life of ordinary people has long been dissociated from academic scholarship. One challenge for public historians is to contribute to reconciling the community of historians with ordinary people and everyday life.

The second consequence of the move from elites to ordinary people has been the changing role of historians. The focus on ordinary people has been accompanied by attempts to foster public participation in history production. In England, historian Raphael Samuel created the History Workshop movement at Ruskin College (Oxford) in the late 1960s as a way to involve ordinary people as both subjects and practitioners of "history from below" (Schwarz 1993). Public participation in storytelling is today made easier by new technology that allows people to record their own materials through phones, cameras, and computers.

This chapter is divided into three parts. The first part explores one specific practice – oral history – and how it can contribute to public history. The second part focuses on some sources about ordinary people used in family and everyday history. The final part explores the challenges – like shared authority and subjectivity – for public historians who are both creators and participants in the projects.

Oral History Practices

Oral history is an incredibly broad activity that cannot be fully covered in one section. In place of comprehensiveness, the aim is to introduce readers to the chief skills necessary to construct, launch, and use oral history. Public historians may also use oral history as sources for exhibitions, TV or radio programs, websites, and so on. Oral history and public history are closely connected through the methodology and the relations with the public. Both oral history and public history involve the public in the construction of representations of the past. However, oral history raises some very specific issues. Public historians need to be familiar with oral history practices since, as specialist in oral history Ronald Grele noted, "Many interviewers are poorly trained and far too many are willing to settle for journalistic standards of usefulness" (1998, 40).

Many tools and resources can help historians to design a project. In addition to the numerous manuals and journals such as the *Oral History Review* and the *Journal of Oral*

Figure 3.1 Oral historian Tanya Finchum interviewing Oklahoma A&M College alumna Ruth
            Myers Lincoln (age 110) at her home in Little Rock, Arkansas, 2007. Courtesy of
            Oklahoma Oral History Research Program, Oklahoma State University Library.

History Society, historians can use different oral history websites (Ritchie 2003, 2011; Perks
and Thomson 2006; Neuenschwander 2009).[1] The Oral History in the Digital Age website
provides lots of resources, especially regarding the different materials historians can use.[2]
The Oral History Association website has useful best practices and guidelines for various
practices.[3] Finally, Baylor University has one of the most important Oral History programs
and designed an *Introduction to Oral History* used in many introductory workshops (2014).

What Does Oral History Bring to Historical Practice?

The Oral History Association (OHA) explains that "Oral History refers both to a method
of recording and preserving oral testimony and to the product of that process" (Oral History
Association 2009). An oral history interview can be an audio or video recording, but it
is crucial that historians focus on first-hand – who have directly witnessed the event –
personal experiences. Both the interviewer and the interviewee have "the conscious intention of creating a permanent record to contribute to an understanding of the past" (Oral
History Association 2009). This last objective is important to distinguish between oral
history and simple recording of past stories.

Oral history has a very long history. During the 1930s and 1940s in the United States, the
Federal Writers' Project recorded thousands of life histories, notably the "slave narratives"

from elderly former slaves living in the South. In spite of this example, some argue that the creation by Allan Nevins of the Columbia Oral History Research Office (COHRO) in 1948 marked the birth of the modern field (Diaz and Russell 1999, 203). Nevins was the first to initiate a systematic and disciplined effort to record on tape, preserve, and make available for future research recollections deemed of historical significance. COHRO became one of the largest archival collections of oral history interviews in the world (Shopes 2002). The Library of Congress American Folklife Center has collected major projects such as the Veterans History Project.[4] Oral history is today a global practice, and the OHA – founded in 1967 in the United States – has organized conferences in Brazil, Turkey, and South Africa, while the International Oral History Association was founded in 1987 in England.

The success of oral history is partly due to the creation of new types of sources. Oral historians collect unique individual experiences that bring depth to our understanding of the past. Oral history not only brings new kinds of sources, but it has the potential for shedding light on issues and historical questions absent from other traditional archives. By focusing on personal accounts, oral historians augment the information provided by more traditional materials such as public records, statistical data, photographs, maps, letters, diaries, and other historical archives. Eyewitnesses bring potential new perspectives that may "fill in the gaps in documentary history, sometimes correcting or even contradicting the written record" (Baylor University 2014, 1). In political history, oral sources can help understand crucial layers of public policy such as alliances, competition, and other mechanisms that one may not find in other public records. Finally, oral history matches the rise of historians' concern for people's history, community, and everyday life.[5] Oral history makes possible the research and production of sources for traditionally underrepresented populations like ethnic minorities, migrants, members of the working class, LGBT, and women.

The oral history format also helps historians to attract new audiences. The personal and often emotional accounts of the past foster public interest. While oral history can attract audiences, it can foster participation as well. In order to create oral history, at least two people must meet: the interviewer and the interviewee/narrator.[6] Alessandro Portelli, one of oral history's most thoughtful practitioners, explains that oral history refers to "what the source and the historian do together at the moment of their encounter in the interview" (1997, 3). This is why the term "narrator" may be preferred to the term "interviewee," which sounds too passive, and why the narrator should be clearly identified in the contents. Unlike journalistic practice, oral historians should refuse the concept of anonymous sources, and make arrangements to deposit their interviews at an appropriate archival repository. Anonymity deprives the narrator of any acknowledgment and prevents other researchers from determining how these sources shaped the historical interpretation.

Starting an Oral History Project

Doing oral history is a long process that requires planning and methodology. Before launching a project, historians should question whether oral history is the best methodology to access the understanding of the past and answer certain questions. What aspects of the topic may have already been covered? What would oral history bring to the understanding of the issue? Has there been any other oral history project/source about similar topics? In order to answer those questions, historians should not hesitate asking local libraries, archivists, historical societies, and using H-Oralhist, the H-Net affiliated listserv. Besides, historians can search university oral history directories such as the Baylor University collections, and the Library of Congress that hold copies of most of the microfilmed oral history collections.

Then, the project must be clearly delimited. Would the project have a topical focus that highlights an event, a period, a person or community, an issue, an organization, or a place? Or would the project have a biographical focus that concentrates on the life experience of one individual? (Baylor University 2014, 8). And how many people would be interviewed for the project? An accurate definition of the project helps choose the materials needed to collect interviews. The blueprint of the project also helps figure out the funding, materials, and timing necessary for implementing it. Unlike most other methodologies used by historians, oral history relies heavily on tools used to collect information. Historians need to choose between audio and video recording (Boyd 2012a). Video recording may be justified by the fact that facial expressions and body language reveal a lot about narrators. Video can also be useful in projects designed for future exhibitions and/or digital uses for which the visual format helps visitors connect with the stories. However, video recording has drawbacks. At least two people must take part – interviewer and video recorder – in the interview. And the more people present during interviews the less confident narrators can become. Video recording also means higher costs for storage and a higher obsolescence of the files. Although more traditional, the audio format is far less expensive and much more flexible. Multiple guides exist to help you choose your materials, microphone, camera, sound recorder, and so on (Boyd 2012a, 2012b; Pennington 2012).[7]

Before the interview starts, historians must think of and decide what to do with the interviews and how, where, and by whom interviews will be preserved. Researchers may use oral history to create source materials for their own writings. Those historians usually focus on the themes and questions relevant for their own research, and they know what they are looking for, and build the project and questions accordingly. However, they often lack the time and resources to create large projects and compile life experiences. Furthermore, they do not always deposit their interviews, notes, and transcripts in archives. The publicness of those projects is therefore limited. Any historian starting an oral history project should collaborate with archives, libraries, or any other repository for their collections.

The second category of oral historians is composed of historians who intend primarily to collect and preserve interviews for future uses. They may concentrate on particular research areas or types of interviews, but they do not attempt to answer questions for specific historical works. Those historians more often record a person's experiences over their lifetime and collaborate with archives that sometimes provide assistance in the form of equipment, appropriate deeds of gift, preservation, and transcribing services. The depositing of interviews in archives where they can be preserved and consulted assures their sustainability and secures the terms and conditions of the copyrights. It is important to know in advance about the recording formats accepted by the repositories to whom you may donate the interviews. It is also necessary to clarify the legal agreements required by the library/archives, and the possible accompanying documents (notes, photographs, maps, etc.).

The choice of recording materials and depository is directly linked to the overall budget of the project. In addition to the materials, historians must take into consideration the organization and number of interviews. A high number of interviews would obviously increase travel costs. Furthermore, any oral history project must plan ahead the possible transcription costs. Transcription is a difficult and time-consuming step in the overall project, but outsourcing the transcription may result in a substantial increase of the budget. Historians may contact state humanities councils that have supported oral history projects. Historians could also ask for funding from universities, local governments, historical societies, and local libraries that may be interested in the local dimension of the project.

Interviews: A Set of Practices

Any good interview depends on serious research that historians undertake before meeting the narrators. In his practical guide on oral history, Donald Ritchie argues that any oral historian should "count on doing as many as ten hours of research for every hour of interview conducted" (2003, 85). Interviewers must be able to design the interview according to existing historical knowledge and loopholes in archive materials. Initial research also helps interviewers to be reactive and create follow-up questions during the interviews. After the initial research, historians can work on setting up the interviews.

Collaboration between interviewers and narrators should be driven by ethics. Baylor University's *Introduction to Oral History* encourages historians to contact narrators – possibly through mail – well in advance in order to explain how and why they have been chosen, what the project is about, and what the output may look like (2014). Oral history is one of the public history practices that contain the most risk for legal issues (Neuenschwander 2009). The fact that oral history is a co-production implies that decisions about the intellectual property, use, and diffusion of the interviews and additional materials collected during the project be discussed and agreed upon. Historians must make sure narrators know about the project and about the recording and its later uses. The *Goals and Guideline* of the OHA stress that "interviewers must insure that narrators understand the extent of their rights to the interview and the request that those rights be yielded to a repository or other party, as well as their right to put restrictions on the use of the material" (Oral History Association 2009). Narrators must give permission to record, reproduce, or distribute their words (Baylor University 2014, 5). An oral history legal release form should include mentions of the donor agreement, of the copyrights, and of the future uses of the materials. For any use, the narrator must transfer copyright ownership to the individual or organization sponsoring the project. The Library of Congress provides a sample of release forms that historians can use (Library of Congress 2009). Finally, colleges and universities that receive federal funds in the United States are required to consult Institutional Review Boards (IRB) – charged by the federal government with protecting the rights, interests, and dignity of human research subjects – to review research protocol (Shopes 2007). Although IRB often only ask for a list of legal issues to be cleared, some IRB have requested historians to submit lists of questions to get authorization (Ritchie 2003, 215–221). This, yet, does not apply to the interview and nothing forces historians to send their questions in advance to the narrators or to let the narrators dictate the orientations of the interview.

Legal issues go beyond the collaboration between interviewers and narrators though. For instance, things said during an interview may be considered as libelous or defamatory and the interviewer or the repository can be sued. Some portions – potentially libelous – of the interview may be restricted for a portion of time. It is also possible for narrators to restrict the access and uses of the sources in the terms and conditions of the copyrights. However, it is very difficult to "enforce restrictions that are linked to the duration of a lifetime, so ask the narrator to specify a particular future date to end the restriction" (Baylor University 2014, 5). Interviewers should avoid making promises over the control of interpretations other than the restrictions stated in the legal release. One recent example that gained notoriety is the Belfast Project undertaken by Boston College in which former members of the Irish Republican Army (IRA) were interviewed. Although promises were made by Boston College that the interviews would not be made public during the narrators' lifetime, partial release was imposed by legal action (Neuenschwander 2012).

When setting up a time and place for the interview, it is important to accommodate narrators' convenience. In Figure 3.1, the historian and Ruth Myers, who was 110 years old, conveniently chose to record the interview at the narrator's home. The length for the interview must be agreed before the interview takes place. It can vary according to the narrators, but interviews are traditionally between one and two hours long. The site conditions can greatly affect the interview. Some oral historians have suggested that the location of the interview subtly influences what a narrator talks about and how they talk about it. Interviews in one person's office, for example, tend to be more formal, less intimate, with the narrator emphasizing public rather than private life (Shopes 2002). During the interview it is important to have the minimum number of persons on site. The presence of other persons may cause discomfort and limit the narrator's willingness to talk about difficult issues. Interaction with relatives may also cause digression or silence. Group interviews are extremely difficult to organize, interpret, and transcribe.

Every interview is different and questions vary according to topics and narrators. However, historians should follow certain rules. For instance, interviews should begin with a general introduction that provides the name of the project, the date and site of the interview, and the name of every person present. Guides of best practices encourage interviewers not to bring ultimate, specific and frozen lists of questions, but to be prepared to be flexible instead. Sticking to specific questions may confine the interview and narrators' memories in too strict formats (Baylor University 2014, 10). Instead, interviewers may use a list of themes or key words they are especially eager to cover. Only one question may be asked at a time. Interviewers should start by asking easy contextual questions and not controversial issues. Potentially difficult topics should be deferred until later in the interview, after the interviewer has established some trust. It is important to ask open-ended questions that leave space for narrators to develop their memories of the events. Active listening is crucial since interviewers should be able to ask follow-up questions (Anderson and Jack 1991). In some cases, historians may decide to stimulate narrators' memory with some visual clues, such as maps or photographs. Nevertheless, interviewers should not intervene too much, and avoid any sound interference. Figure 3.1 demonstrates that the narrator is at the center of the oral history process. Symbolically hidden behind the camera on this image, the historian should limit his/her intervention during the recording. Silent acknowledgment – such as nodding your head – is always preferable to any comment.

Transcription and Preservation of Interviews

There have been many debates about transcription. A transcript represents in print the words and sounds present in the recorded interview, so that the transcriber's goal is to render as close a replica to the actual event as possible (Baylor University 2014, 16). By doing so, transcripts make it easier for users to locate information. However, transcripts are problematic. First of all, they are very time-consuming. The approximate time required to transcribe one recorded hour is 10–12 hours (Baylor University 2014, 16). Outsourcing the transcription is possible but can be very expensive. If transcribing is not an option, the project should at least include an abstract and an index of the recording. It helps document the context of an interview for future uses (Mazé 2012).

The use of transcripts is not without issues. Whether or not transcription may be reviewed by narrators themselves – and possibly corrected – is a major subject of discussion among oral historians (Filene 2011a). What is more, transcripts tend to become the source used by historians to access the narration. Too often, users merely read – or keyword search – transcripts without even listening to the interview. However, spoken and written languages are different. For instance, a transcript may distort what is actually on the sound recording – humor, sarcasm, and other rhetorical aspects may go unnoticed in transcripts. Sound and video are crucial to understand emotions, body language, and other sensitive features. If historians decide to transcribe interviews, training is necessary. Different guidelines can help historians (Baylor University 2015; Concordia University 2013). It is crucial to change as little as possible what the narrators said during the interview.

It is not unreasonable to suggest that the recording and preservation of oral history are undergoing a paradigm shift, as new technologies redefine all aspects of oral history from initial recording to final access and use (Shopes 2012). Digital tools are particularly useful regarding the preservation and sustainability of oral history. Digital technology has greatly enhanced transcription (Shopes 2012). Digital technology allows for the coordination of sound recordings and transcripts. Systems like Automatic Speech Recognition (ASR) technology may in the future replace the time-consuming process of manually transcribing oral history interviews. Nevertheless, ASR is still problematic today since some words are not registered in the list, and particular accents are not recognized (Oard 2012).

Digital technology also has an impact on the collection itself and the amount of materials preserved. Thanks to digital tools, interviews and other recordings can easily be stored, duplicated, edited, and modified. Oral history collections may include – in addition to the interview itself – many different documents. The collection may be composed of an index and transcripts, deed of gift or consent form, materials collected during the research or used for the interviews, such as photographs, maps, or correspondence. It is up to the historian to decide whether (s)he wants to deposit his/her interview notes as well.

It is crucial to have files in a format that can be preserved by the repository. Digital recording creates large digital files. While one hour of high-resolution audio can be 2 gigabytes, high-resolution digital video may go as far as 100 gigabytes per hour. Any compression of the files must be avoided for archival purposes. Indeed, lossy compression – such as MPEG files – aims at reducing the size of the file, and is often done by suppressing sections of the file.[8] While the loss is not perceptible, it still changes the original version. This is not desirable for archival purposes. Compression can only be utilized for presentation on different media such as the web. Sustainability also includes reflection on interoperability. One of the greatest dangers of digital technology is obsolescence.[9] Some files no longer available can prevent the use and preservation of oral history projects. It is important that historians contact repositories early during the project, and avoid proprietary formats and choose a ubiquitous format. Public historians should use open formats as much as possible.

Finally, digital technology fosters direct public access to oral history. Oral history is less and less restricted to archival materials. Exhibitions, e-books, digital apps, and other media now use oral history. The democratization of the access to oral history results in the move from written transcription to original sound and/or video formats. Accessibility in a digital age equates to potential global distribution. Public historians must be aware that as soon as they make oral history public on the web, they reach a potential global public. It has some ethical issues. Especially troublesome is web publication of interviews conducted pre-web without narrators' explicit permission; many feel this violates narrators' rights to decide the level of access to their interviews (Shopes 2002). Providing oral history online allows anybody to access, use, and reuse the sources. This creates new tensions, and renewed debates about oral history ethics and copyright in the digital age (Reeves 2012).

Family, Community, and Everyday Life: Sources for Public Historians

Family History and Genealogy

Oral history practice can deal with particular themes and topics to study people's history. Family stories are among the main popular issues. Very successful in countries such as the United States, England, Italy, or New Zealand, family history has long been dissociated from academic history. Associated with popular culture, family history deals with the lives of everyday people through letters, photographs, objects, and stories. Rosenzweig and Thelen demonstrated in their study of the popular uses of the past that it is the family, not the classroom, that is the principal site for exploration of the past (1998, 9). One popular use of the past is to find out "who exactly our ancestors were, where they came from, and what they got up to" (Colwell 2002, 1). Family memories are major prisms through which people look at and understand the past.

On the one hand, many academic historians – like Eric Hobsbawm – do not consider genealogy as a serious historical practice (Hobsbawm 1998, 270–271). On the other hand, genealogy is certainly the most widespread practice dealing with family history. Genealogy or family reconstitution studies have become very popular since the 1970s. In the United States, the popularity of 1976 Pulitzer Prize winner Alex Haley's book *Roots: The Saga of an American Family* – a novel in which the author traces his African American ancestry back to a tiny village in Gambia, West Africa – has been a turning point (Haley 1976). Today, millions of people read magazines, watch TV shows, are part of clubs, go to festivals, visit archives and historical societies for genealogical research. In the United States, many genealogical repositories – such as the for-profit *Ancestry* – exist online (Crume 2014).

The Church of the Latter Day Saints (Mormons) has one of the most important world collections of genealogical data. Their project is based on reclamation of salvation for their ancestors. According to the Mormons' belief, the dead can be redeemed and baptized into the Church so that families can be united eternally (de Groot 2008, 85). The Genealogical Society of Utah and its website Familysearch.org have collected land, immigration, naturalization, probate, vital, and other public records (Kyvig and Marty 2010, 100). Genealogy is a collaborative practice. With the rise of digital technology, many tools are now available online for democratized genealogical research. With the spread of the Internet, many listservs and forums are now available. In addition to the many websites and software devoted to genealogy, public historians interested in genealogy can contact local libraries and historical or genealogical societies that have copies of census and other certificates, could consult church records, marriage indexes, cemetery records/indexes, and city directories.[10]

Community History

A community is a group of people who share a common sense of identity based on place, religion, activity, or ethnic belonging. Public historians can be involved in many different community projects about, for instance, a Jewish community, same-sex community, or African-American community. Some projects derive from the threat of disappearance. For example, "residents of the rural, mountain community of Ivanoe, Virginia, initiated an oral history project to help save their rapidly disappearing history and revitalize their community" (Ritchie 2003, 223). Likewise, the Tibet Oral History Project aims to record and preserve the life experiences of Tibetan elders according to a wish from the Dalai Lama, who "has emphasized the urgency of conducting interviews of these elders before they pass away and their stories are lost forever" (Tibet Oral History Project undated).

Similar to some family history projects, community projects are great opportunities to involve the public in the production of history. In addition to the recording and preservation of memories, projects can contribute to empowering members of the community. Temple University developed the Discovering Community History Project to encourage residents of different neighborhoods in Philadelphia to document their past.

Everyday Life

One objective of public history is to present the past on a human, even intimate, scale. In order to do so, Jim Gardner suggests providing history "that is about real people, ordinary and extraordinary, dealing with real life and making choices" (Gardner 2004, 16). Along with a new bottom-up history making process, public history started to engage with everyday life (Gordon 2010). Oral history is often the main practice to work on under-documented aspects of everyday life. New topics and new sources have emerged. Everyday life opens up a brand new range of opportunities for public historians. Among them, we can quote food, shopping and consumption, housing, health, criminality, poverty and homelessness.

Food history is perhaps one of the main booming fields in public history (Counihan 2002). Food history fosters public participation and helps connect people with sites. In Figure 3.2, costumed interpreters prepare dishes in the Governor's Palace kitchen at Colonial Williamsburg (CW). The CW's foodways program adds another layer to visitors' experience of the site. About health history, the National Library of Medicine has

Figure 3.2 Colonial Williamsburg's foodways program set out a grand meal in the Governor's Palace kitchen. In front, beef, chicken, and fish dishes anchor a meal that includes vegetables, baked goods, and desserts, 2004. Courtesy of The Colonial Williamsburg Foundation.

developed online and traveling exhibitions about the social and cultural history of science, medicine, and technology. AIDS and ancient killers like tuberculosis have received recent attention from historians. In favor of more historical research about everyday life, historian and Pulitzer Prize winner Michael Wallace mentions the Brooklyn Historical Society that collected oral histories and everyday objects about the AIDS epidemic (Wallace 1996, 46).

Urban criminality is a current public policy issue but has also become the topic of public history projects. In 2006, the Royal Armouries (Leeds, United Kingdom) arranged an exhibition called *Impact*, featuring video interviews and photographs of people caught up in gun crime (Royal Armouries undated). The exhibition put gun crime in historical perspective and raised the issue of how culture glorifies guns – from James Bond to video games. Everyday poverty could also receive more attention, although, as Wallace explains, "One reason museums speak of poverty so sporadically is that the poor leave the least detritus, which in turn has implications for contemporary collecting policy" (Wallace 1996, 45). Through oral history it is yet possible to undertake a major public history project about homelessness (Almutawa 2014).

The history of everyday life has many assets. First of all, it helps to deal with stories more often experienced by the public. The publicness of everyday life history makes it more attractive for people. Megan Elias explains how she associates food and visitors; she "wanted them (visitors) to be able to describe the cooking smells that would have emanated from one particular apartment in the 1870s and to be able to direct visitors to the sites beyond the doors of the museum where once stood the kosher butchers and vegetable carts that supplied those kitchens" (2012, 15). Although not present during the preparation of the dishes in Figure 3.2, visitors to CW can participate in cooking programs organized by the Department of Historic Foodways. Everyday life history also makes the representations of the past less elitist and celebratory. Manon Parry suggests that "historians of medicine have been very supportive of this effort to move beyond triumphant storylines to tell more complex accounts of the history of patients and their practitioners" (2009).

People's History and Personal Experiences: Assets and Challenges for Public Historians

Historians dealing with people's history usually have rich and complex relations with members of local communities. This is especially true for oral historians, whose relations with narrators bring privileged access to memories but raise ethical issues as well. It is necessary to be aware of the assets and limits to the role of public historians.

People's History as Academic Research: The Case of Family Stories

People's history and academic scholarship are not mutually exclusive. Family history – and to some extent genealogy – offer examples of how academic historians can gain from popular sources. For example, historian Mary Stewart argues, "whakapapa, genealogy in traditional Maori oral history, is a vital resource for any historian exploring Maori history" (2012, 249). Throughout her research on her great-great-grandfather, Stewart argues: "I mined my family archive in order to build up a holistic picture of my ancestor and his views upon the world" (2012, 240). In recent years, there have been many examples of family history and personal experiences being used to challenge ways of thinking about broad issues such as migration, nationalism, education, and so on. Through personal archives, family history can make the understanding of the past more complex.

In an article about school education in England, public historian Hilda Kean demonstrates how "material in personal archives, family album and handed down images might well substitute for the absences in the official record" (Kean and Kirsch 2012, 199). Like micro-history, family history can provide an angle to investigate wider historical theories (Magnússon and Szijártó 2013). Stewart asserts that her primary aim was "to use a microhistory of (her) great, great grandfather to engage with debates within the historical academy about migration to New Zealand" (2012, 241). Family history can provide public historians with fantastic alternative sources and representations of the past.

From Public Participation to the Absence of Historian?

Some public historians suggest stepping away from traditional oral history methods to create innovative projects in which public participation is at the core of the oral history practice (Filene 2011a). Through public history projects, historians can invite members of the local community – possibly through public meetings – to express themselves and to take part in the project. Although public participation is one of the public historian's objectives, it may also raise some issues.[11]

First, participation can encounter obstacles. Community members may be reluctant to share memories and materials with outsider public historians. Individuals may refuse to be interviewed by oral historians, especially regarding controversial issues. In addition to the trust that historians can try to develop through multiple meetings, they may use enthusiastic members of the community as intermediaries to collect materials. Trained by oral historians, intermediaries help develop participatory public process.

Another radical step is reached when protagonists directly record stories, with no help/ intervention from oral historians. With the development of digital technology it is easier to produce and record personal testimonies. For instance, the Italian-based Memoro Project has now a global network of participants. Memoro is a bank of memories that records and preserves life stories – through oral stories – from ordinary people all over the world. Stories come from people who record themselves and download the final product on the platform. The Memoro Project's editors review and process all audio and video, but the contents merely come from users. Unlike traditional oral history, the interviewer and the narrator are the same individual. In line with this example, public participation and the role of historians have been at the center of recent debates on the production of oral history.

In the United States, StoryCorps has similarly focused on ordinary people. Since 2003, it has archived more than 50,000 interviews at the American Folklife Center at the Library of Congress. In addition to organized story-booths and door-to-door appointments, participants can use the do-it-yourself process to record themselves.[12] As oral historian Pozzi-Thanner stresses in her review of StoryCorps, all the participant needs is an appointment with StoryCorps, a family member, a friend or acquaintance to serve as the interviewer or interviewee (2005). In his article on the use of StoryCorps, public historian Benjamin Filene details the critical views of some oral historians on StoryCorps (Filene 2011a). He compares the often well-prepared and structured oral history interviews with unfocused self-recorded StoryCorps stories (184). In spite of certain themes – like the testimonies about the 9/11 attacks – the great majority of StoryCorps interviews are not structured according to a theme, event, or group of individuals. The main challenge for StoryCorps – but for oral and people's history at large – is to make individual experiences interesting for people not directly connected to the story. What is more, the narrator has, in StoryCorps, a tremendous amount of control over his/her own image, and can control how (s)he is represented.

This relates to the challenging issues of self-representation and celebration of the past in community and people's history. Historians can help contextualize personal stories into larger narratives.

Historical Practice and Personal Experiences: The Question of Subjectivity

Stories and the Celebration of the Past

Public historians must be careful with the self-representations provided by narrators and community partners about their past. Some people can be very proud and celebratory about their past, and only present the best possible image of themselves. Members of the community may be very reluctant to raise difficult issues about the past. When not at the origins of a project, public historians should discuss and clarify its rationale and objectives. Public historians are also particularly relevant to broaden the traditional notions of what constitutes a community's history. Historians should participate in discussion about the definitions, the boundaries, and changing criteria of a community. More sensible issues such as migration, assimilation of outsiders, and physical, social, and economic mobility can then be investigated for the history of the group. Tensions and conflicts within the community or with outsiders can reveal complex processes, internal values, and authority about the group. In order to avoid celebrating family/community members or merely proposing prosopography (the historical study of the characteristics of a group), historians can question themes such as group relationships, migrations and movements, economics, education, the changing status of family/community members, the respective roles of men and women, or the changing of values and beliefs.

Go Beyond Personal Experience

One of the main reasons for the popular interest in people's history has been the audience's proximity with the historical topic under discussion. This proximity is both an asset – that can create public engagement – and an obstacle in undertaking such public history projects. People's history projects have resulted in attempts to foster very personal interpretations of the past. The challenge for historians is to go beyond simple personal experiences and participate in the construction of stories that have both personal and broader public appeal.

If they do not engage outside the group of study, family history, genealogy, and other oral history projects may have limited relevance for readers. Genealogy is a good example as it may sometimes be limited to the collection of basic facts – date of birth, date of death – about ancestors. Genealogy is, at heart, an introspective research that deals with personal roots. The role of public historians is to set personal roots into larger understandings of the past that are not limited to facts. In addition to bringing information about personal roots, history should be seen as piecing together those facts to help people understand the past. This is where the distinction between pure preservation of memories and historical understanding of the past matters the most.

For example, the BBC broadcast *Who Do You Think You Are?* used genealogy to trace the family history of popular guests through important events. In one of the episodes, the life and genealogy of Jerry Springer – a famous TV host in the United States – was used to discuss 20th century immigration, anti-Semitism, and the Holocaust. Through the show, Springer traced back his family, his grandmother "murdered in the Holocaust," his great-grandfather who "struggled against an anti-Semitic campaign of hate" in 19th century

Poland (*Who Do You Think You Are*). Genealogy can be part of larger public history projects based on biographies, family historic sites, or neighborhoods.

Public historians also serve to contextualize personal relationships in the past. Regarding everyday life and food history, people involved in historic recipe workshops often think that the past is recreated, but no matter how accurate the recipe is there would always be a need for historical contextualization. Elias stresses that the recreation of 19th century Louisiana recipes during cooking workshops should include historical background about who performed the domestic work, the contrast between householders' meals and slave diets (2012, 15). Everyday life topics should not be seen as isolated from other issues, they should be considered in relation with other broad historical topics.

Subjectivity from Narrators and Historians

One final major issue related to the participatory construction of oral history is about the kind of sources produced. Debates exist about the relations between oral historians and their sources. Is the role of historian limited to the creation and deposit of an oral source in a repository? If one considers that the role of historians is simply to create oral history archives, then there is no need for additional work on interviews. However, public historians may feel responsible for the public use and interpretation of oral sources. Historians must verify their findings and place them in an accurate historical context.

Oral historians should be aware of the subjective aspects of their sources. Critics of oral history argue that personal memory – on what oral interviews are based – is failing, so that the information collected is not reliable (Thomson 1998). Narrators may impose their own vision and interpretation of the events they narrate. In other words, sources produced by oral history would not be historical but hearsay. However, the usefulness of sources depends upon the information the historian is looking for, or the questions (s)he seeks to answer (Grele 1998, 41). Even though traditional written primary sources have the advantage of not being influenced by later events or otherwise changing over time, as a narrator might, written documents are also sometimes incomplete, inaccurate, and deceiving (Ritchie 2003, 26). In oral history, what is collected is not the event but its memory through individual experience. In other words, it is important to acknowledge the part played by subjectivity in oral history, and the fact that this does not preclude serious analytical work. Critical analysis helps oral historians better understand what the final product is.

Subjectivity, in itself, does not prevent historical interpretation. Baylor University's *Introductory Guide to Oral History* acknowledges the "subjectivity, which allows interviewers to ask not only, What happened? but also, How did you feel about what happened?" (2014, 1). Historians must try to take into consideration the subjective part of oral sources. What narrators say – as any other source – should not be taken for granted. Just because someone "was there" does not mean they fully understand "what happened" (Frisch 1990, 159–160). Sources must be checked, documentation should be provided, and evidence must be weighed carefully (Grele 1998, 41). Was the narrator an eyewitness of the event (s)he narrates? Is (s)he consistent in her/his depiction of the past? Historical interpretation is based on crossed analysis of sources. Can the narration be corroborated by other sources? A single interview is merely one statement, while an interview in the context of other historical facts can provide a rich understanding of the past.

Subjectivity can lead to particular representations of the past that oral historians should underline. Narrators often recall with great pride their deeds, and tend to downplay external processes. Oral history tends to overemphasize individual acts over broader processes or agencies. Besides, subjective narration can be false. In 1991, Portelli analyzed how oral accounts of the death of an Italian steel worker during a protest in 1949 got the date, place, and reasons for the death wrong (1991). Those errors were facts for Portelli who attempted to understand why narrators were wrong. Subjectivity – through denial, trauma, forgetfulness, and uneasiness – is entirely part of the oral historians' research topic.

Oral history is as much about the narrators as about the events narrated. What is said draws upon the narrator's linguistic conventions and cultural assumptions and hence is an expression of identity, consciousness, and culture. Oral historians must investigate who is saying what, to whom, for what purpose, and under what circumstances. Subjectivity matters and accounts of the same events may vary depending on the narrators. Linda Shopes provides very interesting examples of how the identity of narrators may have an impact on the narration of the past (Shopes 2002). She shows how gender and generational differences affect stories.

Like public history, oral history includes a major self-reflective dimension. Oral historians must reflect on what they collect, how they have collected it, and why. Oral historians should also question the representativeness of the narrators they interview. Since historians select narrators, they could be criticized for choosing one version of the past. The question is not only about knowing whether there is enough testimony to validate evidence, but also to understand to what extent the narrators represent a specific experience of the past. Historians should question how the personal experience they collect relates to broader processes. On the other hand, oral historians should be aware of the possible groups – and experiences – omitted when they select narrators.

Regarding the choice of narrators, the role played by historians – and their impact on the production – must also be questioned (Yow 1997). In *Envelopes of Sound*, oral historians Terkel and Grele argued for an awareness of both the effects of the process on the interviewer and the effects of the interviewer on the process (1975). Public historians must learn how to deal with their own emotions as much as emotions felt by the public. Disgust with perpetrators or empathy with victims may in one way or another affect interviewers (Yow 1997, 76–78). On the other hand, Shopes demonstrates how different interviewers may have different impacts on the narration (2002). Acknowledging that the interviewer is more than a neutral figure explains why information about the interviewer must be provided with the project for future uses and interpretation. An oral historian's agenda should be provided whenever the reader needs this information to evaluate the research.

To conclude, historians' focus on ordinary people and everyday life has attracted a wide public interest. The proximity between the historical issues and present-day audiences has fostered various outstanding public history projects. This proximity and the public participation have also resulted in new challenges for public historians whose training must include practice and reflection on their role in the overall production process. Although recent examples of collection of memories are undertaken without the help of historians, public historians must be able to distinguish between the mere recording of stories and the more complex process of understanding the past in which they are still needed.

Notes

1 See the oral history toolbox: http://dohistory.org/on_your_own/toolkit/oralHistory.html (accessed June 22, 2014) and the National Council on Public History's bibliography http://ncph.org/cms/wp-content/uploads/RRPHC-Oral-History.pdf (accessed July 28, 2015).

2 For instance, the *Ask Doug* page allows users to put in their parameters (price, audio or video, etc.) to receive different suggestions and reviews. See http://ohda.matrix.msu.edu/askdoug/ (accessed July 28, 2015).

3 Since 1968, the Oral History Association has published guidelines and statements about principles and duties for people using this methodology, www.oralhistory.org/about/principles-and-practices/ (accessed September 2014).

4 We can also quote the Veterans History Project of the Library of Congress American Folklife Center. It is an oral history program that collects and preserves the first-hand interviews of America's wartime veterans, www.loc.gov/vets/vets-questions.html#background (accessed July 26, 2015).

5 See below on the new sources for people's history.

6 Issues with self-recording – and the absence of historians – are dealt with below in the StoryCorps example.

7 To choose your digital recorder see also the Baylor Guide's *Choosing Digital Recorder*, 2014, www.baylor.edu/content/services/document.php/66424.pdf (accessed July 12, 2015)

8 Some lossless compression codecs – Apple Lossless Audio Codec (ALE/ALAC) or FLAC (Free Lossless Audio Codec) – exist but are rarely included in recorders' options.

9 See the part on digitization in Chapter 1.

10 The U.S. Superintendent of Documents published a booklet, *Where to Write for Vital Records*, which can help in locating birth, death, marriage, and divorce records in individual states. Besides, guidance on locating information about individuals is available from the Census Bureau (www.census.gov).

11 More details about shared authority and its limits are discussed in Chapter 13.

12 While StoryCorps is unable to archive DIY recordings, the Do-It-Yourself Instruction Guide will show you how to start your own archive, http://storycorps.org/about/faqs/ (accessed July 27, 2015).

Bibliography

Almutawa, Shatha. "Oral Histories of Homelessness." *AHA Today*, April 29, 2014, http://blog.historians.org/2014/04/oral-histories-homelessness/ (accessed July 27, 2015).

Anderson, Katryn and Jack, Dana, eds. *Learning to Listen: Interview Techniques and Analyses*, New York: Routledge, 1991.

Baylor University, Institute for Oral History. *Introduction to Oral History*, 2014, www.baylor.edu/content/services/document.php/43912.pdf (accessed September 2014).

Baylor University, Institute for Oral History. *Style Guide: A Quick Reference for Editing Oral History Transcripts*, 2015, www.baylor.edu/oralhistory/doc.php/14142.pdf (accessed July 27, 2015).

Boyd, Doug. "Audio or Video for Recording Oral History: Questions, Decisions." In *Oral History in the Digital Age*, edited by Doug Boyd, S. Cohen, B. Rakerd, and D. Rehberger, Institute of Library and Museum Services, 2012a, http://ohda.matrix.msu.edu/2012/06/audio-or-video-for-recording-oral-history/ (accessed July 25, 2015).

Boyd, Doug. "Digital Audio Recording: The Basics." In *Oral History in the Digital Age*, edited by Doug Boyd, S. Cohen, B. Rakerd, and D. Rehberger, Institute of Library and Museum Services, 2012b, http://ohda.matrix.msu.edu/2012/06/digital-audio-recording/ (accessed July 28, 2015).

Colwell, Stella. *The Family Records Centre: A User's Guide*, Kew: Public Record Office, 2002.

Concordia University. COHDS, *Interview Transcription*, 2013, http://storytelling.concordia.ca/content/webinar-2-interview-transcription (accessed July 25, 2015).

Counihan, Carol, ed. *Food and Culture in the United States: A Reader*, New York and London: Routledge, 2002.

Crume, Rick. "75 Best Genealogy Websites for US States in 2014." *Family Tree Magazine* (December 2014), http://familytreemagazine.com/article/2014-best-state-genealogy-websites (accessed July 27, 2015).

De Groot, Jerome. *Consuming History: Historians and Heritage in Contemporary Popular Culture*, London: Routledge, 2008.

Diaz, Rose T. and Russell, Andrew B. "Oral Historians: Community Oral History and the Corporate Ideal." In *Public History: Essays From the Field*, edited by James B. Gardner and Peter LaPaglia, Malabar: Krieger Press, 1999, 203–217.

Elias, Megan. "Summoning the Food Ghosts: Food." *The Public Historian*, 34/2 (Spring 2012): 13–29.

Filene, Benjamin. "Listening Intently: Can StoryCorps Teach Museums How to Win the Hearts of New Audiences?" In *Letting Go? Sharing Historical Authority in a User-Generated World*, edited by Bill Adair, Benjamin Filene, and Laura Koloski, Philadelphia: The Pew Center for Arts & Heritage, 2011a, 174–193.

Filene, Benjamin. "Make Yourself at Home—Welcoming Voices in Open House: If these Walls Could Talk." In *Letting Go? Sharing Historical Authority in a User Generated World*, edited by Bill Adair, Benjamin Filene, and Laura Koloski, Philadelphia: The Pew Center for Arts & Heritage, 2011b, 138–155.

Frisch, Michael. *A Shared Authority: Essays on the Craft and Meaning of Oral and Public History*, Albany: State University of New York Press, 1990.

Gardner, James B. "Contested Terrain: History, Museums, and the Public." *The Public Historian*, 26/4 (2004): 11–21.

Gordon, Tammy. *Private History in Public: Exhibition and the Settings of Everyday Life*, Lanham: AltaMira Press, 2010.

Grele, Ronald J. "Movement Without Aim: Methodological and Theoretical Problems in Oral History." In *The Oral History Reader*, edited by Robert Perks and Alistair Thomson, London and New York: Routledge, 1998, 38–52.

Haley, Alex. *Roots: The Saga of an American Family*, Garden City: DoubleDay and Co., 1976.

Hobsbawm, Eric. *On History*, London: Abacus, 1998.

Kean, Hilda and Kirsch, Brenda. "A Nation's Moment and a Teacher's Mark Book: Interconnecting Personal and Public Histories." In *Public History and Heritage Today: People and Their Past*, edited by Paul Ashton and Hilda Kean, London: Palgrave Macmillan, 2012, 187–203.

Kyvig, David E. and Marty, Myron A. *Nearby History: Exploring the Past Around You*, Lanham: AltaMira Press, 2010.

Library of Congress, *Release Form*, Washington, DC, 2009, www.loc.gov/folklife/fieldwork/releaseform. html (accessed September 2014).

Magnússon, Sigurður Gylfi and Szijártó, István M. *What is Microhistory? Theory and Practice*, London and New York: Routledge, 2013.

Mazé, Elinor A. "Metadata: Best Practices for Oral History Access and Preservation." In *Oral History in the Digital Age*, edited by Doug Boyd, Steve Cohen, Brad Rakerd, and Dean Rehberger, Washington, DC: Institute of Museum and Library Services, 2012, http://ohda.matrix.msu. edu/2012/06/metadata/ (accessed July 27, 2015)

Memoro. "The Project." Undated, *Memoro Website*, hwww.memoro.org/us-en/progetto.php (accessed July 28, 2015).

Neuenschwander, John A. *A Guide to Oral History and the Law*, Oxford: Oxford University Press, 2009.

Neuenschwander, John A. "Major Legal Challenges Facing Oral History in the Digital Age." In *Oral History in the Digital Age*, edited by Doug Boyd, Steve Cohen, Brad Rakerd, and Dean Rehberger, Washington, DC: Institute of Museum and Library Services, 2012, http://ohda.matrix.msu. edu/2012/06/major-legal-challenges/ (accessed October 2014).

Oard, Doug. "Can Automatic Speech Recognition Replace Manual Transcription?" In *Oral History in the Digital Age*, edited by Doug Boyd, Steve Cohen, Brad Rakerd, and Dean Rehberger, Washington, DC: Institute of Museum and Library Services, 2012, http://ohda.matrix.msu.edu/2012/06/ automatic-speech-recognition/ (accessed July 28, 2015)

Oral History Association. *Principles and Best Practices: Principles for Oral History and Best Practices for Oral History*, OHA website, 2009, www.oralhistory.org/about/principles-and-practices/ (accessed July 28, 2015).

Parry, Manon. "Divergent Audiences: History and Health for Practitioners and Publics." *NCPH Working Group*, 2009, http://ncph.org/cms/wp-content/uploads/2009/11/Workign-Group-Structur ing-the-Discourse-Case-Statements.pdf (accessed June 2014).

Pennington, Scott. "Video Equipment: Guide to Selecting and Use." In *Oral History in the Digital Age*, edited by Doug Boyd, Steve Cohen, Brad Rakerd, and Dean Rehberger, Washington, DC: Institute of Museum and Library Services, 2012, http://ohda.matrix.msu.edu/2012/06/video-equipment/ (accessed June 15, 2014).

Perks, Robert and Thomson, Alistair, eds. *The Oral History Reader*, London: Routledge, 2006.

Portelli, Alessandro. *The Death of Luigi Trastulli and Other Stories: Form and Meaning in Oral History*, Albany: State University of New York Press, 1991.

Portelli, Alessandro. *The Battle of Valle Giulia: Oral History and the Art of Dialogue*, Madison: The University of Wisconsin Press, 1997.

Pozzi-Thanner, Laura. "StoryCorps: A Review." *The Oral History Review*, 32/2 (2005), http://oralhistory-productions.org/articles/StoryCorps.pdf (accessed July 27, 2015).

Reeves, Troy. "What Do You Think You Own, or Legal/Ethical Concerns." In *Oral History in the Digital Age*, edited by Doug Boyd, Steve Cohen, Brad Rakerd, and Dean Rehberger, Washington, DC: Institute of Museum and Library Services, 2012, http://ohda.matrix.msu.edu/2012/06/what-do-you-think-you-own/ (accessed July 28, 2015).

Ritchie, Donald A. *Doing Oral History: A Practical Guide*, Oxford: Oxford University Press, 2003.

Ritchie, Donald A., ed. *Oxford Handbook of Oral History*, Oxford: Oxford University Press, 2011.

Rosenzweig, Roy and Thelen, David. *The Presence of the Past: Popular Uses of History in American Life*, New York: Columbia University Press, 1998.

Royal Armouries. "Impact." *Royal Armouries website*, undated, www.royalarmouries.org/visit-us/leeds/leeds-galleries/self-defence/leeds-gallery-impact (accessed June 2014).

Schwarz, Bill. "History on the Move: Reflections on History Workshop." *Radical History Review*, 57 (1993): 203–220.

Shopes, Linda. "Making Sense of Oral History." *History Matters: The U.S. Survey Course on the Web*, 2002, http://historymatters.gmu.edu/mse/oral/ (accessed September 2014).

Shopes, Linda. "Negotiating Institutional Review Boards." *AHA Perspectives Online*, 45/3 (March 2007), www.historians.org/perspectives/issues/2007/0703/0703vie1.cfm (accessed July 28, 2015).

Shopes, Linda. "Transcribing Oral History in the Digital Age." In *Oral History in the Digital Age*, edited by Doug Boyd, Steve Cohen, Brad Rakerd, and Dean Rehberger, Washington, DC: Institute of Museum and Library Services, 2012, http://ohda.matrix.msu.edu/2012/06/transcribing-oral-history-in-the-digital-age/ (accessed May 2014).

Stewart, Mary. "Expanding the Archive: The Role of Family History in Exploring Connections Within a Settler's World." In *Public History and Heritage Today: People and Their Past*, edited by Paul Ashton and Hilda Kean, London: Palgrave Macmillan, 2012, 240–260.

Terkel, Studs and Grele, Ronald J., eds. *Envelopes of Sound: Six Practitioners Discuss the Method, Theory, and Practice of Oral History*, Chicago: Precedent Pub, 1975.

Thompson, Edward Palmer. "History from Below." *Times Literary Supplement*, (April 7, 1966): 279–280.

Thomson, Alistair. "'Unreliable Memories?' The Use and Abuse of Oral History." In *Historical Controversies and Historians*, edited by William Lamont, New York: Routledge, 1998, 23–35.

Tibet Oral History Project. "About Us." *TOHP website*, undated, www.tibetoralhistory.org/aboutus.html (accessed July 28, 2015).

Wallace, Mike. *Mickey Mouse History and Other Essays on American Memory*, Philadelphia: Temple University Press, 1996.

Who Do You Think You Are? "Jerry Springer." BBC website, undated, www.bbc.co.uk/whodoyouthink youare/past-stories/jerry-springer.shtml (accessed September 2014).

Yow, Valerie. "'Do I Like Them Too Much?' Effects of the Oral History Interview on the Interviewer and Vice-Versa." *Oral History Review*, 24/1 (1997): 55–79.

Zinn, Howard. *A People's History of the United States: 1492–Present*, New York: Harper & Row, 1980.

Part II

Making Public History
Media and Practice

Making public history is based on traditional historical practice. Historians perform critical analysis of primary sources to produce historical interpretation. However, due to more specific activities – working for and with broad non-academic audiences – public historians have to be familiar with certain practices. Unlike more traditional historians whose production mostly takes the shape of academic articles, monographs, and books, public historians may work with many different media such as television, radio, museums, or video games. This introduction presents three issues that cross the different fields of public history: interpretation, fiction, and sustainability (through protection and fundraising).

Interpretation in Public History

Interpretation is the act or process of explaining or clarifying, translating, or presenting a personal understanding about a subject or object (Dean 1996, 6). Interpretation has become a buzzword in history but also in heritage and communication studies. Cultural institutions can hire interpretive planners or companies like the American History Workshop (AHW) that insure "that interpretive exhibits and presentations reflect new currents of historical research" (AHW undated a). Interpretation is a major step and a key practice in any historical production. Freeman Tilden wrote one of the most well known works on interpretation in 1957. Re-edited multiple times, *Interpreting our Heritage* has become a classic for everyone interested in historical interpretation (Tilden 2008). He defined interpretation as "an educational activity, which aims to reveal meanings and relationships through the use of original objects, by first-hand experience, and by illustrative media, rather than simply to communicate factual information" (2008, 8). The historian can act as the *revealer* who "uncovers something universal in the world that has always been there and that men have not known" (2008, 5). Historians make sense of the past through interpretation.

Even more than historians for whom academic peers are the main audience, public historians must consider the variety of their audiences while interpreting the past. If historians fail to link their interpretation with visitors, Tilden assures that the process will remain "sterile" (Tilden 2008, 9). This is why a basic knowledge of projects' audiences – who they are and what they want – is crucial. Among its *Planning Tools*, the AHW proposes "Community Story Workshops" based on the principle that "Gathering groups representative of local and tourist audiences is a way of learning how key potential themes are currently understood, how diverse communities seek to learn, and what local cultural and organizational resources are available for partnerships" (AHW undated b). Making public history is first of all creating a space for interaction between audiences and the past. Visitors of museums, historic houses, websites, and other public history projects are never empty frames to be filled by instructors. Visitors bring their own knowledge, and historians should take it into consideration. Historians should not consider interpretation as instruction but as provocation to engage audiences with the past (Tilden 2008, 9). Interpretation is about presenting the history that audiences can use to make sense of the(ir) past.

In order to provide a good story about the past, interpreters may try to make the past alive. They can do it through re-enacting the past. For Tilden, the ideal interpretation implies the recreation of the past (2008, 70). The best interpretations also include a sense of physical action for the public. It is extremely different to look at a 16th century musket behind a museum window, and to participate in a re-enactment in which users may hold, load, and ultimately fire the weapon. Even if objects cannot be used, it is important historians recreate the historical context to make the past alive. Historical interpretation must always be designed as a dialogue with the public. In order to strengthen interpretive design, historians can contact and use examples from professional companies such as the AHW or History Associates, associations such as the National Association for Interpretation, or consult the *Journal of Interpretation Research*, or use toolkits such as the one provided by the Interpretive Planning for Historic Trails and Gateways. Readers can also use the National Park Service (NPS) that has played a major role in developing the concept of interpretation in the United States, and still provides useful guidelines.[1] Readers can use the module provided by the NPS as introduction to interpretation (NPS 2008).

History and Fiction

If interpreting the past is a key practice for every historian, several chapters in this part deal with a more controversial issue: the concept of historical fiction.[2] A historical fiction may include real but also fictional characters and events. Types of fiction include historical novels, movies, theater plays, and also documentaries. Historical fictions provide convincing, but not necessarily true, representations of the past (Lee undated). In doing so, historical fiction seems to go against the credo of historical objectivity on which professional history was born in the late 19th century.

Although objectivity and historical truth have been subject to academic debates, the search for accurate narratives based on primary sources is still one major criterion to define history. This is why scholars are usually very critical of historical movies. For instance, in *Past Imperfect*, scholars, mostly but not exclusively historians, critically review 60 movies and discuss their historical accuracy. According to most historians, the best history on screen is based on "accuracy of detail, the use of original documents, appropriateness of music, the looks or apparent suitability of an actor to play someone whose body language, voice, and gestures we can never know from the historical record" (Rosenstone 2003, 61). In comparison with academic historical production, movies, novels, and other works based on fiction are therefore always undermined by inaccuracy. Fiction is, by definition, a distortion of the past. Despite the fact that historical fiction is often written by trained historians, the field remains synonymous with non-reliability in the academic sphere. One could yet wonder whether – and if so how – public historians could write "good" historical fiction. The question greatly matters since historical fiction – movies in particular – is a very popular use of and way to understand the past.

One cannot doubt that history on television, in theaters, or in novels will never reach the academic standards of historical accuracy. As argued by Robert Rosenstone – historian specialist in historical films – we should not expect "films or documentaries to do what (we imagine) books do." He continues:

> Stop expecting them to get the facts right, or to present several sides of an issue, or to give a fair hearing to all the evidence on a topic, or to all the characters or groups represented in a particular situation, or to provide a broad and detailed historical context for events.
>
> (2006, 37)

Historical fiction does not intend to be translated versions of academic books. The production of historical fiction follows different standards and has very specific assets. The task for academic historians is to reach some sort of truth, while the goal of historical movies is to "create a filmic reality that allows the audience to believe a story as if it were true" (Gilden Seavey 2006, 118).

The specific purposes of historical fiction do not mean they are irrelevant for our understanding of the past. Jerome de Groot explains in his book on historical fiction that historical novels are fictional but attempt to present an authentic past (2010, 2). Good historical fictions include archives – objects, pictures, and other sources – as much as possible. Importantly, fiction does not only present what happened, but also things that may have happened and for which we have no trace. The concept of plausibility is here crucial. Natalie Zemon Davis, who worked as a historical adviser on movies, advises, "Let the imagination be guided by evidence, interpreted as best one can, when it is available and, when it is not available, by the spirit or general direction of the evidence" (2003, 48). Historians producing fiction should wonder not only if the things happened, but also whether they could have happened. In his article about historical drama and his experience as screenwriter for Hollywood, Daniel Blake Smith explains that while writing a script he first asks, "Did it happen?" If things can be documented as fact, then he would validate them for inclusion in the script. If the things did not happen, he asks himself "*could* it have happened?" Smith argues that even if a particular moment was not verifiable from the historical record, it could be argued that the scene is "genuinely representative of incidents that often did happen in similar contexts" (2003, 33).

Plausibility must rely on historical accuracy, though. It would be misleading to think that historical fiction delivers authors from doing historical research. However, historical research is not enough to produce a historical fiction. In an article about the reasons why historians should write fiction, Ian Mortimer explains:

> historical fiction requires you to know about many aspects of life you have not thought about before. How do people speak to their children, wash their hair, lock a door, clean their teeth and get undressed for bed? Why was it difficult at low tide to row under London Bridge, did taverns provide meat in Advent in 1567, did physicians wear beards, and so on.
>
> (Mortimer 2011)

If done well, fiction can add much to popular understanding of the past. This explains why historical fiction may be so important for public history.

Research for historical fiction may focus on under-documented ordinary people, events, or sites. Fiction helps depict everyday situations, feelings, and atmosphere that recreate the historical context. Historical fiction adds "flesh to the bare bones that historians are able to uncover and by doing so provides an account that whilst not necessarily true provides a clearer indication of past events, circumstances and cultures" (Sambuchino 2013). Fiction adds color, sound, drama to the past, as much as it invents parts of the past. And Rosenstone argues that invention is not the weakness of films, it is their strength (2006, 38). Fiction can help users grasp parts of the past that have never – for lack of archives – been represented. In fact, Gilden Seavey explains that if producers of historical fiction had rigorously held the strict academic standards, many historical subjects would remain unexplored for lack of appropriate evidence (2006, 124). Historical fiction should, therefore, not be seen as the opposite of professional history, but rather as a challenging representation of the past from which both public historians and popular audiences may learn.

Historical fiction also raises problematic issues. First of all, some historical fictions enter the mind of historical characters through first-person accounts. Academic historians never need to guard against the inconsistency of their characters' traits. Nor do academic historians need to invent ways in which one character influences another. For Mortimer, "Creating fictitious characters who interact with one another goes beyond just imagining the past: it requires you to imagine it and then to change it, gradually and believably, in the reader's imagination" (2011). What historians need here is creativity, and this goes against every principle they have received during their training. Worse, in view of academic standards, writers of historical fiction tell lies. Mortimer admits, "all historical novelists do." Characters of historical fiction say and do things "that they never really said or did" (Mortimer 2011). Invention and fiction overlap. There is unfortunately no general rule as to where the frontier between facts and fiction is, and historians must decide case by case.

Compromises will always have to be found to provide a fictional story. For instance, contemporary language has to be used for the spectator/reader to understand the fiction. The main challenge is not that real and fictional characters cohabit, but that readers and spectators do not always know how to differentiate between fact and fiction. For Zemon Davis, "If major anachronisms are introduced, they should be evident and funny or creative, opening horizons for audiences" (2003, 48). It is important that writers of fiction provide a historical framework through an introduction, an explanatory section, author's notes, footnotes, bibliography, or appendix. For instance, Gregory transcribed historical sources in the annexes of her historical novels. Ideally, the historical framework should stress what is fictional and what comes from proven facts. If done well, historical fiction has the potential to convey history to millions of people.

Copyrights, Protection, and Fundraising

Copyrights

Since audiences are at the center of the field, public history involves some communication issues. Protection is a critical part of every public history project. Through the use of objects and other materials, public historians must be familiar with copyrights. Copyrights have a long – and complex – history that matches legislation. Making history in public, historians may be confronted with different situations and should follow a list of steps. Historians must first determine if permission is requested to use the selected documents and if they are covered by copyright. This step is very complex due to the many exceptions and the fact that copyright laws vary according to different countries.

Historians can use numerous tools. For instance, the University of North Carolina provides a list of situations in which texts pass to the public domain – copyright free. Some websites specialize in copyright-free documents.[3] Likewise, Cornell University lists copyrights for various types of work (Cornell University 2015). According to the status of the object/document, whether it was published or not, and the date of production, historians might be able to use it.

If the document does not belong to the public domain, historians should identify the owner and the rights needed. In case of doubt, historians are encouraged to ask permission. The best option is to directly contact the person or institution where the object is located. Once located, historians can contact the copyright holders to explain their project and purpose for the document, and eventually get a written permission agreement. It is essential not to rely on an oral agreement. It should be also noticed that sound and moving images copyrights are particularly problematic. Rights to use films are extremely expensive. What is more, a photograph or work of art may have entered the public domain, but the available format may not suit the historian's use – especially for an exhibition. There is absolutely no obligation for the owner to provide access to the original or to provide a copy. Historians may have to request – and often pay for – a copy from the owner. Another option is to invoke the fair-use option (United States Copyrights Office 2015). There is no strict definition of fair use but several principles must be filled.[4] The fair-use option allows the use of a document for a limited period of time if it does not interfere with the owner's right (Association of Research Libraries 2012). In other words, commercial uses are excluded. However, fair-use works well for educational projects and projects in which only parts of the document are used.

Even though it is important to make sure historians do not infringe any copyright laws, it is equally important that they know how to protect their work if necessary. On the one hand, public historians should aim to involve the public as much as possible, so they should limit any protection. On the other hand, it is fair to acknowledge some credit for the historian's production. Today, copyright automatically applies to any object that people create (Howard 2011). But copyright does not necessarily mean protection and historians should contact copyright specialists, in particular within university libraries. For public historians, the Creative Commons offers an interesting compromise. Through the website, historians can easily create licence according to their need – allowing or not commercial use for instance. The Creative Commons logo can then be added to the website and other historical production to explain to users what they can and cannot do with the materials (Jackson 2014).

Fundraising and Grant-Application in Public History

The links between history and generating financial resources may, at first, not be obvious. However, public historians very often meet fundraising issues. As administrators, public historians have to secure projects and budgets. In small cultural institutions, fundraising may require public historians to attend meetings with city officials, foundation officers, and other financial sources. Many resources are available for fundraising but this section focuses on those that deal more directly with history and public history. In particular, public historians should know about grant application, which is part of the broader field of fundraising, especially if public funding keeps decreasing.

Sonia Lovine's recent online guideline about grant writing for public historians is extremely useful (Lovine 2013). She presents not only the various resources that public historians can use in grant writing, but also explains the fundamental steps in designing an application. Her guideline is based on two major interrogations: Where can public historians find grants for their projects and institutions? And how can they write successful applications?

One general source on foundations, and a site that public historians should be familiar with, is the Foundation Center. Many websites provide information about grants for (public) historians. They often also contain examples of successful applications.[5] While designing grant applications, public historians should be aware of important steps.

A grant application is a conversation between the founder and the applicant. Like a cover letter, a grant application must be written in close connection with the information provided by the founding institution, often through a document that stresses the deadline, and requirements. The call may be issued through a Request For Application (RFA) or a Request For Proposal (RFP). While you apply to a specific call in the former, you propose your project in the latter.

Lovine stresses several points historians must be careful with while writing grant applications. Historians should identify the problem/goal for which funds are sought. They should make sure the project involves – and is as much as possible about – communities. Grants should use the language and terminology from the call issued by the funding institution. In doing so, historians must make sure they meet the priorities of the founding institution. Finally, Lovine underlines that the project must be feasible, with a strict schedule for completion (2013). Most grant applications are composed of a title, a table of contents, an abstract, a problem statement, a statement of need, goals and objectives, a crucial project narrative that details the various steps, a list of resources requested, a review of the literature about the topic, and possible letters of support (Lovine 2013).

Notes

1 For instance, in 1995, the NPS established standards for its interpreters by creating the Interpretive Development Program (IDP) to "develop effective interpretive skills to facilitate meaningful visitor experiences and encourage stewardship of park resources" (NPS 2009).
2 See Chapters 4, 7, and 9.
3 Google's search tools (usable rights) allow users to find images "labeled for (noncommercial) reuse (with modification)." Other websites such as the American Memory project (Library of Congress) give access to documents from the public domain. Finally, the search engine developed by the Creative Commons permits users to find documents from various sites such as YouTube, Wikimedia Commons, Flickr, or Europeana.
4 The fair-use option is not a legal category and relies most of the time upon interpretation.
5 See the Institute for Museum and Library Services (www.imls.org); the National Endowment for the Humanities (www.neh.gov); the National Historical Publications and Records Commission (www.archives.gov/nhprc); the Mellon Foundation (www.mellon.org); the Alfred P. Sloan Foundation (www.sloan.org/ and www.sloan.org/apply-for-grants/); the Getty Foundation (www.getty.edu/foundation/grants/) (accessed August 13, 2015).

Bibliography

American History Workshop. "Who We Are." AHW website, undated a, www.americanhistorywork shop.com/who-we-are/ (accessed November 11, 2014).

American History Workshop. "Planning Tools." AHW website, undated b, www.american historyworkshop.com/planning-tools/ (accessed September 11, 2015).

Association of Research Libraries. *Code of Best Practices in Fair Use for Academic and Special Libraries*, 2012, www2.archivists.org/groups/intellectual-property-working-group/code-of-best-practices-in-fair-use-for-academic-and-special-libraries (accessed August 11, 2015).

Cornell University. "Copyright Term and the Public Domain in the United States." January 2015, http://copyright.cornell.edu/resources/publicdomain.cfm (accessed September 13, 2015).

Dean, David. *Museum Exhibition: Theory and Practice*, London and New York: Routledge, 1996.

De Groot, Jerome. *The Historical Novel*, New York: Routledge, 2010.

Gilden Seavey, Nina. "Film and Media Producers: Taking History off the Page and Putting it on the Screen." In *Public History: Essays from the Field*, edited by James Gardner and Peter LaPaglia, Malabar: Krieger Publishing Company, 2006, 117–129.

Gregory, Philippa. "Born a Writer: Forged as a Historian." *History Workshop Journal*, 59 (2005): 237–242.

Howard, Jennifer. "What You Don't Know About Copyright, but Should." *The Chronicle of Higher Education*, May 29, 2011.

Jackson, Jason Baird. "Creative Commons and Cultural Heritage." *Archaeology, Museums & Outreach*, August 19, 2014, http://rcnnolly.wordpress.com/2014/08/19/creative-commons-and-cultural-heritage/ (accessed August 11, 2015).

Lee, Richard. "Defining the Genre." *Historical Novel Society*, undated, https://historicalnovelsociety.org/guides/defining-the-genre/ (accessed August 11, 2015).

Lovine, Sonia. D. *Taking Public History for Granted: A Grant-Writing Guide for Public Historians*, Public History Commons, 2013, http://publichistorycommons.org/library/files/original/4a0f2057db2a3399 39b200b7f9770fb5.pdf (accessed April 5, 2015).

Mortimer, Ian. "Why Historians Should Write Fiction." *Novel Approaches: From Academic History to Historical Fiction*, November 2011, http://ihrconference.wordpress.com/2011/11/23/why-historians-should-write-fiction/ (accessed August 12, 2015).

National Park Service. "Meaningful Interpretation: How to Connect Hearts and Minds to Places, Objects, and Other Resources," Washington, DC: National Park Service, 2008, www.nps.gov/parkhistory/online_books/eastern/meaningful_interpretation/mi6m.htm (accessed August 3, 2015).

National Park Service. "Interpretive Development Program." NPS website, November 30, 2009, www.nps.gov/idp/interp/theprogram.htm (accessed September 13, 2015).

Rosenstone, Robert. "The Reel Joan of Arc: Reflections on the Theory and Practice of the Historical Film." *The Public Historian*, 25/3 (Summer 2003): 61–77.

Rosenstone, Robert. *History on Film: Film on History*, Edinburgh: Pearson Education Limited, 2006.

Sambuchino, Chuck. "How to Write Historical Fiction: 7 Tips on Accuracy and Authenticity." *Writer's Digest*, September 2013, www.writersdigest.com/editor-blogs/guide-to-literary-agents/how-to-write-historical-fiction-7-tips-on-accuracy-and-authenticity (accessed August 12, 2015).

Smith, Daniel Blake. "The (Un)Making of a Historical Drama: A Historian/Screenwriter Confronts Hollywood." *The Public Historian*, 25/3 (Summer 2003): 27–44.

Tilden, Freeman. *Interpreting our Heritage*, Chapel Hill: University of North Carolina Press, 2008.

United States Copyrights Office "U.S. Copyright Office Fair Use Index." Copyright.gov, September 2015, www.copyright.gov/fls/fl102.html (accessed September 18, 2015).

Zemon Davis, Natalie. "Movie or Monograph: A Historian/Filmmaker's Perspective." *The Public Historian*, 25/3 (Summer 2003): 45–48.

4   Public History Writing

Writing is the main activity of historians. As Jerome De Groot points out, most historians "still rely on books to establish their authority, to develop their profile, and to make money." He adds that in the UK in 2003, £32 million was spent on history books, accounting for 3 percent of all books sold (2008, 31–32). It is through their writing that most historians connect with the public. Public historians also spend a good deal of time writing, but they distinguish themselves by their large and non-specialist readers. This specificity entails not only different approaches to the sources but also different writing styles. This chapter explores different styles used by public historians to engage with their audiences in writing, the different tools that they use, and the challenge they face in balancing the complexity of the past and simplicity of style when they write.

Academic, Popular, and Public History Writing Styles

Academic (or professional) and popular history styles are often seen as opposed. The difference does not come from the sources used by historians: both styles analyze, interpret, and contextualize primary sources to produce historical narratives. The main difference comes from the respective audiences. Popular history strives "for a very wide audience of non-specialists" (Norton 2013). The dissimilar audiences explain the dissimilar writing styles. For instance, in an article about the links between popular and academic history, Elizabeth Norton – who writes academic and popular history – compares her academic (PhD dissertation) and popular (*England's Queen: A Biography*) works, and how she approaches similar issues in different manners. She argues that academic writing is much more specific and focuses on very delimited issues. She adds that "popular historians often aspire to write in a novelized form – so that the reader can experience and feel the subject's life and times" (Norton 2013).

However, the distinction between academic and popular history writing is increasingly challenged by the rise of public history. Public historians may have graduate training in history, publish monographs, and write articles in peer-reviewed journals such as *The Public Historian* or the *Public History Review*. At least since the launch of the hugely popular history magazine *American Heritage* in the late 1940s, history magazines have also been a major aspect of public history writing. *American History Magazine* in the United States, *History Today* and *BBC History* in the UK, *History Ireland* in Ireland, *Canada's History* in Canada, and *Histoire* in France are other generalist magazines dealing with history. They include articles about a broad variety of topics, and they also review archives, books, and educational materials. Those magazines are important intermediaries between academics and popular audiences.

In order to write in those magazines, historians must often provide reader-friendly approaches to sometimes very complex topics. The popularity of those magazines also demonstrates that well-researched history can be attractive to non-specialist audiences. In addition to magazines, newspapers provide other good examples of historians who wrote for popular audiences. Historians can write columns (Niall Ferguson, *LA Times*, Linda Colley, *Guardian*) or contribute with occasional articles (Jill Lepore, *The New Yorker*). These links explain why a roundtable was proposed for the 2015 annual conference of the National Council on Public History (NCPH) about the "contact zones for historians and journalists" (Laney 2014). Historians often envy the popular interest raised by journalists on certain topics from the past. Much more than in academic articles and books, journalists are able to employ their writing skills to convey passion and emotions.

The lines between academic and popular writing are continually moving. For instance, the University of Massachusetts Amherst created "the Department of History's Writer-in-Residence program (that) facilitates sustained conversation with widely-read authors whose historical work engages broad public audiences."[1] In March 2014, historical non-fiction author Adam Hochschild gave a lecture entitled "Rewriting the Spanish Civil War." One of the questions was "How do you write about a subject on which more than 15,000 books have already been written?" Part of the answer Hochschild gave was that he writes history as scenes, as novelists do (Hochschild 2014). There has been a trend in which academic

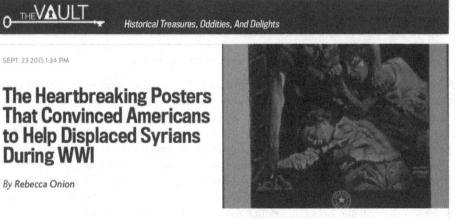

Figure 4.1 Screenshot of *The Vault* (September 23, 2015), Rebecca Onion, Slate.com. Courtesy of Rebecca Onion/Slate.com.

historians want to become more reader-friendly and reach wider audiences. In his book *That Noble Dream*, Peter Novick discusses how academic historians have vacillated between trying to reach wider audiences and shying away from the public (1988). This trend could mean that popular history, public history, and more traditional academic history styles increasingly overlap.

Public historian Alexandra Lord participated in the creation of the Ultimate History Project in which she wanted "to offer a site where historians could get experience writing for a general audience and interact with public historians and the general public" (2012). Likewise, Rebecca Onion runs *The Vault* – see Figure 4.1 – a history blog on Slate.com, and discusses historical items and their interpretations for broad audiences. Figure 4.1 gives an example of the format and assets of digital history writing. Jargon-free, the writer can use hyperlinks – in this case about humanitarian response – and social media – bottom right – to enrich the reading. Those two examples are part of what Jason Steinhauer (communication specialist at the Library of Congress) has recently called "history communicators" who "explain basic historical concepts" as well as "communicate history in a populist tone that has mass appeal across print, video, and audio" (2015). The topic of Rebecca Onion's blog post – here the Syrian refugees in Europe – shows how the links between past and present can help engage popular and academic audiences. However, even though the strict opposition between academic and popular history seems to crack, it is important to be aware that writing for non-specialist audiences is anything but easy, especially for historians who have been trained to write dry, emotion-free texts full of footnotes.

Adopting a Public Style: Writing for Large Non-Specialist Audiences

Public history is a field with many blurry edges and one should wonder whether writing for popular audiences is one of them. Historians may write for very different media (article, blog, panel, leaflet, novel, review) and many different sites (museum, website, national park). The question is to know whether historians who write for broad public audiences are public historians. For instance, is an academic historian who writes a novel a public historian simply because (s)he addresses broad audiences? Although one could argue that not all historians with a public writing style are public historians – because the public engagement is limited – it is true that most public historians adopt very specific writing styles.

The purpose is, here, to discuss what the historians who write for broad audiences have in common. Certain periods and topics are more popular than others, such as World War II, military history in general, or sports (De Groot 2008, 31). It is always very important for public historians to provide a style that does not deter public attention. Writing history for broad audiences does not necessarily involve direct interaction with readers. This does not mean the public is totally absent from the writing process, however. Historians must always have their publics in mind and consider the encounter between their text and their non-historian readers. Texts should be considered – as much as possible – as a dialogue with the public. Historians may wonder what the readers wish to read. History festivals appear as opportunities for historians to discuss and dialogue with their readers and to use the feedback for further writing.[2]

In order to write reader-friendly pieces accessible to broad and non-academic audiences, historians could follow certain principles. In 1946, George Orwell explained six points that writers should follow to engage with their readers (1946, 264). He advised "Never use a long word where a short one will do." Indeed, historians can look at journalism and avoid long sentences and long paragraphs. Various short online articles written by historians are available on the Ultimate History Project. Historians may also check the guidelines provided by George Mason University's History News Network or Duke's Office of News and Communication (History News Network undated; Duke University 2013; Illinois News Bureau undated).

Brevity is crucial in communication and Duke's Office of News and Communication explains that, for op-ed articles, "You have no more than 10 seconds to hook a busy reader, which means you shouldn't 'clear your throat' with a witticism or historical aside" (Duke University 2013). Not every reader would limit reading to ten seconds, but historians should make sure to be straightforward to reach large non-academic audiences. In reader-friendly style, paragraphs should be short, and jargon must be avoided. Orwell proposed to never use a foreign phrase, a scientific word or a jargon word if one can think of an everyday equivalent (1946). Mary Woodsen advises that "Roughly 70 percent of the words in your piece should be one syllable long. Two-and three-syllable words should make up the bulk of the rest. For every multi-syllabic word you write, ask yourself if there's a shorter one that would fit the bill" (undated). Brevity should not yet result in telegraphic style where articles are omitted. The challenge for historians is to convey their arguments in short texts and paragraphs, something very different from the article or dissertation-length practice.

Likewise, the main point/argument should be available in the first paragraph. For example, writers of exhibition panels may consider that visitors sometimes merely read the first sentences or even just the panel's title. The relevance of the introduction goes along with a smart design of the overall layout. Woodsen considers white space very important to break sentences and paragraphs to avoid losing readers' eyes. Studies of Internet users have showed that attention on screens usually follows an "F" pattern. Attention is paid at the first line and then to the bullet points (left part of the page) (Nielsen 2006). It is therefore crucial for writers to think ahead about where the text will be read and by whom. In some cases, people would have to stand to read the text, so it is important to adapt the size and the length of it.

Regarding the style, it seems fair to say that the majority of academic historians struggle with the task of writing dramatically or with empathy. For the sake of objectivity, professional historians in the early 20th century disengaged from their writing (Novick 1988). Professional historians needed to try to be objective and not part of the story they were writing. Historians now have a more nuanced approach to objectivity. Most historians acknowledge critical distance towards their sources while also understanding that they are inescapably positioned when they write about the past.[3]

Historians who intend to reach large non-academic audiences may envisage and practice techniques that graduate history training barely proposes. Several options help historians to engage with their readers. Ian Mortimer – writer of historical fiction – suggests writing a biography of someone as if the writer is that person, as Peter Ackroyd did in his biography of Oscar Wilde (2011). In her blog on the history of crimes, British historian Helen Rogers explains how she piques the interest of readers. Throughout her blog, she acknowledges that, as a historian, she is part of the story she writes. In order to show her own "emotional entanglement in the history and story," she occasionally places herself in the narrative (Rogers 2014).

Why not write the story as a conversation with the readers? This would leave a space for the reader in the text. In his book *A Million Years in a Day*, historian Greg Jenner presents a historical conversation about everyday activities from waking up to going to sleep (2015). Preferably using the active voice – instead of passive sentences – history writing for large audiences can try to make the past alive through emotions, anecdotes, and dialogue. In order to introduce her readers to her stories about the history of crimes, Rogers begins her blog "not with the prison visitor or setting the scene of the gaol but by focusing on how inmates depicted themselves in the tattoos many sported" (2014). She also uses visual and material objects to flesh out the stories. In order to improve their reader-friendly style, historians can use many different tools, exercises, and manuals.[4] The Gunning Fox Index and Flesch Reading Ease measure length, words, and paragraphs, to give some information about the reader-friendly dimension of the text.[5]

Fiction and Historical Novels

Historical fiction is an old writing style that plays on the gaps between known factual history and invention (Maxwell 2012; De Groot 2009). The discussions about historical novels have a lot in common with those on historical movies.[6] The website issued from the historical fiction conference organized in London in 2011 provides an excellent history of the genre (Phillpott 2011). In spite of most academic historians' skepticism toward historical novels, the genre has been through a recent efflorescence and increasing numbers of scholars are contributing to it.[7] Tiya Miles – historian of African American and Native American cultures – used her research to write *The Cherokee Rose*, a historical fiction that explores the narratives of Native American slaveholding. Philippa Gregory, author of historical fiction (especially about Anne Boleyn and the Tudors) sold more than 2.5 million books, and this, argues Beck, has contributed to the "present-day fascination for the Tudors" (Beck 2011, 200, 208).

It is extremely hard to provide a standard definition of historical fiction and the extent to which fiction can balance historical facts. For the Historical Novel Society "a novel must have been written at least fifty years after the events described … or by someone who was not alive at the time of those events (who therefore approaches them only by research)" (Beck 2011, 202). This vague definition results in a wide range of historical novels, from well-researched novels to books that pay little or no attention to history except in the sense of being set in the past (Beck 2011, 202). De Groot lists "thirteen genres which historical fiction can be moulded into: romance, detective, thriller, counter-factual, horror, literary, gothic, postmodern, epic, fantasy, mystery, western, and children's books" (2009, 12). The genre is also composed of many different sub-fields. The Historical Novel Society accepts sub-genres like alternate histories (Robert Harris's *Fatherland*, for instance). Alternate history deals with events that develop differently from the reality (Mitrovich undated).[9] For instance, in *Ruled Britannia*, Turtledove writes as if the 16th century Spanish Armada had been victorious, leading to a now Catholic Britain under Spanish control. Other subfields including pseudo-histories (Umberto Eco's *Island of the Day Before*), time-slip novels (Barbara Erskine's *Lady of Hay*), and historical fantasies (Bernard Cornwell's *King Arthur* trilogy) are part of historical fiction (Beck 2011, 202).

The complexity of the genre does not mean there is no methodology to write good historical novels. First, a good historical novel must be based on intense research. Philippa

Historical fiction raises important questions for historians. In 2011 Novel Approaches conferences highlighted crucial questions about *the popularity of historical fiction, the differences and similarities between historical fiction and academic history*, and whether *the success of historical fiction benefits or threatens academic history?*[8] Instead of discussing whether the concept of historical fiction is valid or not, historians interested in reaching non-academic audiences should work at highlighting what literary authors and academic historians can learn from each other.

Gregory wishes to "offer readers an intellectual challenge as well as an entertainment" and makes clear that "historical accuracy should never be sacrificed for the sake of a good story." She explains "I read everything. I go to museums, I visit the places involved, I even know about the weather" (Beck 2011, 210). Writing historical fictions implies historians need to know about everyday life, and many other details that other academic historians may not have to think about. Gregory also provides author's notes and additional information about the historical sources. Just as with any good historical writing, the most carefully researched and thoughtfully written historical fiction can create space for a broadened understanding and engagement with the past. Another way to do so is to provide additional materials and guidance for readers through a website, DVD, and mobile apps. Digital tools may be very useful in connecting fiction with historical materials and historical interpretation of sources.

However, historical fictions are not merely about facts. Writers should not forget that readers also expect entertainment. Beck argues that the "research process must be treated as a means to an end, not an end in itself" (2011, 203). Research and facts without the addition of fictional components may be difficult to read and far from the ideal fictional entertainment. This is where invention matters. Fiction should be as accurate to the historical records as possible when they are available, but on many occasions, writers need to invent a story. In this case, Gregory stresses that she "chooses the most likely explanation" (Beck 2011, 211). Plausibility does not result from a lack of historical investigation but rather from a pertinent choice of the historian based on a careful understanding of the context.

Another way to catch the reader's attention is to adopt the first-person style, to provide a way for readers to feel connected with the character. This style is particularly problematic for writers trained as historians who are used to the third-person approach, and not being part of the story they tell. This fictional approach – entering the minds of historical characters for instance – is also problematic since it encourages a more narrow and personal perspective of the past. On the other hand, writers of historical fiction cannot easily provide multiple interpretations of the past, they need to provide clear stories for which the first-person style is helpful. Entertainment also forces writers to use what literary critic Lukács called the "necessary anachronism" (De Groot 2009, 182). Language is perhaps the best example. Most writers of historical fiction cannot use the language employed during the events they write about; readers would not understand 16th century English or expressions no longer in use. Modern language is an example of necessary anachronism that is part of the compromises of historical fiction. Writers of historical fiction need to make compromises to attract popular attention, but this should not be done against the available factual knowledge of the past.

Writing historical fiction is a lot of research. In order to penetrate the historical context of the story – language, description, ways of living – historians have to read about sources – diaries, notes, inventories, etc. – written at the time of the story they tell. Historians may, as much as possible, visit the places they write about, visit museums to see the objects, clothes, furniture, and tools they will describe. Private companies such as Research for Writers offer their services to writers as well. In addition to research, historians who want to write fiction could use multiple resources (Sambuchino 2013; Lundoff 2004). Historians may read historical novels to have a better idea of the practice. Furthermore, the Historical Novel Society (HNS) provides a practical guide and a toolkit, and guidelines for short stories (Cook 2011). The writers digest website has tutorials on very specific issues in fiction writing.

Children's Literature, Comics, and Graphic Novels

Children's Books

History for children is not limited to the school system. There is actually a rich literature of history for children. For instance, Terry Deary's *Horrible Histories* have had a global audience since 1993. He has become one of the most popular history writers for children. By no means the sole example, *Horrible Histories* help draw certain features about the field. As many other successful producers of popular history – like Ken Burns – Deary created *Horrible Histories* as a reaction against how he perceived history was taught at schools and in history books: boring and fact-based.[10]

For Deary, history has to be fun, exciting, and engaging. Entertainment is crucial, especially for young readers with a relatively short attention span. It is important to keep children connected to the story. This style of writing highlights how history should be lively to appeal to certain audiences. In *Horrible Stories*, the past is presented in a non-conventional style with jokes and humor. Another way that Deary draws attention to the past is to focus on ordinary people, and ask, for instance, "What did people laugh at a hundred years ago? What made people cry? What did they eat? What games did they play?" (Beck 2011, 232). These everyday topics help connect the readers with the past.

It is important that historians who write for young audiences avoid the strict chronological and encyclopedic approach of the past. Historians should be able to vary documents and activities. History writing can use various types of documents – maps, drawings, pictures – not only to change media, but also to foster visual representation and imagination. The text should not, especially for young audiences whose reading fluency may be an issue, be the sole way to convey the past.

Finally, Deary argues for a conversational style of writing, stating "Hey! You'll never guess what I found out about this period in history" (Beck 2011, 231). Much more than a style, this approach helps bring interactivity. Historians should wonder how their writing can involve readers. From time to time Deary pretends he is discussing with the readers, especially by asking them, "What would you have done?" Interactivity is an incredible challenge for historians who write for large audiences. As for Deary, he uses games, quizzes, and riddles to entertain, to engage with his audiences. Another way is to provide hands-on experiences, recipes from the past that children can undertake, for instance.

Comics and Graphic Novels

Comics and graphic novels can be sources for historians. For instance, Boston College History Department's students arranged an exhibition entitled *Revealing America's History Through Comics* that illustrates "the ways in which comic books reflected American history." It shows how "Captain America grappled with the disillusionment of Watergate, Superman buffed up during the fitness craze of the 1970s, and Batwoman combatted sexism" (Boston College 2014). More challenging is the way historians can use comic strips, manga, cartooning, and other graphic novels to convey interpretations of the past.

Howard Zinn is one of the most famous examples of academic historians who successfully used graphic novels. In 2008, he published *A People's History of American Empire* in collaboration with cartoonist Mike Konopacki. De Groot also mentions Alan Moore as a "key figure in the reinvention of the graphic novel" and Art Spiegelmann's *Maus* as examples of how graphic novels can help to deal with historical horror (De Groot

2008, 223). More recently, Rafe Blaufard published *Inhuman Traffick. The International Struggle against the Transatlantic Slave Trade: A Graphic History* (Blaufard 2014). Comics and graphic novels may help making very complex and difficult pasts more accessible to audiences who are not used to reading history. This media helps historians reflect on how to capture people's (limited) attention and draw them into a more complex and perhaps difficult story.

British historian Claire Hayward focused on *Sally Heathcote: Suffragette* and explains that "Sally's fictional, but her story intertwines with real historical figures of the Suffrage movement, with real events. We see Sally at marches, in Holloway prison being force-fed and at the funeral procession of Emily Wilding Davison" (Hayward 2014). Unlike novels, graphic novels rely heavily on visual depiction. This is an opportunity for historians to link their writing with cultural institutions. For instance, Hayward points out that "The opening page of *Sally* shows an elderly Sally in a nursing home, with a box of Suffragette ephemera open next to her. One of the objects is a medal, bearing Sally's name and the inscriptions 'Hunger Strike' and 'For Valour'." Hayward explains, "these badges were presented to Suffragettes who had endured hunger strikes in prison, in the name of their cause" (Hayward 2014). Well-researched graphic novels can help public historians to recreate the past for their readers.

Digital Public History Writing

Since the professionalization of history in the late 19th century, historians have vacillated between trying to detach themselves from their subjects and reaching out to broader audiences. Monographs and peer-reviewed articles became the norm for academic historians, but there has also been a long history of historians engaging in public education, policy-making, popular entertainment, and non-fiction and fiction writing, even before the age of the Internet. However, much more than any other media, the digital revolution has transformed the knowledge making and sharing process. Digital writing offers one of the only methods to include audiences in the overall process, and as such is a major tool for public historians. With the rise of digital formats to produce history, it is going to be more and more important to develop digital writing skills for the Internet.

The specificity of digital writing first comes from the format itself. Born on the web, available on the web, digital writing takes many different shapes. Reading on a screen is a different practice than reading hard copy. The electronic book (e-book) format has become widespread, and is used by the academic press as well. Nevertheless, although users can flip pages, search the text, and sometimes copy/paste passages, the format is not really different from the one-way communication used for traditional book formats. This is markedly different from the "browsing" that characterizes a good deal of online reading. Many Internet users do not stay long on websites and "bounce" from website to website. More than traditional writers, digital writers need to convince visitors to stay and read their works. Specialists in digital communication traditionally think that the first 20 seconds determine whether a visitor leaves or stays on the website. Digital writers have therefore to adapt their style and the layout of their work on the Internet. Digital writers should make clear what their arguments are, and what their webpage offers to visitors.[11]

The Internet is based on the Hypertext Transfer Protocol (http) in which texts are structured with hyperlinks. Hyperlinks send users toward other webpages or documents by simple clicks. Hyperlinks not only structure the web but also change the overall reading activity. Rather than from top to bottom, digital reading looks now much more like a tree with hyperlinks as branches. For example, it is rare a user of Wikipedia reads the full article without clicking on additional links to other key issues. Digital writers must take this new practice into account. Historians are particularly touched by this evolution since hyperlinks challenge chronological approaches of the past. It seems that hyperlinks work better for thematic production. Hyperlinks can also replace the traditional footnotes, and not render the text too dense.[12]

Digital writing – and hyperlinks – has the capacity to attach multimedia materials to historical narratives. This is particularly relevant for historians working with visual materials and objects. Historians can add video, sound, interactive images, and maps to their writing production, making digital "writing" much more like creating a traditional exhibit, with multiple components and media. A crucial change is that historians can now include primary sources in their historical narratives, so that readers may see, understand, and sometimes challenge the historian's interpretation. This development makes the core historian's activity – his/her interpretation of primary sources – potentially a more public process. The inclusion of primary sources is a risky practice for historians who can then be more openly challenged for their interpretation, but who said that historical narratives should be taken for granted?

This new format brings about collaboration and public participation of the kind that public historians have often sought. Instead of writing in isolation, authors may now have access to each other's drafts and can write books that are more than the sum of their parts. For instance, *Writing History in the Digital Age* was a project supported by the University of Michigan's Library. The *Writing History in the Digital Age* team "made the normally behind-the-scenes development of the book more transparent." Published online – open access – in 2013, the collaborative project details how digital technology has changed the act of writing for historians. An open call for essay ideas was made public during the summer 2011, collecting 60 contributions with 261 comments. Open peer review of 28 essays – with 945 comments from readers and reviewers – was undertaken during the fall of 2011.[13] However, while public in terms of being open and accessible to all, the project was also very conventional in its peer-review system and comments mostly came from scholars. This is why the use of online tools does not always involve broad audiences. In contrast, Wikipedia attracts a much wider range of contributors, making it an often-contentious space of knowledge making.

Created in 2001, Wikipedia has become the symbol of participatory construction of knowledge. Anyone can, if (s)he follows some rules verified during the submission, create and edit articles. As Wolff stresses, Wikipedia "allows any reader to peel away layers of narrative to explore how entries have changed over time, juxtaposing revisions for comparison" (2013). The traces of collaboration are visible. With the reader-friendly style, the inclusion of images and hyperlinks, Wikipedia encompasses many of the digital history attributes stressed above. Public history students' reader-friendly writing style can be tested while submitting a Wikipedia article about one aspect of their research. Historians increasingly seem to be engaging with Wikipedia, for example by having Wikipedians-in-residence or holding edit-a-thons in which they get their institution's collections or materials onto Wikipedia.

Historians writing on the web usually prefer the blog format. According to Stephanie Ho, 75,000 blogs and 1.2 million posts are made daily (2007, 65). Blogs are now entirely part of many public and academic historians' production. The American Historical Association gives annual awards for the best individual, group, and new blogs. A blog is not simply a personal website. What makes a blog a blog is its diary-like style and chronological posts.

Blogs can be research blogs, from institutions, provide points of view about an event, or a project. Starting a blog is an easy thing.[14] Blog editors such as Blogger or Wordpress make the creation and management of blogs easier. Especially relevant for public historians is the capacity to collect comments on their blog and to make their research more interactive.

Micro-blogging, such as Twitter, is part of the different tools that historians can use to interact with wider audiences. The size – posts are limited to 140 characters – of the format limits its use to sharing news, works, conference announcements. However, micro-blogging can also help share digital resources, archives, projects, and websites.[15] Some historians have used Twitter for history projects, asking students to create tweets from historical figures (Moravec 2013). Allwin Collinson's project @RealtimeWWII, or Benoit Majerus's project @RealtimeWorldWar1 offer day-to-day stories on Twitter. It is not simply stories, since Majerus points out that "One of the students' most important aims is to offer reliable source documents for every date they tweet" (undated). History through Twitter is also a way to enhance the publicness of historical archives. The London School of Economics and Political Science provides a detailed guideline for using Twitter in university research, teaching, and impact activities (London School of Economics undated).

It is crucial that historians writing on the web take into consideration who their audiences are. On the one hand, the Internet may allow more visibility for scholars' work among their peers, so that the media does not necessarily greatly affect the historian's writing style. On the other hand, the Internet can help historians reach broader and non-academic audiences. Making a writing piece public on the Internet raises the narratives to potential international and non-academic audiences. In order to reach broad and non-academic audiences, historians may have to adapt their writing style accordingly.

Notes

1 UMass History Annual Writer-in-Residence, www.umass.edu/history/about/writerinresidence. html (accessed August 12, 2015).
2 See the Hay Festival (UK), www.hayfestival.com/ or the Dublin Festival of History, http://dublin festivalofhistory.ie/ (accessed August 16, 2015).
3 See the introduction for the history and debates about historical writing.
4 See www.hemingwayapp.com/ and www.writersdiet.com/WT.php websites (accessed January 10, 2015). Woodsen provides exercises to practice reader-friendly style (undated). Historians can also use manuals such as Peter Elbow's book (Elbow 1998).
5 See Online Utility – Free Online Software Utilities, www.online-utility.org/english/readability_ test_and_improve.jsp; www.online-utility.org/english/help_understand_english_text.jsp (accessed August 13, 2015).
6 See Chapter 7.
7 The Walter Scott prize for historical fiction was created in 2001 in Britain, and the Historical Novel Society was founded in 2007.
8 See the podcasts on YouTube: www.youtube.com/watch?v=i7ahTRWUz5w; www.youtube.com/ watch?v=KHaA9Vag654; www.youtube.com/watch?v=-SoCKyZ9N9s (accessed January 21, 2015).
9 See also the forum www.alternatehistory.com/ (accessed January 23, 2015).
10 About fiction and filmmaking, see Chapter 7.
11 For details about web design and public participation, see Chapter 8.
12 See Chapter 8.
13 http://writinghistory.trincoll.edu/ (accessed August 12, 2015).
14 Among various guidelines, see this website especially devoted to historians: Blogging for Historians, http://bloggingforhistorians.wordpress.com/ (accessed August 16, 2015).
15 Certain websites list historians active on Twitter, www.activehistory.co.uk/historians-on-twitter/ (accessed August 10, 2015).

Bibliography

Beck, Peter. *Presenting History: Past & Present*, London: Palgrave Macmillan, 2011.

Blaufard, Rafe. *Inhuman Traffick: The International Struggle against the Transatlantic Slave Trade: A Graphic History*, Oxford: Oxford University Press, 2014.

Boston College University Libraries. "Revealing America's History Through Comics." January 2014, www.bc.edu/content/bc/libraries/about/exhibits-new/stokeshall/revealing.html (accessed August 8, 2015).

Cook, Myfanwy. *Historical Fiction Writing: A Practical Guide and Toolkit*, London: ActiveSprite Press, 2011.

De Groot, Jerome. *Consuming History: Historians and Heritage in Contemporary Popular Culture*, London: Routledge, 2008.

De Groot, Jerome. *The Historical Novel*, London: Routledge, 2009.

Dougherty, Jack and Nawrotzki, Kristen, eds. *Writing History in the Digital Age*, Ann Arbor: University of Michigan Press, 2013, http://writinghistory.trincoll.edu/ (accessed August 15, 2015).

Duke University's Office of Communication. *How to Write an Op-Ed Article*, November 2013, http://newsoffice.duke.edu/duke_resources/oped (accessed August 13, 2015).

Elbow, Peter. *Writing with Power: Techniques for Mastering the Writing Process*, Oxford: Oxford University Press, 1998.

Hayward, Claire. "Public History in Comic Form: Sally Heathcote: Suffragette." *Exploring Public Histories: Finding Queer History in the Present*, May 12, 2014, https://exploringpublichistories.wordpress.com/2014/05/12/sally-suffragette/ (accessed September 1, 2014).

History News Network. *How Do I Submit an Article to HNN for Publication?* Undated, http://hnn.us/article/41637 (accessed May 3, 2015).

Ho, Stephanie. "Blogging as Popular History Making, Blogs as Public History: A Singapore Case Study." *Public History Review*, 14 (2007): 64–79.

Hochschild, Adam. "Rewriting the Spanish Civil War." March 31, 2014, www.youtube.com/watch?v=VjArQRIeZNI&feature=youtu.be (accessed August 3, 2015).

Hsu-Ming Teo. "Historical Fiction and Fictions of History." *Rethinking History*, 15/2 (2011): 297–313.

Illinois News Bureau. *Op-Ed Guidelines: A Review of Institutional Strategies*, undated, www.news.illinois.edu/about_staff/media_training/Op-ed%20Writing%20and%20Guidelines.pdf (accessed August 13, 2015).

Jenner, Greg. *A Million Years in a Day: A Curious History of Everyday Life*, London: Weidenfeld & Nicolson, 2015.

Laney, Monique. "Contact Zones for Historians and Journalists." *Public History Commons*, June 2014, http://publichistorycommons.org/2015-proposal-contact-zones-for-historians-and-journalists/ (accessed August 13, 2015).

London School of Economics. "Using Twitter in University Research, Teaching, and Impact Activities." Undated, http://blogs.lse.ac.uk/impactofsocialsciences/2011/09/29/twitter-guide/ (accessed August 13, 2015).

Lord, Alexandra. "Writing for History Buffs." *The Chronicle for Higher Education*, July 9, 2012, http://chronicle.com/article/Writing-for-History-Buffs/132755/ (accessed September 2, 2014).

Lundoff, Catherine. "Historical Research for Fiction Writers." *Writing World*, 2004, www.writing-world.com/fiction/lundoff.shtml (accessed August 15, 2015).

Majerus, Benoit. "World War One goes Twitter." H-Europe, undated, http://h-europe.uni.lu/?page_id=621 (accessed Janurary 7, 2015).

Maxwell, Richard. *The Historical Novel in Europe, 1650–1950*, Cambridge: Cambridge University Press, 2012.

Mitrovich, Matt. *Alternate History*, Historical Novel Society, undated, http://historicalnovelsociety.org/guides/alternate-history/ (accessed August 12, 2015).

Moravec, Michelle. "Experiments in LIve Tweeting As a Historical Figure." January 2013, http://

historyinthecity.blogspot.com/2013/01/experiments-in-live-tweeting-as.html (accessed August 12, 2015).

Mortimer, Ian. "Why Historians Should Write Fiction." *Novel Approaches*, November 2011, http://ihrconference.wordpress.com/2011/11/23/why-historians-should-write-fiction/ (accessed August 15, 2015).

Nielsen, Jakob. "F-Shaped Pattern For Reading Web Content." *Nielsen Norman Group*, April 17, 2006, www.nngroup.com/articles/f-shaped-pattern-reading-web-content/ (accessed September 3, 2014).

Norton, Elizabeth. "Writing Popular History: Comfortable, Unchallenging Nostalgia-Fodder." *History Matters*, August 2013, www.historymatters.group.shef.ac.uk/popular-vs-academic-history/ (accessed September 4, 2014).

Novick, Peter. *That Noble Dream: The "Objectivity Question" and the American Historical Profession*, Cambridge: Cambridge University Press, 1988.

Orwell, George. "Politics and the English Language." *Horizon* (April 1946): 252–264.

Phillpott, Matt. "A History of Historical Fiction." *Novel Approaches*, November 25, 2011, http://ihrconference.wordpress.com/2011/11/25/a-history-of-historical-fiction/ (accessed August 15, 2015).

Rogers, Helen. "Blogging Our Criminal Past, Part 3: Public and Creative History." *Conviction, Stories from a Nineteenth-Century Prison*, August 24, 2014, http://convictionblog.com/2014/08/24/blogging-our-criminal-past-part-3-public-and-creative-history/ (accessed August 16, 2015).

Sambuchino, Chuck. "11 Ways to Write More Authentic Historical Novels." *Writer's Digest*, September 17, 2013, www.writersdigest.com/editor-blogs/guide-to-literary-agents/11-ways-to-write-more-authentic-historical-novels-by-a-historian (accessed September 5, 2014).

Steinhauer, Jason. "Introducing History Communicators." *Public History Commons*, January 29, 2015, http://publichistorycommons.org/introducing-history-communicators/#sthash.79jxiRZR.dpuf (accessed August 12, 2015).

Wolff, Robert S. "The Historian's Craft, Popular Memory, and Wikipedia." In *Writing History in the Digital Age*, edited by Jack Dougherty and Kristen Nawrotzki, Ann Arbor: University of Michigan Press, 2013, http://writinghistory.trincoll.edu/crowdsourcing/wolff-2012-spring/ (accessed August 12, 2015).

Woodsen, Mary. "Words at Work: Writing Reader-Friendly, Real-World Prose." *IPM Centers*, undated, www.ipmcenters.org/ipmsymposiumv/sessions/58-0.pdf (accessed August 13, 2015).

5   Editing Historical Texts

The purpose of this chapter is to provide readers with the essential steps to edit historical texts. As Constance B. Schulz – public historian and editor of many collections of historical texts – recently highlighted:

> in this era of Google Books and Wikipedia, of digital libraries that scan manuscripts and put them up on the internet as virtual replicas of the originals, of the ability of anybody with a computer to type up his or her own version of a manuscript ... non-editor scholars may want a reminder of what a scholarly historical documentary edition is and does.
>
> (Schulz 2013, 16)

Although it has become increasingly easy to provide and consult historical texts online, historians who performed historical edition of texts should be – and make users – aware of the value-added component of their work. Scholarly historical editions require specific tasks, and therefore specific skills for historians to guarantee the accuracy, completeness, and contextualization of historical texts. In order to do so, this chapter first presents an overview of modern scholarly documentary editing, and then introduces readers to the step-by-step process.

Introduction to Documentary Editing: Definition, Purposes, and Debates

The Role of Editors

Editing makes documents available for the public, mostly by preparing them for traditional or online publication. Documents can be about an individual, a group of people, an institution, a site, a movement, or any specific issue. Often focusing on political history/leaders, historical edition projects can have many different sizes, from single to multi-volume production (Stevens and Burg 1997, 25–31). Editions of historical documents can have several purposes as well. Editing can serve the preservation – through the multiplication of copies – of the original. The documentary editor preserves history by presenting the full texts, and allowing readers to experience the immediacy of the authentic voice (Falk 2006, 89). Editing can also help bring together documents about a same topic that have been dispersed through different institutions (Stevens and Burg 1997, 17–18). Nevertheless, despite their diversity, editing projects are all connected through their intention to facilitate the access to historical documents.

By definition, editors are public authority (Katz 1995). Editors, as public historians in general, facilitate and democratize access to historical materials. It is therefore not surprising if historical editing was one of the first components of the public history movement (Burke 1982). In addition to public access, the role of historical editors is to add historical value to the primary source. This additional value requires research and particular skills. As Candace Falk argues, "the editor performs the role of both an archivist and a historian in the process of publishing" (2006, 91). Historical editors therefore have strong relations with archivists and manuscript curators (Coles 1994; Eppard 1994; Schulz 1994).

Editors of historical texts pay attention to two main issues: the accurate transcription and the historical context of the document. The tasks of the editor are particularly obvious regarding correspondence. Originally intended for a single reader, correspondence needs an important historical contextualization to be accessed and used by broader non-specialist audiences. The annotation and contextualization are, therefore, highly important. The basic research skills and ability to evaluate evidence are precisely those most useful to any historian doing research (Tarter 1986, 77).

The Birth of Modern Editing

Editing historical documents is an old practice that dates back, for leading figures, to the late eighteenth century (Kline and Perdue 2008, 1–25). In the United States, editors usually mention the edition of Thomas Jefferson's papers – that began in 1943 – as the birth of modern editing though. In 1950, impressed by the edition of Jefferson's papers, U.S. President Harry Truman charged the National Historical Publications Commission (NHPC) to encourage the creation of similar new projects (Massey 2005, 40). Leading figures are, today, still a major subject of historical edition. *Founders Online* gives access to the correspondence and other writings of George Washington, Benjamin Franklin, John Adams, Thomas Jefferson, Alexander Hamilton, and James Madison with more than 160,000 documents. Editing has been highly connected to the history of political leaders.

In terms of methodology, debates emerged between two models in the 1970s. The two models became known as historical (documentary) and literary (critical) editing (Kline and Perdue 2008, 11). According to historian Gordon S. Wood "Unlike literary scholars, who often intensively study the writings of particular authors, many historians are interested in extracting significance from large numbers of documents" (Massey 2005, 48). The historical context is much more important for historical editing through annotations, illustrations, and other explaining materials. Literary editors focus much more on the writing of the authors. For example, they tend to edit only the documents written by the author, and not the letters/documents (s)he received. Despite some disagreements, historical and literary editors share many principles and associations such as the Association for Documentary Editing (ADE), created in 1978, that promotes group identity and exchange of ideas (Massey 2005, 48).

One recent evolution in historical editing came from digital tools. The Internet and the public access to documents have affected editing methodology (Pierazzo 2014). In order to understand the shift, historians can compare the paper and digital editions of John Adams' Papers (Massachusetts Historical Society undated). Although a digital edition follows traditional editing practices, it also involves the use of new tools and approaches. A digital documentary edition (DDE) is the recording of as many features of the original document as are considered meaningful by the editors, displayed in all the ways the editors consider useful for the readers, including all the tools necessary to achieve such a purpose (Pierazzo 2011). This definition includes not only the textual content but also the digital infrastructure (visible to the final user or not) necessary for the publication and exploitation of such content (Pierazzo 2014). For instance, editors of historical documents need to be familiar with XML (Extensible Markup Language), text encoding practice and standards such as the Text Encoding Initiative (TEI).[1]

Digital tools may foster public access (Hajo 2010). The capacity to create searchable texts deeply changed the production and use of text editions. What is more, Web 2.0 offers new opportunities for some public collaboration. Some historical edition projects now use crowdsourcing.[2] Although the practice is subject to debates among historical editors, crowdsourcing gives a role to the public in the collection and transcription of historical texts. Finally, new software like DocTracker (DT) helps provide new opportunities for editors. DT is a content-management database for documentary editions that helps centralize the different steps of the process – search, selection, cataloguing, transcription, storage, metadata creation, annotation, and XML output.

Step-by-Step Historical Editing Process

Editing shares some resemblance to collection management. Both are multi-task processes. Editors have to acquire, access, select, transcribe, verify, annotate, and index materials before they submit them for publication.

Acquisition

Editors start by searching for "all known documents by, to, or perhaps even about the subject of their edition" (Schulz 2013, 16). They need to locate and collect copies of (all the) necessary documents linked to the subject, "including variant versions and editions" (The Association for Documentary Editing undated). In order to locate texts, editors should be aware of the different repositories such as, for instance, the National Union Catalog of Manuscript Collections (NUCMC) in the United States, or the National Inventory of Documentary Sources (NIDS) in the United Kingdom. Both repositories are available through the digital repository Archive Finder.[3] Editors can also use the Online Computer Library Center (OCLC) and its WorldCat service, available at most academic libraries. Other printed resources are provided in Kline and Perdue's guide (2008, 57–58). Search letters can then be sent out to collect copies, including details about the project, and the type of materials needed (Kline and Perdue 2008, 67).

Materials can be collected through different forms such as photocopies or photographs of manuscripts, microform copies, and increasingly digital copies (through cameras or scanners). Sometimes, editors may even have the original manuscript of a text (Schulz 2013, 16). Digital technology and the Internet offer new ways to collect materials for historical editions. Crowdsourcing has greatly enlarged the possibilities for collecting documents. For instance, *Letters of 1916* is creating a crowdsourced digital collection of letters written around the time of the Irish Easter Rising (November 1, 1915 – October 31, 1916). In 2015, the Irish project had collected 1,800 letters from public institution and private collections and has been able to collect texts that comment on the Easter Rising, literature and art, the Great War, politics, business, and ordinary life. Acquisition is, therefore, close to the traditional research undertaken by historians while looking for primary sources.

Accession

Editors need to keep track of the various documents they have located and sometimes collected. The accession helps keep basic information – or metadata – about those documents usually through a database. Categories include the type of document, date and place of creation, creator, recipient, source from which acquired, physical condition, whether or not previously published (and, if so, where), enclosures, docketing or envelope information (Schulz 2013, 17; Kline and Perdue 2008, 46–48). Another important issue to consider is whether or not the documents are under copyright. The existence and the type of copyrights can greatly affect the feasibility of a project. Called a "control file," the database is the first step of cataloguing documents that have been collected. Standards are important to design this database. For instance, the Library of Congress provides the MARC Code List for Organizations that "contains short alphabetic codes used to represent names of libraries and other kinds of organizations that need to be identified in the bibliographic environment" (Library of Congress 2015).

Selection

Selection of the documents applies in two cases: if the quantity of collected documents is too large for the edition project, or if the publisher has limited the number of pages for edition (Schulz 2013, 17). Editors must therefore closely collaborate with the publishers. Editors need to decide with the publishers how extensive the project will be. The project can be comprehensive – so that editors decide to collect every remaining document on/ from one subject – or selective. Comprehensive editions that include every document are rare, so like collection managers, editors usually have to select the documents they want to use (Stevens and Burg 1997, 41–70). Another option is to undertake a hybrid version in which edited texts are associated with facsimile (copy or reproduction of records) (Kline and Perdue 2008, 41–44).

Depending on the scope – comprehensive/selective, themes, authors – editors have to make choices of documents that best carry out the purpose of the project or that bring new understanding of the subject, or that contrast with usual representations. Editors must answer additional questions to select the documents. Are the documents going to be selected because of a common author, theme, period, topic, or geographical area? Do editors want to use documents produced, received, and/or written about the subject? What sort of documents must be dealt with (letters, diaries, speeches, telegrams, memos, etc.)?

Crucial for public historians, editors must define and identify the possible audiences of their work: scholars, enthusiasts, general audience, teachers and schools, or specific organizations (Stevens and Burg 1997, 19). Targeted audiences may affect the edition. Scholarly readers are usually more interested in the information than the readability of the document, whereas editions for schools should insist on brevity and readability (Stevens and Burg 1997, 33).

Regardless of the selection, editors must explain and make their choices available to the users. The editorial method must be made public.[4] If the publication is not comprehensive, editors must decide what to do with the documents not selected for publication. Editors must explain what documents they omitted and the reasons for doing so (copyrights, classified and unavailable, editor's choice). Most editions decide to provide a basic list of documents not published while indicating the date, creator, recipient, and location of the original (Schulz 2013, 17). Editors may also provide information about what other similar documents exist. It helps users to better understand the selection and its representation of the subject/topic. It is therefore necessary that editors have an accurate knowledge of the existing primary sources and historiography.

Transcription

Principles

After having selected documents, editors may choose the appearance of the text. They can provide users with "a literal typeface reproduction of the handwritten text" through some form of photographic or digital surrogate of the original manuscripts (Schulz 2013, 17). In order to do so, they can use photographic facsimile, that is the reproduction of the original text free from alteration, usually through images. This process is fast but the end product may be hard to read for users. Optical Character Recognition (OCR) software can help produce searchable images of texts. A searchable document can be produced through digitization as well. However, those techniques can hardly be used for hand-written documents such as in Figure 5.1a, and unless the edition is published in a format such as microfilm or an online digital scan which reproduces the manuscript image, transcription is needed.

Most of the time editors need to modify the documents through transcription, namely to change "the text of documents from handwriting into type, using established standards for replicating in typeface the essential qualities of each manuscript" (Schulz 2013, 17). Editors must spend lot of time considering the different options, and, if they wish to transcribe the documents, what the transcription policies will be. Transcription is the process of converting textual and non-textual elements of original documents into readable, publishable, typescript form (Stevens and Burg 1997, 71). Images 5.1a and 5.1b show the original manuscript and a preliminary transcription of an 18th century letter. Transcription is never a simple copy of the document, especially with hand-written documents such as in Figure 5.1a. It requires a good knowledge of the rules and conventions (Huitfeldt and Sperburg-McQueen 2008). The key aspect is the accuracy of the transcription (Merrell 2014). It is more difficult than it seems because transcription always implies choices from the transcriber who is part of the production. Like translation, transcription changes the document (Stevens and Burg 1997, 21). The crucial issue is to limit the impact of these changes and not to affect the understanding of the text. The most important rule is to be consistent and to explain the transcription method within the statement of editorial method. To be consistent, editors must apply standards of transcription.

It is critical that editors agree on transcription and emendation policies early in the process, before transcription begins, in order to be consistent. Editors may apply standardization for some elements of the transcription. In general, standardization concerns elements in the source's physical format, and can be employed for salutations, date, and signature (Kline and Perdue 2008, 145). Editors frequently decide to place these items in specific spaces, regardless of where the author originally placed them. Editors also have to decide on policies regarding emendations. Emendations are textual changes made by editors while transcribing original documents (Stevens and Burg 1997, 72). For instance, editors must decide whether they capitalize proper nouns or first words of sentences (even though the author did not). The most obvious decision to be taken is about the spelling. Editors must decide and make clear whether they keep the spelling of the document, even if words are misspelled, or if they change it during the transcription to ease the reading. Likewise, editors must decide what they do with the (lack of) punctuation. Since the 1980s, most historical

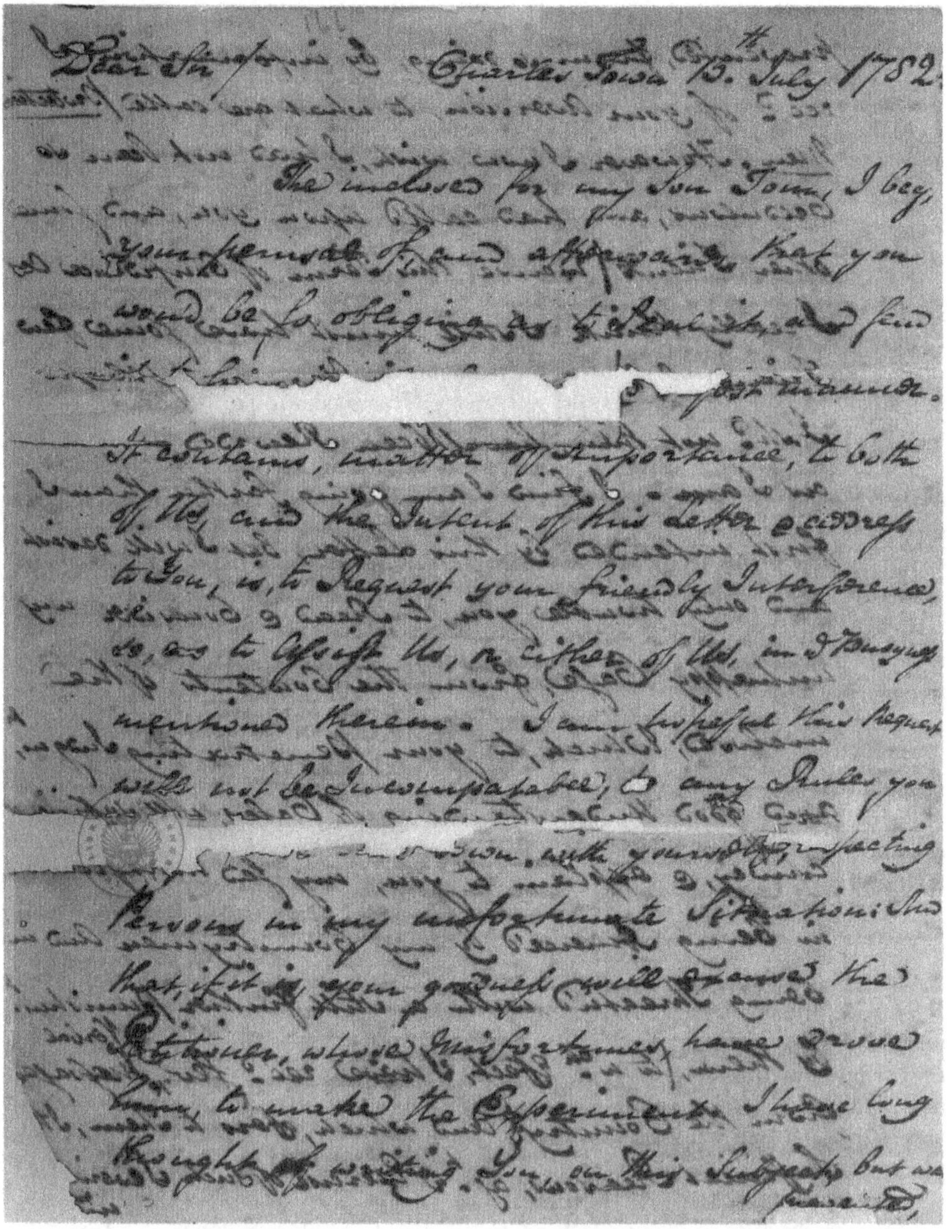

Figure 5.1 Original manuscript and preliminary transcription after tandem reading of a letter from Charles Pinckney (1732–1782) to Charles Cotesworth Pinckney (1746–1825) dated July 15, 1782. Original manuscript is from the public domain, courtesy of the Library of Congress. The transcription is courtesy of the Papers of the Revolutionary Era Pinckney Statesmen.

editions strive to preserve the spelling, the punctuation, the capitalization, superscripts, and strikethroughs exactly as in the original. Editors must make users aware of these choices at the beginning of the edition. However, in order to transcribe documents, editors may have to use specific tags and symbols to transcribe hand-written documents.

CP Sr. to CCP, 15 July 1782, Pinckney Family Papers, Box 6, Folder 3, Library of Congress

Charles Town 15th. July 1782:

Dear Sir

The inclosed for my Son Tom, I beg, your perusal of, and afterwards that you wou'd be so obliging as to Seal it, and send it to him <...> <...> <...> <...>est manner. It contains, matter of Importance, to both of Us, and the Intent of this Letter & address to You, is, to Request your friendly Interference, so, as to Assist us, or either of Us, in ye Busyness mentioned therein. I am hopeful this Request will not be Incompatable, to any Rules you <...> <...> <....> <...> <...>wn with yourself, respecting Persons in my unfortunate Situation; And that, if it is, your goodness will excuse the Petitioner, whose misfortunes, have drove him, to make the Experiment. I have long thought of writing You, on this Subject, but was prevented, from so doing, by information I rec'd of your Aversion, to what are called Protection Men. However I now wish, I had not been so Credulous, and had call'd upon you, and some other Friends (Excuse this Term of Confidence as I really think I still must have some few Friends <...> <.> <...> <...> <...> <...> <...> I sh'd not then, have been Rewarded <...> as I am. I find I am going farther than I first intended by this Letter, but I will desist and only trouble you, to Read and Consider my unhappy, Case, from the Contents of the inclosed; Which, to your Penetrating Judgm't, and good understanding of Cases, will sufficiently convey, & explain to you, my sad <...> In being Amerce'd by my Countrymen And in being Threaten'd with a still further punishm't. by them, (to wch. Effect, I have rec'd sev'. ^Verbal^ messages from the Country) and which, offers to Them, I th<...> Sufficient Reasons, agt. ye Exercise of such Severi<...> Severity <...>

Comparisons, says an old Proverb, are Odious; but who can keep drawing them in such cruel Situations as mine. I don't mention Names because I am happy, in many of my Friends & Fellow Citizens escaping the Punishm't. I have met with, whose Demerits, if Scan'd in a Political View, are certainly more Faulty than <...> or a <...> <...> <...> <...>ting with me: Why then, this Ungenerous Discrimination agt. me? It can't be surely, for having serv'd this Country in many offices, from ye Lowest to some import. ones, without fee or Reward, for near thirty Years past, tho' not Brilliantly yet with the best <...> and I hope not unusefully. Neither can it be, for having Lost Twenty thousand Guineas, or near it, in support of the Cause, (wch. is a hard Truth) <...> <...> <...> <...> <...> have <...> <...> call in to your Assistance; the aid of other Doctors once my Friends, whom I leave to you to name, and have a Consultation, how to Cure my Wound; And may God Almighty grant you Success. I think you may assure

1 of 3

Figure 5.1 (Continued)

Editors must decide what to do regarding a list of common issues such as: undecipherable words, doubt about words, unrecoverable parts, additions and annotations to the original text by the author, underlining, line breaks, non-textual elements such as symbols and drawings, or words in foreign language. Symbols must be transcribed, or a note must be inserted to describe the symbol (Papers of the War Department 2007). There are no general standards, although some editions use [brackets] for undecipherable words, [reading?] when doubt, [...] for unrecoverable gaps, ^addition^ for addition to the original, and *italic* for underlining in the source (Kline and Perdue 2008, 153–159). For instance on the transcription (Figure 5.1b), the editors use <...> to represent missing parts of the manuscript (Figure 5.1a). Likewise, the editors chose to use the word "respecting" (line 7 of the main text) although the three first letters (in green in the transcription) are missing. Editors may consult major projects of historical edition's editorial statement to decide what rules to follow. While adopting rules, editors must consider how the choices and decisions affect the use and understanding of the original document (Stevens and Burg 1997, 21, 121–155).

Crowdsourcing and Transcription

Transcription has become a major part of the editing cost. In a context of lack of funding, editors have explored new ways to transcribe documents. One solution is "to enlist the public to help" (Parry 2012). One example is the project that deals with the documents that perished during the fire of the U.S. War Department in 1800. Collecting copies from various places, historians now have 45,000 documents that need to be transcribed. Crowdsourcing transcription has been undertaken to edit these documents. To do so, the Papers of War Department (PWD) project looks for "transcription associates." PWD uses Scripto, an open-source tool developed by the Center for History and New Media (CHNM). It facilitates community transcription by giving access to certain files and providing a transcription toolbar. Likewise, the Transcribe Bentham project has been developed by University College London (Causer et al. 2012). This collaborative transcription initiative aims to transcribe unpublished documents from the English philosopher (Kaya 2010).

However, the use of crowdsourcing for transcription has raised some issues. Edward G. Lengel, editor of the Papers of George Washington at the University of Virginia, is skeptical about the use of crowdsourcing and argues that it is not as effective or as fast as project managers think (Parry 2012). In a recent article, Causer, Tonra, and Wallace – who have been part of the Transcribe Bentham project – acknowledged that the project had not been as fast as foreseen (Causer et al. 2012). As for other crowdsourcing projects, a handful of people do much of the work.[5] The second main issue is about the transcription practice itself. As seen before, transcribing hand-written papers requires skills and consistency. Sharon Leon from the CHNM explains that editors of the PWD "spend about 30 minutes a day managing the work of these volunteers—comparing transcriptions to the original images, creating accounts, and answering questions" (Parry 2012). To help transcribers, the PWD project provides its transcription associates with "guidelines" about "spelling," "punctuation," "formatting," and "navigation." Likewise, Transcribe Bentham has a "transcription desk" with very detailed guidelines full of examples (Transcribe Bentham undated). In spite of its drawbacks, crowdsourced transcription offers ways to connect the public with primary sources, and gives, as Leon points out, "volunteers a feeling of investment and participation in the work of history" (Parry 2012).

Text Encoding

Text encoding is necessary for all editions that will be published digitally. Text encoding is a process that converts texts into series of code.[6] Encoding makes texts searchable and allows users to undertake new analysis. Texts are usually coded in XML. XML organizes and makes online materials searchable – and therefore usable – by users. XML allows editors to define data such as "name," "date," "site," or any other variable through tags. Tags give indications about the original texts, and can indicate aspects such as physical aspects of the document, proper names, parts of speeches, annotations in margins, or symbols. For example, the XML version of one author's letters and personal writing enables accurate searches by dates, individuals, topics, or any other keywords. Importantly XML-encoded texts can include hypertexts that redirect users to other materials (Kline and Perdue 2008, 272). Text encoding may have become easier and more consistent through the TEI that was created in the late 1980s and that provides a standard and guidelines. However, even with the use of XML tools, text encoding remains a complex practice.

Editors should include a brief explanation of the methods used to digitize and encode the texts (scanning, OCR, manual transcription, XML, etc.). For instance, it may be very useful for editors to include a description of the XML tags used in the edition, and some details about the methods used to tag documents. This is especially important if the edition allows the reader to search for text located within specific tags.[7] For instance, projects can mention whether some models like the Model Editions Partnership (MEP) system have been used (University of South Carolina 2000). Historians can use the many tutorials and online resources that provide information about XML (Vanhoutte and Van den Branden 2009; Morrison 2001; Kasdorf 2003).

Verification, Annotation, Indexing

Verification

Once the document has been transcribed, editors must make sure that an accurate text has been provided. Different techniques exist. Visual collation occurs when a single editor compares two versions of the text visually (Kline and Perdue 2008, 182). Oral proofreading or tandem reading as in Figure 5.1b involves two or more people, where one member checks the new draft of the text while another reads aloud word for word (or letter for letter) and punctuation marks the earlier draft. in Figure 5.1b, the second reader circled words – "Us" with a capital U – that (s)he thinks should be corrected. Any project should have a well-established system for recording corrections of transcriptions and the textual forms that follow; so that records not only document the changes that have been made but also who made them, and when (Kline and Perdue 2008, 183).

Annotation

If transcription raises many literary issues, editions of historical documents also involve historical research. Annotation is "the information added by editors to improve readers' understanding of historical documents" (Stevens and Burg 1997, 157). Annotations are part of the added value of edited documents. They help readers understand the documents, so annotations are crucial in making texts publicly accessible. A large part of annotations intend to clarify the historical context of the text, and provide the opportunity for historians to connect editing and historical analysis. Historians should yet be careful not to create too many annotations. Editors should measure the balance between readability and information.

Annotations answer three sets of questions about the sort of document (provenance notes), about the text (textual notes), and about the meaning (contextual or informational notes) (Stevens and Burg 1997, 22). Annotations clarify and identify sites, individuals, events, and any other passages that require explanation. Provenance notes tell readers where the original document is located and possible additional information about the nature of the document. Textual notes detail the physical appearance of the document, the elements readers cannot see on the document (missing paragraphs, torn pages, multiple authors, notes in the margins) (Stevens and Burg 1997, 22). Informational or contextual notes help readers understand the meaning of the documents and to set them into their historical context. Annotations can be footnotes, endnotes, or be gathered into introductory essays. It seems that footnotes and endnotes are more useful for scholarly editions, while popular audiences tend to prefer introductory essays (Stevens and Burg 1997, 157–198). Information about the context can also appear through additional documents such as maps, tables, chronology, genealogy, or other types of illustrations. It should be noted that crowdsourcing also offers opportunities for annotations. Through tags, participants can provide annotations for texts as they do for images in social media repositories.

Index

The final step in preparing a scholarly edition for publication is the creation of some kind of indexing or retrieval system that gives readers access to the information in the documents for a variety of purposes (Schulz 2013, 18). Not everything can be indexed, so editors need to explain their choices and methodology in a statement of indexing method. Standards and general guides exist (Mulvany 1994; Wellisch 1991). Many editors regard the indexes of the Adams Papers as a model (Kline and Perdue 2008, 284). In order to choose an index and an index methodology, the American Society for Indexing provides resources, especially an Index Finder (American Society for Indexing 2015). The website's section on "Software Tools for Indexing" gives some idea of the choices available for various computer operating systems, web-indexing, and the construction of a thesaurus (a list of terms approved for use in the index). Ultimately, in order to select the main issues to be indexed, editors have to be aware of the historical context, the historiography, and historical debates. So editors are archivists and historians.

Submission

Materials collected and generated by the edition project may then be prepared for submission to the publisher. Editors and publishers must agree on the arrangement of the documents. The entire project may be divided into chapters and volumes, in which documents must be sorted and arranged according to a rationale, that, again, should be explained to the users. Ultimately, editors can sort documents by chronology, typology (correspondence, diary), or by themes. Even though the chronological order may seem less problematic, editors face issues with undated documents, or with more than one document with the same date (Stevens and Burg 1997, 60–61).

Deciding the order in which the documents will be presented should derive from a clear discussion. Documentary editors have adopted standards and conventions for the subdivisions of texts. Although it applies more to literary than historical editing, the Modern Language Association, the Center for Editions of American Authors (CEAA) and later the Committee for Scholarly Editions (CSE) have created guidelines for editors (Modern Language Association undated). The CSE awards the emblems "An Approved Edition" and "An Approved Text" to qualified volumes whose editors wish to submit their work for review. Finally, it is important for editors to explain what the editorial policies have been.

Editors may also decide to add illustrations, maps, and additional documents such as copy editing of original writing (Schulz 2013, 18).

Among the various resources for historians interested in scholarly edition, the open-access *Guide to Documentary Editing* is particularly useful (Kline and Perdue 2008). It provides further reading for the many different issues of historical editing. While older, Stevens and Burg's *Editing Historical Documents* still helps historians in many ways too (1997). Historians can also contact and collaborate with the Association for Documentary Editing (ADE), whose website provides information about conferences, projects, and online resources for historical editors. Historians may subscribe to and consult the email discussion list Scholarly Editing Forum (SEDIT-L). Many journals like the *Journal of Scholarly Publishing* or *Literary and Linguistic Computing* give access to current debates in editing. *Documentary Editing* – renamed *Scholarly Editing* in 2012 – is an open-access journal that provides extensive information, resources, and news about historical editing. In terms of funding, editors can contact their home institutions – especially when projects are based in universities. Major projects have received federal grants from national institutions such as the National Historical Publications and Records Commission (NHPRC) or the National Endowment for the Humanities. Historians can finally attend workshop and summer schools like the annual Institute for the Editing of Historical Documents, sponsored by the ADE and supported with funding from the NHPRC.

Notes

1 See Chapter 8.
2 For an overview of crowdsourcing, see Chapter 8.
3 Archive Founder website, http://archives.chadwyck.com/home.do (accessed August 17, 2015).
4 See for instance the notes on editorial method for the digital edition of John Adams' Papers, www.masshist.org/publications/apde2/view?id=ADMS-06-15-01-0007&mode=fb (accessed May 23, 2015).
5 While 760 people have signed up for accounts for the PWD project, only 125 actively transcribed in the past 90 days (Parry 2012).
6 See Chapters 1 and 8.
7 Minimum Standards for Electronic Editions, http://documentaryediting.org/resources/about/standards.html. The website is no longer available but can be accessed through the Wayback machine (www.archive.org).

Bibliography

American Society for Indexing. "Find an Indexer." 2015, www.asindexing.org/find-an-indexer/asi-indexer-locator/ (accessed August 15, 2015).

The Association for Documentary Editing. "About Documentary Editing." Undated, www.documentaryediting.org/wordpress/?page_id=482 (accessed August 17, 2015).

Burke, Frank G. "The Historian as Editor: Progress and Problems." *The Public Historian*, 4/2 (Spring 1982): 4–19.

Causer, Tim, Tonra, Justin, and Wallace, Valerie. "Transcription Maximized: Expense Minimized? Crowdsourcing and Editing The Collected Works of Jeremy Bentham." *Literary and Linguistic Computing*, 27/2 (March 2012): 119–137.

Coles, Laura Miller. "'Two Souls with but a Single Thought'? The Evolving Relationship Between Archivists and Editors." *Documentary Editing*, 16/2 (June 1994): 43–46.

Eppard, Philip B. "The Archivist's Perspective: Implications for Documentary Editing." *Documentary Editing*, 16/2 (June 1994): 47–50.

Falk, Candace. "Documentary Editors: Not as Boring as It Sounds." In *Public History. Essays from the*

Field, edited by James Gardner and Peter LaPaglia, Malabar: Krieger Publishing Company, 2006, 87–102.

Hajo, Cathy M. "The Sustainability of the Scholarly Edition in a Digital World." *Proceedings of the International Symposium on XML for the Long Haul: Issues in the Long-term Preservation of XML*. Balisage Series on Markup Technologies, vol. 6 (2010), online version, www.balisage.net/Proceedings/vol6/html/Hajo01/BalisageVol6-Hajo01.html (accessed May 12, 2015).

Huitfeldt, Claus and Sperburg-McQueen, C.M. "What is Transcription?" *Literary and Linguistic Computing*, 23/3 (September 2008): 295–310.

Kasdorf, William. *The Columbia Guide to Digital Publishing*, New York: Columbia University Press, 2003.

Katz, Esther. "The Editor as Public Authority: Interpreting Margaret Sanger." *The Public Historian*, 17/1 (Winter 1995): 41–50.

Kaya, Travis, "Crowdsourcing Project Hopes to Make Short Work of Transcribing Bentham." *The Chronicle of Higher Education*, September 13, 2010, http://chronicle.com/blogs/wiredcampus/crowdsourcing-project-hopes-to-make-short-work-of-transcribing-bentham/26829 (accessed August 17, 2015).

Kline, Mary-Jo and Perdue, Susan H., eds. *A Guide to Documentary Editing*, third edition, Charlottesville: University of Virginia Press, 2008, http://gde.upress.virginia.edu/ (accessed August 16, 2015).

Library of Congress. "MARC Code List for Organizations." April 21, 2015, www.loc.gov/marc/organizations/ (accessed August 17, 2015).

Massachussetts Historical Society. "Creation of Digital Edition." Undated, www.masshist.org/publications/apde2/creation (accessed August 17, 2015).

Massey, Gregory D. "The Papers of Henry Laurens and Modern Historical Documentary Editing." *The Public Historian*, 27/1 (Winter 2005): 39–60.

Merrell, James H. "'Exactly as they appear': Another Look at the Notes of a 1766 Treason Trial in Poughkeepsie, New York, with Some Musings on the Documentary Foundations of Early American History." *Early American Studies*, 12 (Winter 2014): 202–237.

Modern Language Association. "Guidelines for Editors of Scholarly Editions." MLA website, undated, www.mla.org/cse_guidelines (accessed August 17, 2015).

Morrison, Alan, Popham, Michael, and Wikander, Karen. *Creating and Documenting Electronic Texts: A Guide to Good Practice*, Oxford: Oxbow Books, 2001, http://ota.ox.ac.uk/documents/creating/cdet/index.html (accessed May 13, 2015).

Mulvany, Nancy C. *Indexing Books*, Chicago: University of Chicago Press, 1994.

Papers of the War Department. "Transcription Guideline." 2007, http://wardepartmentpapers.org/scripto/help.php (accessed August 16, 2015).

Parry, Marc. "Historians Ask the Public to Help Organize the Past." *Chronicle of Higher Education*, September 3, 2012, http://chronicle.com/article/Historians-Ask-the-Public-to/134054/ (accessed May 2, 2015).

Pierazzo, Elena. "A Rationale of Digital Documentary Editions." *Literary and Linguistic Computing*, 26/4 (2011): 463–477.

Pierazzo, Elena. "Digital Documentary Editions and the Others." *Scholarly Editing*, 35 (2014), www.scholarlyediting.org/2014/essays/essay.pierazzo.html (accessed March 17, 2015).

Schulz, Constance B. "Do Archivists Need to Know How to be Editors? A Proposal for the Role of Documentary Editing in Graduate Archival Education." *Documentary Editing*, 16/1 (March 1994): 5–9.

Schulz, Constance B. "Pouring Old Editorial Wine into New Digital Bottles." *Historically Speaking*, 14/5 (2013): 16–18.

Stevens, Michael E. and Burg, Steven B., eds. *Editing Historical Documents: A Handbook of Practice*, Walnut Creek: AltaMira Press, 1997.

Tarter, Brent. "Editing Public Records." In *Public History: An Introduction*, edited by Barbara Howe and Emory L. Kemp, Malabar: Robert E. Krieger Publishing Company, 1986, 70–83.

Transcribe Bentham. "Help:Transcription Guidelines." Undated, www.transcribe-bentham.da.ulcc.ac.uk/td/Help:Transcription_Guidelines (accessed August 17, 2015).

University of South Carolina. "Model Editions Partnership: Historical Editions in the Digital Age." 2000, http://wyatt.elasticbeanstalk.com/mep/ (accessed August 17, 2015).

Vanhoutte, Edward and Van den Branden, Ron. "Describing, Transcribing, Encoding, and Editing Modern Correspondence Material: A Textbase Approach." *Literary and Linguistic Computing*, 24/1 (April 2009): 77–98.

Wellisch, Hans H. *Indexing from A to Z*, Bronx: H.W. Wilson, 1991.

6   Interpreting and Exhibiting the Past

Sites and Purposes of Interpretation

Public Historians and Interpretation

This chapter discusses public access to historical sites and collections via the exhibition medium. In order to make collections and sites accessible the most familiar vehicle is the exhibit "which can take the form of a furnished historic house, a gallery display of similar items, or an interpretive exhibit organized by theme and carrying heavy educational baggage" (Woodhouse 2006, 192). Whether it is hosted by a museum, a website, or a historic house, an exhibition offers a material version of history that is often more accessible to the public than a scholarly article or monograph. Objects and material culture are the core of the exhibition design and help the creation of historical realism (Pearce 1994; Bennett 1998). As Svetlana Alpers underlines, museums and exhibitions are "a way of seeing" the past, the world, and the contemporary societies (1991). This "way of seeing" is based on the process of interpreting the past through objects, images, and space.

The public access to sites and collections makes exhibitions a key activity for public historians. In a recent article on the process of creating exhibitions, Richard Rabinowitz stresses "the vital importance of having historians—and not just designers and media producers—at the center of these creative decisions" (2013, 9). On the one hand, public historians may have to design exhibitions from beginning to end – especially for small institutions – or may have to collaborate with different actors such as curators, designers, interpretive planers, and marketing officers. On the other hand, public historians must remain aware of and willing to collaborate with the public in order to make exhibiting design more collaborative. In order to design exhibitions and interpret historic sites, public historians must know the basic requirements of complex processes (Bennett 1988; Kirshenblatt-Gimblett 2006).

The role of public historians may vary according to the degree of interpretation. In his book on museum exhibition, David Dean distinguishes between displays that "generally refer to a presentation of objects for public view without significant interpretation added," exhibits that "usually mean the localized grouping of objects and interpretive materials that form a cohesive unit within a gallery," and exhibitions that "allude to a comprehensive grouping of all elements (including exhibits and displays) that form a complete public presentation of collections and information for the public use" (Dean 1996, 3). Organizers have to choose between two main sorts of exhibitions: object or idea driven (McKenna-Cress and Kamien 2013, 74–78). An object-driven exhibit is "a presentation of objects purely for the objects' sake; no interpretive information is involved. It is like setting a collection of vases or ceramic figures on a shelf in a home" (Dean 1996, 4). However, it might also be argued that the act of collection and arrangement – through the selection – is one of interpretation, even if no written labels accompany the objects. At the other end of the spectrum, idea-driven exhibits barely rely on objects, and use much more text and graphic design to convey their message (Lord and Piacente 2014, 133–135). Interpretive centers are the best examples of idea-driven exhibitions. They rely on a limited number of artifacts and are usually based on multimedia technology like the 1798 National Visitor Center in Enniscorthy (Ireland), which interprets the 1798 Irish Rebellion through games, multimedia technology, and re-enactment.

Sites and Purposes of Interpretation

The role of public historians depends on the site itself. Exhibitions may be mounted in many different sites. Museums, historic house museums, heritage/interpretive centers, and historic sites are among the main categories. All those sites bear some similarities, but the format of the exhibition may also differ on important aspects. If any site can host exhibitions, historic sites remain the favorite space for non-museum historical exhibitions. The interest largely comes from the fact that historic sites are places where objects can be displayed in their original contexts. Historic places have powerful and provocative stories to tell. As the National Park Service's (NPS) *Teaching with Historic Places* guide stresses, "Places make connections across time that give them a special ability to create an empathetic understanding of what happened and why" (NPS undated). Historic houses offer a privileged site of display as well. Historic house museums have a long history (Butler 2008). Historians can draw on many different studies, guides, and other resources for insight on house museums (Donnelly 2002; Butcher-Younghans 1996; American House Museum 1998).

Interpretation can vary according to the component of the site, but the main difference comes from the purposes of the institution. The purpose can differ depending on whether the site is a public or commercial institution. As Dean explains, while a commercial institution "has as a goal the selling of a product or services for financial gain," exhibits designed by public institutions aim at "informing the public and changing attitudes and behaviors" (1996, 2). In her article "Heritage, Commerce, and Museal Display," Tammy Gordon provides a rich list of exhibition types, and details the different requirements for public historians (Gordon 2008, 2010). According to the site, exhibitions may have several objectives, such as supporting the institution financially by attracting donors and funding; promoting the institution as an appropriate site of conservation/preservation; and/or promoting and engaging with the communities, companies, and ethnic minorities linked to the institution. Regardless of the type of institution, the relevance and weight of marketing policy in the exhibition process has greatly increased since the 1990s. In many large institutions, the marketing department has been the main field of staff increase. One consequence has been the changing definition of exhibition success, sometimes merely depending on attendance and profit figures. Public historians should help balancing marketing strategy with more educational purposes in the definition of success.

Until recently, a large majority of exhibitions have been mounted in museums, so it is important for public historians to understand the concept of interpretation in museums and their changing role while communicating with the public (Hooper-Greenhill 2001). Exhibitions are part of the functions of museums (Lord and Piacente 2014, 8–10). The role of museums – and public exhibitions – has greatly changed since the 1960s (Mason 2006; Marstine 2005; Smithsonian undated). Regarding historic house museums – but the statement can be enlarged to any site of interpretation – McDaniel argues that interpretation "has changed significantly in recent years and has become one of the most challenging areas in which to work" (McDaniel 2006, 244). Exhibitions now include a broader range of interpretive media, and reflect multilayered contents. Interpreting the past has also changed due to the new functions of museums and exhibiting sites. As for public history at large, the concept of access has become highly important.[1] New questions emerged such as what does the museum stand for? Whom is the museum for? Cultural diversity and the variety of approaches in displaying the past became topics of discussion (Karp and Lavine 1991; Carbonell 2004). For instance *Reinventing the Museum* is a collection of articles that address the need for "museums to remain relevant in society" through an ongoing process of internal and external assessment. Reinventing the museum is not just shifting programs, galleries, or financial security, rather, according to editor Gail Anderson, it is a "systemic shift in attitude, purpose, alignment, and execution" to reposition museums as central players in communities (2012, 1). Museums need to better understand their audiences, to provide more participatory experiences, and truly understand educational theory when developing new programming or exhibitions. In other words, "the focus needs to be on the learner, not on the subject to be learned" (Anderson 2012, 128). Public historians who are part of exhibition process must therefore take users into consideration, and know that communicating knowledge and methods of display greatly matter. Exhibition is part of the institution's "communication of meaning" (Lord and Piacente 2014, 10–14).

Collaboration and Public Participation

Exhibitions are collaborative practice so that public historians must be able to work in teams of many different actors. Rules of collaboration, team strategy, and communication are therefore part of exhibition design (McKenna-Cress and Kamien 2013, 7–38). Collaboration is not only interdisciplinary, but can also be international. For instance, the Museums Connect program "strengthens connections and cultural understanding between people in the United States and abroad" (American Alliance of Museums undated). For example, in 2011, the Ben M'Sik Community Museum in Casablanca (Morocco) and the Museum of History and Holocaust Education at Kennesaw (Georgia, USA), collaborated to produce *Identities: Understanding Islam in a Cross Cultural Context*, an online exhibition to increase knowledge about each other's cultural traditions and promote conversations within communities.

Exhibitions can also be undertaken with public participation. As Bill Adair, Benjamin Filene, and Laura Koloski explain in the introduction of their collection on participatory projects, participation has two main origins: first the legacy of the New Social History of the 1960s and its interest in telling history from the bottom-up, and second the more recent development of Web 2.0 that "invites ordinary people to become their own archivists, curators, historians, and designers" (Adair et al. 2011, 11). There is a need to set visitors at the center of attention. In the preface of her landmark work on the *Participatory Museum*, Nina Simon explains that we need this type of institution due to the public dissatisfaction with traditional exhibitions (Simon 2010). According to her, institutions are criticized by visitors for being irrelevant to their life, for never changing, for not including the visitor's voice, and for not allowing visitors to express themselves. One simple answer, for Simon, "is to invite visitors to participate in the construction of the interpretation alongside professionals" (Simon 2011, 20). In putting visitors at the center of the process, exhibit designers echo the current trend of shared authority in public history. This makes exhibitions especially relevant for public historians.

Participatory design is complex and is by no means limited to the use of interactive technology. Participatory experiences are designed to evoke questions, responses, and emotions, to challenge visitors to interact with each other, and build social spaces. Participatory museums not only engage with their visitors, but they make them part of the exhibition process as well (McKenna-Cress and Kamien 2013, 168–170). It is important not only to solicit visitors' opinions, but to give them real work as well (Simon 2015). Visitors become users and participants. Satwicz and Morrissey thus argue for a "public curation" used as "an umbrella term to encompass 'participatory design', 'user-driven content', and the broad and creative range of ways public (or non-professional) audiences are increasingly and collaboratively involved in shaping museum products" (Satwicz and Morrissey 2011, 196). For instance, Nina Simon offers three main options to create a truly participatory experience that reaches a broad audience and redefines the learning environment and educational mission of a museum. In contributory projects, visitors can be "solicited to provide limited and specified objects, actions, or ideas to an institutionally controlled process." In collaborative projects, she argues, "visitors are invited to serve as active partners in the creation of institutional projects that are originated and ultimately controlled by the institution." Finally, in co-creative projects, "community members work together with institutional staff members from the beginning to define the project's goals and to generate the program or exhibit based on community interests" (Simon 2010, ch. 5; McKenna-Cress and Kamien 2013, 170–190).

Each institution has to decide how to implement public participation (MacArthur 2007). The debates are no longer about whether museums are participatory or not, but rather how they can properly apply participatory techniques. As Simon points out, "Not every visitor has a powerful personal story to recount or dizzying expertise to share" (Simon 2011, 22). Participation does not mean turning control to users, but finding a way to convert their contributions into action (Simon 2011, 31). In order to do so, it is possible to foster participatory construction at every step of the exhibition process.

Project Development and Interpretive Planning

Evaluating Institutions and their Audiences

Sites and Institutions

Interpretive planning details the different steps that lead to the interpretation and exhibition of the past (Division of Interpretive Planning 1998, 2). Before going into details about the interpretation and display of the collections, public historians should know about two critical aspects: the institution and its audiences. Historians working in, or commissioned by, an institution should learn about the site itself. Historians must study the institution's mission plan and any possible previous interpretive design in order to understand the role and function of the institution. On the one hand, exhibition can indeed reflect and respect the institutional identity (McKenna-Cress and Kamien 2013, 50–60). On the other hand, exhibition can also play an important part in an institution's efforts to redefine its identities and gain new visitors and community partners. Public historians must know about the collections through an inventory of objects, their conditions, and the required environmental precautions needed for their use (Dean 1996, 16). The accurate knowledge of the collection helps determine the possible external loans necessary to mount the exhibit. This step is particularly important for historic house museums and historic sites. Interpreters must know what the site is about, and how the site would meet the need for audiences (Abramoff Levy 2002, 44). This resource inventory determines what the strengths and weaknesses of the site/museum are.

Audiences

Evaluating audiences is more complex and requires different techniques. In his article about the role of historian in curating exhibition, Rabinowitz admits, "visitors themselves bring the most potent mediating devices—their own experiences, expectations, and habits of mind, not to say the circumstances of the visit and the social interactions they have with companions" (Rabinowitz 2013, 9). It is therefore vital to know more about who visits the institution. This is why Steven Lubar gives the following piece of advice:

> Don't spend all of your time in the back rooms of the museum with the collections or in the library with the researcher or in front of the computer with the designer. Get out there on the museum floor. Watch your visitors. Talk to them. See what works and what doesn't.
>
> (Lubar 2014, 74)

Through evaluation and visitor studies, cultural institutions have been looking for new ways to better understand, serve, and reach their audiences. Evaluation can take several shapes according to the institution's objectives (Dean 1996, 98–102). Evaluations can help institutions to better define their audiences, to know what they want and what they do, and to understand how they learn. In her *Practical Evaluation Guide*, Judy Diamond gives instructions on how to design, implement, and present an evaluation study (1999, 16–17). She introduces three main types of evaluation. The front-end evaluation provides background information for future program planning, the formative evaluation provides information about how a program or exhibit can be improved, and the summative evaluation tells about the impact of a project after it is completed. Although the rise of evaluation is linked to marketing policy, it is important for public historians to use them to adapt exhibition projects.

Audience research first gives institutions a clue about who visits exhibitions (McKenna-Cress and Kamien 2013, 30–33, 40–56). Prior knowledge and personal expectations craft the visitor's experience. Therefore, understanding someone's motivation allows professionals to develop interpretive plans that help meet the needs of diverse visitors and even help to create unique marketing messages to appeal to specific motivation groups. Designing an exhibition for school children, tourists, scholars, engineers, or veterans implies different techniques.

Actors involved in the exhibition process must know how to analyze visitors (Lindauer 2005; Korn 1992, 1994). In addition to a rich literature, public historians can consult journals, associations, research groups, and actors of museum education.[2] Evaluations should be analyzed in line with the literature on visitors regarding their visiting habits, motivations, prior knowledge, and social roles at the time of the visit (Dean 1996, 20–23; Cameron and Gatewood 2000). Museums, according to Faulk and Dierking, "have become ... one of the most important leisure-time venues in the world" (2012, 15). Visitors want to enjoy their time in exhibitions, and a large majority of them want interaction. Interaction limits museum fatigue by creating new relations between visitors and materials. Visits from school groups and children appear particularly challenging for museum professionals. In order to better design exhibitions, professionals must be aware of the specificity of children learning (McRainey and Russick 2010; Vukelich 1984).

It is also necessary to understand what visitors do during exhibitions. As Dean explains, there are three main categories of behaving in exhibitions. There are visitors who move quickly through galleries and show "exitoriented behaviour." They are often casual visitors who are not heavily involved. The second category shows "a genuine interest in the museum experience and the collections … but do not spend much time reading." The third category is composed of a minority of visitors who examine exhibitions with much more attention (Dean 1996, 25–26). With an average read time of ten seconds or less per label, more than 90 percent of visitors do not read museum labels fully. It is therefore necessary to be inventive in terms of design.

In summative evaluations, it is critical to assess what visitors have learned, and how their own background and knowledge have participated in creating meaning during the visits. MATRICE is a recent innovative example of evaluation.[3] This international research group is composed of historians, sociologists, anthropologists, curators, media analysts, designers, psychoanalysts, neuroscientists, and computer scientists. Working with the Peace Memorial Museum in Caen (France), the group uses eye-tracking and captors to understand not only where visitors go in the museum, but also what objects, texts – or part of them – they watch and for how long. The ongoing research helps museum professionals to study questions such as the relations between texts and images for the visitor learning process, the impact of light/design on visitor behavior, and more specific questions such as the attraction/repulsion of historical representations of violence.

Design Brief and Interpretive Planning

Requirements

Interpretive planning is a collaborative process in which historians are part of teams with curators, designers, educators, researchers, and exhibit planners. The role of curators is "to select appropriate objects, contribute to the content of the script, and ensure that collections are displayed with respect for the meaning they convey and their physical preservation" (Woodhouse 2006, 193). Lubar explains that historians may have two main activities: historical and museological. According to him, the historical task is:

> to undertake the research necessary to draw out the historical truth of the object that is, to discover the ways in which history is reflected in it. In doing so, historians may work as or collaborate with curators. The museological task follows closely: to discover ways of exhibiting that history to the museum visitor.
>
> (Lubar 1986, 223)

In other words, the historical part belongs to the creation of the design brief or interpretive planning while the museological role of historians is part of the exhibiting design process.

The design brief or interpretive planning is the document/process that plans and organizes the interpretation and design of the exhibit (Hughes 2010, 24–34). Goal-driven, the interpretive planning helps "make sure that consensus has been reached on the results to be achieved" (Division of Interpretive Planning 1998, 8). One major initial part of the interpretive planning is the definition of the exhibit's big idea (Serrell 1996; Lord and Piacente 2014, 244–249). The big idea provides the key message of the exhibition. The interpretive planning can also contain the different concepts that drive the exhibit (Lord and Piacente 2014, 241–244). The team should be able to sum up the exhibit's big idea into a few sentences. The big idea also has educational value. As Barbara Abramoff Levy explains, "the most effective memorable learning often occurs when we are asked to focus on a few important big ideas that are used as umbrella for smaller ideas ... repetition is a key to retention" (2002, 48). Steven Lubar suggests the option of writing a preliminary press release first, so that the team would know what the exhibit is really about (1986, 221). The necessary clarity of the big idea does not mean the exhibit cannot contain a plurality of interpretations and voices. On the contrary, it is important that the team keeps room for a diversity of representations and for public participation. The specific role of the historian may be to present his/her research on the historical component and interest of the big idea, possibly the historiographical debates, and the links with the institution and audiences.

The big idea and concepts must then be organized into a cohesive narrative, or storyline, for which the role of historian is vital (McKenna-Cress and Kamien 2013, 108–113). The storyline is not simply a linear representation of the exhibit. It may be composed of several elements: a narrative document, an outline of the exhibition, a list of titles and subtitles, and a list of objects (Dean 1996, 103). The narrative document is a well-researched manuscript that includes the sources, archives, and literature about the topic. Based on this document, the outline presents a more simple presentation of the story that must be accessible for every actor of the process. The relevance of the storyline can vary according to sites and exhibitions. Rabinowitz argues for a narrative exhibition that "clusters its documents and artifacts as elements of a single storyline, as would the scenes in a novel or feature film" (2013, 12). The storyline is the glue that makes sense to objects and materials. So, in this case, the storyline affects directly and in a very powerful way the exhibit design.

The storyline also helps selecting objects and materials for the exhibit. The selection is based on the practice of interpreting objects to convey meanings. Public historians may use different resources about objects and historical interpretation (Schlereth 1982; Pearce 1994; Phillips 2005). Using original documents and objects is an asset but also a challenge for institutions. For instance, Rabinowitz underlines that "Conservators often want documents to lie flat (or almost flat) in an exhibit case, which would make them hard for many to read" (2013, 28). For written documents, the challenge is always to decide what pages should be on display since visitors may not access other parts of the work. The opposite situation arises when too few – or no – objects remain about certain aspects of the themes. Historians and curators have to be particularly inventive and rely on specific design, multimedia, or art works (Rabinowitz 2011).

The interpretive planning must also decide the shape of the exhibit. The display can be permanent, changing, or traveling. This decision determines not only the scope but also the design and space of the exhibit (Lord and Piacente 2014, 99–101). As we'll see below, temporary exhibitions have their own logistics and rationale (Lord and Piacente 2014, 197–207).

Visitors and Public Participation

Visitors – at least in terms of target – should be part of every step of the process. The content of the exhibit must be developed with users in mind (McKenna-Cress and Kamien 2013,

89–100). For instance, the USA Visitor Services Association produced a *Bill of Rights* that explains the main obligations of exhibitors regarding visitors (Hughes 2010, 36). The interpretive planning should consider the various ways in which new audiences could be reached and could participate in the process. One way to reach broader audiences is to expand the space of exhibition. This can be done through publications (brochure, catalogues, DVD), social media, or online exhibition (Wallace 2014, 29–39). The exhibit *Modern Wife, Modern Life* at the National Print Museum of Ireland is an excellent example of an exhibit's reach through social media, particularly Twitter, and through a blog.[4]

This can also be done by bringing the exhibit to different communities. Traveling – or portable – exhibits provide new sets of opportunities (Lord and Piacente 2014, 207–217; McKenna-Cress and Kamien 2013, 178–183). Traveling displays expand the space of exhibitions and multiply the opportunities for collaboration. Figure 6.1 shows a 1954 Airstream Trailer used by the University of Louisiana at Lafayette's public history program. Students and faculty refurbished the trailer in 2013 and have been using it to mount and display exhibits in public space. The trailer allows to bring historical exhibits to public libraries (Figure 6.1), schools, festivals, markets, and other public events. The trailer is, itself, an interesting piece of the exhibit as visitors are intrigued by the unusual format. The format of the exhibit helps create public engagement.

New and unusual spaces of exhibition can also be chosen. For instance, De Groot mentions British museums that "put exhibits in shopping centres in order to expand their appeal." Other exhibits, such as the *Curiosity Shop*, were set up in empty units.[5] The entire public space may become a site for curation and exhibition. Obviously, specific challenges such as loan agreements and tour management have to be considered (Lord and Piacente 2014, 210–211, 213–215). But many different resources and examples exist such as the Smithsonian Institution Traveling Exhibition Service (SITES) and Exhibits USA that provide a broad range of temporary exhibitions to museums nationwide (Genoways and Ireland 2003, 156).

Figure 6.1 Museum on the Move, exhibit trailer, in front of the Lafayette Public Library, Lafayette (Louisiana), 2014. Courtesy of the University of Louisiana at Lafayette's Public History program.

Public historians can also contribute to the development of public engagement. The local community is often the most obvious public partner. The community can take part in every step of the interpretive planning and exhibit design. Public participation can be implemented from the initial step of interpretive planning. For instance, the Brooklyn Historical Society set up an advisory group that sent out a call for ideas for its new exhibition (Schwartz and Adair 2011, 113). Responders had to show images and give a sense of what the preliminary checklist would be for the exhibits. The Brooklyn Historical Society's advisory group merely provided technical assistance but no conceptual or content design (Schwartz and Adair 2011, 114–115). Likewise, the Minnesota Historical Society organized the *MN150* project to celebrate the 150th anniversary of the state's founding. *MN150* was a permanent exhibition of 150 topics that "transformed Minnesota." The team of organizers involved communities to give a broader account of the cultural diversity in the state. The team decided to solicit communities to decide what topics should be exhibited. The interpretive planning can, therefore, become a participatory process.

Public participation can also affect the selection of objects. Communities can provide a few selected objects and materials for exhibits. For instance, the London Science Museum mounted an exhibition called *Playing with Science* about the history of science-related toys, for which the museum asked visitors to bring their own toys for special events. Visitors' toys were displayed in vitrines at the end of the exhibit. Contributors were photographed with their favorite toy and wrote short statements. Objects from communities may also become the entire exhibit. The Northern Irish group Healing Through Remembering decided to mount an exhibit about the Northern Irish Conflict. The group solicited the public to avoid unilateral and imposed interpretation on this divisive topic. An artifact audit was undertaken in 2008. Public and private collectors were "invited to lend one artifact that responds to the overall theme and to write a label to accompany their object" (Healing Through Remembering undated). Entitled *Everyday Objects Transformed by the Conflict*, the exhibition was launched in 2011. Public involvement allowed to personalize the display and to connect visitors with objects in many ways.

The public can also help decide what should be on display. Nina Simon mentions the Worcester City Art Gallery and Museum (United Kingdom) that launched *Top 40: Countdown of Worcester's Favorite Pictures*. The team of designers purposefully created the *Top 40* with minimal labels, but included voting stations in the middle of the gallery "where visitors could use paper ballots to vote for a favorite painting and explain their reasoning" (Simon 2011, 24). The staff then used a selection of visitors' comments to rank the paintings the weekly and to design labels. Figure 6.2 shows a similar experience at the Brooklyn Museum in 2008. Developed by Shelley Bernstein, *Click! A Crowd-Curated Exhibition* is a fantastic example of crowdsourcing. Based on the concept that a diverse crowd is often wiser at making decisions than expert individuals, the project began in March 2008 with an open call for photographs depicting the changing faces of Brooklyn. Three hundred and eighty-nine images were collected and then evaluated by the public through online rating tools (Figure 6.2).[6] Public participation therefore influenced both the collection and evaluation of materials. The top 20 percent – according to public rating – of the 389 photographs were selected to be part of the display (Figure 6.2). Importantly, photographs were displayed by size according to their relative ranking within this percentile. Visitors were also able to see how different groups within the crowd evaluated the same photographs. In the end, the Brooklyn Museum merely provided the framework – online and physical – to crowdsourced representations of the past.

Figure 6.2 (a) *Click! A Crowd-Curated Exhibition.* Brooklyn Museum, 2008. Credit: Brooklyn
    Museum photograph. Courtesy of the Brooklyn Museum. (b) Screenshot of the rating
    tools, 2008. Courtesy of the Brooklyn Museum.

A participatory exhibit not only creates interactivity, but also helps connect users to each
other, and ultimately creates new knowledge. It is important to give visitors the possibility
to do something concrete for the exhibit. The interpretive planning may prepare space for
public participation throughout the exhibit with recording devices, stands to write comments, and other practical activities. The relevance of the visitors/users may be even more
direct in the creation of knowledge. For instance, the United States Holocaust Memorial
Museum (USHMM) designed a project/exhibit called *Children of the Lodz Ghetto.* Through
the project, the USHMM invited users all over the world "to help track the paths of several
thousand Polish children affected by the Holocaust." The project/exhibit was conceived to
"get better the more people used it." The designers "addressed the challenge of authenticat-
ing data by involving users in the vetting of each other's work" (Simon 2011, 28–29). The
final exhibit was the result of public participation.

In spite of the benefit of participatory production, it also has some challenges. Howell
argues that "what the public wants out of its history may not always be what the interpreter
feels is best for them." Sometimes, visitors come seeking a reaffirmation of lost ideals
(Howell 2006, 143). Public historians involved in the exhibition design may help facilitate
the dialogue on historical topics and interpretation.[7]

Interpretive Planning at Historic Sites

Interpretive planning is necessary for historic houses and historic sites too. It is "meant to
guide a site in determining what meanings and relationships it wants to reveal, as well as
how and for whom it should do this" (Abramoff Levy 2002, 43). Even more than for traditional museums, knowledge of the site is crucial since it is entirely part of the display and
interpretive process. This is why interpreters at historic houses and historic sites are strongly
encouraged to write a 3–5 page essay on the historical significance of the site (Abramoff

Levy 2002, 47). The essay and the institution's mission statement help to tell the story of the site (Glines and Grabitske 2003).

The difference between traditional museum exhibits and interpretation at historic sites partly comes from the techniques used to deliver messages. It is important for historic houses and historic sites' interpreters to organize an interpretive planning that connects the site, its collections, and visitors. Most historic houses design furnishing plans to create, maintain, and interpret specific objects in the different parts of the house (Brooks 2002). Among the various techniques and activities (traditional display, re-enactment, multimedia devices), tours are by far the most common tools for interpretation (Donnelly 2002, 14). Plenty of tours are available online.[8] One common mistake to avoid is to limit tours to objects and decorative arts (Donnelly 2002, 2). Tours should propose larger frameworks of interpretation. For instance, the site's exterior settings may be included in the interpretive planning. Issues such as the owners' relations with the local community, neighborhood, or town can help enrich the interpretation (Donnelly 2002, 7). It is also important to consider who built the house, who worked in the house, and what their lives were like. For instance, both Stagville State Historic Site in Durham (former plantation in North Carolina) and Whitney Plantation (Louisiana) are sites with a main house and slave dwellings where their tours focus on different spaces as the sites of power negotiation. At the end of the interpretive planning, the team has stories to tell, and it is then necessary to decide how the team can actually tell those stories; this is the role of the interpretive/exhibit design.

Exhibit Design: Space, Objects, and Visitors

Exhibit Space

The obvious main role of historians is to make sure objects are displayed in a historical context that suits the interpretive planning. In order to facilitate historical interpretation, objects can be arranged in contextual settings. The context can appear through period rooms – especially in historic houses – or through documents and items that inform the visitors about the objects' creation and use, or through interpretive documents (labels, panels, video, sound explanation) (Lubar 1986, 224). In addition to the historical context, historians should understand the basics of exhibition design.

Designing an exhibit is a long process (Lord and Piacente 2014, 294–298; Smithsonian undated). Historians can consult lots of different resources (Zotero undated). Public historians must have design skills to understand the whole concept of exhibit space (McKenna-Cress and Kamien 2013, 80–100). Dean defines exhibition design as "the art and science of arranging the visual, spatial, and material elements of an environment into a composition that visitors move through" (1996, 32). Exhibition design is about space. Objects should always be considered in their spatial environment (Communications Design Team 1999). Rabinowitz points out that the design "starts with understanding the physical space of the building and its sequence of distinct areas" (2013, 14). To be more accurate, exhibition design deals with the relationship between space, objects, and visitors. Indeed, while vision remains the principal mediation between objects and visitors, "what people perceive through wholesensory experience is retained far better than that gained through sight alone. A person will remember more about what he or she does" (Dean 1996, 27). Experience is linked to both visitors' spatial environment and their social role in the visitor group, which is why the design needs to accommodate diverse social needs (Leinhardt and Knudson 2004). Figure 6.3 represents a preliminary sketch designed for an exhibition at the National

Figure 6.3 Preliminary concept produced by designers working with an exhibit team at the National Museum of American History in 2007. The exhibit was to be called "Explore American History" but was never completed due to lack of funding. Illustration by Stevan Fisher, concept by Christopher Chadbourne and Associates, 2007. Courtesy of James B. Gardner.

Museum of American History in 2007. The sketch provides information about the relations between objects, space, and visitors. It is necessary to consider the height and angle from which visitors would look at objects, as well as think about the itinerary that visitors would follow throughout the exhibition. The sketch demonstrates that designers should always have visitors in mind while conceiving exhibits.

The size and location of objects matter. For instance, some observers argue that "larger objects and moving objects produce longer viewing times" (Dean 1996, 27). The position of the visitors within the exhibition space has to be considered. Visitors should not feel "overly confined or exposed" (Dean 1996, 42). The standing height, the eye level, and the turning radius help decide where objects should stand (Dean 1996, 39). The alignment of objects – so the spatial relations between objects – equally matters. Too often, the different sensory stimuli – sound, smell, touch, taste – are not considered in the presentation of objects, but they can help visitors engage with the display.

In order to make the exhibit more accessible, the visitor flow must be taken into account as well (McKenna-Cress and Kamien 2013, 146–153). Exhibition strategy requires choosing a path (Hughes 2010, 75–78). Organizers can choose between different patterns: the single path or the multiple paths patterns, the radial pattern, or the star exhibit designed around outstanding objects (Hughes 2010, 75–76). The floor plan can be unstructured – giving freedom of movement to visitors – merely suggested, or directed – imposing a path to the visitors (Dean 1996, 53–54). All those patterns are, themselves, divided into sub-spaces like collection spaces, distributional spaces, or transitional spaces with certain particularities that affect objects and visitors (Dean 1996, 50). For instance, transitional spaces help promote shifts in attention and limit "museum fatigue" (Bitgood 2009). In historic houses, one way to create transitional spaces is to vary the themes of display through the creation of moment-in-time installation (Villa Bryk 2002, 145). Rooms can be furnished according to specific scenes of everyday life or, if allowed by the site, major scenes of the owners' lives. Certain objects and memorabilia – newspapers, calendars, letters, and advertising – can help visitors identify the date and context of the room (Villa Bryk 2002, 146–151).

Besides, in order to choose between the different flows, organizers have to know the basic of traffic strategy. In Western countries (North America and Europe), it seems that visitors tend to turn to the right when entering an open or unstructured area. Once moving to the right, most people will stay to the right, leaving exhibits on the left less viewed (Dean 1996, 51). Likewise, mostly due to visitors' fatigue, objects near the exit received less attention than those at the entrance. According to some observation, while the center of the room is the focus of attention in oriental cultures, it is left as a transactional area in Western cultures (Dean 1996, 51). Although not a scientific rule, this sort of observation helps obtain more attention from visitors. Once chosen, the path can be designed with the various signs and environmental graphics used by organizers to present the exhibit and orientate visitors (Hughes 2010, 56–73). In addition to the variety of signs – maps, icons, and boards – organizers can also use strategies and *mise-en-scène* (Mollerup 2006, 34–42, 48–52, 82–86, 127–193).

Changing the lighting, color, type of objects, types of media, helps create curiosity (Dean 1996, 31). Some knowledge of colors – such as value, texture, balance, line, and shape – and lighting are important (Dean 1996, 33–35; Hughes 2010, 145). A lighting plan may be necessary (Hughes 2010, 130–153). Lighting participates in the construction of attraction/repulsion throughout exhibitions. Although the meaning of colors differs according to cultures, it seems that people tend to avoid dark spaces in museums and historic sites (Laganier and van der Pol 2011). All these components of graphic design help ultimately the fabrication and disposition of display cases/windows (Lord and Piacente 2014, 305–314, 359–373).

Public and Exhibition Design

As for other steps in the exhibiting process, the public can play a role. Instead of delivering the same contents to every visitor, it is important to adapt the exhibition to the different needs and motivations of users (Simon 2011, 21). Ideally, the organizers should strive to layer the exhibit for diverse audiences and accommodate their various needs and learning styles (Lord and Piacente 2014, 253–255; Hughes 2010, 34–56). The *Museum Education Principles and Standards* recommends to "Provide multiple levels and points of entry into content, including intellectual, physical, cultural, individual, group, and intergenerational" (American Association of Museums 2005, 6). The exhibit may be layered for various lengths of visits (short, medium, or long), for different interest groups (experts, children, families, etc.), with various preferred media (texts, sound, visual, hands-on activities) (Hughes 2010, 40–42).

It may also be possible to involve the public to create a plurality of voices within the display. During the presentation of the Guantánamo Public Memory Project at the International Civil Rights Center and Museum in Greensboro, visitors were asked to participate in a poll regarding the use of Guantánamo. Figure 6.4 shows the entrance poll in which visitors were asked to vote – through a token – on the questions "What Should Be

Figure 6.4 Guantánamo Public Memory Project. International Civil Rights Center and Museum, Greensboro, North Carolina (December 12, 2013 – February 14, 2014). Credit: Raina Fox. Courtesy of Guantánamo Public Memory Project.

Done with GITMO?"[9] The repartition of the votes – pretty even among the four possible choices – demonstrated that there was no easy answer to this simple question.

In order to increase visitors' experience, WWI in Flanders Field Museum (Belgium) gives visitors a personal "poppy" bracelet on arrival. The bracelet chip automatically sets the language choice and enables the visitor to discover the collections through one of the four personal stories. Memories – through testimonies, oral history, diaries, and other personal representations – give room to public participation. Through different media, testimonies can be recorded and provided in the display. In his essay on "exhibiting memories," Steven Lubar shows how the use of visitors' memories in exhibitions helps organizers to display the complexity of relations between memory, history, and mythology. As he argues, the "memories revealed a personal history that wasn't in the textbooks" (Lubar 1997, 20–21). Likewise, for its new exhibition in 2006 on the history of wars in Ireland, the National Museum of Northern Ireland (Belfast) used public memories to interpret and display the particularly divisive gallery on the Northern Irish Troubles. Instead of presenting a unilateral representation of the Troubles (1969–1998), the museum solicited public curation. The museum asked different groups of victims to choose objects from its collections – it could be a weapon used by paramilitary groups, a political poster, a photograph of the 1972 Bloody Sunday March, etc. – and to give their own memories associated with the objects. The voices were recorded and served as labels – through audio presentations – for the objects. This process contributed to the multiplicity of interpretations of the Troubles.

Another way to foster participatory process in exhibit is to display certain objects to spark discussion. For Nina Simon, "Social objects are the engines of socially networked experiences, the content around which conversation happens ... (they) allow people to focus their attention on a third thing rather than on each other, making interpersonal engagement more comfortable" (2010, ch. 4). One interesting use of provocative objects was at the Science Museum of Minnesota in 2007. Curators used stacks of money to represented income disparities between races and the stacks became a focal point for visitor discussions. "The powerful physical metaphor [of the stacks] made the information presented feel more spectacular without dumbing it down or overdressing" (Simon 2010, 131–132). Another excellent use of this is the Eastern State Penitentiary's *The Big Graph*, which visually conveys increasing incarceration rates in the United States (Eastern State Penitentiary 2015).

Interpretive Texts

Contrary to what some curators may argue – especially in art museums where the staff often intend to limit intermediaries between art works and visitors – objects do not speak for themselves. Interpretation is needed. Interpretive tools for creating immersive environment – walking tours, multimedia devices, virtual reconstruction, and museum theater – are explored in Chapter 9; this part discusses the use of texts in interpretive design. Writing texts for exhibits and historic sites requires public historians to adopt specific rules (NPS 2008; Australian Museum 2008). In *Writing for Museums*, Margot Wallace breaks with traditional academic writing and encourages readers to consider not only their audience but also the medium of delivery and mode of consumption for their writing.[10] She details the different writing activities in museums such as social media, learning outcomes, newsletters, and so on (Wallace 2014). Panels and labels are the heart of exhibition texts.[11] For a long time, they were the main media between objects and visitors. Texts need to be part of the entire organizing process and not left for the end. Besides, texts should be connected to each other. For instance, the outline of the exhibition and storyline should be used to choose a title and to write texts (panels and labels) for the different sections.

Obviously, the first rule in writing interpretive text is an appropriate use of language. Many resources provide stylistic rules and guidelines, but these rules are not enough (Strunk and White 1999; Flaherty 2010). Texts must be clear and attract visitors' attention. Wallace offers some writing techniques from an institutional marketing and audience perspective (Wallace 2014). If historians want to write exhibit texts, they must work as text writers whose purpose is to collect content and research documents and to reduce the many pages of information into coherent and clear summaries. In doing so, it is important to write for an average visitor who has no previous knowledge of the topic. Collaboration is, again, vital. Texts should be submitted to collaborators and possibly to visitors for evaluation.

Texts for exhibitions are divided into three main categories: title, head texts and panels, and labels (Lord and Piacente 2014, 275–281). The title is an important piece of communication for the exhibition. As Dean underlines, the title "sets the tone and parameters of the exhibition and serves as a major part of the curiosity 'hook' needed to attract visitors into the gallery" (Dean 1996, 109). According to Dean, the title should not exceed ten words, and should not be designed to provide information but rather grab attention through thematic approach (Dean 1996, 112). Head texts act as guides through the exhibition. They need to present the key concepts and sub-fields of the exhibit in a few words.

In order to design panels, organizers must be able to write short summaries and "tell a story in a 100 words" (Borowsky undated). They tell visitors why they should care about the story in the gallery. Introductory panels for the exhibition may be between 50 and 200 words divided into short 75-word paragraphs. The introductory panel presents the big idea of the exhibit. Other panels vary from 75 to 150 words and are more associated with one theme or group of objects (Dean 1996, 113–114). Section texts relate to more specific sections of the exhibit. "They introduce a cluster of documents and interpretive devices and explain what brings them all together" (Rabinowitz 2013, 25). For each panel it is good practice to have about two or three good quality related images, which will engage visitors and give them a visual sense of life in this period.

Beverly Serrell's *Exhibit Labels* provides an exhaustive approach for writing panels and labels (Serrell 1996). Labels describe items or group of items. They "try to provide visitors with some way of seeing and interpreting a historical object" (Rabinowitz 2013, 27). They must be plain and concise, from the specific to the general (Bitgood 2000). Labels have to be written according to audiences. If most of the visitors are scholars or experts in the field, labels tend to be technical since visitors would know the basic concepts. However, if the visitors are mostly school groups, labels have to be reader-friendly and avoid technical terms (Genoways and Ireland 2003, 282). Usually, the 75-word limit also applies to label writing. Informative labels should not be confused with an identity tag or ID label that is a set of descriptive data about the object (name, title, date, origin, and catalogue number). Like for the graphic design, organizers must pay attention to the public access to the texts in terms of size, disposition, and position. Panels and labels must be visible to several visitors from different standpoints. The style, font, and size of labels should not be neglected (Dean 1996, 120–131). Another category of texts that should not be forgotten about is distributed materials. The variety of publications – catalogues, leaflets, school activities, websites, and other printouts – help broaden public access to exhibitions. They may simply present the exhibition as an event or provide more technical information for further use of the display.

Curating Public Space: Art and Public History

In order to expand their exhibiting space, museums have increasingly worked beyond their walls. Museums and historic sites try to link their collection to the institution's external environment. As McDaniel points out, "interpretation at historic house museums is increasingly extending beyond the walls of the building to include the landscape and the people who shaped it, used it, and saw it from different perspective" (McDaniel 2006, 245). The landscape, the neighborhood, and the community become a context of interpretation (Howett 2002). This process is symbolic of public history projects that have taken place in public space. In 2014, the Stadsmuseum in Ghent (Belgium) brought Ghent's colorful history of migration to life – not in the museum but in the city itself. The city became the space of exhibition. Likewise, the history of the city of Montreal (Canada) is projected onto city walls, making public space a site of exhibition (Bruemmer 2015). Those different examples demonstrate that spaces of exhibition have greatly diversified.

Exhibiting and curating in public space brings the relations between public history and art to the foreground. In their post on the future of historic house museums, Bill Adair and Laura Koloski stress the numerous recent projects that work with contemporary artists of all disciplines. For instance, Figure 12.1 shows the statues of slave children at Whitney Plantation. Artist Woodrow Nash created these 40 statues and contributed to the emotional aspect of remembering slavery. Based on historical research, this artistic production allows the presence of people for whom the lack of sources has often resulted in the absence of historical representation. At Kuerner Farm, the staff invited sound artist Michael Kiley to create a short piece that visitors to the site experienced in addition to the regular tour activities (Adair and Koloski 2015). Historic sites have become privileged spaces for collaboration too. In 2015, Rebecca Bush, curator at the Columbus Museum, wrote a post for the annual NCPH conference entitled *Bringing Art into History: Interdisciplinary Approaches*. She explains that collaboration is particularly useful for public historians dealing with contemporary issues (undated).

Although most historical institutions own and display art works, historians and artists do not collaborate very often.[12] In order to foster collaboration, historians should first understand the fundamental differences between the disciplines of art and history. Indeed, historians and artists do not usually conceive and describe their projects in similar terms. Melissa Rachleff used Fred Wilson's *Mining the Museum* at the Maryland Historical Society, in 1992, to explain both the differences of the two disciplines and the reasons why historians and artists should collaborate (2011). According to her, the exhibit "has come to be recognized as the quintessential artist-history exchange" (2011, 217). As an artist, Wilson explored the relationship of people of color to the museum collections and questioned "the conventions of display and connoisseurship reinforced a Eurocentric view of history and culture" (Stanton 2005, 24). Instead of a linear narrative, Wilson's exhibit was "fragmentary, suggestive, theatrical/performative, and based in a dialectic rendering between the past (objects) and the present (display)" (Rachleff 2011, 219). For instance, the piece entitled "metalwork" arranged several pieces of silverware with slave shackles in order to address the link between the two, namely the fact that prosperity derives from the work of slaves. Usually the historical context is at best evoked by artists but often remains unimportant. Likewise, historical accuracy may not be part of artists' ethics (Koloski 2011, 266). These differences make any collaboration a problematic venture for historians.

Artists – much more than historians – are creators. As Cathy Stanton learned from her interviews with visitors to collaborative projects between artists and historians, "Several of my respondents seemed to be judging the art purely on its aesthetic merits, while others seemed drawn to one work or another entirely by its appearance" (2005, 30). A risk exists of objects being uncritically aestheticized. Stanton therefore advises public historians "to make sure they take an active role in presenting the artworks to their various audiences" (2005, 30).

Collaboration with artists can turn out to be very useful for historians and institutions in order to create attractiveness. While reviewing public history practice in Massachusetts, Stanton perceived that art projects were linked to grassroots movements "with open studio tours, artists loft developments, and designated arts districts emerging across the landscape." In consequence, she saw many public history institutions that try "to ally themselves with the dynamism of the present-day arts world, and to broaden their own horizons and audiences in the process" (2005, 23). Collaboration with artists can bring new audiences to public history projects.

In the initial steps, collaboration can also "provide the exhibition or organization staff with a new perspective on the material, possibly even influencing the choice of themes or storylines for the exhibition." Artists can help understanding the challenges of making ideas take physical form (Koloski 2011, 266, 279). Artists are able to produce "striking, memorable images with the power to provoke viewers into thinking in new ways about the past and how we know about it" (Stanton 2005, 28). Cultural institutions have invited artists to reimagine their collections and broaden their public reach. Much more than historians, artists are sensible to emotions and creativity. Some artists use and manipulate objects "to create new meanings or reveal hidden ones" (Stanton 2005, 23). Art appeals to senses other than the visual. As Andrea Witcomb explains:

> the project becomes not so much about the delivery of information (and a kind of very simplistic communication model that underpins that) but a process where you can use the senses and aesthetic practices to think about different ways of achieving the exhibition's aims.
>
> (Koloski 2011, 279)

At Kuerner Farm, the artist was invited "to enhance the multi-sensory aspect of visiting the farm" (Adair and Koloski, 2015).

Artists are fully aware of the multiple interpretations that their work can create. Rachleff argues that the collaboration seems "to offer history museums an avenue for making history appear human, more relatable for contemporary sensibilities" (2011, 219). It can provide visitors with new ways of understanding the historical content and themes of the project (Koloski 2011, 266). At the Portland Art Museum, artist Rebecca Keller designed *Object Stories*, for which she created videos that personified objects and gave them a voice. Collaboration with artists forces institutions, historians, and viewers to consider the process by which different meanings have been attributed to objects. For instance, pop culture exhibits are excellent crossover vehicles for engaging both social history and art. An early example would be Experience Music Project's *Disco: A Decade of Saturday Nights* and the Victoria and Albert Museum's *David Bowie Is* (Gordon 2013).

To conclude, interpreting and exhibiting the past offer many opportunities for public historians to interact with actors and audiences. Exhibitions inherently fulfill public history's objective of making the past accessible. Like public history at large, exhibitions and interpretation in historic sites have become more and more participatory. Although this chapter only focused on interpreting and exhibiting the past, it is also important for public historians to be aware of the different public uses of the historical narratives. The chapters on shared authority and activism continue the discussion on the applications of history and the role of historians and historical institutions in contemporary societies.

Notes

1 See the numerous journals about museums: among others, *Museum News, Curator, Museum and Society*.
2 *Visitor Studies* journal; the Visitor Studies Association, www.visitorstudies.org; the Committee on Audience Research and Evaluation – Standing Professional Committee of AAM, www.care-aam. org; the Australia Evaluation and Visitor Research Group, http://amol.org.au/evrsig/index.html; the Group for Education in Museums (GEM), www.gem.org.uk/; the *Journal of Museum Education*, www.mer-online.org; Hein (1998); Hooper-Greenhill (1999).
3 Memory Analysis Tools for Research Through International Cooperation and Experimentations.
4 The author wants to thank Tammy Gordon for sharing this example.
5 For example, the mobile museum entitled the *Curiosity Shop* was set up in empty units in Redcar and Stockton (UK) (De Groot 2008, 244).
6 According to the website, 3,344 people participated in the evaluation process by casting 410,089 evaluations. Each of the 389 works was viewed approximately 1,054 times. www.brooklynmuseum.

org/opencollection/exhibitions/3168/Click!_A_Crowd-Curated_Exhibition (accessed September 26, 2015).

7 See Chapter 11 to go further on the challenge of participatory processes.

8 For historic houses, see for instance http://thehistoricinterior.com/blog/ (accessed August 19, 2015).

9 Visitors could choose between: (1) Return it to the Cuban government; (2) Memorialize it or make it a museum; (3) Keep it as U.S. territory, with the detention center open; (4) Close it as a detention center, but keep the territory.

10 For an overview of writing for broad audiences, see Chapter 4.

11 See the label writing competition for the best labels, https://aam-us.org/docs/default-source/awards/view-the-2013-winners.pdf?sfvrsn=0 (accessed May 2, 2015).

12 Rebecca Keller, Professor at the School of Art Institute of Chicago, is teaching the annual public history short course at Arizona State University, https://asunews.asu.edu/20150109-keller-public-history-short-course (accessed September 2, 2015).

Bibliography

Abramoff Levy, Barbara. "Interpretation Planning: Why and How." In *Interpreting Historic House Museums*, edited by Jessica F. Donnelly, Lanham: AltaMira Press, 2002, 43–61.

Abramoff Levy, Barbara, Lloyd, Sandra, and Schreiber, Susan. *Great Tours! Thematic Tours and Guide Training for Historic Sites*, Lanham: AltaMira Press, 2002.

Adair, Bill and Koloski, Laura. "Imagining a Future for Historic House Museums." History@Work, May 18, 2015, http://publichistorycommons.org/imagining-a-future-part-1/#sthash.fWOMGUQK.dpuf (accessed May 2, 2015).

Adair, Bill, Filene, Benjamin, and Koloski, Laura, eds. *Letting Go? Sharing Historical Authority in a User-Generated World*, Philadelphia: Pew Center for Arts & Heritage, 2011.

Alpers, Svetlana. "The Museum as a Way of Seeing." In *Exhibiting Cultures: The Poetics and Politics of Museum Display*, edited by Ivan Karp and Steven D. Lavine, Washington, DC: Smithsonian Books, 1991, 25–32.

American Alliance of Museums. "Museums Connect: Building Global Communities." Undated, www.aam-us.org/resources/international/museumsconnect (accessed August 19, 2015).

American Association of Museums. *Excellence in Practice: Museum Education Principles and Standards*, Washington, DC, 2005, www.aam-us.org/docs/default-source/accreditation/committee-on-education.pdf?sfvrsn=0 (accessed August 19, 2015).

American House Museum. Athenaeum Symposium, Philadelphia. 1998. James C. Rees, "Forever the Same, Forever Changing: The Dilemma Facing Historic Houses," and Frank E. Sanchis, "Looking Back or Looking Forward? House Museums in the 21st Century," and John M Groff, "To Think Own Self Be True: The Small House Museum in the 21st Century," www.philaathenaeum.org/hmuseum/ (accessed May 1, 2015).

Anderson, Gail, ed. *Reinventing the Museum: The Evolving Conversation on the Paradigm Shift*, Walnut Creek: AltaMira Press, 2012.

Arthur, Paul. "Exhibiting History: The Digital Future." *reCollections: Journal of the National Museum of Australia*, 3/1 (2008), http://recollections.nma.gov.au/issues/vol_3_no_1/papers/exhibiting_history/ (accessed March 27, 2015).

Australian Museum. "Writing Text and Labels." 2008, http://australianmuseum.net.au/writing-text-and-labels (accessed August 18, 2015).

Bautista, Susana. *Museums in the Digital Age: Changing Meanings of Place, Community and Culture*, Lanham: AltaMira Press, 2013.

Bennett, Tony. "The Exhibitionary Complex." *New Formations*, 4 (Spring 1988): 73–102.

Bennett, Tony. "Pedagogic Objects, Clean Eyes, and Popular Instruction: On Sensory Regimes and Museum Didactics." *Configurations*, 6/3 (1998): 345–371.

Bitgood, Stephen. "The Role of Attention in Designing Effective Interpretive Labels." *Journal of Interpretation Research*, 5/2 (2000): 31–45.

Bitgood, Stephen. "When Is 'Museum Fatigue' Not Fatigue?" *Curator: The Museum Journal*, 52 (April 2009): 193–202.

Borowsky, Larry. "Telling a Story in 100 Words: Effective Label Copy." *AASLH Technical Leaflet 240*, undated, https://gpmproject.files.wordpress.com/2012/09/6-borowsky-telling-a-story-in-100-words.pdf (accessed April 28, 2015).

Brooks, Bradley C. "The Historic House Furnishings Plan: Process and Product." In *Interpreting Historic House Museums*, edited by Jessica F. Donnelly, Lanham: AltaMira Press, 2002, 128–144.

Bruemmer, Rene. "Montreal's History to be Projected onto City Walls throughout Old Montreal and the Old Port." *Montreal Gazette*, April 27, 2015, http://montrealgazette.com/news/local-news/montreals-history-to-be-projected-onto-city-walls-and-on-your-smartphone (accessed August 18, 2015).

Bruggeman, Seth. *Here, George Washington was Born: Memory, Material Culture, and the Public History of a National Monument*, Athens: University of Georgia, 2008.

Bush, Rebecca. "Bringing Art into History: Interdisciplinary Approaches." *Public History Commons*, undated, http://publichistorycommons.org/2015-proposal-bringing-art-into-history/ (accessed May 3, 2015).

Butcher-Younghans, Sheery. *Historic House Museums: A Practical Handbook for Their Care, Preservation, and Management*, Oxford: Oxford University Press, 1996.

Butler, Toby. "'Memoryscape': Integrating Oral History, Memory and Landscape on the River Thames." In *People and their Pasts: Public History Today*, edited by Paul Ashton and Hilda Kean, London: Palgrave Macmillan, 2008, 223–239.

Butley, Patrick H. III. "Past, Present, and Future: The Place of the House Museum in the Museum Community." In *Interpreting Historic House Museums*, edited by Jessica F. Donnelly, Lanham: AltaMira Press, 2002, 18–43.

Cameron, Catherine M. and Gatewood, John B. "Excursions into the Un-Remembered Past: What People Want from Visits to Historical Sites." *The Public Historian*, 22/3 (Summer 2000): 107–127.

Carbonell, Bettina, ed. *Museum Studies: An Anthology of Contexts*, Malden: Blackwell, 2004.

Communications Design Team, Royal Ontario Museum. "Spatial Considerations." In *The Educational Role of the Museum*, edited by Eilean Hooper-Greenhill, London and New York: Routledge, 1999, 178–190.

Cunningham, Kay Mary. *The Interpreters Training Manual for Museums*, Washington, DC: American Association of Museums, 2004.

Dean, David. *Museum Exhibition: Theory and Practice*, London and New York: Routledge, 1996.

Dean, David. "The Exhibition Development Process." In *The Educational Role of the Museum*, edited by Eilean Hooper-Greenhill, New York and London: Routledge, 1999, 191–200.

De Groot, Jerome. *Consuming History: Historians and Heritage in Contemporary Popular Culture*, London: Routledge, 2008.

Diamond, Judy. *Practical Evaluation Guide*, Lanham: AltaMira Press, 1999.

Division of Interpretive Planning, Harpers Ferry Center. *Planning for Interpretation and Visitor Experience*, Harpers Ferry, West Virginia, 1998, www.nps.gov/hfc/pdf/ip/interp-visitor-exper.pdf (accessed August 19, 2015).

Donnelly, Jessica F., ed. *Interpreting Historic House Museums*, Lanham: AltaMira Press, 2002.

Durbin, Gail, ed. *A Teacher's Guide to Learning from Objects*, London: Department of National Heritage, 1991.

Eastern State Penitentiary. "The Big Graph." 2015, www.easternstate.org/visit/regular-season/history-artist-installations/big-graph (accessed August 17, 2015).

Faulk, John and Dierking, Lynn. *Museum Experience Revisited*, Walnut Creek: Left Coast Press, 2012.

Flaherty, Francis. *The Elements of Story: Field Notes on Nonfiction Writing*, New York: Harper Perennial, 2010.

Gallas, Kristin and Perry, James. *Interpreting Slavery at Museums and Historic Sites*, Lanham: Rowman & Littlefield Publishers, 2014.

Genoways, Hugh H. and Ireland, Lynne M. *Museum Administration: An Introduction*, Walnut Creek: AltaMira Press, 2003.

Glassberg, David. "Rethinking the Statue of Liberty: Old Meanings, New Contexts." Amherst: University of Massachusetts, 2003, https://archives.iupui.edu/bitstream/handle/2450/678/RethinkingTheStatue-Glassberg.pdf (accessed August 17, 2015).

Glines, Timothy and Grabitske, David. *Telling the Story: Better Interpretation at Small Historical Organizations*, AASLH Technical Leaflet #222, 2003.

Gordon, Tammy S. "Heritage, Commerce, and Museal Display: Toward a New Typology of Historical Exhibition in the United States." *The Public Historian*, 30/3 (August 2008): 27–50.

Gordon, Tammy S. *Private History in Public: Exhibition and the Settings of Everyday Life*, Lanham: AltaMira Press, 2010.

Gordon, Tammy S. "Exhibit Review: *David Bowie Is*, Victoria and Albert Museum." *The Public Historian*, 35/3 (August 2013): 116–119.

Healing Through Remembering. "Everyday Objects Transformed by The Conflict." Undated, www.healingthroughremembering.org/projects/Everyday_Objects (accessed August 19, 2015).

Hein, George E. *Learning in the Museum*, London: Routledge, 1998.

Hooper-Greenhill, Eilean, ed. *The Educational Role of the Museum*, London: Routledge, 1999.

Hooper-Greenhill, Eilean. *Museums and the Interpretations of Visual Culture*, New York: Routledge, 2001.

Howell, Mark. "Interpreters and Museum Educators: Beyond the Blue Hairs." In *Public History: Essays from the Field*, edited by James Gardner and Peter LaPaglia, Malabar: Krieger Publishing Company, 2006, 141–156.

Howett, Catherine. "Grounds for Interpretation: The Landscape Context of Historic House Museums." In *Interpreting Historic House Museums*, edited by Jessica F. Donnelly, Lanham: AltaMira Press, 2002, 111–128.

Hughes, Philip. *Exhibition Design*, London: Laurence King, 2010.

Karp, Ivan and Lavine, Steven D., eds. *Exhibiting Cultures: The Poetics and Politics of Museum Display*, Washington, DC: Smithsonian Books, 1991.

Kirshenblatt-Gimblett, Barbara. "Exhibitionary Complexes." In *Museum Frictions: Public Cultures/Global Transformations*, edited by Ivan Karp, Corinne A. Kratz, Lynn Szwaja, and Tomas Ybarra-Frausto, Durham, NC: Duke University Press, 2006, 36–45.

Knowles, Anne Kelly, ed. *Past Time, Past Place: GIS for History*, Redlands: ESRI Press, 2002.

Koloski, Laura. "Embracing the Unexpected: Artists in Residence at the American Philosophical Society." In *Letting Go? Sharing Historical Authority in a User-Generated World*, edited by Bill Adair, Benjamin Filene, and Laura Koloski, Philadelphia: Pew Center for Arts & Heritage, 2011, 266–282.

Korn, Randy. "Visitor Studies and History." *Mosaic: Newsletter of the Center on History-Making in America*, 1 (Spring/Summer 1992): 10–11.

Korn, Randy. "Studying Your Visitors: Where to Begin." *History News*, 49/1 (January/February 1994): 23–26.

Laganier, Vincent and van der Pol, Jasmine, eds. *Light and Emotions: Exploring Lighting Cultures*, Basel: Birkhäuser GmbH, 2011.

Lavin, Meggett B. "Building a Tool Kit for Your Interpreters: Methods of Success from Drayton Hall." In *Interpreting Historic House Museums*, edited by Jessica F. Donnelly, Lanham: AltaMira Press, 2002, 251–269.

Leinhardt, Gaea and Knudson, Karen. *Listening in on Museum Conversations*, Lanham: AltaMira Press, 2004.

Levinson, Stanford. *Written in Stone: Public Monuments in Changing Societies*, Durham, NC: Duke University Press, 1998.

Lindauer, Margaret. "The Critical Museum Visitor." In *New Museum Theory and Practice: An Introduction*, edited by Janet Marstine, Oxford: Wiley, 2005, 203–225.

Lord, Barry and Piacente, Maria, eds. *Manual of Museum Exhibitions*, second edition, Lanham: Rowman & Littlefield Publishers, 2014.

Lubar, Steven. "Public History in a Federal Museum: The Smithsonian's National Museum of

American History." In *Public History: An Introduction*, edited by Barbara J. Howe and Emory L. Kemp, Malabar: Krieger Publishing Company, 1986, 218–228.

Lubar, Steven. "Exhibiting Memories." In *Exhibiting Dilemnas: Issues of Representation at the Smithsonian*, edited by Amy Henderson and Adrienne L. Kaeppler, Washington, DC: Smithsonian Institution Press, 1997, 15–27.

Lubar, Steven. "Curator as Auteur." *The Public Historian*, 36/1 (February 2014): 71–76.

MacArthur, Matthew. "Can Museums Ever Allow Online Users to Become Participants." In *The Digital Museum: A Think Guide*, edited by Herminia Din and Phyllis Hecht, Washington, DC: American Alliance of Museums Press, 2007, 57–65.

MacArthur, Matthew. "Get Real! The Role of Objects in the Digital Age." In *Letting Go? Sharing Historical Authority in a User-Generated World*, edited by Bill Adair, Benjamin Filene, and Laura Koloski, Philadelphia: Pew Center for Arts & Heritage, 2011, 56–68.

McDaniel, George W. "At Historic Houses and Buildings: Connecting Past, Present, and Future." In *Public History: Essays from the Field*, edited by James Gardner and Peter LaPaglia, Malabar: Krieger Publishing Company, 2006, 233–256.

McGraw, Marie Tyler. "Southern Comfort Levels: Race, Heritage Tourism, and the Civil War in Richmond." In *Slavery and Public History: The Tough Stuff of American History*, edited by James Oliver Horton and Lois E. Horton, New York: New Press, 2005, 151–160.

McKenna-Cress, Polly and Kamien, Janet A. *Creating Exhibitions: Collaboration in the Planning, Development, and Design of Innovative Experiences*, Oxford: Wiley, 2013.

Mackenzie Lloyd, Sandra. "Creating Memorable Visits: How to Develop and Implement Theme-Based Tours." In *Interpreting Historic House Museums*, edited by Jessica F. Donnelly, Lanham: AltaMira Press, 2002, 210–231.

McRainey, Lynn and Russick, John. *Connecting Kids to History With Museum Exhibitions*, Walnut Creek: Left Coast Press, 2010.

Marstine, Janet. *New Museum Theory and Practice: An Introduction*, Oxford: Wiley, 2005.

Mason, Rhiannon. "Cultural Theory and Museum Studies." In *A Companion to Museum Studies*, edited by Sharon Macdonald, Oxford: Wiley, 2006, 17–32.

Miller, Lige Benton. "History on the Drawing Board: The Historian as Developer of Interpretive Media." In *Public History: An Introduction*, edited by Barbara J. Howe and Emory L. Kemp, Malabar: Krieger Publishing Company, 1986, 199–210.

Mollerup, Per. *Wayshowing: A Guide to Environmental Signage, Principles and Practices*, Zurich: Lars Muller, 2006.

National Park Service. "Teaching with Historic Places." *Heritage Education Services*, undated, www.nps.gov/nr/twhp/whyplaces.htm (accessed August 18, 2015).

National Park Service. "Benchmark Competency Standard Effective Interpretive Writing." 2008, www.nps.gov/idp/interp/230/module.htm (accessed August 19, 2015).

Pearce, Susan M. *Interpreting Objects and Collections*, New York: Routledge, 1994.

Phillips, Ruth. "Re-Placing Objects: Historical Practices for the Second Museum Age." *Canadian Historical Review*, 86/1 (2005): 83–110.

Rabinowitz, Richard. "Curating History's Silences: the Revolution Exhibition." In *Revolution! The Atlantic World Reborn*, edited by Thomas Bender, Laurent Dubois, and Richard Rabinowitz, New York: New-York Historical Society, 2011, 247–268.

Rabinowitz, Richard. "Eavesdropping at the Well: Interpretive Media in the Slavery in New York Exhibition." *The Public Historian*, 35/3 (August 2013): 8–45.

Rachleff, Melissa. "Peering Behing the Curtain: Artists and Questioning Historical Authority." In *Letting Go? Sharing Historical Authority in a User-Generated World*, edited by Bill Adair, Benjamin Filene, and Laura Koloski, Philadelphia: Pew Center for Arts & Heritage, 2011, 208–230.

Satwicz, Tom and Morrissey, Kris. "Public Curation: From Trend to Research-Based Practice." In *Letting Go? Sharing Historical Authority in a User-Generated World*, edited by Bill Adair, Benjamin Filene, and Laura Koloski, Philadelphia: Pew Center for Arts & Heritage, 2011, 196–206.

Schlereth, Thomas J., ed. *Material Culture Studies in America*, Walnut Creek: Rowman AltaMira Press, 1982.

Schwartz, Deborah and Adair, Bill. "Community as Curator: A Case Study at the Brooklyn Historical Society." In *Letting Go? Sharing Historical Authority in a User-Generated World*, edited by Bill Adair, Benjamin Filene, and Laura Koloski, Philadelphia: Pew Center for Arts & Heritage, 2011, 112–124.

Serrell, Beverly. *Exhibit Labels: An Interpretive Approach*, Lanham: AltaMira Press, 1996.

Simon, Nina. *The Participatory Museum*, Santa Cruz: Museum 2.0, 2010.

Simon, Nina. "Participatory Design and the Future of Museums." In *Letting Go? Sharing Historical Authority in a User-Generated World*, edited by Bill Adair, Benjamin Filene, and Laura Koloski, Philadelphia: Pew Center for Arts & Heritage, 2011, 18–34.

Simon, Nina. "Some Other Wild Ideas About the Participatory Museum." March 12, 2015, http://engagingplaces.net/2015/03/12/slideshare-some-other-wild-ideas-about-the-participatory-museum/ (accessed August 19, 2015).

Smithsonian Museum. *Museum Studies: A Brief Introduction to Theory, Role, History, and Philosophy*, undated, http://museumstudies.si.edu/Header2b.html (accessed August 19, 2015).

Stanton, Cathy. "Outside the Frame: Assessing Partnerships between Arts and Historical Organizations." *The Public Historian*, 27/1 (Winter 2005): 19–37.

Strunk, William Jr. and White, E.B. *The Elements of Style*, London: Longman, 1999.

Tallon, Loic and Walker, Kevin, eds. *Digital Technologies and the Museum Experience*, Lanham: AltaMira Press, 2008.

Villa Bryk, Nancy E. "I Wish You Could Take a Peek at Us at the Present Moment: Infusing the Historic House with Characters and Activity." In *Interpreting Historic House Museums*, edited by Jessica F. Donnelly, Lanham: AltaMira Press, 2002, 144–168.

Vukelich, Ronald. "Time Language for Interpreting History Collections to Children." *Museum Studies Journal* (Fall 1984): 43–50.

Wallace, Margot. *Writing for Museums*, Lanham: Rowman & Littlefield Publishers, 2014.

Woodhouse, Anne. "Museum Curators." In *Public History. Essays from the Field*, edited by James Gardner and Peter LaPaglia, Malabar: Krieger Publishing Company, 2006, 187–202.

Zotero. "Museum Exhibits." Undated www.zotero.org/groups/brown_amcv2220_museum_exhibits/items (accessed August 19, 2015).

7 Radio and Audio-Visual Production

Audio-visual history production has become one of the most popular means for accessing the past. David Thelen and Roy Rosenzweig explained in *The Presence of the Past* that movies and television broadcasts are far more successful than academic texts in reaching broad and non-specialist audiences (Thelen and Rosenzweig 2000). For instance, 40 million individuals in over 24 million homes watched Ken Burns's *Civil War* documentary during the week of its initial broadcast in September 1990 (Glassberg 2001, 92). In spite of its popularity, historians do not usually participate in the production of history through radio, film, or documentaries. Most historians remain "outside of the picture" and act as film critics (Carnes 1995). Historians are often absent from one of the most influential and popular sources of historical knowledge.

Public historians, however, seem more intrigued – and perhaps more armed – to deal with this media. For instance, *The Public Historian* – the journal of the National Council on Public History – published an entire issue dedicated to "History, Historians, and Cinematic Media" in 2003. This chapter explores the ways history is produced through sound and audio-visual media. In doing so, we might consider the qualities of "good" audio-visual history, what part the historian should/can play in the overall production, and what skills public historians must have to launch such projects.

History on Air: Radio and Sound Archives

History programs are popular on radio. The Organization of American Historians curated significant radio programming through the summer of 2006, and the archived episodes continue to provide historians with podcast materials and the opportunity to study the medium (Talking History 2012). In Europe, *This Sceptred Isle* was a popular 216-episode program about British history broadcast on Radio 4 (UK) in 1995 and 1996, and which generated a large audience.

The asset of radio programs comes first from their relatively – in comparison with audio-visual media – inexpensive production. In the 1980s, David Dunaway – who produced radio history programs – stressed, "whereas professionally produced film or television documentaries cost from $1,500 to $5,000 per minute of finished product, radio's costs are approximately an eighth of that amount" (1984, 80). What is more, radio is a fantastic medium for public historians. Radio stations are often very interested in stories from local communities, which also serve as a basis of interest for public history. On radio since 1972, Dunaway has produced history programs and documentaries such as *Writing the Southwest* (1995), *Across the Tracks: A Route 66 Story* (2001), and *Pete Seeger* (2009). Despite such successes, historian producers remain the exception. For instance, *This Sceptred Isle* was produced by Pete

Atkin, a songwriter and radio producer who had no history background. Most of the time radio producers come from journalism or communication, not history, and their background focuses on technique and technology. It is crucial, therefore, that public historians gain familiarity with the techniques and specific issues of radio production.

Public historians willing to produce radio programs should study the ins and outs of oral history and sound archives.[1] Sound archives can provide lively materials for history programs. In 2003, American RadioWorks broadcasts of *The President Calling*, for example, featured excerpts from the informal, taped conversations of former U.S. presidents (Lyndon Johnson conversing with Kennedy's widow Jaqueline, for instance) (American RadioWorks undated). Also notable was the 2002 collaboration between American RadioWorks and Washington University (St. Louis) for a project on African American veterans of the Korean War. Entitled "Korea: The Unfinished War," the project utilized many oral history sources.

The use of oral history through radio programming gives access to voices people rarely hear. Migrants, ethnic minorities, and ordinary people become voices to the past and tell compelling stories that deepen and make more complex traditional historical interpretations. Radio programs can bring life to and reconstruct the atmosphere of the past to create an effect of intimacy for the listeners. Another advantage of radio is the possibility to transport "the listener to distant, imaginative terrain the way great travel writing delivers the reader to a faraway land" (Biewan and Dilworth 2010, 135). In addition to facts and primary resources, public historians involved in radio programming must consider the use of emotional components. In order to give a sense of being there (in the past), producers can use first-person narratives and interviews with people who lived through the events.[2]

Although historical radio programs and oral history may work together, they also maintain distinctive methods. As seen in Chapter 3, historians who interview witnesses for the creation of oral history archives tend not to intervene in the story and leave the floor to their narrators. Radio producers work differently. They make choices and select the parts of the interviews they want to broadcast according to the themes and format of the program. Besides, pacing is crucial. If the interview or recorded sound archive is too slow or too fast, it may very well not match the radio format. The quality of the media does not matter much for archives but it is crucial for broadcasting issues. Too much hesitation, such as "hmmm" or silences, and strong accents may render the interview unfit for radio. As Dunaway argues, "Preparing a program for the general public involves balancing faithfulness to historical content with the need for an effective, moving presentation" (1984, 86). Oral historian Michael Frisch notes that when oral history is used as a mere source of data, it undercuts ordinary people as shapers and interpreters of their own experience (1990). Historian-producers should certainly know about how to communicate the past but should not forget that sources have to be interpreted and contextualized. Too often, oral testimonies are seen as mere illustrations, although they should be discussed to provide meaning about the past. This is why public historians should not limit themselves to the role of consultants, but should aim at producing their own programs as well.

Film and Documentary: Introduction to History on Screen

While dealing with "unofficial sources of historical knowledge" British historian Raphael Samuel gave television "pride of place" (1994, 13). Television and movie theaters give access to aspects of the past that would barely reach popular audiences. For instance, *Le Retour de Martin Guerre* – a movie about 16th century France – has been seen by millions of people "who otherwise would have only the vaguest idea about the sixteenth century and how peasants lived and felt in the past" (Zemon Davis 2003, 45). In spite of the success of history on screen, historians are at best advisors and more often only critics who review movies. When we consider history on screen "it is easy to be critical of what we see ... But ask what we expect a film to be or do, and basically we, historians, don't know, other than to insist that it adhere to 'the facts'" (Rosenstone 2003, 65). Very few producers have history backgrounds. The absence of historians is not necessarily due to academic mistrust. Most of the time, production companies want historians to validate facts, not to produce a scenario (Smith 2003, 44).

Misunderstanding arises from the different goals of filmmakers and historians. As Gilden Seavey explains in her essay on history and audio-visual media, "The task for historians is to arrive at some kind of truth ... the goal for the filmmaker, on the other hand, is to first and foremost ... create a filmic reality that allows the audience to believe a story as if it were true" (2006, 118). Historians and filmmakers, therefore, have contrasting agendas. Filmmakers seek to entertain, to connect past and present, and ultimately to make money (Beck 2011, 173). Besides, their definition of truth differs from traditional historical practice. "The 'truth' for the historical filmmaker lies in the idea of a 'general truth about the subject' not in its specifics" (Gilden Seavey 2006, 124). Filmmakers use historical sources to provide general representations – a sense – of the past. Historians are used to dealing and writing about historical complexity, and this does not fit history on screen. Indeed, history on screen rarely fits the detailed presentation of complex events (Gilden Seavey 2006, 121). Conveying history to a broad audience inevitably involves a degree of simplification or, in the case of most Hollywood films, downright distortion. The question for historians is to know how – and to what extent – they can produce entertaining and historically accurate representations of the past on screen.

Historical films are produced for TV or cinema. Topics of historical films often deal with war (*The Pianist*, Roman Polanski, 2002; *Schindler's List*, Stephen Spielberg, 1993) or its consequences. Rachid Bouchared explored the conduct and aftermath of the Algerian War in *Outside the Law/Hors la loi* (2009). Another widespread type of historical film deals with biography, especially about monarchs – see Stephen Frears's *The Queen* (2006) or Patrice Chereau's *La Reine Margot* (1994). Films, much more than documentaries, add fictional parts and sometimes reinforce the representations of the past in terms of "goodies and baddies" and simplistic interpretation (Beck 2011, 175). Films are certainly not the best media to represent the past with academic accuracy but they can help the public better understand emotions, interpersonal relations, and personal motivation (Toplin 1996, 2).

Over the past two decades the production of historical documentaries has exploded. A documentary is a work that derives its contents from actual (rather than imagined) events, persons, and places (Juel undated). Unlike historical fictions for which the past is staged, documentaries are fact-based and show what once was there or would have been there even without the camera. A crucial difference between film and documentary is the use/absence of sources and historical materials. In addition to American documentaries such as *The American Experience*, or Ken Burns's documentaries, British producers – especially the BBC – have a long tradition of historical documentaries (*The Great War* (1964), *Grand Strategy of World War II* (1972), and more recently Simon Schama's *History of Britain* (2000)).

Making History on Screen

"Quit complaining about bad films; write your own" (Smith 2003, 28). Making history on screen forces historians to reconsider their role and position and to move from their comfort zone – as critics – to become part of historical production. There are two main options for historians. First, they may produce their own film/documentary. For instance, Daniel Walkowitz, a specialist in U.S. labor and social history, produced *Molders of Troy*, about industrial workers in New York State, a fiction film based on his research for *Worker City, Company Town* (Toplin 1996, 8). The second and more common option is for historians to develop consulting services for production houses. Due to the capital investment and specialist crews that film production requires, it can be worthwhile for historians to learn how to work with already existing production companies. Consulting historians can have a major role in the selection of historical sources, the historical arguments, and the overall narrative of the film/documentary. In order to produce history or to act as historical consultants, historians must have a few critical skills and clear ideas about what fiction can bring to the understanding of the past and about the limits to invention (Toplin 1996, 2).

Study, Review, Advise the Works of Others

Historians who intend to produce history on screen should start by studying and reviewing the works of others. Historians can write short film reviews for local/online journals, or might write op-ed pieces in which they analyze the kind of historical narratives produced through film, series, or documentaries. Instead of complaining about the difference between academic writing and history on screen, they can focus on how sources are used by producers. Mark Freeman's *Guide to the Study of Documentary Film* invites historians to concentrate on a few key issues like cinematography, sound, *mise-en-scène*, and editing (Freeman 1997).

Regarding cinematography, it is important to pay attention to the framing (what is included and excluded), the composition (angle of view, visual distortion), and color (black and white for historical documents versus color to give a sense of realism). Attention should also be paid to sound and voices in the way the story is narrated, the importance of dialogue and silence in the construction of the narratives, and the place given to music. Ronald Blumer particularly encourages historians to pay attention to "the narration that sets the background and attempts to explain to the audience what exactly is going as clearly and succinctly as possible without color" (2002). Regarding documentary films, historians should discuss the use and presentation of "primary witnesses" and other primary sources such as photographs, artifacts, and films. *Mise-en-scène* refers to the setting, costuming, décor, lighting, and acting. Re-enactment or re-creation of sites is particularly relevant to give life to the past. Blumer explains how, in order to re-create scenes of the 18th century urban landscape of London and Paris, he had had to shoot in Vilnius, Lithuania, which still had un-renovated 18th century urban streets (2002).

The last, but very important, element of the initial review is the role given to historians in the narratives. Historians have two different roles. They can be interviewed by the producer or serve as advisors. Producers are usually keen to interview historians to bring authority to the narratives. Historians also help to set the subject into broader historical contexts. However, as Nina Gilden Seavey reminds us, these interviews are also a matter of "casting the right character for the role" (2006, 123). The producer may choose historians according to his/her conception of the topic. Gilden Seavey thus takes the example of Ken Burns, who chose Shelby Foote for his Civil War documentary partly because of his "lyrical southern drawl, his scruffy comportment, and his verbal facility with the intricate detail of Civil War life" (2006, 123). Reviewing all these aspects should help historians become familiar with the different styles and possible ways to represent the past on screen.

Production of "Good" – and Popular – History on Screen

Historians may have more impact on film production as advisors. Natalie Zemon Davis – who worked as advisor for *Le Retour de Martin Guerre* – argues for a strong acknowledgment of the role of historical advisors and suggests that they should be part of "all the visual and sound perspectives and aspirations of filmmakers, the qualities and movement of actors, and costs." This allows, "first, constructing an image of a past time and place that is plausible, and second, following the lines of the historical plot so that it does not do serious violence to what evidence we have" (Zemon Davis 2003, 47). However, historical advisors do not directly produce narratives. In order to produce popular history, historians should understand what audiences like about history on screen.

In 1991, for research on documentaries about the Civil War, David Glassberg and one of his students analyzed the multiple letters received by Ken Burns for his Civil War documentary. The objective was to understand what people had liked and how this could be applied to other historical production. "What did Americans see when they watched *The Civil War*? What did they learn from the series?" (2001, 95). The study of the letters revealed three key issues: the role of direct and emotional connection, the relevance of real places, and family history. More than one out of every four letters praised Burns for offering a sense of direct, emotional connection with the past (Glassberg 2001, 99). One challenge for public historians is therefore to produce an accurate yet also lively account of the past.

In order to do so, historians must be aware of the different formats. Will the story follow one specific character? Will a single narrator, an actor, or a historian tell the story? Historians should be aware though that this format personalizes the representation of the past and makes any complex interpretation more difficult. If Burns adopts the multiplicity of voices, Simon Schama assumes "the instrumental role of 'author-presenter' seeking to engage, inform, educate and entertain a television audience" (Beck 2011, 102).

Historians should not abuse description and analysis. In order to maintain the interest of the audience, narratives should not consume more than one-quarter of the program's length (Gilden Seavey 2006, 127). Like public history writing in general, the beginning of the script is crucial. Smith argues that there "is often a '10-10' rule: if readers aren't hooked by the first and last ten pages of a script, the rest never gets read" (Smith 2003, 32). Furthermore, Donald Watt reminds us that "the tempo is different, there can be no recall, no flipping back of the page, no elaborate parallel themes by footnotes or parenthesis" (Gilden Seavey 2006, 126). The story must be straightforward and not confusing to the readers/viewers.

The main difference between films and documentaries is the use of primary source materials to construct the narrative. Historians can use different archives, letters, diaries, photographs, footage, artifacts, objects, works of art, eyewitness testimonies, or sounds. This broad range of materials allows producers to give life to the past. According to Glassberg, the use of photographs contributes to the reality effect in Burns's documentary (2001, 100). As he revealed, the proximity with the past can be even more powerful when the past is placed in the context of family history (2001, 104). Family history serves as a lens through which to understand the past.

Sites are also very important in history on screen. Documentary and film rely a lot on re-enactment and visual reconstruction. In these instances, producers may turn to film techniques (Computer Generated Images/Computer Assisted Design) to create scenes or places from the past. Frequently these scenes are quite effective in creating a sense of mood or place, drawing the documentary away from the traditional use of evidence and bringing the viewer into experiencing the past (Gilden Seavey 2006, 125). Nevertheless what most persuaded Burns's viewers that the history they saw was real were the present-day scenes of battlefields such as Antietam and Gettysburg. It was important for people that Burns went to the "places where the past happened" and listened "for ghosts and echoes of the event" (Glassberg 2001, 101). Burns filmed his contemporary footage at exactly the same location, season, and time of the day as the important historical event he was narrating. Materials and sites gave spectators a sense of proximity with the past.

Finally, as Toplin stresses, "Excusing any manipulation in the name of artistic license is indefensible" (1996, 10). Historians must be aware of the danger of producing pure fiction. Having said that, it is extremely difficult to judge the part that fiction and historical facts should play in history on screen. It really depends on the objectives, and historians and producers may have conflicting agenda. What is certain, though, is that public historians may play the role of intermediary.

It is also important that historians help producers consider sources not as mere illustration of the narratives. As in any historical production, each piece of evidence should be weighted alongside others to determine its veracity in the broader historical context (Gilden Seavey 2006, 122). This critical analysis of historical materials is often omitted in documentaries since the producer may only seek to find the right kind of documents to support the narratives. Historian-producers should at the very least place the materials into a historical context and not take for granted information extracted from the sources. It is especially important for witnesses whose voice may sound like the uncontested – and unique – interpretation of the past. The visual representation of the past is even more problematic when historians face a shortage of documents as, for example, on Greek or Roman Antiquity. Historian producers must then use art works, lithographs, etchings, archaeological findings, artifacts, and other sources – sometimes even not contemporary from the period under consideration – to help create a sense of reality. Those sources are often indirect and require even more contextualization.

The struggle over historical accuracy on screen presents enduring challenges for historians. Zemon Davis gives two examples of historical compromises she made for the movie *Le Retour de Martin Guerre*. She stresses that, as historian, she could accept a minor mistake about the color of the judges' clothing during a trial scene but criticized the fact that the movie presented the trial as a public event rather than a more accurately private event because it gives a false representation of 16th century public life. She explains, "If major anachronisms are introduced, they should be evident and funny or creative, opening horizons for audiences" (2003, 47). We touch here upon a crucial aspect of history on screen. Inaccuracy may be tolerated in certain cases. Toplin invites us to question whether the "manipulation of evidence is developed out of genuine and laudable efforts to communicate broad truths" (1996, 12). What matters ultimately – especially for films – is the capacity to convey a particular historical message about the event, and not the few historical inaccuracies. Rosenstone argues that to be judged "historical," "a film must somehow engage the discourse of history, the already existing body of writing, arguments, debates, memories, images, moral positions, and data surrounding the topic with which it deals" (2003, 76). However, very few films meet this expectation. Public historians should focus and strive for films and documentaries to provide a historical understanding of the past.

History on Screen as Public and Participatory History?

Public history invites public participation. One way to do so for historians involved in audio-visual production is to create links between the past and the present. Producers can punctuate films and documentaries with contemporary debates. Another option is to allow – as Simon Schama did for *History of Britain* – contemporary witnesses to become an integral part of the narrative (Beck 2011, 105). Similarly useful are productions that foster public historical debates. Public debates that followed *Schindler's List*, *Lincoln*, or *Selma* are part of the public history production. Another example is *Days of Glory* (*Indigènes* in French) produced by Rachid Bouchared in 2006 that brought light to men from the French colonies who got drafted to fight during World War II. In spite of their service, those veterans faced systematic discrimination and successive French governments even froze their pensions. The film and the debates that followed contributed to a public acknowledgment of the colonial troops and to the changing pension system.

Entertainment and Reality (History) Television

British producer Simon Schama argues that television has contributed to the downfall of "the usual hierarchy of authority" and has provoked "a democracy of knowledge" (Schama 2004, 27). To some extent, the public can now participate in history programs. If radio programs can animate live discussion with audiences, television is more conservative in the role of its audiences. Too often, the public only passively consumes what television producers provide them with. This passivity demonstrates the problems innate in using television as an education medium (De Groot 2008, 152).

Television can offer a broad range of historical programs. Certain channels like The History Channel (USA), Discovery History (UK), or Histoire (France) specialize in history programs. As for screened history in general, historical programs on TV often favor certain topics such as wars and military history, monarchs and "great men," or sports. Mostly encountered in the United Kingdom, costume drama is a fictional story based on romance or adventure. Costume drama, like *Jane Eyre* (BBC, 2006) or *Anna Karenina* (Channel 4, 2000), is often an adaptation of novels from, for instance, Dickens, Tolstoy, or Flaubert. Although fictional, the genre relies on reconstruction of the past through visual aesthetic. Other series based on history emerged in the 2000s. Produced by the American HBO network, *Rome* was broadcasted from 2005 to 2007. This very expensive ($100 million budget) series depicted the city of Rome in the years 49–31 B.C.E. Composed of detailed visual representation of the city, *Rome* contains bad language, violence, and sex. According to Jonathan Swamp, consultant and co-producer of the series, the most important thing to do was to "evade the clichés of Holy Rome, all white pillars and white togas" (De Groot 2008, 199). Historical fictions provide – through emotions, adventure, and drama – the entertaining aspect of television.

Entertainment might also lead to audience participation. Quiz shows such as *Are You Smarter than a Fifth Grader?* (Fox, 2007) or *University Challenge* (BBC, 1994–) have increased in popularity since the 1990s. Game shows present history as a set of facts that are correct or not, with right and wrong answers. History has to match the marketing presentation of the game, to be fast, straight to the point, and entertaining.

A new sort of program emerged in the 2000s. In relation to the strategy to foster emotion, experience, and reality, television producers attempted to increase interaction with audiences through reality TV. Reality TV became famous with the production of *Big Brother* in Holland in 1999, and started to diffuse into many different sub-fields, among them reality-history programs. De Groot defines reality-history as:

> the suite of programmes which somehow involve and enfranchise the audience into historical experience, either by allowing them to participate in history through the

game-style re-enactment of the "House" format (in which a group of people are placed in a particular setting for a set amount of time and forced to act in the style of a historical period), or through interactivity of various forms such as voting, nominating, or commenting.

(2008, 165)

The purpose is not to reach accurate interpretation of the past, but to provide "experiences" of the past based on re-enactments and to invite viewers to identify with the protagonists (De Groot 2008, 165). Shows like *100 Greatest Sporting Moments* in the UK (1999), or *The Greatest Frenchman of all Time* in France (2005) asked audiences to vote and to participate in the creation of history. Endemol, the company responsible for *Big Brother*, also produced *Restoration* in 2003 on the BBC (UK), in which the public chose and voted for which historical building should be saved. Other shows directly involved participants.

The BBC produced *Destination D-Day: The Raw Recruits* in 2004 in which volunteers participated in the reconstitution of the Normandy landings. Emphasis was put on experiencing the past. An important feature of reality-history is the connection with the present. The BBC produced *The Trench* in 2002 as a recreation of the World War I trench experience, through the 10th Battalion of the East Yorkshire Regiment on the Western Front in 1916. The volunteers came from the same area as that of the 1916 regiment and spent two weeks in a trench system in France created for the show.

One interesting aspect for public historians is the current attention paid to everyday life history. In the United States, *Colonial House* was broadcasted on PBS in 2004 and attempted to recreate daily life in 17th century Plymouth colony. Reconstructing the past implies serious research for historical advisors on furniture, food, hygiene, clothing, and work. British public historian, Juliet Gardiner, worked as historical advisor for *The 1940s House*, a 2001 show produced for Channel 4 (UK) that asked a modern-day family to experience the life of a family in London during World War II. Reality-history TV can obviously be criticized in its attempt to re-create the past. Despite historical details, participants of *The Trench* hardly experienced what World War I soldiers went through. The relevance of the shows should not be fully rejected, however. Supporting and interactive materials – especially websites presenting historical documents, quizzes, and interviews – can help non-specialist audiences to better understand the past.

Partners, Training, and Tools

Perhaps even more than for other types of historical production, history on air and on screen requires collaboration. Producing a radio program, a documentary, a film, or a TV series involves many different production roles and positions that historians must engage and collaborate with. For instance, a historian who intends to make a documentary for a radio or TV program should discuss his/her needs with an array of technicians and be ready to deal with sound and visual issues. Productions, for example, require extensive content, sound, and effects editing. As Dunaway stresses regarding radio programs, "it is not unusual to use only a minute of an hour's interview in the final production." (Dunaway 1984, 83). Editing is achieved through a variety of techniques, including montage, the superimposition of sounds, interviews, and narration. Video editing for a documentary may require weeks or months of work. Dunaway points out that 10–25 hours per minute are necessary for radio documentary editing (1984, 87). Depending upon the size and budget of the production, video editing can range from the use of relatively simple and free editors (such as iMovie for Mac), to more elaborate software (such as FinalCut Pro, Adobe Premiere), to the hiring of documentary/ video editing companies, yet it remains a crucial aspect for all productions.

Public historians can also contact various organizations that promote video editing. The Visual History Summer Institute (VHSI) at Georgia Southern University provides special training for historians to learn the basic tools of media production (Georgia Southern University undated). The VHSI has sessions such as "Working with Camera" and "Working with Natural and Artificial Lights." In Figure 7.1, Graciela Cano practices different techniques that historians must learn if they want to move from advisor to producer of historical documentary films. It is particularly relevant to understand how primary sources can be filmed and represented.

Historians can also follow and attend The World Congress of Science and Factual Producers (WCSFP), or the International Documentary Association (IDA), The Credits and the Documentary Educational Resources that provide resources, showcase, courses, and funding. Furthermore The International Association for Media and History is an organization of filmmakers, broadcasters, archivists, and scholars dedicated to historical inquiry into film, radio, television, and related media. The Documentary Center sponsors a wide range of programs devoted to documentary film, an annual six-month Institute for Documentary Filmmaking, the International Emerging Filmmakers Fellowship, a Center Screen documentary showcase, and a course outline that help users to sharpen their approach to documentaries at large.

Public historians should talk to others with experience as historical advisors or filmmakers. Historians may also consult websites of historical advisors, or consult different books on the production of documentaries (Freeman 1997; Barnouw 1993; Barsam 1992). The *Historical Journal of Film, Radio and Television* also offers very useful advice and case studies. *Current* is a website that covers public television and radio with information about legislation, future events, links to sites, professional organizations related to the media, journals, and media activist organizations.

Historians who want to produce their own films face additional constraints. Daniel Smith details the steps he encountered and warns, "one of many lessons we learned in dealing with

Figure 7.1 Graciela Cano during the 2015 Visual History Summer Institute, Georgia Southern University. Courtesy of Graciela Cano, Michael Van Wagenen (VHSI/Georgia Southern University).

Hollywood is that unless you have a hugely attractive high-concept movie, development and decisions take a *lot* of time" (2003, 36). Historians have to find producers and submit the script to "development executives" who "figure out whether they can risk pursuing a project" (Smith 2003, 36). Smith used the *Hollywood Creative Directory*, which lists producers, their projects, and their contacts, to find a director for his project. Once the historian has found a director and a production company, (s)he enters the stage of development. Smith explains that "Development is the time when a screenplay gets read in very serious ways – perhaps for the first time – by everyone from network executives to prospective directors and actors." This process involves different partners with different roles:

> Executives read a script with an eye toward targeting a large audience while keeping the budget low; directors are trying to visualize the story, eliminating excess dialogue and exposition; actors are looking for juicy characters to play with dramatic "character arcs" and stunning snatches of dialogue.
>
> (Smith 2003, 39)

The road leading to the production of historical films is long and this is why historians are usually limited to the role of advisors whom producers consult and – sometimes – listen to.

To conclude, historians may use and take advantage of radio and audio-visual production to increase public access to the past. Sound and audio-visual media allow historians to vary the format of historical interpretation and make the past alive. It is also critical for historians to encourage contextualization and historical analysis of sources so that the latter do not remain pure illustrations. In doing so, historians can participate in the creation of entertaining and accurate historical productions.

Notes

1 See Chapter 3.
2 See Chapter 9.

Bibliography

American RadioWorks. "The President Calling – FINAL SCRIPT." Undated, http://american radioworks.publicradio.org/features/prestapes/transcript.html (accessed August 20, 2015).

Barnouw, Erik. *Documentary: A History of the Nonfiction Film*, Oxford: Oxford University Press, 1993.

Barsam, Richard. *Nonfiction Film: A Critical History*, Bloomington: Indiana University Press, 1992.

Beck, Peter. *Presenting History: Past & Present*, London: Palgrave Macmillan, 2011.

Biewan, John and Dilworth, Alexa, eds. *Reality Radio: Telling True Stories in Sound*, Chapel Hill: University of North Carolina Press, 2010.

Blumer, Ronald. "So You Want to Make a History Documentary?" *History News Network*, November 4, 2002, http://hnn.us/article/1033 (accessed August 20, 2015).

Carnes, Mark C. *Past Imperfect: History According to the Movies*, New York: Henry Holt and Company, 1995.

De Groot, Jerome. *Consuming History: Historians and Heritage in Contemporary Popular Culture*, London: Routledge, 2008.

De Groot, Jerome. "'Perpetually Dividing and Suturing the Past and Present': *Mad Men* and the Illusions of History." *Rethinking History*, 15/2 (2011): 269–285.

Dunaway, David K. "Radio and the Public Use of History." *The Public Historian*, 6/2 (Spring 1984): 77–90.

Edgerton, Gary R. and Rollins, Peter C., eds. *Television Histories: Shaping Collective Memory in the Media Age*, Lexington: The University Press of Kentucky, 2001.

Freeman, Mark. "A Guide to the Study of Documentary Films." 1997, www-rohan.sdsu.edu/~mfreeman/images/DOCFILMS.pdf (accessed August 20, 2015).

Frisch, Michael. "Oral History, Documentary, and the Mystification of Power: A Critique of *Vietnam: A Television History*." In *A Shared Authority: Essays on the Craft and Meaning of Oral and Public History*, edited by Michael Frisch, Albany: State University of New York Press, 1990, 159–178.

Georgia Southern University. "Visual History Summer Institute." Undated, http://class.georgiasouthern.edu/history/home/public-history-program/vhsi/ (accessed August 20, 2015).

Gilden Seavey, Nina. "Film and Media Producers: Taking History Off the Page and Putting It On Screen." In *The Public History: Essays from the Field*, edited by James B. Gardner and Peter LaPaglia, Malabar: Krieger Press, 2006, 117–129.

Glassberg, David. *Sense of History: The Place of the Past in American Life*, Amherst: University of Massachusetts Press, 2001.

Juel, Henrik. "Defining Documentary Film." Undated, http://pov.imv.au.dk/Issue_22/section_1/artc1A.html (accessed August 20, 2015).

Plane, Ann Marie, ed. "History, Historians, and Cinematic Media." *The Public Historian*, 25/3 (Summer 2003): 5–6.

Rosenstone, Robert. "The Reel Joan of Arc: Reflections on the Theory and Practice of the Historical Film." *The Public Historian*, 25/3 (Summer 2003): 61–77.

Rosenstone, Robert A. *History on Film/Film on History*, Harlow: Pearson, 2006.

Rosenthal, Alan, ed. *New Challenges for Documentary*, Berkeley: University of California Press, 1988.

Samuel, Raphael. *Theatres of Memory: Past and Present in Contemporary Culture*, London: Verso, 1994.

Schama, Simon. "Television and the Trouble with History." In *History and the Media*, edited by David Cannadine, Basingstoke: Palgrave Macmillan, 2004, 20–33.

Smith, Daniel Blake. "The (Un)Making of a Historical Drama: A Historian/Screenwriter Confronts Hollywood." *The Public Historian*, 25/3 (Summer 2003): 27–44.

Talking History. "Aural History Productions." 2012, www.talkinghistory.org/radioarchive.html (accessed August 20, 2015).

Thelen, David and Rosenzweig, Roy. *The Presence of the Past: Popular Uses of the Past in American Life*, New York: Columbia University Press, 2000.

Toplin, Robert. *History By Hollywood: The Use and Abuse of the American Past*, Chicago: University of Illinois Press, 1996.

Watt, Donald. "History on the Public Screen I." In *New Challenges for Documentary*, edited by Alan Rosenthal, Berkeley: University of California Press, 1988, 435–436.

Zemon Davis, Natalie. "Movie or Monograph? A Historian/Filmmaker's Perspective." *The Public Historian*, 25/3 (Summer 2003): 45–48.

8 Digital Public History

"The Past was analog. The Future is digital." The shift is purposefully over-simplified, but this assertion from Roy Rosenzweig and Dan Cohen – founders of the Center for History and New Media (CHNM) – encourages historians to explore the impact of new technology on the history-making process (Cohen and Rosenzweig 2005). Digital tools are transforming the work of historians in many different aspects. Lots of primary sources are now available online. New tools – GIS and network analysis for instance – allow historians to undertake new analysis of historical sources. Historians can now publish their research through websites, blogs, and social media.

This section does not aim to cover the whole field of digital history, but explores the links between digital history and public history. On the one hand, since any online historical product can potentially be accessed all over the world, the Internet can help create digital public history. Public historians should be comfortable with Web technology since it can help connect and collaborate with large audiences. On the other hand, Sharon Leon – historian at the CHNM – argues that "historians employing digital methods might make their work publicly available, yet accessibility does not mean the work is inherently public history" (Leon 2015). In other words, making history public through the Web does not guarantee public interaction. This chapter explores how digital history and public history overlap.

The Rise of Digital Practices

Digital Humanities

It is spectacular to see how digital practices have affected not only history but also the whole field of humanities. The use of computers in humanities has a history that dates back at least to the 1950s. The first part of A Companion to Digital Humanities usefully details the history of humanities computing (Siemens et al. 2004). Father Roberto Busa – an Italian Jesuit priest – is often seen as a pioneer in using computing for humanities (in this case, text analysis) in the 1950s and 1960s. Busa's work contributed to developing the "computer as instrumental tool" and "text as object" (Svensson 2009). Humanities computing developed in the 1960s, the Computers and the Humanities journal was created in 1966, and the Association for Computers in the Humanities (ACH) was founded in the 1970s (McCarty 2005). Humanities computing dealt mostly with texts and linguistics. As Patrik Svensson underlines in his article on the move from humanities computing to digital humanities, the journal Literary and Linguistic Computing, the Association for Literary and Linguistic Computing (ALLC), and their focus on textual and text-based literary analysis, were symbolic of the domination of text analysis in the initial use of computers by human-ists (Svensson 2009).

More recently, humanities computing representatives have appropriated the term digital humanities (Svensson 2009). The term digital humanities came to widespread usage with the 2004 publication of *A Companion to Digital Humanities*, which proposed the term as a replacement for "humanities computing." The new name was also an attempt to "broaden the tent beyond the literary disciplines that had grown up under that earlier term" (Scheinfeldt 2014a, 2014b). New associations such as the Alliance of Digital Humanities Associations (ADHO), new journals like *Digital Humanities Quarterly*, and new websites like digitalhumanities.org prove the success of the shift.[1]

Digital manifestos flourished in Europe and North America.[2] The 2009 Digital Humanities Manifesto 2.0 stressed that:

> Digital Humanities is not a unified field but *an array of convergent practices* that explore a universe in which: a) print is no longer the exclusive or the normative medium in which knowledge is produced and/or disseminated; instead, print finds itself absorbed into new, multimedia configurations; and b) digital tools, techniques, and media have altered the production and dissemination of knowledge in the arts, human and social sciences.
>
> (*The Digital Humanities Manifesto 2.0* 2009)

If humanities computing mostly focused on literary studies – embodied by the Text Encoding Initiative founded in the late 1980s – digital humanities have a broader agenda that includes visual representations and public participation (Svensson 2010).

Digital History

Digital history is part of the digital humanities, so that historians can certainly consult the rich bibliography on digital humanities. In order to know more about the rise of digital humanities, their internal debates, and different practices, readers can use multiple resources (Berry 2012; Gold 2012; Svensson 2009, 2010, 2012; Terras et al. 2013; Zotero undated). Historians can also participate in THATCamps. The Humanities and Technology Camp is an un-conference originally created by the CHNM in 2008. Different from traditional academic conferences, THATCamps insist on the participation of attendees who create the program and sessions, discuss the links between humanities and digital technology, and propose workshops and training. Although digital history shares some tools and practices with other sub-fields of the digital humanities, it also has its own problematic. For instance, in a 2014 post, Stephen Robertson – director of CHNM – sheds light on the "opportunity to emphasize what makes digital history different from digital literary studies and 'dh' (digital humanities)." (Robertson 2014).

In 2008, the *Journal of American History* published a discussion between digital history practitioners on the "promises of digital history" (Cohen et al. 2008). Participants defined digital history as "anything (research method, journal article, monograph, blog, classroom exercise) that uses digital technologies in creating, enhancing, or distributing historical research and scholarship." Digital history is based on the use of new media and computers in order to analyze and understand historical information and/or to communicate its results.

Historians using computers should have a basic knowledge of the machine (Laue 2004). Any course about digital history may start by an introduction to the history and functioning of computers. The Computer History Museum's website offers useful timelines and exhibitions that visualize the history of computers. For example, a course could start by "dissecting" a computer in order to identify the main components, or hardware. Learning how computers work also involves software, namely, the machine-readable instructions that make the computer's processor perform operations.[3]

From the first computers in the 1930s and 1940s to the first desktop computers in the 1970s and the use of computers for historical research in the 1980s and 1990s, it is interesting to discuss the impact of technology on the "historical imagination" (Thomas 2014). Until the late 1980s, digital history – or historical computing as it was called – was limited to quantitative research.[4] Historical computing had therefore no public engagement. Statistics, economy, and quantitative analysis benefited the most from computing history. However, the move from analog to digital has produced numerous changes in the overall process of cultural production.

Digital history is not simply a set of practices; it is also a new format to produce history, with new actors and new results (Ayers 1999). Initiated by the University of Virginia, the Valley of the Shadow project presented the experiences of Union and Confederate soldiers during the U.S. Civil War. The creators of the project (William G. Thomas III and Edward L. Ayers) used digital media to present their historical research through massive searchable archives. Created in 1994 at George Mason University, the CHNM has been a major actor in defining digital history and its public uses. The main work on digital history was written in 2005 by Dan Cohen and Roy Rosenzweig and is one of the major works in the field (2005).

One specific aspect of digital history in comparison with digital humanities is the lesser attention paid to text and linguistic analysis. Tom Scheinfeldt points out that "as an historian, the story of Father Busa, of Humanist, and even of cliometrics is not my story … as a digital historian who isn't much involved in textual analysis, it isn't a story I can much identify with" (Scheinfeldt 2014a, 2014b). Instead, Scheinfeldt argues that digital history is much more connected to cultural issues through oral history and folklore studies. More than literary studies, digital history is the inheritor of collecting and archiving practice. It is no coincidence that the subtitle of Cohen and Rosenzweig's book is "gathering, preserving and presenting the past on the web." The creation, preservation, and visualization of historical data have been at the core of digital history.[5] Visualization of historical data offers many new opportunities for historians to present their work (Catt 2015). According to Robertson, the second practice more specific to digital history is the area of digital mapping (Robertson 2014). He mentions the first two winners of the AHA's Roy Rosenzweig Prize for Innovation in Digital History, which were mapping projects.[6] Those practices more specific to digital history explain why Scheinfeldt argues that "the digital humanities family tree has two main trunks, one literary and one historical, that developed largely independently into the 1990s" (2014a, 2014b). Dan Cohen underlines three major aspects of digital history: searching and researching sources through digital technology; the manipulation (and creation) of digital documents (visualization, mapping, and so on); and the new audiences provided by digital sharing (Cohen et al. 2008). The latter aspect has been deeply connected to the rise of the Internet.

The World Wide Web's opening in 1993 with the creation of HTML and browser technologies offered historians a new medium in which to present their work (Thomas 2014). Almost every historical archive, museum, library, and society now have their own website. However, the first websites were merely static pages providing contents that could be changed and updated by webmasters. A new generation of websites emerged in the early

2000s, known as Web 2.0 (O'Reilly 2005). Sometimes referred to as the transformation from the read-only to the read-write web, Web 2.0 is the evolution of the Internet from a place where websites disseminated information to users, to a platform (a place to run computer applications) that enables and encourages collaboration among users. Users can interact between each other, and interact with the contents themselves. Webpages are no longer purely static but can change according to users' choices. Web 2.0 also allows users to be involved as web actors and interact with the webpage.[7] The possibility to involve Web users in the production of digital public history project will be discussed below.

Digital Public History and User-Generated Contents

From Digital History to Digital Public History

In a post on the future of digital history, digital historian William G. Thomas underlined that:

> By digital we should mean something much more than big data or computation, we should mean an engagement with the medium that challenges us to rethink, re-configure, re-conceptualize, and reimagine the forms of historical expression and historical knowledge, suitable to the digital tools, networks, and machinery at our disposal.
> (Thomas 2014)

Digital tools, networks, and media affect the public component of historical practices. In the introduction to their digital history guide, Cohen and Rosenzweig list the seven qualities of digital media and networks that potentially allow to do things better: accessibility and interactivity are among them (2005). Digital tools, technology, and media can help the development of public history.

Digital history – and digital humanities at large – have a public component that resonates in public history. The Internet is certainly the main aspect that gives digital history a public space. Technically, every website can reach the public in every part of the world. The links between the Internet and public access explain why one could argue that history online is by definition public, since it may be accessed by anybody who has an Internet connection. In other words, digital history has the potential to become the typical public activity for historians.

However, it is clear that not all digital history projects are public history. Digital history projects may have no public engagement at all and may primarily target academic audiences. Digital tools can be used to study materials or to provide new layers of interpretation without any public access or engagement. Through the Internet, historians can create websites, blogs, apps, and use social media to make their research public. Historians can also participate in forums and public discussions about their projects. In 2015, a session was organized at the annual conference of the National Council on Public History (NCPH) about digital public history. As Jason Heppler expressed, "There is a difference between 'public-facing' digital projects and digital projects of public engagement" (undated). Sheila Brennan argues that "if our questions are driving our projects, then the project is not public. It's our project" (Cantwell 2015). There is a difference between public access and public engagement. Besides, it is not because an online project, a website, or a blog has the potential to reach millions of Internet users that it actually does. For example, many online historical exhibitions designed by students, historians, or even institutions are barely visited.

Are historians whose blogs, websites, and online projects are merely visited by a couple of users, digital public historians? When does digital history become public digital history? The publicness – the type of audiences, their engagement with the project – of digital history is a major source of discussion.

In order to allow public participation, sources should be available. While most academic production relies on footnotes to provide information on primary sources, digital historians have other options. Digital media allows historians – mostly through hyperlinks – to provide "opportunity for people to evaluate sources, and, consequently, the historian's interpretation of them" (Foster 2014). Added to online historical projects, online primary sources allow users to understand how historians analyze documents and construct their interpretation. This creates better trust among users who may also construct their own interpretation. Through digital media, there is a possibility to make historians' methodology publicly available. The question remains, though, to know who the audiences are. Users may be scholars who discuss the work of their peers or non-specialist and/or broader audiences interested in the topic. The online presentation of the project and the writing style would vary according to the targeted audiences.[8] The public participation from scholars, community, collection managers, and other users in the digital public history project should not be limited to public feedback. Audiences can help shape the historical questions and approaches about the project. This participates in the distinction between digital history and digital public history. Scheinfeldt encourages digital humanists at large to release early and often through digital platforms. He argues that public release through blogs, websites, and digital publications gives opportunities for other scholars and non-academic audiences to give feedback early in the production and, therefore, to be part of the project (2014a).

Many works have been published on digital humanities and – to some extent – on digital history, but digital public history has been much less explored (Zotero undated; Noiret 2013, 2015; Heppler undated). Leon regrets that "the most recent edited collection that focused on digital history [Nawrotzki and Dougherty 2013] only includes one essay that addresses public history" (Leon 2015). Digital public historians work at making history accessible and usable to diverse audiences (Hillman 2015). Digital public historians also contribute to making the public an actor of history projects through user-generated contents. As Leon argues, "this notion of user-centered history is the key factor that makes digital public history stand apart both from academic digital history and other work in digital humanities" (Leon 2015). Through public engagement and participation, digital history can become digital public history. It is critical to pay attention to the process and tools by which public participation can take place.

In order to do digital public history, it is important to try to define whom one is collaborating with and who the audiences for specific types of projects are. Digital public historians have to build audiences (Cohen and Rosenzweig 2005, 141–159). The different chapters of this textbook go into more specific details regarding digital audiences for online collection, exhibitions, apps, and other projects. Specific audiences affect digital public history projects. Some targets can be identified at the beginning of projects – for instance clients, community, scholars, family members, or museum visitors. The relative anonymity of the Internet makes it challenging to identify audiences. Some tools exist to track and assess digital audiences (Cohen and Rosenzweig 2005, 141–159). Web analytics also provide solutions to better know the online users (Beasley 2013).

The Web 2.0 has facilitated user engagement where anyone with access to the Web is able to contribute to history projects (Noiret 2013). In a 2014 article, Meg Foster thus analyzes the complex and powerful relationship between the Internet and public history (Foster

2014). She argues that thanks to Web 2.0, "the status of public historians as the producers and 'laypeople' as the audience of history is shifting." She continues, "Ordinary people are using online technologies to shape the past, while historians are reporting, commenting and contributing to these changes" (Foster 2014). Whether Web 2.0 has so strongly affected the role of public historians remains an issue of discussion, however it is clear that the Internet offers a way to reunite digital history and public history.

Crowdsourcing and Digital Public Engagement

Public history is not only history for a large audience but involves public participation as well. In spite of Web 2.0, the Internet does not always make audiences active. The risk for digital public historians is to create history that is enjoyed but not engaged with by audiences. Instead of simply asking for final comments from users, historians can involve audiences early in the process. The relations between digital public historians and users raise questions about the role of historians in participatory processes. On the one hand, the Internet has fostered a democratization of access and made user participation possible. On the other hand, the Internet has also resulted in an absence of authenticity. As Gertrude Himmelfarb stressed in her article against the use of the Internet:

> the Internet does not distinguish between the true and the false, the important and the trivial, the enduring and the ephemeral ... Every source appearing on the screen has the same weight and credibility as every other; no authority is "privileged" over any other.
> (1996)

Everybody may, today, tag and comment on documents online. What can be the role of historians in the effervescence of opinions about the past? Those questions have been particularly important in the rise of crowdsourcing activities.

The term "crowdsourcing" was first used by Jeff Howe in 2006 and defined as "the act of taking work once performed within an organization and outsourcing it to the general public through an open call for participants" (Ridge 2014, 1; Howe 2006). Crowdsourcing is a process by which practice – and to some extent authority – is delegated to individuals or groups through digital tools. In Figure 8.1, users are invited to contribute to the transcription of Jeremy Bentham's manuscript. Similar to a military draft, the poster shows how crowdsourcing relies on volunteers to accomplish some digital tasks, in this case, digital transcription. Crowdsourcing is, at first, a reflection on roles and practices in historical production (Owens 2012).

Historians and institutions can use crowdsourcing for many different projects in which different users can participate. Crowdsourcing can be used for transcription and correction in which users transform texts into machine-readable format (Marston 2015). For instance, for *What's on the Menu* users help the New York Public Library to transcribe the "historical restaurant menus, dish by dish, so that they can be searched by what people were eating back in the day" (Orville 2005). Crowdsourcing can also be about the identification of places, people, and other items (Marston 2015). *Placeography* is a project created by the Minnesota Historical Society in 2007. The project invites users to provide personal stories about the history of sites, buildings, neighborhoods, or any other place to which they have a personal connection. Other crowdsourcing projects ask users to provide contents – stories, artifacts – for digital collections. *Parallel Archives* is a project in which historical documents related to life under communism in Eastern Europe are collected from audiences. The result is the digitization of everyday materials directly coming from the public involvement in the project. Finally, crowdsourcing can also be utilized to manage existing collections. Users are asked to process, describe, and tag items. Since 2008, cultural institutions all around the world (U.S. Library of Congress, National Library of New Zealand, the National Archives UK, for instance) have participated in the *Flickr Commons*, a project in which visitors could share, tag, and comment on photo archives online. Likewise, the U.S. National Archives uses the notion of "citizen archivists" who can tag, transcribe, and edit items related to the records of the U.S. National Archives.

Crowdsourcing encapsulates the challenges of digital public historians. On the one hand, it enhances public participation in historical projects. Public participation can help manage very large amounts of material in archives and libraries, especially for small, under-staffed institutions. Crowdsourcing can allow existing communities to be actively involved in the collection of their heritage. It also helps institutions to know better what users want to collect and preserve.[9] Crowdsourcing raises theoretical and practical issues about historians' role and authority as well.[10] In crowdsourcing, only what participants know and do matters, not who they are. This meritocracy can be prolific, but it can also trigger unexpected consequences. Quality control is an issue to be considered. Everybody can comment on the Internet, it does not mean that every statement is true or even relevant. Crowdsourcing might result in an absence of authenticity and authority. The fruits of the absence of authority should be balanced with the need for critical understanding of sources. The challenge for historians is to avoid the replacement of knowledge and analysis by opinions. Digital public historians have to work at the creation of knowledge and scholarship, and not to the multiplication of pure opinions (Grove 2009).

Digital public construction of history works better when crowdsourcing is done through commitment guided by rules, like in transcription projects. Crowdsourcing is here not limited to tagging pictures but implies a personal investment. This commitment leads to the creation of citizen (digital) history in which volunteers assist scholars in conducting scholarly research. Scientists have used crowdsourcing (citizen science) to create platforms in which users help scholars study natural phenomena. For *Old Weather*, users help reconstruct the climate by transcribing old weather records from ships' logs. As Mia Ridge argues, "Building a successful crowdsourcing project requires an understanding of the motivations for initial and on-going participation, the characteristics of tasks suited to crowdsourcing and the application of best practices in design for participation, content validation, marketing and community building" (2014, 2). Creators of projects must decide what role is given to the crowd. Can users only provide documents? Can they comment and interpret the items? Or can the users even change the format and research questions of the project? In the last category, the project becomes co-creative. Rose Holley gives useful tips to be considered before launching a crowdsourcing project (2010).

Regardless of the project, it is important to maintain critical analysis of sources. For instance, *PhotosNormandie* is a crowdsourcing project that re-documents D-Day and subsequent military campaign photographs through new captions (Peccatte 2012; Cade 2013). Public participation is asked and users help identify sites, weapons, regiments on photographs. However, comments are not taken for granted. This is where crowdsourcing offers space for historical analysis. Users are encouraged – as for any historical production – to provide evidence for their comments. Sources are compared and cross-analyzed. Historians in crowdsourcing projects must not act as cultural missionaries, bringing knowledge to the crowd, but should encourage to apply historical analysis to documents. Crowdsourcing can then become a fantastic way not only to share documents but also to reach and interpret the past. It is as important to enhance public practice as to involve the non-academic public in history production. As for public history at large, crowdsourcing is first of all a community of practice.

Programming, Web Design, and Systems for Digital Public Historians

Programming

There have been many debates among practitioners about the skills historians need to perform digital (public) history. One is about programming. Computers are machines that make millions of operations according to programs designed by humans. Designed as a set of lines of coding, programming (or coding) is basically a set of instructions given by humans to computers. Coding is a language in which humans and computers can interact. Should historians know coding and programming in order to create digital public history projects? The short answer is "maybe not." Historians can be very effective through the simple use of software and digital tools. The Institute for Historical Research (London, UK) proposes multiple introductions to the use of digital tools and technology for historians. Furthermore, many editors exist today to design a website (wordpress, dreamweaver), to curate online exhibitions (Omeka), to manage archives (pastperfect), that do not need historians to code.

Many digital history and digital public history projects are collaboration between historians and other experts like computer scientists. Digital historians may not be able to design entire programs and set of codes, but they should be able to figure out what programs do in order to better understand what computers and computer scientists can do for history. Each programming language may be associated with a particular use (Pinola 2013). Software programming such as C, C++, C#, Python, or Ruby, is complex and requires specific skills.[11] C, C++, and Python can be used to develop software, applications, or video games as well. They are particularly useful for creating an immersive environment.[12] In a talk about the Perseus Digital Library, Gregory Crane talked about the future of the humanities and the need for "polyglots" or "connectors" – "people who can stand between humanities and computer scientists – who can guide the digital channels." (Manan 2006). Indeed, what matters is ultimately not the program but its use to produce history.

It is important for historians to understand what digital tools and software do and imply for the production of (public) history. Historians may consult the numerous online tutorials about programming.[13] Simply using tools without understanding the issues at stake may limit the historian's set of action. Historians should not be digitally passive users. Since computers and digital tools are the media that link the different actors of digital public history projects, historians should be able to understand their functioning.

Web Design

The creation of websites has become a crucial step in digital public history. Websites may be public platforms that allow interaction. Although some historical institutions outsource Web design activities, public historians should at least be aware of the process in order to communicate with Web designers. Digital public historians may know about programming languages that appear useful to foster public interaction.

HTML, CSS, JavaScript, PHP, Flash, or AJAX are used to program on the Web and to design websites and applications. HTML (HyperText Markup Language) is the *lingua franca* for the Web. Invented by Tim Berners-Lee in the late 1980s, HTML basically tells the Web browser what content to display thanks to tags that format the contents of the page.[14] If they need to design websites, historians should start with HTML and CSS.[15]

Public historians should also be aware of design issues and must pay particular attention to the accessibility and usability of websites. Part of general Web design recommendations, accessibility is fundamental to make digital history a public and participatory process.[16] Usability, navigation, interactivity, and user-focused design should be at the core of digital public history websites (Petrik 2000; Cohen and Rosenzweig 2005, 51–58). Colors, size, and font choices also matter (Petrik 2000). Historians must give substantial consideration to who would use the website, in order to design a more appropriate interface. Would users want to download (crowdsourcing projects), comment, or transcribe items? Would the website be primarily used by scholars or by non-academic audiences? For the latter, it may be useful to provide reader-friendly short texts.[17] Today, historians can easily use software designed specifically to produce a website. HTML editors usually have a visual "what you see is what you get" (WYSIWYG) interface that helps create usable websites.

Creating Usable Digital Sources: Database and Text Encoding

Access to sources has become a key element for collection management.[18] However, the number of sources can undermine public access, especially when there is no straight-forward way to find specific information. In order to present hundreds or thousands of documents online, digital public historians can use two main approaches: database and XML (Extensible Markup Language). The main asset of database and XML is to organize and make online materials searchable – and therefore usable – by users. They both allow historians to define data as "name," "date," "site," or any other variable, and to encode historical materials according to these variables. For example, the creation of a database of one author's letters and personal writing enables accurate searches from users by dates, individuals, topics, or any other keywords.[19]

A database is a stored collection of data (Ramsay 2004). In addition to basic database management systems (Excel, Access), digital public historians can use more complex tools to increase the usability of historical sources.[20] A relational database is able to understand how lists and the objects within them relate to each other, so make searches more accurate. In order to make online searches possible, historians have to create web databases on servers (an Excel database on a historian's computer desktop would not be available for online search).[21] Web database therefore requires scripting languages such as PHP to link information from the database and webpages.[22]

Like HTML, XML is a markup language.[23] It means that it wraps contents into tags. Computers are only able to process binary data (lists of 0 and 1). So, they need tags to make sense of data. Words have to be encoded in order to be processed by computers. Tags that are used to encode a text are the markup language (XML), and the application of the markup language to a text is called text encoding. While databases make queries possible by storing information in lists of data, XML transforms texts and other documents into searchable items.[24] XML is, more than database, appropriate for written primary sources.

The difficulty of XML is its extreme flexibility. In XML, each element has to be defined by the creator of the document. This may result in a great variety of encoded texts. Text encoding has been made easier and more consistent through the Text Encoding Initiative (TEI). The TEI is an international organization founded in 1987 to develop guidelines for encoding machine-readable texts in the humanities and social sciences (Cummings 2007). Digital public historians have used the TEI and text encoding to make huge corpus

Figure 8.1 "Transcribe Bentham Needs You!" Transcribe Bentham, A Participatory Initiative, 2015. Image created by Kris Grint. Courtesy of Tim Causer/UCL Transcribe Bentham.

searchable. Among numerous projects, the University of College London launched Transcribe Bentham – see Figure 8.1 – in which the hand-written manuscripts of the British philosopher are transformed into searchable document through XML and TEI guideline.

To conclude, the digital media, tools, and systems may greatly affect historians' public practices. Public historians do not need to know and use every aspect of digital history, but may focus on what helps increase the public components of their projects. Digital tools and media can certainly inspire public historians to create digital spaces of public interaction. This is why most of the chapters in this textbook deal with specific digital tools and technology that contribute to public engagement in collection management, exhibitions, oral history, or video games. In particular, readers can consult Chapter 9, which explores how digital tools can create an immersive environment for historians and their audiences.

Notes

1 The Institutionalization of the Digital Humanities was also proved by the establishment of the Office of Digital Humanities by the National Endowment for the Humanities (U.S.) in 2008 (Svensson 2009).
2 See for instance the Manifesto for the Digital Humanities issued at the 2010 THATCamp Paris.

3 Historians should know the basics of the binary numeral system, the creation of data, and the functioning of the operating system (OS) and browser (Zemanek and Chitty 2015). Andrea Laue provides a useful introduction on how computers work (Laue 2004).

4 British historians were at the forefront of historical computing. The Association for History and Computing (AHC) was founded at Westfield College, University of London, in 1986, and has sponsored several large conferences and published proceedings (Thomas 2014).

5 The Institute of Historical Research provides an online browser of different digital tools according to the historian's need, www.history.ac.uk/history-online/tools (accessed November 2014).

6 See Valley of the Shadow, http://valley.lib.virginia.edu/VoS/choosepart.html; Digital Harlem: Everyday Life, 1915–1930, http://digitalharlem.org/; and Going to the Show, http://docsouth.unc.edu/gtts/ (accessed August 9, 2015).

7 Forums and tags are some of the most famous changes in Web 2.0. The creation of Wikipedia in 2001 is one of the most famous examples of the participatory digital construction of knowledge.

8 See Chapter 4.

9 See Chapter 1.

10 See Chapter 11.

11 Wiki tutorials for Python, https://wiki.python.org/moin/ and forum http://www.python-forum.org/ (accessed December 2014).

12 See Chapter 9.

13 A useful project for historians interested in coding is called The Programming Historian. See in particular Code Academy, www.codecademy.com/, w3schools, www.w3schools.com/ (accessed January 20, 2015).

14 To see the HTML code of any page on the Internet, use the right button of the mouse and then select "view page source." Historians can use the World Wide Web Consortium to see the different HTML tags, www.w3.org (accessed August 10, 2015).

15 While HTML controls the structure of the document, Cascading Style Sheets, or CSS, is used to control the visual presentation of webpages.

16 The W3C has issued a helpful series of white papers, guidelines, and techniques to make websites more accessible for a variety of people, www.w3.org/WAI/ (accessed January 2015).

17 See Chapter 4.

18 See Chapter 1.

19 For an introduction to XML, see www.tei-c.org/release/doc/tei-p5-doc/en/html/SG.html. The Institute for Historical Research (IHR) provides an introduction for historians to Semantic Markup, as well as an introduction to Text Mining, www.history.ac.uk/research-training/courses/digital-tools. The IHR also provides tutorials for historians to build and use databases: www.history.ac.uk/research-training/courses/building-databases and www.history.ac.uk/research-training/courses/designing-databases (accessed November 2014).

20 Microsoft Excel is a basic example in which users can create simple databases such as a list of data sorted by name, age, and so on. More complex database management software (like Access) can be used to create non-numerical lists of data.

21 Digital historians who wish to build online relational databases may use the expensive Oracle software or – for more modest projects – MySQL that is an open-source software. For instance, MySQL is used to handle the rich database of the September 11 Digital Archives.

22 See the Appendix in Cohen and Rosenzweig, http://chnm.gmu.edu/digitalhistory/appendix/index.php (accessed November 2014).

23 For an introduction to the XML ground rule, see http://teibyexample.org/modules/TBED00v00.htm (accessed November 2014).

24 Historians can therefore use text editors such as Notepad (Windows) or TextEdit (Mac) to create XML documents.

Bibliography

Ayers, Edward. "The Pasts and Futures of Digital History." Virginia Center for Digital History, 1999, www.vcdh.virginia.edu/PastsFutures.html (accessed September 23, 2015).

Beasley, Michael. *Practical Web Analytics for User Experience: How Analytics Can Help You Understand Your Users*, Burlington: Morgan Kaufmann, 2013.

Berry, David M., ed. *Understanding Digital Humanities*, Houndmills and New York: Palgrave Macmillan, 2012.

Cade, D.L. "PhotosNormandie: An Online Archive of 3,000+ CC Photos from WWII." *PetaPixel*, April 6, 2013, http://petapixel.com/2013/04/06/photosnormandy-a-collection-of-over-3000-cc-photos-from-wwii/ (accessed August 9, 2015).

Cantwell, Chris. "Public History as Digital History as Public History." *DH&PH*, April 2015, http://dh-ph.tumblr.com/ (accessed August 3, 2015).

Catt, Braden. "Visualizations." digitalpublichistory.com, last modified April 30, 2015, www.digitalpublichistory.com/dph-in-action/visualizations/ (accessed August 8, 2015).

Cohen, Daniel and Rosenzweig, Roy. *Digital History: A Guide to Gathering, Preserving, and Presenting the Past on the Web*, Pittsburgh: University of Pennsylvania Press, 2005.

Cohen, Daniel J., Frisch, Michael, Gallagher, Patrick, Mintz, Steven, Sword, Kirsten, Murrell Taylor, Amy, Thomas III, William G. and Turkel, William J. "Interchange: The Promise of Digital History." *The Journal of American History*, 95/2 (September 2008), www.journalofamericanhistory.org/issues/952/interchange/ (accessed January 2014).

Cummings, James. "The Text Encoding Initiative and the Study of Literature." In *A Companion to Digital Literary Studies*, edited by Ray Siemens and Susan Schreibman, Oxford: Blackwell Publishing, 2007, 451–476.

The Digital Humanities Manifesto 2.0. 2009, www.humanitiesblast.com/manifesto/Manifesto_V2.pdf (accessed August 10, 2015).

Foster, Meg. "Online and Plugged In? Public History and Historians in the Digital Age." *Public History Review*, 21 (December 2014): 1–19, http://epress.lib.uts.edu.au/journals/index.php/phrj/article/view/4295 (accessed August 7, 2015).

Gold, Matthew K., ed. *Debates in the Digital Humanities*, Minneapolis: University of Minnesota Press, 2012.

Grove, Tim. "New Media and the Challenges for Public History." *Perspectives on History*, May 2009, www.historians.org/publications-and-directories/perspectives-on-history/may-2009/intersections-history-and-new-media/new-media-and-the-challenges-for-public-history (accessed January 2015).

Heppler, Jason. "Digital & Public History." Personal blog, undated, http://jasonheppler.org/digital/ (accessed August 4, 2015).

Hillman, Meghan. "Defining DPH." DigitalPublicHistory.com, May 8, 2015, www.digitalpublichistory.com/about (accessed August 7, 2015).

Himmelfarb, Gertrude. "A Neo-Luddite Reflects on the Internet." *Chronicle of Higher Education*, November 1, 1996.

Holley, Rose. "Crowdsourcing: How and Why Should Libraries Do It?" *D-Lib Magazine*, 16/3/4 (March–April 2010), http://dlib.org/dlib/march10/holley/03holley.html (accessed August 10, 2015).

Howe, Jeff. "The Rise of Crowdsourcing." *Wired*, June 2006, www.wired.com/wired/archive/14.06/crowds_pr.html (accessed August 8, 2015).

Journal of Digital Humanities. "Bibliography." *Journal of Digital Humanities*, 1/4 (2012), http://journalofdigitalhumanities.org/1-4/bibliography/ (accessed August 7, 2015).

Laue, Andrea. "How the Computer Works." In *A Companion to Digital Humanities*, edited by Ray Siemens, John Unsworth, and Susan Schreibman, Oxford: Wiley-Blackwell, 2004, www.digitalhumanities.org/companion/ (accessed November 2014).

Leon, Sharon. "User-Centered Digital History: Doing Public History on the Web." *Bracket*, March 3, 2015, www.6floors.org/bracket/2015/03/03/user-centered-digital-history-doing-public-history-on-the-web/ (accessed August 4, 2015).

McCarty, Willard. *Humanities Computing*, New York: Palgrave, 2005.

Manan, Ahmed. "The Polyglot Manifesto." *History News Networks*, May 21, 2006, http://historynewsnetwork.org/article/25354 (accessed November 2014).

Marston, Emma. "Crowdsourcing and Funding." *Digital Public History*, May 2015, www.digitalpublichistory.com (accessed August 8, 2015).

Nawrotzki, Kristen and Dougherty, Jack, eds. *Writing History in the Digital Age*, Ann Arbor: University of Michigan Press, 2013.

Noiret, Serge. "Digital History 2.0." In *L'histoire contemporaine à l'ère numérique – Contemporary History in the Digital Age*, edited by Frédéric Clavert and Serge Noiret, Brussels, Bern, Berlin, Frankfurt am Main, New York, Oxford and Wien: Peter Lang, 2013, 155–190.

Noiret, Serge. "Digital Public History: Bringing the Public Back In." *Public History Weekly*, 3 (2015), http://public-history-weekly.oldenbourg-verlag.de/3-2015-13/digital-public-history-bringing-the-public-back-in/ (accessed August 7, 2015).

O'Reilly, Tim. "What Is Web 2.0: Design Patterns and Business Models for the Next Generation of Software." *O'Reilly*, September 30, 2005, www.oreilly.com/pub/a/web2/archive/what-is-web-20.html (accessed August 5, 2015).

Orville, Vernon Burton. "American Digital History." *Social Science Computer Review*, 23/2 (Summer 2005): 206–220, http://chnm.gmu.edu/essays-on-history-new-media/essays/?essayid=30 (accessed November 2014).

Owens, Trevor. "The Key Questions of Cultural Heritage Crowdsourcing Projects." Trevorowens.org, July 31, 2012, www.trevorowens.org/2012/07/the-key-questions-of-cultural-heritage-crowdsourcing-projects/ (accessed August 10, 2015).

Peccatte, Patrick. "PhotosNormandie a cinq ans – un bilan en forme de FAQ." *Déjà vu*, January 27, 2012, http://culturevisuelle.org/dejavu/1097 (accessed September 23, 2015).

Petrik, Paula. "Top Ten Mistakes in Academic Web Design." *Essays on History and New Media*, May 2000, http://chnm.gmu.edu/essays-on-history-new-media/essays/?essayid=3 (accessed August 4, 2015).

Pinola, Melissa. "Which Programming Language Should I Learn First?" *lifehacker*, December 5, 2013, http://lifehacker.com/which-programming-language-should-i-learn-first-1477153665 (accessed January 10, 2015).

Ramsay, Stephens. "Databases. Introduction." In *Companion to Digital Humanities*, edited by Ray Siemens, John Unsworth, and Susan Schreibman, Oxford: Blackwell Publishing Professional, 2004, www.digitalhumanities.org/companion/ (accessed August 1, 2015).

Ridge, Mia, ed. *Crowdsourcing Our Cultural Heritage*, Farnham: Ashgate, 2014.

Robertson, Stephen. "The Differences between Digital History and Digital Humanities." May 23, 2014, http://drstephenrobertson.com/blog-post/the-differences-between-digital-history-and-digital-humanities/ (accessed August 7, 2015).

Rogers, Brent. "Bibliography." *Digital History Project*, September 27, 2010, https://digitalhistory.wordpress.com/2010/09/27/bibliography/ (accessed August 5, 2015).

Scheinfeldt, Tom. "Getting into Digital Humanities: A Top-Ten List." *Found History*, August 18, 2014a, http://foundhistory.org/digital-humanities/getting-into-digital-humanities-a-top-ten-list/ (accessed November 2014).

Scheinfeldt, Tom. "The Dividends of Difference: Recognizing Digital Humanities' Diverse Family Tree/s." *Found History*, April 7, 2014b, http://foundhistory.org/2014/04/the-dividends-of-difference-recognizing-digital-humanities-diverse-family-trees/ (accessed August 10, 2015)

Siemens, Ray, John Unsworth, and Susan Schreibman, eds. *Companion to Digital Humanities*, Oxford: Blackwell Publishing Professional, 2004, www.digitalhumanities.org/companion/ (accessed August 1, 2015).

Svensson, Patrik. "Humanities Computing as Digital Humanities." *Digital Humanities Quarterly*, 3/3 (2009), www.digitalhumanities.org/dhq/vol/3/3/000065/000065.html (accessed August 6, 2015).

Svensson, Patrik. "The Landscape of Digital Humanities." *Digital Humanities Quarterly*, 4/1 (2010), http://digitalhumanities.org/dhq/vol/4/1/000080/000080.html (accessed August 6, 2015).

Svensson, Patrik. "Envisioning the Digital Humanities." *Digital Humanities Quarterly*, 6/1 (2012), http://digitalhumanities.org/dhq/vol/6/1/000112/000112.html (accessed August 6, 2015).

Terras, Melissa, Julianne Nyhan, and Edward Vanhoutte, eds. *Defining Digital Humanities: A Reader*, new edition, Farnham and Burlington, VT: Ashgate, 2013.

Thomas, William G. III, "The Future of Digital History, #rrchnm20." Personal blog, November 16, 2014, http://railroads.unl.edu/blog/?p=1146 (accessed August 5, 2015).

Zemanek, Alysha and Chitty, Ethan R. "Data." *DigitalPublicHistory.com*, April 29, 2015, www.digitalpublichistory.com/fundamentals/data/ (accessed August 1, 2015).

Zotero. "Reading List on Digital Public History." Undated, www.zotero.org/groups/digital_public_history_dot_com (accessed August 2, 2015).

9 Immersive Environments or Making the Past Alive

Immersive Environment and the Recreation of the Past

Immersion, Living History, and Re-Enactment

> All understanding interpreters know as well as I what the ideal interpretation implies: re-creation of the past, and kinship with it. The problem is how to achieve this desirable end.
>
> (Tilden 1984, 70)

As Freeman Tilden explained in his groundbreaking book on historical interpretation, historians – as other interpreters – should be familiar with the practice and challenge associated with the recreation of the past. Experience and recreation of the past can take various shapes such as, for instance, living history sites, re-enactments, or role-playing games. These formats are based on a common principle: to allow people to step back in time in immersive environments. Immersive environments create a perception – through various tools and techniques – of being physically present in a recreated space/time (Robertson et al. 2006). For instance, the international organization Bridging Ages – Figure 9.1 – aims at "bridging the past with the present" and "recreating the past in an educational setting." Its website states that "Time Travels is an educational method where the participants research and take part in the life of another historical time period."[1] Immersive environment and recreation of the past is interactive and can foster a public and personal engagement with the past. In order to recreate the past, sites and organizations rely mostly on three principal tools – tours, multimedia and digital technology, and live activities – that we will cover in this chapter.

Recreating the past is largely associated with one category of sites (living history sites) and one activity (re-enactment). Living history is a simulation of life in the past (Anderson 1984). Often associated with museums and historic sites, living history has a long history and an extensive literature (Handler and Gable 1997; Magelssen 2007; Magelssen and Justice-Malloy 2011). Living history may be restricted to specific spaces in a museum like the *Trench Experience* in the Imperial War Museum (London). The spread of period rooms – in which artifacts from the same period are on display – in the early 20th century emerged as a result of the desire to provide visitors with the "atmosphere" of the past. Living history may also apply to whole sites. For instance, open-air museums developed in Scandinavian countries to recreate historic structures and lost heritage (Anderson 1984, 17–33). Projects vary in size, subject, and format but open-air museums mostly depict rural and pre-industrial life. In Europe, open-air museums usually only display buildings and artifacts, but in the

United States there is great interest in the recreation of activities as well. The Iowa Living History Farms recreate individual farmsteads, while other projects like the Old Sturbridge Village in Massachusetts aim at recreating communities.

Two of the most famous living history museums in the United States are Colonial Williamsburg and Henry Ford's Greenfield Village. Financed by John D. Rockefeller, William Goodwin purchased the entire area that had formed Williamsburg, restored and furnished surviving colonial buildings, built replicas, recreated gardens, and opened the town to the public.[2] Likewise, in the 1920s, Henry Ford created another major open-air museum near Detroit. Ford wanted Greenfield Village "to have something of everything with the intention of creating a museum to 'reproduce the life of the country in its every age'" (Durel 1986, 231).

Living history sites often connect with artifacts and material culture issues. Houses and other buildings on living history sites are usually furnished. It helps ground the audience in the time and place being portrayed (Peers 2007, 91). Living history sites aim to make objects alive through the recreation of the past and activities for visitors: cooking, cleaning, harvesting, and many other crafts. Considerable research is often applied to identifying authentic techniques and often recreating replica tools and equipment.

Unlike the museums that present the lives of elites and outstanding events, living history sites often focus on ordinary people and everyday life. For example, Old Sturbridge Village presents "resources for understanding the pasts of people who left little formal documentation" (Becker and George 2012, 84). Likewise, the Tenement Museum in New York City focuses on the life of migrants in the Lower East Side.

Re-enactment is a practice based on an intention to recreate the past in the present through the performance of certain actions (Samuel 1994, 139–168). For instance, more than 10,000 people participated in the re-enactment of the Battle of Gettysburg in 1998. Re-enactments rely heavily on personal experiences among participants (Johnson 2014). There is, therefore, a difference between living history and re-enactment. While re-enactment is based on the participation of re-enactors, visitors of living history sites may simply "consume" history with limited engagement. Visitors are not necessarily participants.

Re-enactment is a global practice with groups in the United States, Australia, Britain, Germany, Namibia, and Brazil (Agnew 2004, 328). Wikipedia provides the list of events and groups of re-enactors all around the world.[3] In addition to books, magazines, and articles, re-enactment is the subject of many handbooks, how-to tutorials, YouTube demonstration, and guides of good practice from scholars, re-enactors, and groups.[4] Historians can also contact organizations like the Society for Creative Anachronism. Although many different events or periods can be re-enacted, re-enactors favor certain popular themes like the Vikings, medieval tournaments, pirates, or pilgrims. War-related re-enactments are without doubt the most popular events. In the United States, the Civil War has the largest number of re-enactors. Re-enactments can be about a specific event (Gettysburg) or about a much broader period (the Middle Ages). When focusing on a specific battle, it can be a combat demonstration, a battle re-enactment, or a tactical combat. While the battle re-enactments execute the same actions, demonstration is a public event in which re-enactors present troops, weapons, and stories without necessarily fighting. Finally, re-enactors of tactical combats have no script to follow, and fight the battle "again" with on-site judges deciding winners and losers. Another specific practice is the re-enactment of the past through music. The point is not to perform classical music but to use historical instruments through Historically Informed Performance (Butt 2002). Based on a combination of research and performance, music re-enactment attempts to recreate historical works.

Challenges for Living History Sites

One crucial aspect about immersive environment deals with the relation between education, entertainment, and commercial purposes. An increasing number of sites have developed immersive environments in order to attract more visitors. As William Pretzer points out in his essay on history and performance, "it makes a huge difference … if the institution is publicly supported or market oriented." According to him, the latter would be more concerned with "'visitors' satisfaction than with scholarly approbation" and therefore would give more room to entertainment (1999, 274). At Colonial Williamsburg (CW), pushing the entertainment angle was expected to increase visitation by building up the off-season business and by encouraging visitors to stay longer and come back often. Cary Carson, who has worked as historian at CW, argues that "Colonial Williamsburg made a marriage between education and entertainment long before it aspired to emulate libraries or art museums" (1998, 16). In his book on *Mickey Mouse History and Other Essays on American Memory*, Mike Wallace is very critical of the place given to entertainment in historical shows, for instance in the Hall of Presidents at Disneyland (1996). For "Disney Realism" the past is merely entertainment, designed more according to what designers think the public wants than any historical reality (Wallace 1996, 135–137). The challenge for historians is to create entertaining and immersive narratives that also engage the public in an understanding of the past.

Historians who participate in immersive and living history projects must pay extreme attention to the site. Different cases are possible regarding the authenticity of the sites. First, sites can be real emplacement of historic sites like CW or the Sloss Furnaces National Historic Landmark in Birmingham (Alabama). The sites can be part of historic preservation projects like Strawbery Banke in New Hampshire that saved and preserved 30 buildings from demolition in the 1950s. Projects can also reconstruct buildings and structures on their sites of origin (CW). The second case deals with sites that are not historical – in the sense that they have little or nothing to do with the artifacts and buildings reconstructed. The project removes the structures from their original sites to the living history site. For example, the Firestone Farm was relocated from its original location in Columbiana County, Ohio, to the Greenfield Village. In this scenario, the team must discuss at length what structure – and why – must be removed. For instance, removing a structure usually makes it difficult for any historic preservation nomination.[5]

Trying to recreate the past can be very problematic. Recreating the past always faces the fact that the past is gone and that any recreation can only, by definition, be incomplete. Other issues come from present-day selection. For instance, public historians David Kyvig and Myron Marty underline that while trying to recreate the past in Greenfield Village, Henry Ford "mistook the phony for the real, removed objects from the setting that gave them meaning, and failed to organize his vast collection so that the process of development over time could be appreciated" (2000, 1). Historians must be aware of the limits to the recreation of the past – visitors never fully experience what people went through in the past – and of the danger of displaying objects out of their historical context. For example, Strawbery Banke used to present in the same site the Sherburne House (restored to its early 18th century period), with other 19th century historic buildings, while other houses had not been restored at all, but simply adapted for modern use, retaining 20th century features (Durel 1986, 235). The public may have trouble making sense of the different time periods. Providing a sense of historical context is essential. One solution is for the site to focus on one specific space, theme, or topic to investigate over time. Another solution is to clearly show the different historical changes of the same building, such as Carter's Grove – an 18th century plantation within CW – that displays its development since its original 17th century site.

Performing the Past in Immersive Environments

Performing history includes many different activities such as tours, theater, and costumed character interpretations that involve acting. The actors of the performance – or interpreters – are very important in public history. In many aspects, interpreters are re-enactors of the past. It is important not only to understand how performing history can be done, but also what it can bring to the field of public engagement with the past.

Theater, First-Person Interpretation, and Historical Performance

In his *Theater 101 for Historical Interpretation*, Dale Jones – founder of Making History Connections, which helps institutions offer programs to connect with visitors – argues that "if the goal of historical interpretation is to engage and inform visitors, then some of the best tools for achieving those goals come from the world of theater" (Jones undated). Although theatrical representations of the past have been studied by theater and performance studies scholars, historians have preferred to focus on historical re-enactments in living history sites, museums, or on film and television (Dean 2012, 21).[6]

Many historical – or history-based – plays attempt to recreate the past on stage. Production teams sometimes undertake historical research. For instance, David Dean shows in his article on theater and public history how, in order to prepare a historical play about the 1917 Battle of Vimy, "the production team, and later the acting company, visited the Canadian War Museum for a tour of the First World War galleries and to examine artifacts and accurate reproductions used by the living history interpreters in the museum" (2012, 32). The collaboration between research and performance may give birth to very lively historical narratives. Dale Jones provides an interesting guideline to use theater for historical interpretation in different institutions such as museums and historic sites (undated).

Theater, as live interpretation, can also be a formidable tool to create immersive environments and to engage visitors through objects. Many resources are now available to develop museum theater and live interpretation (Bridal 2004; Hughes 1998).[7] Live interpretation is a term used to denote activities that provide active, face-to-face contact between the interpreter and the visitor (Risk 1994). Live interpretation and acting can help interpreters create immersive environments for their publics.

Tours and Performance

Tours – guided or not – are certainly the main interpretive tool to engage visitors in museums and historic sites. In her essay on successful tours in historic houses, Barbara Abramoff Levy presents several case studies (Abramoff Levy et al. 2002, 194–198). As for any historical enterprise, guides/interpreters must assemble facts (Abramoff Levy et al. 2002, 7–11). In addition to information about the historical context, a tour can use references to biographies. It helps connecting visitors to individual stories and, for historic houses, to the owners and different categories of actors who have had a historic role. The main challenge for the interpreter is to connect the site, material culture, and visitors.

In living history sites, live interpretation often takes the form of costumed historical interpretation. For instance, Figure 11.1 shows two interpreters at CW – Hope Smith (left) and Imani Turner (right) – before the latter runs to freedom. Live interpretation is done through first-, second-, or third-person interpretation techniques. In the three cases, trained presenters use costumes, effects, and objects to convey historical narratives. With third-person interpretation, interpreters are not necessarily portraying a character. They are educators or lecturers explaining people, events, or places and answering questions from the perspective of the present. Interpreters acknowledge they are present-day actors dressed with historical costumes. They can, therefore, provide information about the historical context and the difference with the present. Third-person interpreters have to be good storytellers, use colorful language and quotes from primary sources (Jones undated). Like the National Museum of American History or the Canadian Museum of Civilization, sites can develop scripted dialogues to address certain controversial issues (Tzibazi 2012, 167).

First-person interpretation is very different. In "'first person' interpretation, the interpreter thinks 'I/We' first, (s)he assumes the role of a person from the past and converse from the perspective of the past. (s)he portrays a person who does not yet know how things are going to turn out" (Salicco undated). While some sites allow interpreters to move in and out of their characters to answer questions from visitors, others – like the Ukrainian Cultural Heritage Village near Edmonton – forbid it (Markewicz 2013a). The first-person interpretation techniques may be very difficult to process; so historians should explore the rich literature and guidelines to find out about the requested skills (Roth 1998). Training, flexibility, and improvisation are crucial (Jones undated).

First-person interpretation can also be problematic. For example, awkward situations may arise when visitors mention/use a present-day reference that the interpreter is not supposed to know about. Furthermore, a historical interpreter cannot always fully adopt the views of the past and react to visitors accordingly. For instance, in her comparison between first- and third-person interpretation practices, Markewicz wonders "How would someone who was really from 1880 react to an immodestly dressed set of strangers barging into their farm house and interrogating them about their livestock and insisting upon eating some of their food?" (2013a, 2013b) One solution is to use what is termed loose first-person interpretation. Although interpreters speak in the first person, they are allowed to break the spirit and provide historical knowledge and interpretation to answer visitor questions. However, this solution also faces the risk of confusing visitors when the interpreter breaks the character with going back and forth between past and present.

Since guides and interpreters are the main media between the collections, the sites, and the visitors, it is necessary to provide them with appropriate training (Cunningham 2004). It is vital to spend significant time on training interpreters and staff members, and conduct exhaustive interpretive research (Abramoff Levy et al. 2002, 61–81). Guides should receive and be familiar with certain documents such as the institution's mission statement and historical significance, the interpretation guidelines, fact sheets, education program materials, but also more administrative documents such as the policies and procedures, and the safety and security protocols (Lavin 2002, 254). Interpreters must be able to adapt the tour to different audiences, to work with visitors from different ages (Abramoff Levy et al. 2002, 109–112).

Training is especially relevant for institutions dealing with difficult and controversial pasts. In one chapter of *Interpreting Slavery at Museums and Historic Sites*, Gallas and Perry discuss staff training, unconscious racial bias, and "racial baggage" (2014, 21–26). They explain that the training should consider visitors but also interpreters' learning crisis, namely, the reluctance to cope with topics and issues that create discomfort and/or go against personal opinions. If unresolved, interpreters' learning crisis may pass along many of their own feelings about slavery, race, and their racial baggage. More importantly, it risks reproducing dominant historical narratives and myths to visitors. It is the interpreter's role not only to educate, but also to "help visitors achieve comfort with their discomfort." This role requires interpreters to become familiar with the historical sources and to be confident to manage interpretation that inherently causes discomfort among visitors (Gallas and Perry 2014, 28, 98).

Audience Participation

Like other public history practices, performing the past should consider public participation. Giving visitors access to objects and materials from the past is crucial to create links between past and present. Objects have more meaning when used and set back in their context. Already in the late 19th century, Skansen Museum in Sweden used musicians and craft people to recreate the past (De Groot 2008, 117). Participation can be encouraged by hands-on activities like cooking, sewing, or any other crafts experienced by visitors. In addition, some sites allow participation in historical research. In the early 1980s, Strawbery Banke opened a dig to the public.[8] Many people were eager to learn the techniques of researching the history of a house, a family, or a landscape (Durel 1986, 237). Those activities aim to recreate the past through the manipulation of objects.

Second-person interpretation is another form of interpretation in which visitors may adopt a character and participate in hands-on activities (Magelssen 2006). For instance, the Lower East Side Tenement Museum (New York City) started a new public program called Tenement Inspectors. After a tour talk, participants get a questionnaire and inspect the apartments of the museum to "demand answers from costumed historic re-enactors with strong Yiddish accents" (Larson 2014). Through time travel, visitors can be "sent" to the past and attributed roles. For instance, Conner Prairie Interactive History Park in Indiana created the "Follow the North Star" program in which participants become a runaway on the Underground Railroad, fleeing from captivity, risking everything for freedom. Participants may have to follow historical guidelines or can – less often – make their own choices, although it might result in anachronism and poor historical reconstruction if not done properly.

Re-Enactments

Re-enactment has become – as seen in Figure 9.1 – very popular and can help make the past alive for museums, films and documentaries, and school programs (Johnson 2015). However, few historians participate in re-enactments (Gapps 2003). One reason may be that participants are sometimes more inclined to perform and celebrate than analyze the past. De Groot explains "They (re-enactors) often see their work as commemoration of those who died in battle, as a dedication to their memory" (De Groot 2008, 107). Re-enactments may sometimes be disconnected from any historical context, avoiding taking any stance vis-à-vis historical interpretation. Vanessa Agnew stresses in her definition of re-enactment, "regardless of whether it is the Waffen SS or Allies, European voyagers or indigenous peoples, reenactors evince a bipartisanism that rests on a general indifference to political specificity" (2004, 334). Re-enactments are mostly individual and group experiences of the past.

Historians can participate as historical advisors. In order to be familiar with the different strategies, historians can visit the multiple websites devoted to re-enacting the past, read handbooks, and watch tutorials. Ultimately, historians may contact and discuss

Figure 9.1 Re-enactment of the Battle of Waterloo (1815), French soldiers attack (right side) the English troops (left side), at Hougoumont Farm. Bicentenary of the 1815 Waterloo Battle (Belgium) (Day 1, June 19, 2015). Courtesy of Serge Noiret.

with re-enactors, and participate in re-enactments (71st Pennsylvania Volunteer Infantry undated; Civil War Reenactment Headquarters for Civil War Reenacting Events undated). Re-enactments can be useful for historical research too. Re-enactments help make the past alive by recreating historical situations. In Figure 9.1, during the bicentenary of the Battle of Waterloo, participants recreated the battle for the Hougoumont Farm in which the French attempted to bypass the English troops. Re-enactors studied in detail the site and its geography and connection with military strategy. Historians and participants can learn about the past in ways non-achievable by other means. There is a space for public historians to learn from, to collaborate with, and to improve the recreation of the past (McCalman and Pickering 2010).

Historians need to know the different types of re-enactors. The credibility of each re-enactor is measured through his/her fidelity with the past – in terms of materials and action (Agnew 2004, 330). There are the novices (referred as "farbs" in the jargon) who are at the entry level. They "undergo trials, acquire skills and experience, and are finally inducted into a community of dedicated reenactors" (Agnew 2004, 331). In addition to mainstream re-enactors, hardcore re-enactors are very strict about authenticity. In *Confederates in the Attic*, Tony Horwitz explains how some re-enactors went on extreme diets to look and feel as real Confederate soldiers (1998, 7–8, 12–13).

Re-enactments are based on collaborative practices and many actors can collaborate in major re-enactments. Re-enactments not only involve re-enactors, but also advisors, event planners, sponsors, and sometimes spectators as seen in the background of Figure 9.1.[9] The field also includes re-enactment societies – for instance Sealed Knot, the British largest re-enactment society – companies specializing in period costumes, accessories, event-planning agencies providing scripts and historical advice. Most of the societies produce their own guidelines, from which historians could learn.

As advisors, historians should also be prepared to pay particular attention to daily-life details (clothes, diet, weapons), as well as behavior and military strategy. By accomplishing tasks in a recreated historical context, historians can also test and practice research hypotheses about the past. However, re-enactments are often based on experiences and leave little space for interrogation and interpretation. Historians may face several specific challenges. Battle re-enactments usually follow a linear script devoid of complexity and sometimes even devoid of historical context. For instance, slavery is hardly discussed as a cause of the U.S. Civil War among Confederate re-enactors. In spite of the few black units, such as the 54th Massachusetts Volunteer Infantry and the 1st South Carolina Volunteers, re-enacting is basically a white activity. Re-enactors are often free to act autonomously within the script, "governed by their knowledge of what could have happened more than what actually did happen" (Thompson 2010, 162). The reconstruction of the past then becomes dependent on personal skills, choices, and interpretation.

(Video) Games and Immersive Environments

Games and Time Travels

Making history is a serious intellectual process. But does it mean there is no place for games and amusement? Is it possible to play with/in the past? As Abigail Perkiss and Mary Rizzo explained about their working group on games and public history, play has become "a central method through which the public connects with history" (2015). They created a Zotero reading list on public history and games (Zotero undated). The number of popular quizzes, TV shows, and role-playing activities present a specific aspect of public history. In the working group on public history and games, participants discussed the different types of games and how playing can help engage audiences (Rizzo 2015). Games can be very efficient activities to engage young audiences whose attention span is limited. In the United States, Reacting to the Past (RTTP) emerged in the 1990s as an alternative way of learning history through games. Designed mostly for instructors, RTTP provides a series of games to study various periods of history.

Games can also be designed in collaboration with historic sites. For instance, Bridging Ages is an international organization that utilizes local history to understand present-day life and society, and recreate the past in an educational setting. The organization uses Time Travels as a way to combine historical research, historic sites, and games in order to make history come alive for participants. In Figure 9.2, historical first-person interpreter Stephanie Steinhorst enrolls students through games and activities in the re-enactment of a campaign to secure women's suffrage in a Time Travel to 1912. Initially developed by the Educational Department at Kalmar läns Museum (Sweden), the international group provides a strict historical methodology (choice of a site, research in archives, oral history, landscape interpretation), training days, and subject teaching, before undertaking the Time Travel itself. Participants role-play those historical persons they have studied in a frozen point in the past, and join specific activities on site (Westergren 2006). For instance, Jon Hunner's class at New Mexico State University researched the 1930s, developed characters and activities, and then time-travelled with local schools to learn about the Great Depression. Bridging Ages not only works at the links between past and present, but also strengthens the links between universities, schools, museums, historic sites, and landscape.[10]

Video Games

Many video games are set in the past. Through online network, participants can now compete and interact with each other (Howard 2015). However, most of them passively

Figure 9.2 Time Travel course at New Mexico State University. Stephanie Steinhorst enrolls 5th grade students in the campaign to secure women's suffrage in a Time Travel to 1912, 2014. Credit: Jon Hunner. Courtesy of the public history program at New Mexico State University.

use the past to set the game in a different context. For example, *Call of Duty* (supposedly taking place during World War II) could entirely work without any historical context, and both the Allies and Axis could be replaced by any other actors without changing the game (Wilkinson 2014). Other video games have recently emerged as part of the Serious Games category.[11] For instance, *Pox and the City* is a role-playing game developed by a collaborative digital history project. Authors say they wanted a game – based on medical history (vaccination against smallpox) in 19th century Edinburgh – that "allowed an exploration of the social history of medicine rather than just a recapitulation of accepted theories" (Zucconi et al. 2012).

While giving space to entertainment, historical video games can be based on research (the Historical Collections of the College of Physicians of Philadelphia for *Pox and the City*) and provide understanding of the past. Another potential use of video games is to train users to analyze historical visual/written documents in their context. For instance the free game *Totem's Sound* is based on the journals of Norwegian explorer Johan Adrian Jacobson. Players must collect artifacts from coastal First Nations people (Priestman 2014). Games can help recreate the context in which artifacts should be analyzed. The role-playing dimension can also foster reflection about historical issues and engage users into various understandings of the past. In role-playing games, users may have to confront historical problems and historical complexity. Unlike mainstream games like *Call of Duty*, Serious Games do not adapt a historical context to a playing scenario but start with historical understanding of the past that they adapt to role-playing activities.

Video games can allow the reconstruction of periods and societies that no longer exist and can provide accurate representations through immersive environments. For instance,

Pox and the City uses streets that can be located on historic maps. More recently, Ubisoft's *Assassin's Creed* has received attention for its depiction of Paris during the French Revolution (Sliva 2014). Users can visit historic buildings and ordinary houses. The study of more than 150 maps by historians working for Ubisoft has informed the virtual reconstruction of Paris. However, the format of the games and the wish to provide a vision of Paris that matched users' expectation led to some distortions (Bastille, Notre-Dame Cathedral, for instance). One designer acknowledges, "the aim is not to be 100 per cent historically accurate ... It's to convey a believable setting, a believable city" (Webster 2014). As Maxime Durand, Ubisoft's in-house historian, explains, "In the single player story, the history is a backdrop ... but they (users) are seeing real people from the French Revolution like Gabriel Riqueti, the comte de Mirabeau" (Kamen 2014). Similarly to film advisors, historians have to decide whether the distortions in video games change the overall understanding of the past they wish to convey.

Historians interested in historical video games can explore the various blogs and websites devoted to the field.[12] They can also play different games and analyze how they engage users with representations and interpretations of the past. More and more digital humanists are interested in video games and now write useful analyses and tutorials. For instance, *Playing with the Past* studies the representations of history in video games and how games engage users. In particular, Elliott and Kapell's introduction informs readers of the different options to recreate a historical past through video games (Elliott and Kapell 2013).

3D Virtual Reconstruction

History in 3D

In recent years, more and more digital humanists have been using 3D technology.[13] Projects can be university-based, such as the Virtual World Heritage Laboratory (University of Virginia) that aims to apply 3D digital tools to provide new analysis of historic sites. The recreation of the past through 3D technology can also help cultural institutions to propose new experiences to their visitors. For instance, Colonial Williamsburg (CW) has launched Virtual Williamsburg.

3D technology is particularly relevant to recreate and preserve the past through digital format. Buildings and their interiors can be fully recreated through 3D technology. For instance, CW has used 3D technology to recreate 18th century Drayton Hall (Danaparamita 2013). It is especially relevant for virtual archaeology that deals with events and sites long gone (Frischer and Dakouri-Hild 2008).[14] Virtual archaeologist Bernard Frischer explains that with the 3D reconstruction of archaeological sites:

> we can virtually preserve the site through 3D data capture as we dig it up. And, once we model the 3D data gathered in the field, we can allow our colleagues to retrace our decisions and to test the validity of our conclusions with more precision and confidence.
>
> (Frischer undated, v)

Rome Reborn is an international project that creates 3D models of ancient Rome from the first settlement (ca. 1000 B.C.E.) to the depopulation of the city in the early Middle-Ages (ca. 550 C.E.). Through 3D modeling, several international research centers have compiled research to recreate the city. Rome Reborn only displays the sites with enough archival documentation for an appropriate analysis. There is no place for invention. 3D reconstruction helps research the city space, the relations between buildings, and ultimately the recreation of the city organization. Designers also assert that "it can be used to run urban or architectural experiments not otherwise possible, such as how well the city or the buildings within it functioned in terms of heating and ventilation, illumination, circulation of people" (Rome Reborn 2013).

Another asset of virtual reconstruction is the fact that a digital model is progressive and can be updated with new historical discoveries. Buildings can be added to Rome Reborn according to historical progress. 3D projects can also facilitate the collaboration between various repositories. For instance, 3D historical buildings can host 3D replicas of collections housed in various museums, and help institutions display objects usually hidden from the public (Danaparamita 2013). Access to digital copies of objects makes possible the manipulation – by historians and by the public – of artifacts usually not available.[15] Through virtual 3D reconstruction, users can interact with and manipulate the contents (Forte 2011, 8). For instance, while it is not available for visitors on site, users of the virtual environment can access the narrow staircase at Drayton Hall that enslaved people used in the past.

Process, Technology, and Tools

In order to develop 3D projects, historians may have to deal with several challenges. Regarding the virtual recreation of historic buildings, it is first important to discuss and decide the historical period. Rome Reborn's team decided to choose 320 c.e. as the date for the city modeling. Since 3D reconstruction is based on remaining information about the site/building, the decision should come from the amount of available materials. When attempting to reconstruct the Renault (car factory) assembly line, French historians decided to focus on the year 1922 because they could take advantage of multiple photographs, newspaper articles, and other visual documents (Michel 2009). Historians must have a clear idea of their path of action, especially when they deal with poorly documented sites. When the amount of information is limited, would historians display unfinished buildings or present a version of what they think is close to the reality?

Historians who participate in virtual reconstruction are particularly helpful in the collection of information. For instance, the team in charge of the virtual reconstitution of medieval Cluny monastery in France has been composed of several historians (Père et al. 2010, 156). Likewise historian Marie-Pierre Besnard participates in the virtual reconstruction of Notre-Dame as it was before World War II (Figure 9.3). Research of materials includes multiple formats, so historians should not limit their research to written documents. In addition to the traditional archives, historians must go on site for the different measurements and eventually for archaeological remains. Historians should also be prepared to look for depictions such as works of art, photographs, and literary descriptions of the site.

In addition to historical research, any accurate virtual reconstruction of sites must be based on on-site measuring. The layout of the site can first be designed through CAD (Computer-Assisted Design) software. Called a hand-made model, this format is designed according to the measurements taken on site. To be more accurate, teams can use 3D scanners. If objects and buildings still exist, 3D scanners – contact or non-contact – can be used to create scan models.[16] After the collect, it is necessary to use the point cloud to extrapolate the shape of the items and produce the 3D model used for the reconstruction of the past. Notre-Dame Reborn provides models such as Figure 9.3 that is based on scanning, and modeling through 3DSmax. Created in 1982 by Autodesk, AutoCAD is the most famous CAD software to design buildings, products, or public spaces, without having to draw up

Figure 9.3 Digital representation of the church Notre-Dame, Saint-Lô (France) as it was before
World War II, 2015. Courtesy of Marie-Pierre Besnard/Notre-Dame Reborn, SO
NUMERIQUE.

plans by hand. Other 3D modeling software examples are Google SketchUp and Blender
(free) that offer polyvalent 3D design. Maya and 3D Studio Max are more complete but also
more expensive and more complex to use.

There are two options to design a 3D object. Historians can use CAD software to apply
on-site measurements and photographs to create the object. The second option is to use
the point cloud collected with 3D scanners to create CAD models.[17] Meshing or mesh
modeling is the action of converting points – but also suppressing overlapping points, gaps,
and irrelevant points – into meshes (forms). 3D mesh modeling software is then useful.[18] In
their article on the modeling of the Cluny monastery (France), Père, Landrieu, and Rollier-
Hansellman offer a very interesting example of the different steps of 3D model construction
(Père et al. 2010, 155).

It is important that historians are part of the 3D modeling design as well. The results of
the 3D creation must be verified and compared with existing historical sources (archaeological remains, various visual depictions such as paintings and eventually photographs,
written descriptions, and so on). For instance, for the missing part of the Cluny monastery,
historians completed the model by using examples of monasteries from the same time
period, by using written descriptions, and archaeological dig (Père et al. 2010, 153–154).
Conflicting views may exist not only between historical depictions and the 3D model, but
also between historical depictions themselves (Struck et al. 2008, 116). The role of historians is essential to overcome those issues.

In order to go further in the virtual reconstruction of the past and to make projects more interactive, historians can participate in immersive environment design. Figure 9.3 is part of the interactive virtual visit of the church created by the Notre-Dame Reborn project. Interiors of building can be enriched with objects digitized by other institutions. The role of the historian may be to select appropriate objects according to the period and site of the reconstruction. More difficult is the rendering of light, shadow, and eventually acoustic effects. Thanks to 3ds Max software and photographs from the site, the virtual reconstruction team added light and shadow to the virtual Drayton Hall (Danaparamita 2013). Another very impressive example is the project about the ruins of the monastery of Georgenthal in Germany (Struck et al. 2008). The interactive project uses sound to allow users to enter an immersive environment of the 16th century. For instance, the 1525 attack of the monastery is recreated and users "can locate each voice of the attackers and victims moving past and through each other in surprising acoustic transparency" (Struck et al. 2008, 116). Users follow the young monk Domenicus during the attack. Interactivity helps foster the personal presence of users in the virtual world. In order to move from a mere 3D reconstruction of a building to something more interactive with an immersive environment, historians need to be familiar with more complex software like Unity. For the monastery of Georgenthal project, the team had to record scenes against blue screen, and fused them with matching camera (connected in Maya software) takes of the virtual background.

To conclude, recreation of the past through immersive environments can help historians attract and engage popular audiences. Although virtual reconstruction has become one of the main techniques, immersive environments can be designed for many different sites through games, walking tours, activities, and interpretation. Historians can be very helpful in making objects come alive through the recreation of historical contexts and sceneries. Due to the complexity of the tools (digital) and skills requested (performance), historians are strongly encouraged to enter collaborative projects. As historians, it is important that they accept the need for fun and entertainment while not relegating historical understanding of the past to a secondary purpose.

Notes

1 Bridging Ages website, www.bridgingages.com/ (accessed November 12, 2014).
2 Before the American Revolution Williamsburg was an important political and social center, the capital of the province of Virginia. In 1780, the government moved to Richmond (Durel 1986, 230).
3 See Wikipedia, http://en.wikipedia.org/wiki/List_of_historical_reenactment_events; http://en.wikipedia.org/wiki/List_of_historical_reenactment_groups (accessed November 12, 2014).
4 See magazines such as *Skirmish* or *Call to Arms*.
5 See Chapter 2.
6 See also the American Alliance for Theatre and Education (AATE).
7 See also the International Museum Theatre Alliance, www.imtal.org (accessed November 15, 2014).
8 See Chapter 2.
9 See the website about the re-enactments organized for the bicentenary of the Battle of Waterloo (1815–2015), www.waterloo2015.org/en (accessed August 18, 2015).
10 Trainings, workshops and courses are provided by the Kalmar läns Museum, through the newsletter, and during annual conferences, www.bridgingages.com (accessed November 10, 2015).
11 See the Serious Games Initiative, www.seriousgames.org/ (accessed November 12, 2015).
12 See, for instance, www.playthepast.org/ and http://killscreendaily.com/about/ (accessed November 13, 2015).

13 See Chapter 8 for an overview of digital humanities, digital history, and digital public history.
14 See also the *Digital Applications in Archaeology and Cultural Heritage* online journal.
15 See for instance the 3D model of Lincoln's death mask at the Smithsonian Museum, http://3d.
    si.edu/explorer?modelid=27 (accessed August 22, 2015).
16 The scanner creates a point cloud – placed on a 3D coordinate system – of geometric samples at
    the surface of the object. There are contact or non-contact 3D scanners. Contact scanners are
    more simple but are not appropriate for fragile or big objects. There are two main categories of
    non-contact scanners: Time of Flight or by triangulation. Time of Flight scanners can be removed
    from the subject, so they are convenient for landscape or historical buildings. The reconstruction
    of the Virtual Cluny monastery in France used this type of scanner. Scanners by triangulation
    are more accurate and can be used for small objects. See for instance the Digital Michelangelo
    Project, a databank of statues by Michelangelo in Florence created by computer scientist Marc
    Levoy at Stanford with a triangulation 3D scanner, http://graphics.stanford.edu/projects/mich/
    (accessed August 25, 2015).
17 Generally, the point cloud cannot directly generate a 3D model, some intervention – called mesh-
    ing – is needed. The form (polygon mesh) is composed of vertices, edges, and faces.
18 For instance, MeshLab is an open source, portable, and extensible system for the processing and
    editing of unstructured 3D triangular meshes, http://meshlab.sourceforge.net/; see also Geomagic
    Studio, Rhinoceros 3D, and CATIA that provide a function to switch directly from a point cloud
    to a CAD model.

Bibliography

71st Pennsylvania Volunteer Infantry. *Beginner's Handbook Beginner's Guide*, undated, www.71st
  penncob.org/attachments/013_71st_MembershipPack_JGC.pdf (accessed August 25, 2015).

Abramoff Levy, Barbara, Lloyd, Sandra, and Schreiber, Susan. *Great Tours! Thematic Tours and Guide
  Training for Historic Sites*, Lanham: AltaMira Press, 2002.

Agnew, Vanessa. "What is Reenactment?" *Criticism*, 46/3 (2004), http://digitalcommons.wayne.edu/
  cgi/viewcontent.cgi?article=1151&context=criticism (accessed August 20, 2015).

Anderson, Jay. *Time Machines: The World of Living History*, Nashville: American Association for State
  and Local History, 1984.

Becker, Jane and George, Alberta Sebolt. "Teaching with the Past at Old Sturbridge Village: An
  Interview with Alberta Sebolt George." *The Public Historian*, 34/1 (Winter 2012): 83–111.

Bridal, Tessa. *Exploring Museum Theatre*, Walnut Creek: AltaMira Press, 2004.

Butt, John. *Playing with History: The Historical Approach to Musical Performance*, Cambridge: Cambridge
  University Press, 2002.

Carson, Cary. "Colonial Williamsburg and the Practice of Interpretive Planning in American History
  Museums." *The Public Historian*, 20/3 (Summer 1998): 11–51.

Civil War Reenactment Headquarters for Civil War Reenacting Events. *How to Get Started in Civil
  War Reenacting*, undated, www.reenactmenthq.com/beginners.php (accessed August 25, 2015).

Cook, Alexander. "The Use and Abuse of Historical Reenactment: Thoughts on Recent Trends in
  Public History." *Criticisms*, 46/3 (2004): 487–496.

Cunningham, Kay Mary. *The Interpreters Training Manual for Museums*, Washington, DC: American
  Association of Museums, 2004.

Danaparamita, Aria. "Coming to Drayton Hall: Historic Preservation in 3D." *PreservationNation Blog*,
  July 22, 2013, http://blog.preservationnation.org/2013/07/22/coming-to-drayton-hall-historic-
  preservation-in-3d/#.VJckBf8Ae (accessed November 22, 2014).

Dean, David. "Theatre: A Neglected Site of Public History?" *The Public Historian*, 34/3 (Summer
  2012): 21–39.

Dean, David, Meerzon, Yana, and Prince, Kathryn. *History, Memory, Performance*, London: Palgrave
  Macmillan, 2014.

De Groot, Jerome. *Consuming History: Historians and Heritage in Contemporary Popular Culture*,
  London: Routledge, 2008.

Durel, John. "The Past: A Thing to Study, A Place to Go." In *Public History: An Introduction*, edited by Barbara Howe and Emory Kemp, Malabar: Krieger Publishing Company, 1986, 229–241.

Elliott, Andrew B.R. and Kapell, Matthew Wilhelm. "Introduction: To Build a Past that Will 'Stand the Test of Time': Discovering Historical Facts, Assembling Historical Narratives."In *Playing With The Past: Digital Games and the Simulation of History*, edited by Andrew B.R. Elliott and Matthew Wilhelm Kapell, New York: Bloomsbury Academic, 2013, 1–30.

Forte, Maurizio. "Cyber-Archaeology: Notes on the Simulation of the Past." *Virtual Archaeology Review*, 2/4 (May 2011): 7–18, http://varjournal.es/doc/varj02_004_14.pdf (accessed August 25, 2015).

Frischer, Bernard. "From Digital Illustration to Digital Heuristics." In *Beyond Illustration: 2D and 3D Digital Technologies as Tools for Discovery in Archaeology*, edited by Bernard Frischer and Anastasia Dakouri-Hild, British Archaeological Report, undated, v–xxiv, www.frischerconsulting.com/frischer/pdf/Frischer_Heuristics.pdf (accessed August 25, 2015).

Frischer, Bernard and Dakouri-Hild, Anastasia. *Beyond Illustration: 2D and 3D Digital Technologies as Tools for Discovery in Archaeology*, Oxford: Archaeopress, 2008.

Gallas, Kristin and Perry, James. *Interpreting Slavery at Museums and Historic Sites*, Lanham: Rowman & Littlefield Publishers, 2014.

Gapps, Stephen. "Performing the Past: A Cultural History of Historical Reenactments." PhD diss., University of Technology, Sydney, 2003, www.phansw.org.au/author/stephengapps/ (accessed November 3, 2014).

Glassberg, David. *Sense of History: The Place of the Past in American Life*, Amherst: University of Massachusetts Press, 2001.

Hadden, Robert Lee. *Reliving the Civil War: A Reenactor's Handbook*, Mechanicsburg: Stackpole Books, 1999.

Handler, Richard and Gable, Eric. *The New History in an Old Museum: Creating the Past at Colonial Williamsburg*, Durham, NC: Duke University Press, 1997.

Horwitz, Tony. *Confederates in the Attic*, New York: Pantheon, 1998.

Howard, Josh. "Public History and Video Gaming: Spontaneous Digital Remembrance." *Public History Commons*, June 2, 2015, http://publichistorycommons.org/public-history-and-video-gaming/#sthash.IYbyPbGJ.dpuf (accessed August 25, 2015).

Hughes, Catherine. *Museum Theatre: Communicating with Visitors Through Drama*, Portsmouth, NH: Heinmann, 1998.

Jackson, Anthony. "Inter-Acting with the Past: The Use of Participatory Theater at Heritage Sites." *Research in Drama Education*, 5/2 (2000): 199–215.

Johnson, Katherine. "Performing Pasts for Present Purposes: Reenactment as Embodied, Performative History." In *History, Memory, Performance*, edited by David Dean, Yana Meerzon, and Kathryn Prince, London: Palgrave Macmillan, 2014, 36–52.

Johnson, Katherine. "Rethinking (Re)Doing: Historical Re-Enactment and/as Historiography." *Rethinking History: The Journal of Theory and Practice*, 19/2 (2015): 193–206.

Jones, Dale. "Theater 101 for Historical Interpretation." *Making History Connections*, undated, www.makinghistoryconnections.com/docs/Theater%20101%20for%20Historical%20Interpretation.pdf (accessed August 24, 2015).

Kamen, Matt. "Assassin's Creed Historian on Merging the Past with Fiction." *Wired*, October 23, 2014, www.wired.co.uk/news/archive/2014-10/23/assassins-creed-unity-interview-maxime-durand (accessed August 26, 2015).

Kyvig, David E. and Marty, Myron A. *Nearby History: Exploring the Past Around You*, second edition, Walnut Creek: AltaMira, 2000.

Larson, Sarah. "Congratulations: You're a Tenement Inspector." *The New Yorker*, August 18, 2014, www.newyorker.com/culture-desk/sarah-larson/congratulations-youre-tenement-inspector (accessed November 13, 2014).

Lavin, Meggett B. "Building a Tool Kit for Your Interpreters: Methods of Success from Drayton Hall." In *Interpreting Historic House Museums*, edited by Jessica F. Donnelly, Lanham: AltaMira Press, 2002, 251–269.

McCalman, Iain and Pickering, Paul, eds. *Historical Reenactment: From Realism to the Affective Turn*, London: Palgrave Macmillan, 2010.

Magelssen, Scott. "Making History in the Second Person: Post-Touristic Considerations for Living Historical Interpretation." *Theatre Journal*, 58/2 (2006): 291–312.

Magelssen, Scott. *Living History Museums: Undoing History through Performance*, Lanham: Scarecrow Press, 2007.

Magelssen, Scott and Justice-Malloy, Rhona, eds. *Enacting History*, Tuscaloosa: University of Alabama Press, 2011.

Markewicz, Lauren. "First Person Versus Third Person Interpretation." *History Research Shenanigans*, August 31, 2013a, https://historyboots.wordpress.com/2013/08/31/first-person-versus-third-person-interpretation/ (accessed August 25, 2015).

Markewicz, Lauren. "Challenging Visitors and Challenging Visitor Expectations." *History Research Shenanigans*, August 31, 2013b, https://historyboots.wordpress.com/2013/09/12/challenging-visitors-and-challenging-visitor-expectations/ (accessed August 25, 2015).

Michel, Alain. "The Virtual Reconstruction of a Renault-Billancourt Workshop in Inter-War France: Historical Sources, Methodology and Perspectives." *Documents pour l'histoire des techniques*, 18/2 (2009): 23–36, http://dht.revues.org/56 (accessed August 25, 2015).

O'Brien Backhouse, Meghan. "Re-Enacting the Wars of the Roses: History and Identity." In *People and Their Past: Public History Today*, edited by Paul Ashton and Hilda Kean, Basingstoke: Palgrave Macmillan, 2009, 113–130.

Peers, Laura. *Playing Ourselves: Interpreting Native Histories at Historic Reconstructions*, Lanham: AltaMira Press, 2007.

Père, Christian, Landrieu, Jeremie, and Rollier-Hansellman, Juliette. "Reconstitution virtuelle de l'église abbatiale Cluny III : des fouilles archéologiques aux algorithmes de l'imagerie." In *Virtual Retrospect 2009*, edited by Vergnieux and Delevoie, Bordeaux: Archeovision, 2010, 151–159, http://archeovision.cnrs.fr/pdf/vr09_pdf/09_Landrieu.pdf (accessed August 24, 2015).

Perkiss, Abigail and Rizzo, Mary. "Can Public History Play? A Conference Pop-up Preview." *Public History Commons*, April 13, 2015, http://publichistorycommons.org/can-public-history-play/#sthash.Ih4VOORb.dpuf (accessed August 25, 2015).

Pretzer, William S. "At Historic Sites and Outdoor Museums: A High Performance Act." In *The Public History: Essays From the Field*, edited by James B. Gardner and Peter LaPaglia, Malabar: Krieger Press, 1999, 257–279.

Priestman, Chris. "Totem's Sound Takes a Cynical Look at American Colonialism." *Kill Screen*, October 8, 2014, http://killscreendaily.com/articles/totems-sound/ (accessed August 25, 2015).

Risk, Peter. "People-Based Interpretation." In *Manual of Heritage Management*, edited by Richard Harrison, Oxford: Butterworth-Heinemann Ltd, 1994, 320–330.

Rizzo, Mary. "Can Public History Play?" *Storify*, April 2015, https://storify.com/rizzo_pubhist/can-public-history-play (accessed August 25, 2015).

Robertson, Toni, Mansfield, Tim, and Loke, Lian. "Designing an Immersive Environment for Public Use." In *Proceedings of the Ninth Conference on Participatory Design: Expanding Boundaries in Design*, New York: ACM, 2006, 31–40.

Rokem, Freddie. *Performing History: Theatrical Representations of the Past in Contemporary Theatre*, Iowa: University of Iowa Press, 2000.

Rome Reborn. "About." 2013, http://romereborn.frischerconsulting.com/about.php (accessed August 24, 2015).

Roth, Stacy. *Past into Present: Effective Techniques for First-Person Historical Interpretation*, Chapel Hill: University of North Carolina Press, 1998.

Salicco, John. "Some Thoughts on First Person Interpretation of Historical Persona." Brodmoore: There Was A Time, undated, www.therewasatime.net/First%20Person%20Interpretation%20of%20Historical%20Persona.pdf (accessed August 25, 2015).

Samuel, Raphael. *Theatres of Memory: Vol.1, Past And Present In Contemporary Culture*, London: Verso, 1994.

Sliva, Marty. "Assassin's Creed Unity Review." *IGN*, November 11, 2014, www.ign.com/articles/2014/11/11/assassins-creed-unity-review (accessed August 25, 2015).

Struck, Georg, Böse, Ralk, and Spierling, Ulrike. "Trying to Get Trapped in the Past: Exploring the Illusion of Presence in Virtual Drama." In *First Joint International Conference on Interactive Digital Storytelling*, November 26–29, 2008, Berlin: Springer Berlin Heidelberg, 2009, 114–125, http://link.springer.com/chapter/10.1007%2F978-3-540-89454-4_18#page-1 (accessed November 22, 2014).

Thierer, Joyce M. *Telling History: A Manual for Performers and Presenters of First-Person Narratives*, Walnut Creek: AltaMira Press, 2009.

Thompson, Jenny. *War Games: Inside the World of 20th Century War Reenactors*, Washington, DC: Smithsonian Books, 2010.

Tilden, Freeman. *Interpreting Our Heritage*, third edition, Chapel Hill: University of North Carolina Press, 1984.

Tzibazi, Vasiliki. "Museum Theatre: Children's Reading of 'First Person Interpretation' in Museums." In *Public History and Heritage Today: People and Their Pasts*, edited by Paul Ashton and Hilda Kean, London: Palgrave Macmillan, 2012, 163–183.

Wallace, Mike. *Mickey Mouse History and Other Essays on American Memory*, Philadelphia: Temple University Press, 1996.

Webster, Andrew. "Building a Better Paris in 'Assassin's Creed Unity': Historical Accuracy Meets Game Design." *The Verge*, October 31, 2014, www.theverge.com/2014/10/31/7132587/assassins-creed-unity-paris (accessed Augut 25, 2015).

Westergren, Ebbe. *7 Steps Towards in-Depth Teaching in Historic Environments: Time Traveling as an Educational Method*, Kalmar läns Museum (Sweden), 2006, www.bridgingages.com/site/assets/files/1476/7_steps_booklet.pdf (accessed August 25, 2015).

Wilkinson, Alex. "History and Video Games: A Brief Thought." *Digital/Public History*, January 15, 2014, http://5702x.graeworks.net/?p=172 (accessed August 25, 2015).

Zotero. *Play and Public History Reading List*, undated, www.zotero.org/groups/play_and_public_history (accessed August 25, 2015).

Zucconi, Laura, Watrall, Ethan, Ueno, Hannah, and Rosner, Lisa. "Pox and the City: Challenges in Writing a Digital History Game." In *Writing History in the Digital Age*, edited by Jack Dougherty and Kristen Nawrotzki, Ann Arbor: University of Michigan Press, 2012, http://writinghistory.trincoll.edu/evidence/zucconi-etal-2012-spring/#fn-3124-1 (accessed November 13, 2014).

Part III
Collaboration and Uses of the Past

Public history can help change the way historians traditionally work. In addition to the production of historical narratives, public historians deal with the collection and preservation of sources. As agents in cultural institutions, public historians may also be in charge of more administrative tasks such as fund-raising or marketing audiences. Another major component of public history is the awareness and consideration of the multiple uses of the past by different audiences. The role of audiences – not only as consumers but also as actors of the production of history – has greatly affected the role and duties of public historians.

In his blog *On Public Humanities*, Steven Lubar argues that "If we want the humanities to be more than academic – if we want them to make a difference in the world – we need to change the way we work" (2014). He gives seven suggestions that can help historians make history practices more public and collaborative. The first rule is that public humanities are "not about you." Lubar suggests "Start not by looking at what you, your discipline, or the university needs and wants, but by what individuals and communities outside the university need and want" (2014). Public history implies collaboration, and historians should work in close connection with communities. Working with communities does not mean historians should bring their expertise to others – like missionaries would bring truth and knowledge – but should instead collaborate with partners to design richer interpretations of the past. In many public history projects, public engagement is not limited to the final steps, but is at the core of practices through constant interaction.

One critical subject of controversy regarding public history has been about the use of the past. In some cases, historians provide services for communities, associations, institutions, historic sites, and clients. Public historians may have to answer questions asked by someone else. This service may contrast with some more traditional academic historians who strongly argue they are the sole deciders in their research projects. Is a historian hired by clients to produce a narrative that they can use for non-academic purposes and sometimes for financial profit breaking any ethical rule? Is a historian still a public historian if (s)he works merely for a company's internal uses of the past? And how do the uses of the past affect the historian's role and practices? Public historian Rebecca Conard points out that:

> historians who enjoy a constitutional right of free speech, supported by an academic tradition that encourages the open expression of ideas, have license to protest when this freedom is threatened. Public historians, in contrast, are likely to find that their freedom of expression is constrained in one way or another.
>
> (2006, 75)

As the previous examples demonstrate, ethical issues have been at the center of public historians' activities.[1] This part of the textbook explores the various challenges and ethical issues that public historians may face while working for communities, public institutions, and clients. Conard rightly argues that "We serve the field of public history best if we prepare students not just to accept unintended consequences philosophically, but to think about possible consequences in advance and to act responsibly" (2006, 79).

While historians may have to work for clients, they may also have to manage teams and institutions. For instance, public historian and the former Director of the Truman Library, Michael Devine, stresses that many historian become administrators and directors of historical agencies and other similar organizations (2006, 46). Historians may have to work as intermediaries between staff, boards, and other support groups. History training programs offer little help for historians who become managers. Most of those historians have to learn the job by themselves. Devine explains that the historical profession has:

> been controlled by academics who, secure in their tenured positions, see themselves as the trainers of others who will serve as academics like themselves … and that many who instruct students in our university public history programs have no administrative experience outside of the university.
>
> (Devine 2006, 53–54)

Public historians may have to diversify their skills and be able to collaborate with non-traditional actors who might question their authority.

Note

1 The National Council on Public History (NCPH) published a code of ethics in 1986. Theodore Karamanski edited *Ethics and Public History* in 1990 (Karamski 1990). The new NCPH *Code of Ethics and Professional Conduct* was adopted in 2007 and a special edition of *The Public Historian* was published in 2006. In addition to these codes and guidelines, readers can consult the multiple examples published by other fields such as archives, museums, or oral history.

Bibliography

Conard, Rebecca. "Roundtable: Ethics in Practice: Editor's Introduction." *The Public Historian*, 26/1 (2006): 75–79.

Devine, Michael. "Administrators: Students of History and Practitioners of the Art of Management." *The Public History: Essays From the Field*, edited by James B. Gardner and Peter LaPaglia, Malabar: Krieger Press, 2006, 45–56.

Karamanski, Theodore, ed. *Ethics and Public History: An Anthology*, Malabar: Krieger Publishing Company, 1990.

Lubar, Steven. "Seven Rules for Public Humanists." *On Public Humanities*, June 5, 2014, http://steven lubar.wordpress.com/2014/06/05/seven-rules-for-public-humanists/#comments (accessed August 26, 2015).

10 Teaching Public History
Creating and Sustaining University Programs

There is a growing academic interest in public history training. More and more history departments propose courses for public history careers. Originally located in North America, public history programs are now present worldwide. The National Council on Public History's (NCPH) *Guide to Public History Programs* listed 220 university programs around the world in 2013.[1] In 2013, the author of this textbook organized a working group at the NCPH annual conference in which public history training was compared around the world. Unlike tenure track academic jobs in history, openings for public history positions have been rising in the last ten years.[2]

Despite this vitality, teaching public history faces many challenges (Kelley 1987; Welch 2003; Miller 2004). Instructors often lack materials, guidelines, and arguments to open and develop public history programs. The rise of public history programs is debatable too. Public historian at Eastern Washington University, Larry Cebula, wonders "if we are about to flood a shallow job market with too many graduates," since, he argues, public history jobs are not so abundant, and the competition is high to obtain a job in historic institutions (Parsons 2012). Before creating a public history university program, historians and administration must answer questions such as why they should start a public history program at all; what it takes in terms of staff, resources, collaboration, and mission statement; if it should be restricted to grad students or open to undergraduates; and what the fields taught in the program should be. This chapter explores some issues about why and how public history training could be designed.

Creating Public History Programs

Reasons to – or not to – create public history programs vary according to whether one is a faculty member, part of an administration, a history student, or a local partner. Nevertheless, doing history in public, collaborating with non-academic partners, and sharing authority may not be natural skills for historians, so it is important for history students to be better prepared. Public history training does not only prepare students for certain jobs, but also offers opportunities for academic reflectivity. Historians who work outside academia often do not have time to discuss, explore, and read about theories and practices of public history. Public history training can provide a space and time for critical attitudes and self-reflectivity in which both practice and theories are covered. Even if students do not get a full-time history job outside academia, they may have to collaborate with partners and work with a broad public. In that case, a basic introduction to public history can be a positive experience. This is why every history department could provide, at the least, an introductory course to the public practices of history. History instructors can adopt public history assignments for more traditional survey classes as well.

Notwithstanding the benefit of teaching public history, Jay Price – who directs the Public History Program at Wichita State University – sees that "too many programs have been created primarily to boost enrollment in history departments, not because there was a need in the community for professionals with certain skills" (Cebula 2013). Although important, enrollment should not hide the necessary requirements to develop a public history program. Historians and departments considering the creation of a public history program can consult the various best practice guides and the discussions about creating new programs (National Council on Public History 2008a, 2009a, 2010).

In line with what Noel Stowe – founder of the public history program at Arizona State University – recommended during a panel entitled *Developing a Public History Program* at the 2000 NCPH conference, any department considering opening a public history program should ask and answer a series of specific questions (Brandimarte 2000).[3] First of all, public history programs need funding to pay for faculty, field trips, materials, guest speakers, projects, internships, communication, etc. Although guest speakers may sometimes be useful options, history departments cannot assume only one faculty member would handle public history courses. But no matter how big the department is, not every field of public history practice can be covered.[4] One solution is to identify potential instructors in other departments (anthropology for cultural resources management, visual arts for video and documentary editing, libraries for archives management, for instance) and local institutions. Students can also attend courses outside of the history department to broaden their skills (budget management, law, computer science, and so on). Public history instructors can bring guest speakers who share their expertise in more specific fields.[5] Ideally public history organizations like the NCPH or the International Federation for Public History (IFPH) could provide lists of online public history speakers to represent their respective fields.[6] So it is crucial that departments review their strengths and potential hiring opportunities before creating any public history program.

Success really depends on the program's connection with local networks. Any creation of a public history program should take into consideration the existence of other public history centers that could be competitors in terms of recruitment. Before opening a program, the local networks of libraries, museums, archives, and other cultural institutions should be evaluated and contacted. In her comments on best practices for public history programs, Carrie Barske urges to take into consideration the local opportunities for internships and the possible organizations that the program could partner with. If those resources are limited, creating a public history program may be doomed to fail (Cebula 2013). To know about the local resources is important to list the potential places and length of internships, but also to have a better idea of potential employment for public history students. Are there any particular needs for local history sites (cultural resources management, digital production, interpretive design, etc.)? In other words, as Jay Price points out, "is your program filling a recognized need in the area or just pumping out graduates who need to compete in an already saturated job market?" (Cebula 2013).

Even though careers in public history go well beyond local networks, location is a critical aspect in deciding whether or not a public history program should be created. Some sites are privileged. For instance, Deborah Welch writes in her article on public history teaching that "Universities of North Carolina at Greensboro, with its close proximity to the original eighteenth-century Moravian settlement at Old Salem, are able to proffer strong graduate programs in preservation and museum studies" (Welch 2003, 72). She also uses state universities as examples, ultimately showing how the location within a state capital can allow programs to propose courses in archival studies. Programs located close to (state) capitals

– like Carleton University's public history program in Ottawa (Canada) – national parks, presidential libraries, heritage parks, historical societies, major museums are at a distinct advantage in terms of opportunities for internships, research, networking. To some extent, the use of digital tools and media can help go beyond the local limitations. International collaborative teaching allows students (and instructors) from different parts of the world to interact with each other and with public history practitioners.[7]

How to Create an Appropriate Public History Program?

Opening a public history program is a very complex process. The Curriculum and Training Committee of the NCPH has published a very useful draft about "Best Practices for Establishing and Developing a Public History Program" that provides guidance on subjects, such as funding, hiring practices, tenure and promotion, curriculum development, and areas of specialization (Vivian 2015). History departments can also get help from "academic program reviewers" who "offer expert advice to university and college departments or programs in public history" (National Council on Public History undated). International collaboration exists too. For example, the public history programs at the University of York and Royal Holloway University in London influenced the creation of the master's in public history at Trinity College Dublin (Ireland). In order to convince departments and university colleagues of the interest of a public history program, historians must clarify the market segment at which the program would be aimed. The first question is to know whether public history would be limited to regular (with a history training) students – if so only graduate or undergraduate students as well – or if it would be available to existing practitioners (who may not have a history training) through continuing education.

Most public history training is done through master's programs because students need a solid historical methodology.[8] Another option is to include public history practice in traditional courses through specific assignments. Material culture, oral history, history games, and mapping are especially useful. This solution has the merit of introducing the concept of public history without the creation of a specific program/structure. The NCPH warns historians considering opening public history courses for undergraduates that "first and foremost in any undergraduate history program should be an emphasis on teaching students the best methods in researching and writing history" (National Council on Public History 2009a). Students must develop solid historical bases (historiography, writing, archive analysis) before approaching public history.

Opening public history courses to undergraduates presents certain advantages too. It helps broaden students' historical practices, shows them that there is a public interest in historical subject matter, and fosters interdisciplinary teaching in which colleagues from other department and guests from outside academia can intervene. Furthermore, Welch indicates that by integrating public history techniques throughout the undergraduate curriculum, students became more engaged in their classes, and the number of students who declare history as their major increased significantly as well (2003). Some research shows that undergraduates who participate in hands-on research have a better chance of graduating with a higher grade point average (Association of American Colleges and Universities 2008). Historians and departments interested in creating undergraduate courses in public history can use existing resources and case studies (National Council on Public History 2009a, 2009b).

Another major interrogation about the creation of a public history program deals with the fields of study. Departments must choose between programs that introduce students to a broad range of public history areas and more specialized programs that focus on one (or more) of the core activities (archives, museums and material culture, historic preservation, and more recently digital history). In 2000, within a panel about *Developing a Public History Program*, John Hunner – from the public history program at New Mexico University – "spoke about the merits of generalist public history training that equips his graduates with many skills adaptable to the broad field of public history" (Brandimarte 2000). Jay Price conversely argues that "career paths become ever more specialized, with greater demands that graduates bring specialized skills" (Cebula 2013). Daniel Vivian – editor of the *Best Practices for Establishing and Developing a Public History Program* – agrees, and further explains, "as public history training becomes more common, specialized areas of emphasis will distinguish graduates of one program from others" (Cebula 2013). Of course, the choice depends on the size of the department and the faculty's fields of expertise. Large programs can offer a wide range of courses in collection management, oral history, digital history, and historic preservation while more limited programs may need to develop a particular "niche" in one specific field.

Teaching Theory and Practice

There is little agreement on public history teaching and possible common curriculum. As for the discipline at large, public history teaching depends on its audiences: students and employers. Instructors should know their students, their experience in public history, and the career they wish to pursue. It is crucial for instructors to be aware of their students' strengths and weaknesses when they design a course. Instructors must also investigate the other side: employers. What do employers need from public history students and how can instructors train students to match the offers? The survey entitled *Public History Employers – What Do They Want?* published by Philip Katz in 2003 is a useful resource.[9] Instructors can also have a look at the report of a working group named Imagining New Careers in Public History, which gives a better view of the job market (Blackbourn 2012). Finally, a more recent survey from the NCPH presents the skills employers consider the most useful (Scarpino and Vivian 2015). If traditional skills such as historical research and writing, historical and historiographical knowledge, public programming and interpretation, public speaking, and editing are critical, less traditional skills like fundraising and digital media are highly desirable and will remain so in the future (Scarpino and Vivian 2015). Based on the local opportunities for collaboration and internship, on the faculty's skills, on the orientation that departments want to give to the program, it is important to design a realistic plan about what students need to learn to be successful.

In a recent post, Suse Cairns – from the Baltimore Museum of Art – asked "is it still beneficial to read books on sociology, cultural theory, or philosophy, when instead that time could be used to read up on new technologies and business practices?" Applied to public history training, the question is to know whether theory is useful for students who would likely be hired for their skills. Cairns also wonders "whether having a well-developed theory about museums actually makes someone a better practitioner" (Cairns 2014). The relations between theory and practice are not easy to assess. In public history training one of the main challenges is to balance historical research, archival analysis, and to learn how to deal with broad and non-academic audiences. Public history students are no "bad historians" turning to public practice to get a job. In order to balance theory, historical methodology and public practice, instructors need to adapt their assignments. Most public history programs include an introduction to public history course in which students become familiar with the specificity and debates in the field. On the other hand, programs also provide skill-based courses based on practice. Nevertheless, the distinction between theory and practice is not always clear-cut, and history departments should be able to design courses that provide both theory and practice.

Instructors can require their students to design individual or collective public history projects that force them both to do history in public and to reflect on the issues at stake. Collective projects are potentially more rewarding in public history since they enable students to experiment with collaborative and collective work. Students may work on exhibit proposals, documentary film treatment, website development plans, and other production of public history narratives (National Council on Public History 2008a). It is also important that students be in contact with non-academic partners/clients for the development of their project. Students encounter different approaches and uses of the past that can greatly differ from the academic world. Project-oriented public history courses and collaboration with non-academic partners are difficult to manage, however. First, work schedules in and outside academia vary. Although instructors may want to follow academic agendas and design projects according to semesters, non-academic organizations usually work in different timelines and at a much quicker pace.

Projects help students to practice public history and can serve to apply certain theories – like shared authority or public involvement – discussed in class. Projects can enhance public history's reflective aspect as well. For each step of a project, it may be useful for students, instructors, and eventually partners, to re-examine basic principles and issues. As Stowe argues, "Teaching reflective practice techniques throughout the curriculum distinguishes public history from traditional fields" (2006, 40). Reflective practice can take place after the production, so during a phase of debriefing in which students do not apply theories to hands-on projects but propose theories based on their practice of public history. Public history instructors should therefore have a flexible and multi-directional conception of the links between theory and practice.

Public historians' work is based on collaboration with actors who may have a very different agenda and conception of history that require compromises. Problem-solving sessions can turn out to be very helpful for public history instructors. In those sessions, students, instructors, or guest speakers present and share problems they have faced in their public activities. The role of the instructors is to connect the problematic case studies to broader key public history issues. Some instructors utilize case studies in public policy drawn from Richard Neustadt and Ernest May's *Thinking in Time: The Uses of History for Decision Makers* (Stowe 2006, 60). For example, Middle Tennessee State University has proposed a museum management seminar that "includes advanced problem-solving for museum staff and consideration of ethical issues such as repatriation of artifacts."[10] Problem-framing, implementation, and improvisation are the keywords of problem-solving learning for which students will develop "their own repertoires of skills and understandings" (Stowe 2006, 54). Any public history students should at least be familiar with the problem-solving aspect of his/her potentially future job. It is therefore important for students to be introduced to situations where no ready answers exist, in order to become as flexible as possible and armed to manage difficult situations.

Internship is another assignment/practice very specific to public history. Figure 10.1 shows Eric Scott, by then a graduate student in the public history master's program at the University of Louisiana at Lafayette, during his internship at the Levine Museum at the New South, Charlotte, North Carolina in 2013. Internship is crucial since it allows students to gain hands-on experience, to practice collaborative works, and help them to create

Figure 10.1 Eric Scott (University of Louisiana at Lafayette) during his internship at the Levine
Museum at the New South, Charlotte, North Carolina, 2013. Courtesy of Eric Scott/
Levine Museum at the New South.

their own networks of public practitioners. Internship can, as Figure 10.1 shows, also allow
students to be in direct contact with audiences through tours. Internships can take place
on many different sites, such as archives and libraries, museums, battlefield heritage centers,
neighborhood and community preservation projects, or radio/television broadcasting. But
internships should also be opportunities to connect theory and practice. The NCPH argues
that internships provide students with "opportunities to reflect on their activities and connect their practical experience with the skills and knowledge gained in their public history
training" (National Council on Public History 2008a). Internships are also opportunities
for history students to critically reflect on projects and institutions they have been part of.
The work of students during internships is also useful to preserve the networks of small local
heritage sites whose limited funding does not allow to hire professional historians. This is
especially true for institutions that have no access to federal funding and that mostly rely on
donations and volunteering (Miller 2004, 186).

However, an internship is not a traditional assignment in academic history, so instructors
must observe a few rules. The benefit and purpose of the internship must be discussed early
in the process. An on-site internship advisor/supervisor and a faculty advisor/supervisor
should be assigned to any student. They should, with the student, agree on the conditions of
employment (dates, schedule, eventual wage, travel). The NCPH recommends that "every

effort should be made to see that interns receive compensation for their work commensurate with the qualifications required for a position" (National Council on Public History 2008a). Guidelines should also be clear about the student's activities on site, the regular meetings with his/her advisors, the various duties, and the assignments (s)he may have to submit to the program. Students should, as much as possible, do a variety of different work (Scarpino and Vivian 2015).

Evaluation is especially challenging for internship. It partly comes from the definition of a successful internship. Objectives should be clear from the beginning for the student. Most public history programs ask students to submit reports or diaries about their on-site activities. Based on a reflective practice, the reports should force the student to reflect on his/her personal skills and involvement in broader collaborative projects, and the different activities practiced. Besides, some programs associate internships with specific courses or seminars. With readings, meetings, discussions, presentations, those courses attempt to connect the practical experience of an internship with broader discussion in the field of public history. However, not every internship will fulfill student expectations. In some cases, an intern's activities may be limited to basic daily administrative tasks such as sorting documents, updating files, sending emails, or doing photocopies. While important, these administrative tasks should not be the core of the internship. This is why it is important for advisors to agree on the intern's activities beforehand. Internship is not a solution for jobs no one wants to do in under-staffed institutions. So, finding and supervising useful internships is very time-consuming for public history instructors who need to build trust and know their local actors well.

Notes

1 Although non-exhaustive, the list demonstrates the extreme predominance of English-speaking countries: 193 programs were located in the United States, 8 in Great Britain, 7 in Canada, 5 in Australia, 2 in Ireland, 1 in India, 1 in China, 1 in Belgium, 1 in Holland, and 1 in Germany. However, other programs do exist in South Africa, Switzerland, and Germany, for instance, http://ncph.org/cms/education/graduate-and-undergraduate/guide-to-public-history-programs/ (accessed March 18, 2014).
2 In 2008, the number of job announcements for public historians rose by 27.9 percent and in 2013 the number of postings rose significantly again (Parsons 2012).
3 According to Stowe, historians should ask: "What is your niche – what role will you fill in your local, state or regional public history community? How healthy are your networks within that community? Are you up to date on relevant historiography? What are the philosophical underpinnings of the new program? and How does the public history program relate to the needs, strengths and priorities of the History department? How does it benefit the department?" (Brandimarte 2000).
4 It is interesting to note that the first public history master's program in Italy (University of Modena and Reggio Emilia) offers an impressive range of courses and practices (Noiret 2015).
5 Although it may be difficult to pay guest speakers, digital tools (especially video and sound software) now permit more flexibility and more opportunities for online discussions.
6 Another solution could be to create a pool of public history instructors who could help each other on certain aspects of the field, in order to mutualize public history training.
7 See for instance the Committee on International Public History Teaching designed by Thomas Cauvin and Tammy Gordon for the International Federation for Public History.
8 Historical research is defined as the main skill requested by employers at entry level (Scarpino and Vivian 2015).
9 See www.historians.org/publications-and-directories/perspectives-on-history/september-2003/public-history-employers-what-do-they-want-a-report-on-the-survey (accessed September 5, 2015).
10 Middle Tennessee State University, *Graduate Courses in Public History*, www.mtsu.edu/publichistory/Coursework.php (accessed August 29, 2015).

Bibliography

Association of American Colleges and Universities. "The Student as Scholar: Undergraduate Research and Creative Practice." 2008, www.aacu.org/meetings/undergraduate_research/index.cfm (accessed March 30, 2008).

Bingmann, Melissa. "Advising Undergraduates about Career Opportunities in Public History." *Perspectives on History* (March 2009), www.historians.org/publications-and-directories/perspectives-on-history/march-2009/advising-undergraduates-about-career-opportunities-in-public-history (accessed March 12, 2014).

Blackbourn, Nick. "Imagining New Careers in Public History: A Working Group." *Public History Career Blog*, April 17, 2012, http://publichistorycareers.wordpress.com/ (accessed August 30, 2015).

Brandimarte, Cynthia. "Developing a Public History Program." *CCWH Newsletter*, 31/2 (Summer 2000).

Cairns, Suse. "Do Museum Professionals Need Theory?" *Museum Geek*, June 10, 2014, https://museum geek.wordpress.com/2014/06/10/do-museum-professionals-need-theory/ (accessed September 17, 2014).

Cebula, Larry. "'Make it so' but How? Best Practices for Public History Programs." *Public History Commons*, February 11, 2013, http://publichistorycommons.org/best-practices-new-public-history-programs/#more-2064 (accessed March 12, 2015).

Kelley, Robert. "On the Teaching of Public History." *The Public Historian*, 9/3 (Summer 1987): 38–46.

Miller, Marla R. "Playing to Strength: Teaching Public History at the Turn of the 21st-Century." *American Studies International*, 42/2,3 (June–October 2004): 174–212.

National Council on Public History. *Program Review Process*, undated, http://ncph.org/cms/education/graduate-and-undergraduate/program-review-process/ (accessed August 28, 2015).

National Council on Public History. *Best Practices in Public History: Public History Internship*, 2008a, http://ncph.org/cms/wp-content/uploads/2010/08/Internship-Best-Practice.pdf (accessed March 17, 2014).

National Council on Public History. *Best Practices in Public History: The M.A. Program in Public History*, 2008b, http://ncph.org/cms/wp-content/uploads/2010/08/Grad-Best-Practice.pdf (accessed March 18, 2014).

National Council on Public History. *Best Practices in Public History: Public History for Undergraduate Students*, 2009a, http://ncph.org/cms/wp-content/uploads/2010/08/Undergrad-Best-Practice.pdf (accessed March 18, 2014).

National Council on Public History. *Public History for Undergraduates Compilation*, 2009b, http://ncph.org/cms/wp-content/uploads/2009/11/Public-History-for-Undergraduates-compilation.pdf; http://ncph.org/cms/wp-content/uploads/2009/11/Public-History-for-Undergraduates-compilation2.pdf (accessed August 28, 2015).

National Council on Public History. *Best Practices in Public History: Certificate Programs in Public History*, 2010, http://ncph.org/cms/wp-content/uploads/Best-Practices-in-Certificate-Programs-approved.pdf (accessed March 18, 2014).

National Council on Public History. *Best Practices for Establishing a Public History Program*, 2013, http://publichistorycommons.org/library/items/show/9 (accessed August 26, 2015).

Noiret, Serge. "Italy's First Master's Degree in Public History Starts in September 2015." International Federation for Public History website, June 29, 2015, http://ifph.hypotheses.org/748 (accessed August 27, 2015).

Parsons, Anne. "Help Wanted: Thoughts on the Recent Boom in Academic Public History Jobs." *Public History Commons*, September 17, 2012, http://publichistorycommons.org/help-wanted-thoughts-on-the-recent-boom-in-academic-public-history-jobs/#sthash.1GGCIxPS.dpuf (accessed August 26, 2015).

Scarpino, Philip and Vivian, Daniel. "Report from the Task Force on Public History Education and Employment." *Public History Commons*, April 14, 2015, http://publichistorycommons.org/report-public-history-education-and-employment/#sthash.22TomL0j.dpuf (accessed August 27, 2015).

Stowe, Noel. "Public History Curriculum: Illustrating Reflective Practice." *The Public Historian*, 28/1 (Winter 2006): 39–65.

Vivian, Daniel, ed. *Draft: Best Practices for Establishing and Developing a Public History Program*, April 2015, Public History Commons, http://publichistorycommons.org/best-practices-public-history-program/ (accessed August 25, 2015).

Welch, Deborah. "Teaching Public History: Strategies for Undergraduate Program Development." *The Public Historian*, 25/1 (Winter 2003): 71–82.

11 Shared Authority
Purposes, Challenges, and Limits

Public History and Shared Authority

Doing public history raises questions about the role, the authority, and the expertise of historians. Public historians need to discuss about who owns the past (Graham 1995). The question of authorship mostly emerged in the 1960s in line with the new social history. History from below – or "people's history" as defined by Raphael Samuel in Britain – was part of a new focus on popular history and ordinary people. Associated with new techniques such as oral history, social history asked for a more popular and participatory construction of history. In line with this request, Michael Frisch popularized the concept of shared authority in the late 1980s (Frisch 1990). Initially focused on oral history in which the narrator participates in the construction of the narratives, the concept of shared authority helps turning people from mere consumers into active participants. Frisch explains that "a Shared Authority … suggests something that 'is' – that in the nature of oral and public history, we are not the sole interpreters. Rather, the interpretive and meaning-making process is in fact shared *by definition*" (2011, 127).

However, if most historians would today agree that they can collaborate with many different partners, they do not easily share their authority. As public historian Jim Gardner regrets, "we (historians and curators) still, for the most part, think of the public essentially as the audience, the recipients" (2004, 14). If the definition of a shared authority is important, the process of "sharing authority" guides public historians' practices. The title of a recent book – *Letting Go? Sharing Historical Authority in a User-Generated World* – puts emphasis on the need to share the production of history (Adair et al. 2011). More than 20 years after his first book on shared authority, Frisch explains in this new book that "sharing Authority suggests this is something we do – that in some sense we 'have' authority, and that we need or ought to share it" (2011, 127). But who is the "we" used by Frisch? Is the "we" made of historians and publics? What is the role of historians and who owns the past?

Sharing authority can be done, for instance, through inviting visitors attending exhibitions to share their stories and interpretations of the collections, through collaboration with narrators in creating oral history sources, or through developing online crowdsourcing projects. As Steven Lubar warns in his blog on public humanities, "Having that conversation [about sharing authority] is not easy. Finding the right balance is tricky. The humanist needs to be not only an expert, but also a facilitator, and a translator. Seeking that balance is part of the work of every project" (2014). Most of the time, history training does not lend itself to shared authority. Students are not required to share authority on their production, and collaborative writing remains rare.[1] But some solutions exist. For instance, the National Park Service developed a public training program called "Co-Creating Narratives in Public

Spaces," based on the manner in which shared authority affects day-to-day work in heritage sites.[2] Sharing authority is not limited to the final phase of the history production. It could be applied to the design of the project, the research questions, the collection of documents and artifacts, and – even more radically – to the interpretation of those holdings. The presence of multiple voices from community and individual partners is an alternative to unquestioned official histories and helps empower people, especially underrepresented minorities. In turn, multiple voices enhance diversity in historical narratives. Historical research cannot always match the stories and topics the different publics want to hear. By including public participation in their work, public historians can attract broader audiences.

Historians and Emotions

If public historians want to share authority, they need to grasp how people use and make sense of the past. One aspect that historians sometimes choose to ignore is the relevance of feelings and emotions. Traditionally, historians have been trained to avoid any personal involvement in their writing and personal connection with the subject of their research. The argument has long been made that scientific and professional history shall be produced through emotion-free research (Novick 1988). What is more, as Amy Tyson argues in her book on emotions in public history, any activity associated with emotions is often "perceived as feminized (even when it is performed by men), the value of which is not only widely unappreciated on a social level but often goes unarticulated even within one's own organization" (2013, 5). Nevertheless, the distance between historians, their sources, and the readers is challenged in public history where historians are often in close contact with partners and audiences. Roy Rosenzweig and David Thelen's study of the uses of the past demonstrated that the more the public feels connected with the story, the more they engage and participate (1998). Identity, family history, and personal experiences are therefore major reasons for public participation. The public wants to "feel" history, or – as David Glassberg underlines – to have a "sense of the past" (2001). The participatory history-making process can hardly proceed without dealing with emotions (Frevert 2011).

Many public historians, especially interpreters, are on the front line and in dialogue with non-specialist audiences. Those public practitioners must be aware that communication and emotions are part of their job. Figure 11.1 shows first-person interpreters at Colonial Williamsburg during a "Run to Freedom" scene in which a slave (Kate, played by Imani Turner) is about to run for freedom. Overwhelmed and in tears, the interpreter goes through personal emotions linked to the re-enactment. Those emotions are also a way to connect with audiences. Tyson explains that *The Staff Administrative Handbook* informed trainees at Historic Fort Snelling that "feelings and attitudes and facial expressions are highly communicable to the visitor. Active staff members who obviously are enjoying their job create an ideal environment for learning" (2013, 14). Likewise, Alderson and Low's *Interpretation of Historic Sites* provides a list of "Do's and Don't's of Interpretation" that helps interpreters manage their personality and emotions in their interactions with visitors (Alderson and Low 1986). The job of public historians is not to give way to emotions but to be aware, contextualize, and problematize emotions in historical understanding of the past. Certain emotions are, for example, more difficult than others to handle. Public interpreters may experience discomfort, or even disgust, with certain historical topics. James Oliver Horton interviewed interpreters who participated in the 1994 controversial "Estate Sale" program arranged at Colonial Williamsburg (CW), whose aim was to re-enact a slave auction. He reported that African American interpreters experienced "strong emotions – anger and extreme sadness,

Figure 11.1 "Run to Freedom" scene at the Peyton Randolph property. Eve, portrayed by Hope
Smith (left), hugs Kate, portrayed by Imani Turner (right) before she runs to freedom
with the British as Cornwallis leaves Williamsburg for Yorktown. 2008. Credit: David
M. Doody. Courtesy of The Colonial Williamsburg Foundation.

as well as pride at being part of this bold historical statement" (Tyson 2013, 147). Rather
than denying emotions, public practitioners must be ready to acknowledge – and problematize the fact – that feelings affect the production of collaborative public history.

   In addition to their feelings, public historians have to deal with public emotions. Leaving
the ivory tower, historians enter the world of reactions, emotions, (dis)agreements, and
discussions. Some public historians may have to deal with very sensitive issues and must
learn how to handle them. There is no single solution, and no training whatsoever can fully
prepare public historians to act appropriately, but historians, if exposed to public reactions
in their training, may anticipate certain issues. For example, Tyson mentions three possible
ways to deal with historical oppression: "minimizing oppression content, rejecting all content of oppression, and explicitly including oppression content." The people she interviewed
noted the extent to which they would choose to minimize, reject, or include painful histories
based on comfort cues that they perceived from visitors (Tyson 2013, 152). When she was
working at Fort Snelling, Tyson remembers there was a manual available to interpreters
about African American history in which happy role models were put forward (Tyson 2013,
154). Public practitioners tweak the story according to the level of (dis)comfort they perceive among the visitors. The point is not to deny the validity of public interpretation of the

past – every historian adopts a different stance whether (s)he discusses with peers, students, or specialists – but to explore how feelings affect practices and narratives, and act accordingly to preserve historical integrity. Silencing difficult aspects of the past is clearly not ideal, and public historians should be prepared to find better solutions to discuss controversial issues.

Practitioners who are in direct contact with audiences can consult workshops, guidelines, and best practices. Tyson quotes a handbook called *Language & Ethnicity* that provides interpreters with "Appropriate" and "Non-appropriate Terms" – and explanations – to deal with controversial issues. This initiative helps historical practitioners engage the public in potentially charged topics while minimizing the risks (Tyson 2013, 162). This is true across most societies. Take for example the various controversies surrounding the interpretation of the history of Anglo-Irish relations in Northern Ireland. Many historic institutions in Ireland have had to work to find acceptable ways to represent the past. During the Northern Irish Peace Process in the 1990s, the Community Relations Council – funded by the Irish and British governments as well as the European Union – organized workshops, published guidelines, and supported projects to help practitioners produce and interpret a history that both Catholic Nationalists and Protestant Unionists could hear and share (Cauvin 2011).

Celebrations of the Past: Historians and Pride

Identity and History: Celebration versus Commemoration

Historians have complex relations with commemorations (Bodnar 1993). On the one hand, commemorations create lots of opportunities to engage the public. On the other hand, some historians are reluctant to participate in events that are sometimes highly politicized and dominated by political agendas. The broad range of actors involved in commemorations also results in a certain competition of interpretations. People and groups use the past for different – and sometimes competing – purposes, and this makes the concept of shared authority even more difficult to handle for historians. The competition is partly due to the relevance of commemorations – and more broadly history – for identity issues. The past has been used to shape our sense of ourselves, so that historic sites are not only dealing with the past, but with present identity issues as well. One critical challenge for historians is to deal with celebratory representations of the past.

Although the distinction between celebration and commemoration is not always obvious, the difference comes from their purposes (Gillis 1994). While commemoration might be defined by its educational and more critical purpose, celebration focuses exclusively on positive, rewarding, and identity-based aspects of the past. Celebrations are therefore associated with pride, glory, martyrs, and heroes. Some museums are now called "memorials" based on the memories – and sometimes the celebration – of the past (Williams 2008). Unlike celebrations, commemorations may include aspects that some actors do not want to remember. By selecting the aspects of the past to be remembered, celebrations often leave out many actors of the past. In Northern Ireland, the ethnic divisions between Catholic Nationalists and Protestant Unionists led to different choices about what part of the past should be remembered. While Catholic Nationalists mostly chose to remember revolts against the British rule like the 1798 Rebellion or the 1916 Easter Rising, the Protestant Unionists largely celebrated the Union with Britain through William of Orange or the Battle of the Somme (Cauvin 2011). Through these examples, certain events are selected and celebrated while others are purposefully forgotten.

Celebration's positive and proud representations of the past can make the work of historians very difficult. A vivid example was the 1994/1995 Enola Gay controversies. The Smithsonian National Air and Space Museum intended to mount an exhibition on the B-29 aircraft Enola Gay and more largely on the bombing of Japan. However, some groups of veterans found the way the event was reportedly going to be represented offensive and anti-patriotic. Discussing the appropriateness of the bombing was going against the traditional celebration of the U.S. involvement in World War II and against the museum's long-time celebratory focus on aviation and technology. This has become a major example of the debates about shared authority. Could curators of a national institution choose interpretations of the past without external intervention, or should the public – in that case groups of veterans – have their say as to how the past should be remembered? (Linenthal 1997). In spite of some adjustments, the exhibition was ultimately cancelled. The interpretations of World War II, and in particular the role of the military, are part of celebratory narratives used by American veterans to construct and reflect on their identity.

Among the celebratory narratives, those dealing with the nation appear to be particularly controversial. In particular, the links between museums and national identity have been the subject of numerous studies (Fladmark 2000; Kaplan 1994). Historians working in national institutions may very well feel the pressure of restricted definitions of the nation that are not open for discussion (Ostow 2008, 3–15). Jim Gardner points out that it is often a "tough sell" and quotes critics who "questioned why NMAH [National Museum of American History] as the nation's history museum did not do more positive, more celebratory exhibits." According to him, it has been even more complicated to engage the public with the complexity of the past since the 9/11 attacks and the U.S. presence in the Middle East that raised the risk of "being deemed unpatriotic, failing to foster the unity essential to the nation in a time of crisis" (2004, 12). But public historians dealing with the national past should strive to engage audiences, to challenge stereotypes, and to explain the complexity of the past. In other words, the challenge for historians who work in national institutions is to question any celebration of the past, any forgetting of the dark aspects, while also taking into consideration the variety of public demands.

Public Historians as Actors of Commemorations: A Quest for Pluralism

Instead of celebrating the past, historians should strive to understand it as it really was, not as what people want it to be, and by doing so should endeavor to create a space for discussion about the past. The most important role for historians is, according to Linenthal, to participate in the construction of "demilitarized zones of public conversation where people can engage various, perhaps even irreconcilable, interpretations of our past" (1997, 45). Different voices and interpretations of the past must be heard without fearing any prejudice. This is the first step to help people to understand the multiple meanings and interpretations of the past. This also contributes to broadening the voices heard during commemorations in terms of age, sex, ethnic identity, neighborhood, affiliation, and so on. Commemorations should start with public debates in which multiple voices could be heard. Although groups of veterans were, at one point, involved in the Enola Gay exhibition project, perhaps they could have collaborated earlier in the process in order to address controversies. Plurality of voices does not mean absence of tensions, but it helps implement the concept of shared authority.

Fostering the plurality of voices includes bringing underrepresented topics to the foreground.[3] For example, during discussions about the 150th anniversary of the U.S. Civil War, some historians argued for moving away from the exclusively political and military events, and to also embrace "sites that reflect significant economic, social, and cultural processes and trends" (Feller 2010). During similar discussions at the National Council for Public History conference, Elizabethada Wright stressed that:

> the glory of Gettysburg is far more enticing with its stories of sacrifice and heroism; however, we need to hear stories about the freemen and women who ran from the Gettysburg area because they knew what the approaching Confederates would do to them.
>
> (Wright 2011)

Likewise, through its exhibition called *Broken Bodies, Suffering Spirits: Injury, Death, and Healing in Civil War Philadelphia*, the Mütter Museum of the College of Physicians of Philadelphia was able to engage the public with ordinary actors of the past usually underrepresented in the historical narratives of the Civil War. Historians can help provide interpretation of everyday life, ethnic minorities, and other underexplored subjects during commemorations.

Finally, it is important that historians help actors of commemorations consider long-term issues and not single decontextualized events. Too often commemorations result in the celebration of a single moment in history, without paying attention to the long-term consequences. For instance, the 150th anniversary of the U.S. Civil War's theme was "Civil War to Civil Rights" and offered an opportunity to discuss the various cultural and social issues that are still central to life in the United States. In the same vein, the NMAH organized, for the 200th anniversary of Lincoln's birth, discussions in which some issues of Lincoln's presidency were compared to present-day debates. Through the links between past and present, historians not only engage audiences but they spread critical thinking to issues usually detached from historical interpretation.

The Limits to Shared Authority

Sharing authority does not mean historians should give up critical analysis of the past. As for any historical activity, it is necessary to wonder about the reliability of the sources, not least when they come from the public. Dan Cohen, founder with Roy Rosenzweig of the Center for History and New Media – stresses how some of the photographs collected from the public for the 9/11 archives had been digitally edited and modified (Mihm 2008). Likewise, Roy Rosenzweig – through a study of Wikipedia – wonders how we know that the people contributing to projects know what they are talking about (2006). Wikipedia offers multiple examples of false documents and "facts." The problem is not about shared authority but about the uses of the past and the role public historians can play in the process. Dickson reflects that:

> ultimately, what I learned from my inadvertent Wikipedia hoax was not that Wikipedia itself isn't reliable, but that so many people believe it is. My lie – because that's what it was, really – was repeated by dozens of sources, from bloggers to academics to journalists.
>
> (Dickson 2014)

The public need historians to better use and interpret the past, and therefore to improve shared authority.

The Difficult Past

Sharing authority implies collaboration with different actors who may have very different feelings about the past. Sharing authority not only brings a plurality of voices and a more participatory historical production, but it also makes the process more controversial. It is especially true regarding what some historians have called "difficult past" (Schwartz and Kim 2010). In a blog post entitled "When is Your Audience Ready for the Tough Stuff?" Linda Norris highlights how some topics like concentration camps in Germany, the European responsibility in the consequences of colonization in Africa, Native American history, or communist violence in Eastern Europe are still taboos (2014). Violent, sectarian, and divisive events remain difficult to interpret and create controversies in the present. Despite substantial literature, historians often remain unarmed to deal with those topics.[4]

In some cases, historians are confronted with a public unwillingness to talk about certain aspects of the past. Public interpreters may face uncomfortable silences from audiences when they raise certain controversial aspects. If silences may result from individual choice, they can also come from institutional decisions. For example, there are sites where slavery is actually silenced and not discussed. In Louisiana, most plantation tours focus on planter families, their success story, and the richness and magnificence of the home furniture. For a long time Oak Alley Plantation (Louisiana) had hardly spoken of slavery at all, and the slave cabins were only added in 2013. Its website invites visitors to "come enjoy her [Plantation] beauty & dream of her rich past!"[5] Historians can help historical sites to acknowledge that slavery is entirely part of the past and should not be silenced (Gallas and DeWolf Perry 2014). It would be a mistake to think that audiences cannot cope with the history of slavery.

Another very challenging question is knowing whether – and if so how – historians should represent historical violence (Sontag 2003). For example, curators of the different exhibitions mounted about the 9/11 attacks on the World Trade Center have had to decide whether or not to include representations of the hijackers, of the civilians who jumped into the void, and other testimonies of sufferings.[6] There is no obvious solution to the question of whether or not historians should display violent representations of the past to facilitate historical understanding, but historians could discuss the objectives and public uses of the display. For instance, for the section on "Mobile Killing Squads" in its permanent exhibition, the United States Holocaust Memorial Museum (USHMM) set up privacy barriers to prevent children from free access to violent images (USHMM 1993–1995). The more disturbing images are shown on monitors that are screened by three-foot high concrete walls. Besides, the USHMM posted a warning outside a new exhibit about the crimes against humanity in Syria, which reads "the videos presented in this room contain difficult imagery. Parental guidance is strongly advised."[7] The idea was to shield young audiences who may not be prepared to see those images.

When Sharing Authority is Impossible

If historical violence can trigger tough debates about what should and what should not be represented, the situation can become even more complex when historians deal with what Sharon Macdonald has called "Undesirable Heritage." Some people do not want to be associated with certain aspects of the past. Macdonald asks, for instance, how historians – and the community at large – can today deal with fascist material culture (2006). In other terms, what should Germans do with the physical remains of the Third Reich? The fascist

Figure 11.2 Entrance of the Documentation Centre Nazi Party Rally Grounds, Nuremberg (Germany), in the north wing of the former Congress Hall of the former Nazi party rallies, 2015. Credit: Marcus Buck. Courtesy of Dokumentationszentrum Reichsparteitagsgelände.

heritage is quite the opposite of the cherished and celebratory past people may want to commemorate, but it also raises questions about the dangers and attraction of the dark past.

There is a tension between the wish to distance oneself from the horrors of World War II and the need to recognize them for educational purposes. Should historians work at the preservation – or even reconstruction – of the remaining Nazi buildings? If so, historians may be criticized for making the Nazi past worth remembering, "risking returning the buildings to their former glory." Any museum putting on display Nazi artifacts similarly confronts the problematic aesthetization of the past. This raises the possibility that sometimes the creation of a museum might be counter-productive. However, should we destroy the sites at the risk of losing historical materials? Doing nothing or using these buildings for other non-related purposes may be seen as "'failure' to face up to the past" (Macdonald 2006, 18). Historians should be very careful to adopt an educational – and not at all celebratory – purpose. One option is to develop educational projects. Macdonald explains that a Documentation Centre of fascist studies was opened in 2001 in a former Nazi building. Figure 11.2 shows the entrance of what used to be the Congress Hall of the Nazi Party in Nuremberg. Designed by Albert Speer, the chief Nazi architect, the building has not been destroyed. Instead of preserving it as such, the original message and architecture of the Nazi has been challenged by the new purpose – Documentation Centre – and architecture of the site. In 1998, Architect Günther Domenig added a diagonal glass and steel passageway that contrasts with the plain Nazi style. Similarly, plans had started (but were recently abandoned) to transform the H-Block – from the Maze Prison in Northern Ireland where Republic and Loyalist terrorists were sent – into an international Peace Centre. The plan was to make the site not a museum devoted to the prisoners but a center of interpretation that gives more flexibility to discuss the complex peace process in Northern Ireland and abroad.

Historians may also meet open reluctance to mention certain aspects of the past. Robert Weyeneth published an interesting article in 1994 about the "Challenges of Public History in a Community with a Secret" (1994). His research about a 1919 violent labor confrontation that killed at least six people turned out to be more challenging than he expected. He explains that "the absence of commemoration was intentional, and I found myself disturbed by this effort to ignore, if not obliterate, the past" (Weyeneth 1994, 52). Can – and should – a public historian (especially as an outsider) play a catalytic role, Weyeneth asks. Following the concept of shared authority, historians should not see themselves as agents of catharsis. They are merely actors – and not missionaries – within the whole process of interpreting the past. But they definitely can work at creating public spaces of discussion. In this particular case, Weyeneth used the nominating process of the National Register of Historic Places to open discussion. He argues that he "anticipated that some of the ghosts of 1919 might be exorcised by the public hearings required by the nomination process and the publicity they tend to generate" (Weyeneth 1994, 56). In any case, historians should be prepared to attend passionate – and sometimes hostile – public meetings that are necessary to share authority. This is why the simple fact of taking part in such public discussion is of great value for the community as well as the historian.

Difficulty may arise when certain actors do not want to share authority with historians who may not be welcome in public debates. Historians may be excluded from public debates when they support interpretations of the past that are considered not appropriate by certain powerful actors. Some actors feel they own a sort of cultural copyright that makes them the true – and unique – interpreters of their past. As Weyeneth brilliantly wrote, "the assumption is that a community or group who were historical participants – authors of the past – enjoy some right of copyright that gives them control over the 'fair use' of the past" (Weyeneth 1994, 65). The power relations here are critical. Actors may struggle for the control of the interpretations of the past. Their objective is by no means to share authority but to impose their views on the process, especially when historians mention and explore inconvenient events and interpretations. For example, Weyeneth explained how local actors campaigned to suppress his book and silence his inconvenient history (2003).

Another example was the exhibition organized by the Canadian War Museum (CWM) about the Combined Bomber Offensive or Bomber Command, the Allied campaign in which some 10,000 Canadian airmen died between 1943 and 1945. One question the display intended to ask was about "the efficacy and the morality of the … massive bombing of Germany's industrial and civilian targets." Although the CWM received positive feedback from four prominent historians and had consulted some veterans' groups early in the process, the museum became the target of an intense critical campaign from other veterans' groups. The campaign resulted in parliamentary sub-committee hearings that forced the CWM to make changes to the display (Dean 2009, 1–2). The main question of the controversy became: Who has authority in interpreting Canadian military history, the veterans who lived the events or historians/curators who research the past (Dean 2009, 9)? Veterans can be both wonderful and problematic resource/partners for historians. Dubin points out in his book on memory and power relations that "the certainty of lived experience is a powerful credential to invoke and it is virtually impossible for someone else to rebut without seeming arrogant or insensitive" (1999, 5). The power of the witness/actor can be overwhelming for historians. The unwillingness to make certain aspects of the past public can also come from official policy. Li Na, who teaches public history in China, recently explained how the concept of doing history in public is in itself controversial in her country. She stresses that "it all boils down to the idea of authority-sharing. Official history is still authoritative and controlling" (Torres 2014).

A final limit to shared authority comes from possible counter-productive reactions. To give just one example, an instructor in charge of a course on nuclear history – and her students – wanted to share class discussion with the public through web posts. However, they faced harsh criticism. The instructor explains how the blog became – unexpectedly – very popular. But "it was not long before the blog began attracting comments from people who were angered by the post and who responded by directly attacking my student" (Rumiel 2012). The point here is not to detail the reasons for what she called a "witch hunt" but to underline that by sharing their work, historians and students can become the target of heavy criticism. Sharing authority is a type of practice that must be discussed and prepared beforehand, and with the knowledge that there is a risk of being overwhelmed by the amount of reaction, however predictable or unpredictable it may be.

Radical Trust

Historians should not turn their back on the complexity and ambiguity of the past because of the public debates. Shared authority is a difficult concept also because there is little agreement on its possible limits. Historians have struggled to define their role in this participatory process. Can every user be his/her own historian? Some historians have seen important limits to the concept of shared authority. For instance, Jim Gardner opposes what he calls "radical trust," the act of "looking to the public for content and direction." For him, radical trust "means letting the public … determine the future of public history" (2010, 53). As he argues, knowledge and opinion are not similar, and "we need to resist the current impulse to welcome (and thereby validate) any and all opinions" (Gardner 2010, 54). Sharing authority does not mean adopting relativism as a standpoint. Everyone can participate in public history, but not every opinion is equal. Besides, opinions may sometimes be counter-productive, ill-informed, and/or offensive. For instance, Gardner points out that the NMAH "has had to deal with individuals who deny that Japanese Americans were wrongly interned during World War II" (2010, 55). There is a difference between sharing and giving up authority. Historians definitely have a role to play in the participatory conception of history and its quality control.

Already in 1995, NMAH curator Steve Lubar warned that:

> sharing too little authority means that the audience will lose interest in or be unable to follow the narrative; it over privileges the curator's point of view. Sharing too much authority, on the other hand, means simply telling the audience what they already know, or what they want to know, reinforcing memory, not adding new dimensions of knowledge, new ways of approaching problems, new understanding.
>
> (1995, 46)

Historians should not see themselves as missionaries bringing the truth, but they should not underestimate their role either. Historians could work at providing historical interpretation of the past. History makes meaning of the past, and historical interpretation is based on critical analysis of primary materials.

Historians could, for instance, consider asking more critical and constructive questions rather than providing ready-made answers to the public. Historians need to take risks.

Historians need to stick to their duty of challenging stereotypes and assumptions about the past. As Roger Simon states about exhibitions, history becomes difficult – or risky – when it "confronts visitors with significant challenges to their museological expectations and interpretive abilities" (Simon 2011, 433). For example, any national institution could keep a space for the discussion of what it means to be part of this nation. Nations – and political borders – have a rather recent history to which the past does not always correspond. Cultural – and above all national – institutions could encompass different geographical scopes such as local, regional, or transnational frameworks. Challenging the national representations may be disturbing for popular audiences, but it ultimately helps understand the complexity of the past. By exhibiting objects, museums can be at the foreground of transnational interpretations of the past. Objects travel and do not respect national barriers, so why should history represented in museums impose a national interpretation on the collections? Gardner reckons that "rather than try to concoct a simple story of shared experiences, we should share many stories, from multiple points of view, exploring the complexity and richness of the American Past" (2004, 17). Historians are not afraid to question aspects of the past – and of societies – that are usually silenced. For instance, the NMAH arranged in 1994 an exhibition called *Claiming a Public Place: Gay, Lesbian, and Bisexual Pride, 1969–1994*, and the Smithsonian National Portrait Gallery an exhibition called *Hide/Seek: Difference and Desire in American Portraiture (2010–2011)*, that questioned long-standing taboos in American history. Likewise, in a revealing post called "sacrificing comfort for complexity: presenting difficult narratives in public history," Rose Miron explains how the project *Fort Snelling and Guantánamo: Corresponding Histories, Disparate Rememberings* provides a risky while challenging comparison between the two sites. The project highlights that "Fort Snelling was used as a concentration camp for Dakota people during the winter of 1862–1863" and "seeks to draw on the similar histories of detention at Fort Snelling and Guantánamo, asking why the two sites are remembered so differently today, and what this might tell us about larger narratives of empire and imperialism" (2014). Shared authority must foster participation and collaboration, but must not annihilate critical and challenging interpretations of the past.

Historian Ed Linenthal argues that what the public wants is not a simple story. On the contrary, he thinks that there is space for complex and rich stories. Historians must resist, according to him, "the insidious and dangerous attempts to sanitize or romanticize history" (Linenthal 1994, 990). The now-abandoned Museum of French History project aimed to start by asking people what French identity meant for them. The survey was supposed to help curators design the new institution. This attempt would have symbolized how historians could share authority without ignoring the need to develop public critical analysis of the past.

Shared authority does not mean historians' inactivity. A tendency noticed by Gardner is that public historians are becoming more timid, refusing to take risks (2010, 56). Just because certain actors may not warmly welcome historians and their interpretations does not mean that historians should return to the comfort of the ivory tower. The audiences need to know more about what history is and how historians work. Weyeneth realizes that disputes also come from the fact that people have little understanding of the interpretive nature of history. Historians could explain how they ask questions about sources, how they attempt to think critically about the past, and how they contextualize the past (Weyeneth 2003, 1–2). An understanding of the historian's craft could help people share authority more easily. In other words, to foster shared authority, historians could share not only the final results but also their interpretive activities. The objective is not to make history more opinion-based, but to make public understanding of the past more critical.

Notes

1 See Chapter 4.
2 See videos and archives of the training, http://connectlive.com/events/publicspaces/ (accessed September 3, 2015).
3 See Chapter 12.
4 The NCPH provides a short list of case studies reading for controversial events, http://ncph.org/cms/wp-content/uploads/RRPHC-Controversies.pdf (accessed January 17, 2015).
5 See Oak Alley Plantation website, www.oakalleyplantation.com/learn-explore/what-shes-all-about#sthash.5LBygSQF.dpuf (accessed January 17, 2015). It greatly contrasts with the Whitney Plantation (that opened in Fall 2014), which is defined as "a genuine landmark built by African slaves and their descendants." The site is dedicated to the interpretation of slavery along the River Road, www.whitneyplantation.com/ (accessed May 13, 2015).
6 The first exhibition mounted at New York State Museum (Albany) refused to include such photographs.
7 I would like to thank Robert Ehrenreich from the USHMM for the information.

Bibliography

Adair, Bill, Filene, Benjamin, and Koloski, Laura, eds. *Letting Go? Sharing Historical Authority in a User-Generated World*, Philadelphia: The Pew Center for Arts & Heritage, 2011.

Alderson, William T. and Low, Shirley Payne, eds. *Interpretation of Historic Sites*, Lanham: AltaMira Press, 1986.

Bodnar, John. *Remaking America: Public Memory, Commemoration, and Patriotism in the Twentieth Century*, Princeton: Princeton University Press, 1993.

Cauvin, Thomas. "Quando è in gioco la Public History: musei, storici e riconciliazione politica nella Repubblica d'Irlanda." *Memoria e Ricerca*, 37 (2011): 53–71. English translation: www.fondazione casadioriani.it/modules.php?name=MR&op=body&id=550 (accessed January 21, 2015).

Dean, David. "Museums as Conflict Zones: The Canadian War Museum and Bomber Command." *Museum and Society*, 7/1 (2009): 1–15.

Dickson, E.J. "I Accidently Started a Wikipedia Hoax." *The Daily Dot*, July 29, 2014, www.dailydot.com/lol/amelia-bedelia-wikipedia-hoax/ (accessed January 23, 2015).

Dubin, Steven C. *Displays of Power: Memory and Amnesia in the American Museum*, New York and London: New York University Press, 1999.

Feller, Laura. "Doing History in NPS Classroom." *Perspectives on History*, May 2010, www.historians.org/publications-and-directories/perspectives-on-history/may-2010/controversy-in-the-classroom/doing-history-in-nps-classrooms (accessed January 23, 2015).

Fladmark, Magnus, ed. *Heritage and Museums: Shaping National Identity*, Shaftesbury: Donhead Publishing, 2000.

Frevert, Ute. *Emotions in History: Lost and Found*, Budapest: Central European University Press, 2011.

Frisch, Michael. *A Shared Authority: Essays on the Craft and Meaning of Oral and Public History*, Albany: SUNY Press, 1990.

Frisch, Michael. "From A Shared Authority to the Digital Kitchen, and Back." In *Letting Go? Sharing Historical Authority in a User-Generated World*, edited by Bill Adair, Benjamin Filene, and Laura Koloski, Philadelphia: The Pew Center for Arts & Heritage, 2011, 126–138.

Gallas, Kristin L. and DeWolf Perry, James. *Technical Leaflet: Developing Comprehensive and Conscientious Interpretation of Slavery at Historic Sites and Museums*, American Association for State and Local History, 2014, http://resource.aaslh.org/view/developing-comprehensive-and-conscientious-interpretation-of-slavery-at-historic-sites-and-museums/ (accessed January 12, 2015).

Gardner, James. "Contested Terrain: History, Museums, and the Public." *The Public Historian*, 26/4 (Fall 2004): 11–21.

Gardner, James. "Trust, Risk and Public History: A View From the United States." *Public History Review*, 17 (2010): 52–61.

Gillis, John R. *Commemorations: The Politics of National Identity*, Princeton: Princeton University Press, 1994.

Glassberg, David. *Sense of History: The Place of the Past in American Life*, Amherst: University of Massachusetts Press, 2001.

Graham, Otis L. Jr. "Who Owns American History?" *The Public Historian*, 17/2 (Spring 1995): 8–11.

Kaplan, Flora, ed. *Museums and the Making of "Ourselves": The Role of Objects in National Identity*, London and New York: Leicester University Press, 1994.

Linenthal, Edward T. "Committing History in Public." *Journal of American History*, 81 (December 1994): 986–991.

Linenthal, Edward T. "Problems and Promise in Public History." *The Public Historian*, 19/2 (1997): 45–47.

Linenthal, Edward T. and Englehardt, Tom. *History Wars: The Enola Gay and Other Battles for the American Past*, New York: Metropolitan Books, 1996.

Lubar, Steven. "In the Footsteps of Perry: The Smithsonian Goes to Japan." *The Public Historian*, 17/3 (Summer 1995): 25–59.

Lubar, Steven. "Seven Rules for Public Humanists." On Public Humanities, June 5, 2014, http://stevenlubar.wordpress.com/2014/06/05/seven-rules-for-public-humanists/ (accessed September 3, 2015).

Macdonald, Sharon. "Undesirable Heritage: Fascist Material Culture and Historical Consciousness in Nuremberg." *International Journal of Heritage Studies*, 12/1 (2006): 9–28.

Mihm, Stephen. "Everyone's a Historian Now: How the Internet – and You – Will Make History Deeper, Richer, and More Accurate." Boston.Com, May 25, 2008, www.boston.com/bostonglobe/ideas/articles/2008/05/25/everyones_a_historian_now/?page=full (accessed January 28, 2015).

Miron, Rose. "Sacrificing Comfort for Complexity: Presenting Difficult Narratives in Public History." *Public History Commons*, April 24, 2014, http://publichistorycommons.org/sacrificing-comfort-for-complexity/#sthash.m3gRT1St.dpuf (accessed August 30, 2015).

Norris, Linda. "When is Your Audience Ready for the Tough Stuff?" *The Uncatalogued Museum*, September 22, 2014, http://uncatalogedmuseum.blogspot.co.uk/2014/09/when-is-your-audience-ready-for-tough.html (accessed January 29, 2015).

Novick, Peter. *That Noble Dream: The "Objectivity Question" and the American Historical Profession*, Cambridge: Cambridge University Press, 1988.

Ostow, Robin, ed. *(Re)Visualizing National History: Museums and National Identities in Europe in the New Millennium*, Toronto: University of Toronto Press, 2008.

Rosenzweig, Roy. "Can History be Open Source? Wikipedia and the Future of the Past." *The Journal of American History*, 93/1 (June 2006): 117–146, http://chnm.gmu.edu/essays-on-history-new-media/essays/?essayid=42 (accessed January 30, 2015).

Rosenzweig, Roy and Thelen, David. *The Presence of the Past: Popular Uses of History in American Life*, New York: Columbia University Press, 1998.

Rumiel, L. "On Learning." *Nuclearhistorymatters*, April 3, 2012, http://nuclearhistorymatters.wordpress.com/2012/04/03/on-learning/ (accessed January 28, 2015).

Schwartz, Barry and Kim, Mikyoung, eds. *Northeast Asia's Difficult Past: Essays in Collective Memory*, London: Palgrave Macmillan, 2010.

Simon, Roger I. "A Shock to Thought: Curatorial Judgement and the Public Exhibition of 'Difficult Knowledge'." *Memory Studies*, 4 (February 2011): 432–449.

Sontag, Susan. *Regarding the Pain of Others*, London: Macmillan, 2003.

Torres, Victoria. "Public History or Public Toilets in China?" *History News Network*, April 20, 2014, http://historynewsnetwork.org/article/155294#sthash.IIylPTLu.dpuf (accessed September 3, 2015).

Tyson, Amy M. *The Wages of History: Emotional Labor on Public History's Front Lines*, Amherst: University of Massachusetts Press, 2013.

USHMM. "Photo Archives." 1993–1995, http://digitalassets.ushmm.org/photoarchives/detail.aspx?id=1092929&search=permanent+exhibition&index=3 (accessed September 2, 2015).

Weyeneth, Robert R. "History, He Wrote: Murder, Politics, and the Challenges of Public History in a Community with a Secret." *The Public Historian*, 16 (Spring 1994): 51–73.

Weyeneth, Robert R. "The Risks of Professionalizing Local History: The Campaign to Suppress My Book." *Public History News*, 4 (Fall 2003): 1–2.

Williams, Paul. *Memorial Museums: The Global Rush to Commemorate Atrocities*, London: Bloomsbury Academic, 2008.

Wright, Elizabethada. "The Choices We Make: Public Historians' Role in the Commemorations of the Sesquicentennial of the American Civil War." *Civil War Case Statement*, NCPH, 2011, http://ncph.org/cms/wp-content/uploads/Combined-Civil-War-Case-Statements.pdf (accessed January 23, 2015).

12 Civic Engagement and Social Justice
Historians as Activists

From Civic Engagement to Social Justice

By working not only with but also for their audiences, public historians perform a public service. The uses of the past and the historians' public service can take several formats. Historians may understand their public service as coming from the research of the truth. The uses of the past are an inescapable part of public historians' professional ethics. In the 1990 collection of essays on *Ethics and Public History*, Theodore Karamanski argued that the research of the truth "strengthens the characters of individual and empowers institutions to achieve their goals" (1990, 10–11). The past can have some very practical uses; it can, for instance, contribute to group/individual identity.[1]

Activist historians argue that history can be used to improve the present and – therefore – the future (Korza and Schaffer Bacon 2005). According to this definition, there is a long tradition of activists among historians. Public historian Rebecca Conard recalls that James Harvey Robinson articulated the concept of "useful history" in 1912 when he "called upon historians to 'exploit' their methods of research and analysis to advance the 'general progress of society'" (2015, 116). History has a wonderful potential to examine contemporary issues and social concerns in the light of the past, so that history can help people understand the complexity of the present (Korza and Schaffer Bacon 2012). This objective translates in historians' role in civic engagement. According to public historian Mary Rizzo, the concept of civic engagement is at the core of the public humanities. She wrote:

> When the American Academy of Arts and Sciences makes the case for federal support for the public humanities in its Heart of the Matter report, it relies on arguments about the potential for civic engagement. AAAS contends, for example, that the humanities encourage "civic vigor" and prepare citizens to be voters, jurors, and consumers.
>
> (2014)

In other words, historians can help people to become better citizens.

What appears to be more recent is the shift from civic engagement to social justice. In a 2014 conference arranged at North Carolina State University, public historians discussed the move "From Civic Engagement to Activism: Public History as Civic Responsibility." The move from civic engagement to social justice and activism has become central in public history debates. Some public historians consider their role as social activists and advocate for a multitude of groups who have been marginalized, economically and/or socially, and whose histories have been devalued or ignored by mainstream history, in the preservation of historic places, and in the interpretation of history for the public.[2] In the United States, social activism received more attention during the 1960s and 1970s along with the civil rights movement and related rights movements. In history, the main consequence was a new research focus on people's history.[3] In her article on the pragmatic root of public history, Rebecca Conard points out that "'people's history' was introduced in 1986 with the appearance of an edited collection of essays under the title of *Presenting the Past: Essays on History and the Public*" (2015, 115). British historian Raphael Samuel influenced the authors of this collection. In the United Kingdom, Samuel's History Workshop at Ruskin College in Oxford greatly affected the people's history movement. As activist, Samuel worked at empowering ordinary people through history. Through different tools and practices – for instance, participatory museums and digital crowdsourcing – some public history projects inherited Samuel's objectives to empower individuals and communities by making them actors of historical production.

In a 2014 National Council on Public History's (NCPH) working group entitled "Toward a History of Civic Engagement and the Progressive Impulse in Public History," Denise Meringolo and Daniel Kerr questioned how public historians could more effectively use historical work to foster change (NCPH 2014). One answer was to produce more inclusive and more diverse representations of the past. The 2007 NCPH Code of Ethics and Professional Conduct highlights that "a public historian should welcome opportunities to represent cultural diversity in his or her work and to enfold members of underrepresented groups into the profession" (NCPH 2007). Likewise, the Social Justice Alliance for Museums explains, "we acknowledge that many museums have for many years failed to operate for the wider public benefit, and instead have catered primarily for educated minorities. We reject this approach."[4] The objective is not to adapt the past to present issues, but to provide more complex representations by giving voice to underrepresented aspects and actors of the past. This creates richer interpretations of the past as well as empowers underrepresented groups in the present.

Public historians can also be more interventionist and act to change societies. In the 1980s, Michael Wallace argued that museums could be activist in different ways, "by intervening directly in inter-community conflicts; by presenting alternatives on issues of public policy, and by promoting historically informed planning initiatives." For instance, he proposed that:

> a museum could present a full-rigged exhibition on a controversial subject, and conclude by presenting various proposed solutions, perhaps screening short video presentations by spokesperson for alternative approaches. Visitors could then vote, and a computer terminal would tally and present updated results.
>
> (1996, 51–52)

More recently, a conference in 2008 entitled "Active History: History for the Future" resulted in the creation of Active History, an organization that intends to "make a tangible difference in people's lives" through a "history that makes an intervention and is transformative to both practitioners and communities."[5] In those cases, public historians would not only foster cultural diversity, but would also participate in public policy and present-day social justice.

Before going more into detail about practices, it is necessary to stress that historians' activism is controversial since it is often based on their personal convictions. In a blog post about activism, public historian Cathy Stanton explains, "most public historians are reluctant to describe themselves as advocates, activists, or political actors per se." One reason is that "deeply-held values within the historical profession still tend to place advocacy in direct opposition to analytical rigor" (2015). The NCPH's Code of Ethics and Professional Status warns, "a public historian should critically examine personal issues of social conscience as distinct from issues of ethical practice" (NCPH 2007). As Ludmilla Jordanova points out in her book on history in practice, "feelings are not always a very good guide because, by their very nature, they make people uncritical." However, she does not condemn activism, but suggests that "the moral commitments of historians and the nature of their human values need to be made explicit whenever possible and tempered by evidence that is open to scrutiny" (2000, 169). The least historians should do is to be aware of the impact of activism on their work. This helps, according to Jordanova, "to explain more openly to a wider public the processes through which historical judgments are reached" (2000, 171).

Public History as a Source of Social Empowerment for Underrepresented Groups

The range of underrepresented groups in historical narratives is way too broad for an exhaustive presentation in this chapter. The purpose is not to cover every topic but to propose some practices and examples to inform public historians about their role in social empowerment.

Native Populations

In settler societies (the United States, Australia, New Zealand, South Africa, among others), the voices of native populations have – for a long time – often been silenced in mainstream culture. In his history of the history profession in America, Ian Tyrrell explains how the rise of a national "scientific" and professional history in late 19th and early 20th century America resulted in the "distancing of American history from what came before the arrival of Anglo settlement" (2005, 231). The study of Native American peoples shifted from history to anthropology (Conn 2004). Historians established a clear distinction between Indians' and settlers' past. For a long time, historians not only silenced the history of natives, but also participated in the destruction of their heritage. According to David Neufeld, "the practice of public history with aboriginal peoples in North America over the past century and a half has been generally destructive of their communities and identities." In collecting "relics" – including the bodies of ancestors – museums participated in the looting of native communities (Neufeld 2006, 117). History was done without, and to the detriment of, native populations.

Historians and cultural institutions need to collaborate with and empower native populations (Lawlor 2006; Peers 2007). Public historian Amy Lonetree has recently argued for decolonizing museums (2012). In other words, historians should fight the colonial views on native populations that have been conveyed by books, movies, museums, and other media. Historians should reconsider the view of a superior and dominant culture, should acknowledge the history of native populations, and collaborate with natives more often. There are now numerous sites where public land management have established agreements with native groups (Kelman 2013; Spence 2000). For instance, the Washita Battlefield National Historic Site in Oklahoma tells the story of an attack on a Cheyenne village by General George Custer and the 7th U.S. Cavalry. Historians can help shed light on parts of the past that have been ignored.

Shared authority is essential.[6] Historians and political actors should not speak in place of native populations. In 1989, the U.S. Congress passed a law establishing a National Museum of the American Indian (NMAI) as part of the Smithsonian Museum.[7] More than 25,000 Native Americans attended the opening of the museum in 2004. It is important that museums, exhibitions, documentaries, and archives should not just be about native populations, but also be produced with them. Historians may consider the creation of committees that include representatives of native populations (Neufeld 2006, 119). Amanda Cobb explains:

> The NMAI staff held dozens of community consultations at different sites in Indian Country. At each consultation, participants voiced their ideas for the building, landscape, and overall tone of the museum, going far beyond what was originally asked of them.
>
> (2005, 490)

Collaboration could apply to the various steps of history projects, from the creation to the final production. For example, the objects and exhibitions at the NMAI have to be managed in conjunction with representatives of Native Americans. Cobb stresses that: "As a result of such collaborative curation, the museum employs 'nontraditional' (by museological standards) methods of care and preservation, display, and classification, and privileges Native conceptualizations of history and truth." Some of these techniques result from "the belief that many cultural objects are alive rather than inanimate and often require curators to allow them to 'breathe' rather than suffocate in sealed plastic containers." Finally, the NMAI provides "tribal citizens with the ability to visit their objects and to 'feed' them, often with pollen, or perform ceremonies with them" (Cobb 2005, 493). Shared authority helps empower native populations and to enrich public history methodology.

Some public historians go further and strive to acknowledge the present-day consequences of colonial history. For example, some projects focus on the long-term consequences of residential schools in Canada (Regan 2011). The Truth and Reconciliation Commission of Canada (TRCC) highlights that "For over 100 years, Aboriginal children were removed from their families and sent to institutions called residential schools ... to eliminate parental involvement in the spiritual, cultural and intellectual development of Aboriginal children." In order to "revitalize the relationship between Aboriginal peoples and Canadian society" the TRCC gathers "statements from former students of the Indian Residential Schools and anyone else who feels they have been impacted by the schools and their legacy."[8] Likewise, the TRCC's Missing Children project presents research on the numerous Aboriginal children who, after having been sent to residential schools, never returned to their home communities. This public history project addresses the traumatic experience of parents who never found out about their children.[9] History and education at large are, in this case, seen as cultural reparation, making people aware of past injustice.

Looting and Repatriation

Colonial dominant actors have, for a long time, been looting native populations' heritage (Fine-Dare 2002). As a consequence, public debates have discussed the issue of repatriation of human remains and sacred objects. In 1990, the U.S. Congress passed the Native American Graves Protection and Repatriation Act (NAGPRA) to encourage the identification and the return of human remains and sacred items to their communities of origin. All public and private museums that have received federal funds must obey NAGPRA.[10] Historians working in such institutions must know the complex repatriation process that is composed of identification, inventory, and consultation with descendants (Mihesuah 2000).[11]

The process of repatriation is by no means limited to native populations. In addition to the now famous controversy between Greece and the British Museum over the ownership of the Panathenaic Frieze, international discussions emerged about the role of historians in the repatriation process. The 2009 Athens conference on the "Return of Cultural Objects" discussed case studies in Zimbabwe, Greenland, Ethiopia, and Iraq (Museum International undated).

Repatriation can also result from more recent periods. The Nazis plundered and collected a huge number of cultural artifacts (Kurtz 2009). Louis Marchesano, curator at the Getty Research Institute argues, "we are very aware that tens of thousands of looted objects were never properly repatriated or returned to their lawful owners" (1999). The topic is extremely complex since works of arts were looted by the Nazis but were later brought back by the Allies. Historians can help, through their research, to find the owners of those artifacts. Historians must question how the Nazis obtained the items, from whom, when, and under which circumstances. The United States Holocaust Memorial Museum (USHMM) provides a very useful list of resources for historians interested in Nazis' looted art, and lists the current projects by country (USHMM undated).

Migrants

Migrants are another group whose voices are barely heard in public historical debates. While debates on immigration have, by definition, international and transnational components, the issue is also extremely powerful at the local scale. In 2014, for the project Dialogues on Immigration, 20 history museums and heritage centers organized public discussions in the United States. Sometimes museums are even physically concerned. In 2010, immigrants who were applying for legal documents, occupied La Cité de l'Immigration (the French Museum of Immigration) (Labadi 2013).

Museums and heritage sites have the potential to become spaces of public discussion for controversial topics. For example, although it represents 40 percent of the population, the Hispanic community of Tucson (Arizona) seldom visits the Saguaro National Park. In order to remedy this, the park created an outreach project and undertook a study of its early Hispanic homesteads to connect with the Hispanic community (NPS 2009, 25). Museums can also be at the origins of projects that take place beyond their walls. In 2014, Ghent (Belgium) Stadsmuseum arranged an exhibition on the history of migration outside of its walls, through highlights in the city. The project contributed to recovering the city's migration past and to give it a space (STAM undated).

In the 1980s, Michael Wallace suggested to make exhibitions about the history of "guest workers," Mexicans in the United States, Africans in France, or Turks in Germany (1996, 48). In the same vein, the Bracero History Archive – a collaborative project between the Center for History and New Media at George Mason University, the National Museum of American History, and the UTEP Institute of Oral History – collects and makes available the oral histories and objects related to the eponymous program that facilitated the migration of millions of Mexican guest workers in the United States between 1942 and 1964.

Historians can help the public understand how important immigration has been for societies. In New York City, the Lower East Side Tenement Museum has now become a traditional example of public history. The museum has developed a program that "engages new immigrants in dialogue about contemporary immigration-related issues, and helps them to strategize about actions they can take to shape those issues" (Ševčenko and Russell-Ciardi 2008, 12). Historians can participate in debates on immigration and identity. For instance, in their project "At Home in Holland" students from the University of Amsterdam respond "to the way that hostile reactions to immigrants have undermined the traditional idea of Dutch tolerance and hospitality in recent years." Students investigated the changing attitudes towards refugees and new migrants in Holland. They noticed how "the language of the debate has shifted, from refugee, to asylum seeker, to illegal immigrant, to criminal" (Foulidis et al. 2014). Following the 9/11 attacks on the World Trade Center, the Arab American National Museum designed an exhibition entitled *Patriots and Peacemakers* about the history of Arab Americans in the U.S. Army and institutions. Historians should not design the past according to their opinions in present-day debates, but they can help demonstrate how the past is often much more complex than some simplistic views argue.

Slavery and Segregation

Slavery has always been an international phenomenon. In 2007, the International Slavery Museum opened in Liverpool (UK), giving a large space to the Transatlantic Slave Trade. In Louisiana, Whitney Plantation is the site of a slavery museum whose academic director – Dr. Ibrahima Seck – is a historian from Cheikh Anta Diop University in Dakar (Senegal). Seck has worked on international collaboration, in particular with the House of Slaves (Maison des Esclaves) on Gorée Island, two miles off the coast of the city of Dakar.[12] Figure 12.1 shows one of the most striking components of Whitney Plantation. The "Children of Whitney" are 40 statues of children designed by artist Woodrow Nash

Figure 12.1 "Children of Whitney." Statues of slave children designed by artist Woodrow Nash for Whitney Plantation, Louisiana, 2015. Courtesy of Whitney Plantation.

for Whitney Plantation. Their purpose is first to remind visitors that slavery was not just about adults but also greatly affected children. The focus on children also comes from the fact that Whitney Plantation uses oral testimonies of former slaves from the U.S. Federal Writers' Project in the 1930s. The majority of these former slaves were children at the time of emancipation. The use of these sources by Whitney Plantation participates in a more general focus on children during slavery.

Nevertheless, historian of slavery, James Horton, underlines that "The history of slavery and its role in the formation of the American experience is one of the most sensitive and difficult subjects to present in a public setting" (1999, 20). The United States has a World War I national museum (Kansas City), a World War II national museum (New Orleans), the United States Holocaust Memorial Museum, a museum devoted to the 9/11 attacks, but there has been no national slavery museum. Historian Eric Foner recently stressed that:

> It's something I bring up all the time in my lectures … If the Germans built a museum dedicated to American slavery before one about their own Holocaust, you'd think they were trying to hide something. As Americans, we haven't yet figured out how to come to terms with slavery.
>
> (Amsden 2015)

In Louisiana, as in most Southern states, until very recently, visitors to plantations could not learn much about the slaves whose history was absent from the narratives that focused on rich white families and decorative history.

Several types of public history projects attempt now to preserve the trace of slavery. Archaeology has been critical in the recent reinterpretation of slavery. The Digital Archaeological Archive of Comparative Slavery was initially based on sites like the archaeology programs at Monticello (Thomas Jefferson's plantation), Mount Vernon (George Washington's plantation), and Andrew Jackson's Hermitage.[13] Another new and very interesting project is the Periwinkle Initiative, which aims to build a National Burial Database of Enslaved Americans.[14] Likewise, Joseph McGill Jr. is the founder of the Slave Dwelling Project. He spends nights in many different slave dwellings in order to bring attention to those sites that are often neglected. Like for plantations in Louisiana, McGill stresses that "Americans tend to focus on the 'big house,' the mansion and gardens, and neglect the buildings out back … If we lose slave dwellings, it's that much easier to forget the slaves themselves" (Horwitz 2013). However, it is important not to forget that slavery was not a unique Southern issue, but belongs to American history. In 2006, the New-York Historical Society mounted an exhibition called *Slavery in New-York* to show that slavery was not a uniquely Southern phenomenon.

The Thirteenth Amendment to the U.S. Constitution (1865) did not mean that the consequences of slavery were no longer visible. In the introduction of his book on slavery and public history, Horton argues that "what we understand today as racism is largely a legacy of the slavery that formally ended nearly a century and a half ago" (Horton and Horton 2006, x). Some historians extend the period of their studies from slavery to its long-term impact and significance. The International Slavery Museum in Liverpool explains that "our vision is to create a major new International Slavery Museum to promote the understanding of transatlantic slavery and its enduring impact … on Africa, South America, the USA, the Caribbean and Western Europe."[15] Another famous example is District Six that used to be, before the 1970s, an example of cultural diversity in South Africa. Opened in 1994, the museum is located in Cape Town, in an area where

60,000 people were forced to move during the Apartheid in the 1970s. The mission of the museum is to "mobilize the masses of ex-residents and their descendants into a movement of land restitution, community development and political consciousness." The creation of the museum was an act of activism for which "the recovery and restoration of memory is just as important as, and needs to be a vital component of, the recovery and restoration of land" (Prosalendis et al. 2013, 284, 286). The District Six Museum offers a way for people to discuss and challenge the impact of the Apartheid. For historians, reparations for past injustices may not be about money or legal actions, but rather through the shape of educational projects to fight oblivion.

Women and Gender History

Women are by no means a minority, but they are often underrepresented in historical production. One excellent example is the Women's Rights National Historical Park that has been interpreting the struggle for women's equality since it opened in 1982 (Conard 2012). However, as Dubrow and Goodman point out, relatively few properties significant in women's history are listed on the U.S. National Register of Historic Places (Dubrow and Goodman 2002, 3). Besides, when part of the narratives, women are often confined to the history of domestic tasks. Historians have participated in producing male-defined and male-centered representations of the past. Women's history can help historians and the audiences develop new interpretations and new understandings of the past.

In order to bring women back to the front of the historical scene, it is first necessary to undertake surveys. Such surveys about women's part in historical institutions have been done in Wisconsin and Georgia. Georgia's Historic Preservation Division was the first state agency to address gender issues related to the identification, documentation, and evaluation of historic properties through its Women's History Initiative (Dubrow and Goodman 2002, 11). Surveys in states or in specific institutions could enable public history actors to enrich historical narratives. For example, *Raising Our Sights: Women's History in Pennsylvania* was a project of the Pennsylvania Humanities Council in 1992 that worked for the inclusion of women's history in more than a dozen historic sites. Historians in charge of collection and interpretation should always ask themselves if both male and female experiences are represented.

Debates about a possible National Women's History Museum reveal how difficult it is to reach an agreement on women and gender history (Michel 2014). Cathy Stanton wonders where the next generation of gender studies in public history is. She argues, "what's being said and done in public history interpretation of gender and sexuality remains firmly within the model of adding neglected or 'subaltern' histories into mainstream or 'official' narratives" (Stanton 2013). Historians can go further than simply incorporating women's experiences into traditional narratives. Sometimes, the overall historical narrative is driven by male representations. In this case, it is important to rethink the whole interpretation of the past. One option may be – like through the creation of the National Collaborative for Women's History Sites – to adopt women's point of view as the central frame of reference for the narrative. For instance, *HerStories* is an oral history archival project that focuses on mothers' experiences and representations in Sri Lanka.

Karen Nickless and Heather Huyck from the National Collaborative for Women's History Sites have detailed the steps for "Putting Women Back in History" (2015). They give three very useful pieces of advice. First, "Every single historic site is a women's history site – including the ones you don't think are." Interpreters should also "See women both independently and as part of a greater whole" and "Let the women speak for themselves" (Nickless and Huyck 2015). Likewise, Edith Mayo argues that historians should redefine the meaning of objects "placing them within a framework of women's history" (Mayo 2002, 121). Historians can also provide a space where visitors can discuss their own representations of gender relations. For Stanton, "masculinity—the foundation of much of that structure—remains the elephant in the room that nobody's really talking about" (2013). It may be extremely challenging for historians to make users and visitors think about mainstream categories in the past and present.

LGBT, Queer, and Sexual Practices

In terms of sexual practice and identity, historical narratives have mostly been conservative and preferred focusing on traditional family relations. As Alison Oram demonstrates in her article on historic houses:

> the stress on the genealogy of the elite families who have inhabited them is strongly heteronormative, and they have certainly been less permeable to the now well-established social histories of class, gender, colonialism and sexuality than other popular genres of history.
>
> (2011, 192)

Homosexuality, bisexuality, and transgender relations remain globally absent from public historical narratives. It is still problematic to find funding for events that deal with what has been called LGBT (Lesbian, Gay, Bisexual, and Transgender).

Notwithstanding this general reluctance, the history of the LGBT movement developed since the 1960s and has now global networks (Hayward 2015). History became an important tool for the LGBT movement. Gays and lesbians, Lauren Gutterman argues, "see history as capable of teaching them not only about themselves, but also about the potential for political transformation" (2010, 96). Likewise, Oram explains that "Naming key historical figures as lesbian or gay instead of glossing over or denying their sexuality was akin to the politics of coming out. Gay activists claimed a positive historical narrative of homosexuality, critiquing the heterosexist bias of existing history-writing" (2011, 195). Historians interested in LGBT projects can now access and use many different resources, such as the Center for Lesbian and Gay Studies (CLAGS) at the City University of New York.

Similar to women history that challenges the male-centered representations of the past, LGBT public history could challenge the implicit heterosexual norm of historical production. Historians can work at preserving archives. The Society for American Archivists' Gay and Lesbian Archives identifies LGBT archives and collections all over the United States. With the Internet, it becomes easier to bypass the lack of funding to create online repositories. For instance, gay activist Jonathan Ned Katz founded OutHistory.org in 2003, a wiki to allow users to upload and curate materials.

Through archival works, historic preservation, and exhibitions, historians can foster more inclusive narratives. For instance, the United States Holocaust Memorial Museum had an exhibition called "Nazi Persecution of Homosexuals, 1933–1945." Likewise, a memorial to homosexuals persecuted under Nazism was created in Berlin in 2008. The GLBT Historical Society has been working on a comprehensive study of queer historic sites in San Francisco. It is important for historians to show how materials about the past construct and convey definitions of sexual practices and sexual norms.

Mainstream History

The links between public history and underrepresented groups raise questions about what mainstream history is. The main question is to know whether ethnic minorities and under-represented groups should be more acknowledged in mainstream institutions or whether it is necessary to design specific sites and narratives. The National Museum of the American Indian now represents Native Americans, and the National Museum of African American History and Culture is scheduled to open in 2016. However, some historians like Jacki Thompson Rand – historian specialist in American Indian and Native Studies – consider that "the museum represents a lost opportunity to integrate American Indians into the national consciousness" (Rand 2007). Similar debates took place regarding the project of a national women's history museum (NWHM). One criticism has been about the relative lack of presence from historians in the NWHM's project that would rather be a "Women's Hall of Fame."[16] Are such museums the sign that African Americans, American Indians, and women are still not fully part of the mainstream national history?[17]

Outside the United States, the Te Papa Tongarewa Museum (New Zealand) is extremely interesting. As one of the Dominions within the British Empire, New Zealand received European populations and became a settler country. As other settler societies, the representa-tions of the relations between Europeans and native populations (Maori) have been contro-versial in New Zealand. In 1998, the Museum of New Zealand Te Papa Tongarewa opened as the new national museum and art gallery of New Zealand. The name itself reflects a focus on biculturalism and on the contribution of the Maori to the national culture and history. The museum is based on the concept of biculturalism, "the recognition of the historical interaction of two peoples, Mäori (the indigenous people) and Päkehä (the settler population)" (Bozic-Vrbancic 2003, 295). Although somehow artificial, the two distinct cultures became the prism through which the past has been represented in the museum. In this case, the museum displays "two mainstreams of tradition and culture" (Paku undated). The museum offers an example of how historians not only have to reckon with history as a source of empowerment for minorities but also with the overall concept of mainstream and national history.

Public Historians and Everyday Suffering

The relations between the past and the present are at the center of public history. It is critical for public historians to take into consideration what the present motivations and demands of the public are. Like historians, historic sites, museums, and other cultural insti-tutions cannot live in an ivory tower. In a recent post Linda Norris asked whether museums need disaster plans for people not only to take care of the collections but also to help the communities (Norris 2014). Public historians might consider how they could help relieve communities from some everyday suffering.

Criminality, Incarceration, and Prison Memories

In his 1996 book on American memory, Mike Wallace was convinced that "Urban crime is both an indisputably sexy subject and a matter of immense contemporary concern" (1996, 44). Historians may address those issues not only because they are "sexy," but also because they reveal the complexity of the past. New projects such as the Prison Public Memory Project use history to create forums where different actors "can come together to engage in conversation and learning about the complex role of prisons in communities and society" (Prison Memory Project undated). In a recent interview with Martha Swan, public historian Mary Rizzo discusses the use of history in creating public understanding of complicated contemporary issues such as mass incarceration (Rizzo and Swan 2014). Created by Swan in 1999, *John Brown Lives!* is a public history project – in the memory of Abolitionist John Brown – that deals with mass incarceration and drug laws and encourages "people to question the narrative of American history, the meaning of freedom, the role of policy in racial issues, and the connections between history and place" (Rizzo and Swan 2014, 61). The *John Brown Lives!* project shows how the links between past and present are crucial for public historians. The project examines the effects of the 1973 Rockefeller drug laws on mass incarceration, on the people who work in prisons, and on the communities where prisons are built (Rizzo and Swan 2014, 62). The approach is very similar to the work of Heather Ann Thomspon and Michelle Alexander, who argue that mass incarceration and the disproportional percentage of African Americans in prison is the consequence of a persistent system of racial inequality (Thompson 2010; Alexander 2010). The issue here is not to agree or disagree with their argument but rather to demonstrate the need for public history projects on issues that continue to affect everyday life.

Incarceration can lead historians to deal with long-term issues. The Guantánamo Public Memory Project (GPMP) was launched in 2009 and aims at building public awareness of the long history of the station on the island of Cuba. The project goes further than the mere history of the site; it includes examples and interpretations from various actors, on-site workers, detainees, and staff, and shows the complexity of the different perspectives. Different universities participate in the project and help broaden the historical narratives.[18] For example, Brown University's students designed a panel questioning what a refuge is, and what makes a refugee. The project also fostered interaction by proposing users to vote on questions such as "Is the U.S. an Empire?"[19] The project shows how incarceration can help historians and students to question much broader aspects of everyday life. GPMP extended to other sites of detention. The University of Minnesota created a digital project to accompany the GPMP. Named GTMO in MSP (Minneapolis-Saint Paul), the project examines "immigrant detention in Minnesota along with increased surveillance of the Somali American community in Minneapolis since 9/11" (University of Minnesota 2014). It demonstrates how the tactics used to detain suspected terrorists have had actual consequences in Minneapolis and St. Paul (Taparata 2014). Incarceration and criminality are but two examples of everyday suffering, that public historians could deal with in order to explain the complexity of the past and present.

Poverty and Exclusion

Another sort of everyday suffering that historians have recently dealt with is poverty and homelessness. Among the voiceless actors of the past, poor and homeless people are certainly the most difficult for historians to research. Those topics are extremely difficult to deal with because of the lack of sources and materials. Nevertheless, public historians have proved to be inventive and to use new techniques to give space to poverty and homelessness.

The Museum of the City of New York mounted an exhibition in the 1990s on the history of homelessness (Wallace 1996, 45). More recently, Daniel Kerr – public historian at the American University – published *Derelict Paradise: Homelessness and Urban Development in Cleveland, Ohio*. Oral history is very effective at dealing with poverty and homelessness and producing a bottom-up analysis (2003). The Cleveland Homeless Oral History Project demonstrates how public historians can give a voice to the homeless population as well as to provide social change (Kerr 2012). Kerr explains how oral history and social justice are linked. Likewise, since 2008, the Oral History of Homelessness Project has collected hundreds of stories from people across the state of Minnesota.[20]

In addition to giving a voice to homeless people, oral history can be used by historians to help isolated communities to recover social links. The Shenandoah Valley Oral History Project works both at preserving and strengthening social links for marginalized communities. For the project, Kerr's students interviewed "poultry farmers and processing workers, labor and civil rights activists, Native Americans, Latino immigrants, ex-offenders, homeless people, gays, lesbians and bisexuals throughout the Shenandoah Valley" (James Madison University undated).

Another example is about history projects that deal with how people affected by diseases have been excluded from societies. The Brooklyn Historical Society has collected oral histories and materials about the AIDS epidemic. They have collected "photographs, medical records, t-shirts, phone bills, herbalist bottles, workshop pamphlets, and the sickroom contents of a man felled by the disease" (Wallace 1996, 46). Since 1986, Victoria Harden – member of the History Office of the U.S. National Institutes of Health – has worked on an AIDS History Project based on oral history "to ensure that the American people were given an accounting of what the NIH had done to deal with this disease" (Harden 2000). Similar to their work with ethnic minorities, historians can contribute to conveying the history of voiceless people who suffered from everyday violence, and empower people to fight isolation.

History for Peace: Human Rights, Apologies, and Reconciliation

Human Rights and Coming to Terms with the Past

The links between human rights and history have strengthened in the last two decades. History and historians have been asked to help people come to terms with the past. First used to enable Germans to deal with their Nazi past, the expression is also about making peace with the past. In order to do so, actors first have to acknowledge their violent past. One example was the creation of the International Coalition of Historic Site Museums of Conscience in 1999. Sites of conscience are historic places that foster public dialogue on pressing contemporary issues in historical perspective. The founding members "believed that remembering sites of both abuse and resistance [was] critical in the transition to democracy" (Ševčenko 2008, 9–10). Representing and discussing the history of human rights – and their violation – has a direct connection with democratic engagement. The argument is that coming to terms with the violent past can help populations overcome past tensions and move towards better democratic systems.

Among the various partners and projects of the International Coalition, *Memoria Abierta* sheds light on the human rights abuses during the dictatorship in Argentina. *Memoria Abierta* encourages public discussion "about what should be done with the clandestine detention centers where torture was perpetrated." In Czech Republic, the Terezin Memorial is about Nazi atrocities; it "involves children into dialogues about contemporary examples of racism such as the attacks on the Roma people and the rise in neo-Nazi nationalist youth groups" (Ševčenko 2008, 12–13). In Romania, the Institute for the Investigation of Communist Crimes and the Memory of the Romanian Exile (IICCMER) aims at collecting online archives, at organizing exhibits, and providing student programs to support public awareness on the history of communism in Romania. Historians can also work in commissions, like Latvia's History Commission that studies the Crimes against Humanity

Figure 12.2 Villa Grimaldi, international day for the victims of enforced disappearances, Santiago (Chile), 2015. Courtesy of Villa Grimaldi. www.villagrimaldi.cl/.

Committed in the Territory of Latvia from 1940 to 1956 during the Occupations of the Soviet Union and National Socialist Germany.

Figure 12.2 was taken at Villa Grimaldi in Santiago (Chile) in 2015 during the international day for the victims of enforced disappearances. Villa Grimaldi is part of the International Sites of Conscience network. In operation from 1974 to 1978, Villa Grimaldi was used during Augusto Pinochet's regime by the Dirección de Inteligencia Nacional (DINA), the Chilean secret police, as a site of interrogation and torture for political prisoners. Among the 4,500 detainees brought to Villa Grimaldi, more than 200 disappeared, likely assassinated by DINA. During Operation Colombo at least 119 political dissidents disappeared. Figure 12.2 shows the faces of those disappeared in Villa Grimaldi as well as the list of names in the wall panel.[21] The Corporación Parque por la Paz Villa Grimaldi (Corporation Peace Park at Villa Grimaldi) was created in 1996 in order to recover the history of the disappeared and atrocities committed in the villa. In addition to the historical research necessary to recover the roots of Villa Grimaldi, historians participate in the creation of a larger historical perspective. Recent panels deal with the history of DINA all over Chile. Historians also participate in present-day civic engagement through education programs that address discrimination, torture, political violence, and human rights.

The International Coalition wants to use the past to reach a better future. Their website asserts that:

> By analysing the underlying factors that resulted in the Holocaust we might find ways to prevent genocide today; by walking in the shoes of past generations of immigrants, we might better understand immigration struggles today; and in unravelling the mechanisms of past dictatorships, we can fight repression today.
>
> (International Coalition of Sites of Conscience undated)

Through training, funding, and international networks, the International Coalition is representative of how history has become a tool to build democracy.

Apologies

Debates about apologies have emerged in countries such as the United States (for the enslavement of African Americans), in France (for the participation in the deportation of Jews during World War II), or in Australia (for the uprooting of natives by settlers) (Bookspan 2001; Maier 2003). Apologies are often political acts, coming from governments or parliaments.[22] Governments can, like in Australia, set aside a day to remember an injustice. In 1998, the Australian government created a "Sorry Day" to acknowledge that the government "had forcibly removed Aboriginal children from their families on the assumption that their culture was doomed" (Weyeneth 2001, 14). Those political acts are partly designed to appease present-day political tensions. For instance, in 1996 Tony Blair accepted English responsibility in the 1850s Irish Famine. He did so, in the heart of the Northern Irish Peace Process, as a way to close the past and to make the current political situation in Northern Ireland more suitable for peace.

Apologies may also have financial components through the payment of reparations. While the prospect of German reparations has recently been raised by the Greek government, the German government already announced in 1999 the establishment of a "Remembrance, Responsibility, and the Future Fund" to compensate the victims of exploited labor by private companies during the Nazi era. In the United States, Congress passed a law in 1988 about Japanese Americans interned in camps during World War II. The law "apologized for the incarceration and paid $20,000 to each survivor of the camps" (Weyeneth 2001, 18–19). The New York Attorney Deadria Farmer-Paellmann founded the Restitution Study Group that examines "innovative approaches to securing justice for injuries inflicted upon oppressed people." Considering that slavery and segregation have left indelible marks in all areas of the lives of people of African descent, the group favors "a humanitarian trust funded by parties that participated in and benefited from slavery [that] would address the capital needs of African Americans" (Restitution Study Group undated).

Apologies raise many questions for historians. First, are apologies valid historical processes or are they more political and activist issues from which historians should exclude themselves? Questions also deal with the format. Regarding the uses of the past, remembering past injustices may also revive present-day tensions. There have been so many crimes and acts of injustice in the past that apologizing can become an endless process. Another interrogation is about responsibility. When asked whether the United States should apologize to Japan for dropping atomic bombs on Hiroshima and Nagasaki in 1945, President George Bush answered, "War is war. There is nothing to apologize for" (Weyeneth 2001, 27). More broadly, can and should present-day actors apologize for events they did not directly participate in? For instance, who could, today, apologize for slavery in the United States?

Work from historians and historical committees can lead to apologies. Historian Jan Gross published *Neighbors: The Destruction of the Jewish Community in Jedwabne, Poland* in 2001. The book focused on the massacre that took place at Jedwabne in July 1941. The massacre against Polish Jews was not undertaken by the Nazis, but by non-Jewish neighbors. This work led the president of Poland, Aleksander Kwasniewski, to publicly ask pardon in the name of Polish people. Historians can play a role in establishing a deconflicted space of discussion with critical analysis of the past.

Reconciliation

In an article about historians and reconciliation, Elzar Barkan explains:

> because group identity is shaped by historical perspectives, historical narratives have an explicit and direct impact on national identities. Thus, by playing an adjudicatory role in the creation of such narratives and ensuring adherence to ethical norms, historians can contribute to reconciliation among nations.
>
> (Barkan 2009, 900)

Institutions like the United States Institute for Peace (USIP), the International Center for Transitional Justice, the Institute for Historical Justice and Reconciliation, or Facing History and Ourselves support public history projects. For instance, created in 1984 by the U.S. Congress, USIP undertook a history initiative that aimed to explore how divided societies recovering from violent conflict have been teaching the conflict's history to participate in a larger process of social reconstruction and reconciliation (Cole and Barsalou 2006).

However, judges and lawyers, not historians, dominate most of those institutions. As a consequence, Greg Grandin argues that "In most truth commissions, history was not presented as a network of causal social and cultural relations but rather as a dark backdrop on which to contrast the light of tolerance and self-restraint" (2005, 48). Partly due to this lack of historical thinking, the process of reconciliation has had the tendency to use the past as a mere background in which injustice took place. For instance, some Chilean historians have criticized the Report of the Chilean National Commission on Truth and Reconciliation for "its insistence on the need to establish moral equivalency between the Left and the Right" (Grandin 2005, 48). Historians should be aware that the primary purpose of truth and reconciliation commissions is not historical research but rather to provide the basis for a new shared identity.

Nevertheless, historians from different origins have participated in reconciliation. For example, they can help create archives of truth commissions and other processes (Peterson 2005). Historians can also help contextualize representations of conflict (Blom 2007). Led by historians Charles Ingrao and Thomas Emmert, historians from different countries and different cultures met and worked in teams to confront the Yugoslav controversies about the past. Subjects such as the dissolution of former Yugoslavia, but also ethnic cleansing, were discussed (Ingrao and Emmert 2012). The diversity of historians provides a rich account to be used for reconciliation. Likewise, in order to deal with the issues of expropriation during World War II, Austria created a commission with historians from different countries and invited Jewish representatives (Barkan 2009, 900). The Alliance for Historical Dialogue and Accountability also seeks to give individuals the tools to deconstruct historical narratives for themselves, to challenge past myths. Historians could become examples for collaborative works that can lead to reconciliation.

Historians involved in post-conflict and reconciliation processes must be particularly careful with the consequences and uses of historical production. Barkan asks several questions about how historians should address contested versions of the past.

> Does constructing a "shared" narrative mean giving equal time to all sides? How do the goals of delegitimizing the nationalist historical myths that feed ethnic hatred and conflict converge with the aim to construct, through history, a new national identity?
>
> (2009, 903)

One aspect is to delegitimize nationalistic and xenophobic uses of the past for present-day political uses. Historians could also work at providing space for competing popular interpretations of the past. In Northern Ireland, Healing Through Remembering (HTR) has provided public spaces to discuss the different interpretations of the Northern Irish conflict. In *Everyday Items Transformed by Conflict*, HTR enabled people to provide and comment on everyday objects that they thought symbolized the conflict. The multiple voices and interpretations present the complexity of the conflict and the multiple perspectives. Those historical approaches are particularly interesting to design history textbooks in divisive societies (Cole and Barsalou 2006).

Notes

1 See Chapter 13.
2 The author thanks Rebecca Conard for her comments on the shift from civic engagement to social justice.
3 See Chapter 3.
4 Social Justice Alliance for Museums, http://sjam.org/about-us/. See the case studies at http://sjam.org/case-studies/ (accessed November 15, 2015).
5 Active History website, homepage, http://activehistory.ca/ (accessed August 27, 2015).
6 See Chapter 11.
7 The law was introduced by Senator Daniel Inouye of Hawai'i and Representative Ben Nighthorse Campbell (Northern Cheyenne) of Colorado.
8 The Truth and Reconciliation Commission of Canada's website, www.trc.ca/websites/reconciliation/index.php?p=312 (accessed November 13, 2014).
9 Missing Children Project, TRCC's website, www.myrobust.com/websites/trcinstitution/index.php?p=823 (accessed August 31, 2015).
10 Likewise, the NMAI has a Repatriation Office to work on Native American objects, http://nmai.si.edu/explore/collections/repatriation/ (accessed November 12, 2014).
11 About identification, in 2009, 38,671 individual human remains, 998,731 funeral objects, 144,163 unassociated funerary objects, 4,303 sacred objects, 948 objects of cultural patrimony, and 822 objects that are both sacred and patrimonial had been registered and published by the NAGPRA program, www.nps.gov/nagpra/FAQ/INDEX.HTM#What_is_NAGPRA? (accessed August 31, 2015).
12 Opened in 1962, the House of Slaves intends to memorialize – through its Door of No Return – the final exit point of the slaves from Africa. See the virtual tour, http://webworld.unesco.org/goree/en/index.shtml (accessed September 5, 2015).
13 See Chapter 2, pp. 66–67.
14 The author would like to thank Rebecca Conard for the suggestion.
15 The Liverpool museums website, www.liverpoolmuseums.org.uk/ism/about/index.aspx (accessed September 5, 2015).
16 There is actually already a National Women's Hall of Fame in Seneca Falls (NY), www.womenofthehall.org/ (accessed August 30, 2015).
17 To know more about the arguments in favor of the NWHM, see www.nwhm.org/about-nwhm/#; to know more about their exhibits, see www.nwhm.org/online-exhibits/ (accessed November 21, 2014).
18 For a list of university partners, see http://gitmomemory.org/televisual-monitor/?panel=5&refresh=5 (accessed November 13, 2014).
19 For the list of questions, see http://gitmomemory.org/televisual-monitor/?panel=10&refresh=5 (accessed November 27, 2014).
20 The Oral History of Homelessness's website, http://ststephensmpls.org/oralhistory/project.html (accessed August 31, 2015).
21 "El olvido está lleno de memoria" can be translated as "oblivion is filled with memory."
22 See, for instance, Jacques Chirac's recognition, in 1995, of France's responsibility for deporting thousands of Jews to Nazi death camps during the German occupation in World War

II. As well, the U.S. "Congress issued a formal apology to native Hawaiians in 1993 for the overthrow of the Kingdom of Hawaii by the United States government in 1893" (Weyeneth 2001, 13).

Bibliography

Alexander, Michelle. *The New Jim Crow: Mass Incarceration in the Age of Colorblindness*, New York: The New Press, 2010.

Amsden, David. "Building the First Slavery Museum in America." *New York Times Magazine*, February 26, 2015, www.nytimes.com/2015/03/01/magazine/building-the-first-slave-museum-in-america.html (accessed August 31, 2015).

Barkan, Elazar. "AHR Forum: Truth and Reconciliation in History. Introduction: Historians and Historical Reconciliation." *The American Historical Review*, 114/4 (2009): 899–913.

Blom, Hans. "Historical Research Where Scholarship and Politics Meet: The Case of Srebrenica." In *Contemporary History on Trial*, edited by Harriet Jones, Kjell Ostberg, and Nico Randeraad, Manchester: Manchester University Press, 2007, 104–122.

Bookspan, Shelley. "History Means Often Having to Say You're Sorry." *The Public Historian*, 23/3 (Summer 2001): 5–7.

Bozic-Vrbancic, Senka. "One Nation, Two Peoples, Many Cultures: Exhibiting Identity at Te Papa Tongarewa." *Journal of the Polynesian Society*, 112/3 (September 2003): 295–313.

Cobb, Amanda. "The National Museum of the American Indian as Cultural Sovereignty." *American Quarterly*, 57/2 (2005): 485–506.

Cole, Elizabeth A. and Barsalou, Judy. "United or Divided? The Challenges of Teaching History in Societies Emerging from Violent Conflict." A Special Report from the U.S. Institute of Peace, #163, Washington, DC (June 2006): 1–16.

Conard, Rebecca. "All Men and Women Are Created Equal: An Administrative History of Women's Rights National Historical Park." Washington DC: Organization of American Historians, April 2012, www.nps.gov/wori/learn/historyculture/upload/Women-s_Rights_NHP_Administrative_History.pdf (accessed August 31, 2015).

Conard, Rebecca. "The Pragmatic Roots of Public History Education in the United States." *The Public Historian*, 37/1 (February 2015): 105–120.

Conn, Steven. *History's Shadow: Native Americans and Historical Consciousness in the Nineteenth Century*, Chicago: University of Chicago Press, 2004.

Dubrow, Gail Lee and Goodman, Jennifer B. *Restoring Women's History through Historic Preservation*, Baltimore: Johns Hopkins University Press, 2002.

Fine-Dare, Kathleen. *Grave Injustice: The American Indian Repatriation Movement and NAGPRA*, Lincoln: University of Nebraska Press, 2002.

Foulidis, Anna, van Kessel, Hanneke, van de Reep, Arvid, and Verkleij, Roos. "Project Showcase: At Home in Holland." *Public History Commons*, June 6, 2014, http://publichistorycommons.org/project-showcase-at-home-in-holland/#sthash.4Zg8N4hS.dpuf; www.athomeinholland.uva.nl/ (accessed August 31, 2015).

Grandin, Greg. "The Instruction of Great Catastrophe: Truth Commissions, National History, and State Formation in Argentina, Chile, and Guatemala." *American Historical Review*, 110/1 (2005): 46–67.

Gutterman, Lauren. "OutHistory.org: An Experiment in LGBTQ Community History-Making." *The Public Historian*, 32/4 (2010): 96–109.

Harden, Victoria. "The Challenge of 'Too Much' History: The AIDS History Project at the National Institute of Health." *Public History News*, 20/2 (Winter 2000): 3–4, http://ncph.org/cms/wp-content/uploads/PHN-Vol-20-No-2.pdf (accessed November 2, 2014).

Hayward, Claire. "International Approaches to LGBTQ Public History." *Public History Commons*, February 17, 2015, http://publichistorycommons.org/international-approaches-to-lgbtq-public-history/ (accessed August 31, 2015).

Herbert, John and Estlund, Karen. "Creating Citizen Historians." *The Western Historical Quarterly*, 39/3 (Autumn 2008): 333–341.

Horton, James Oliver. "Presenting Slavery: The Perils of Telling America's Racial Story." *The Public Historian*, 21/4 (Autumn 1999): 19–38.

Horton, James Oliver and Horton, Lois. *Slavery and Public History: The Tough Stuff of American Memory*, New York: The New Press, 2006.

Horwitz, Tony. "One Man's Epic Quest to Visit Every Former Slave Dwelling in the United States." *Smithsonian Magazine*, October 2013, www.smithsonianmag.com/history/one-mans-epic-quest-to-visit-every-former-slave-dwelling-in-the-united-states-12080/#0CAUxutl5lphziSy.99 (accessed November 13, 2014).

Ingrao, Charles and Emmert, Thomas A., eds. *Confronting the Yugoslav Controversies: A Scholars' Initiative*, second edition, West Lafayette: Purdue University Press, 2012.

International Coalition of Sites of Conscience. "Approach." Undated, www.sitesofconscience.org/approach/ (accessed August 31, 2015).

James Madison University. "Shenandoah Valley Oral History Project." Undated, www.jmu.edu/history/shenandoah-valley-oral-history-project.shtml#sthash.BD3UK3kO.dpuf (accessed August 31, 2015).

Jordanova, Ludmilla. *History in Practice*, London and New York: Oxford University Press, 2000.

Karamanski, Theodore J., ed. *Ethics and Public History: An Anthology*, Malabar: Robert E. Krieger Publishing Company, 1990.

Kelman, Ari. *A Misplaced Massacre: Struggling over the Memory of Sand Creek*, Cambridge, MA: Harvard University Press, 2013.

Kerr, Daniel. "'We Know What the Problem Is': Using Oral History to Develop a Collaborative Analysis of Homelessness from the Bottom Up." *Oral History Review*, 30/1 (2003): 27–45.

Kerr, Daniel. "How Oral History Can Facilitate Movement Building." Columbia University podcast, January 6, 2012, www.youtube.com/watch?v=NHRkPuJfasg (accessed August 31, 2015).

Korza, Pam and Schaffer Bacon, Barbara. *History as a Catalyst for Civic Dialogue: Case Studies from Animating Democracy*, Washington, DC: Americans for the Arts, 2005.

Korza, Pam and Schaffer Bacon, Barbara. "History Organizations and Engagement." In A Working Guide to the Landscape of Arts for Change, Americans for the Arts, 2012, http://animating democracy.org/sites/default/files/HistoryOrg%20Trend%20Paper.pdf (accessed November 12, 2014).

Kurtz, Michael. *America and the Return of Nazi Contraband: The Recovery of Europe's Cultural Treasures*, Cambridge: Cambridge University Press, 2009.

Labadi, Sophia. "The National Museum of Immigration History: Neo-Colonialist Representations, Silencing, and Re-Appropriation." *Journal of Social Archaeology*, 13/3 (2013): 310–330.

Lawlor, Mary. *Public Native America: Tribal Self-Representations in Museums, Powwows, and Casinos*, New Brunswick: Rutgers University Press, 2006.

Lee, Antoinette. "Cultural Diversity in Historic Preservation." *Preservation Forum*, 6 (July/August 1992): 28–41.

Linenthal, Edward T. "The National Park Service and Civic Engagement." *National Park Service Centennial Essay Series*, George Wright Forum, 25/1 (2008): 5–11.

Lonetree, Amy. *Decolonizing Museums: Representing Native American National and Tribal Museum*, Chapel Hill: University of North Carolina Press, 2012.

Maier, Charles. "Overcoming the Past? Narrative and Negotiation, Remembering, and Reparation: Issues at the Interface of History and the Law." In *Politics and the Past: On Repairing Historical Injustices*, edited by John Torpey, Lanham: Rowman & Littlefield Publishers, 2003, 295–304.

Marchesano, Louis. "Classified Records, Nazi Collecting, and Looted Art: An Art Historian's Perspective." National Archives, 1999, www.archives.gov/research/holocaust/articles-and-papers/symposium-papers/an-art-historians-perspective.html (accessed August 31, 2015).

Mayo, Edith. "Putting Women in Their Place: Methods and Sources for Including Women's History in Museums and Historic Sites." In *Restoring Women's History through Historic Preservation*, edited by Gail Lee Dubrow and Jennifer B. Goodman, Baltimore: Johns Hopkins University Press, 2002, 111–131.

Michel, Sonya. "A Women's History Museum Without Women's Historians." *Public History Commons*, May 12, 2014.

Mihesuah, Devon Abbott. *Repatriation Reader: Who Owns Native American Indian Remains*, Lincoln: University of Nebraska Press, 2000.

Museum International. *Return of Cultural Objects: The Athens Conference*, undated, http://portal.unesco.org/culture/en/ev.php-URL_ID=39227&URL_DO=DO_TOPIC&URL_SECTION=201.html (accessed September 1, 2015).

National Council on Public History. *Code of Ethics and Professional Conduct*, 2007, http://ncph.org/cms/about/bylaws-and-ethics/ (accessed August 31, 2015).

National Council on Public History. *Call for Working Group Discussants*, 2014, http://ncph.org/cms/wp-content/uploads/Call-for-Working-Group-discussants.pdf (accessed August 31, 2015).

National Park Service. *Stronger Together: A Manual on the Principles and Practices of Civic Engagement*, Woodstock: National Park Service, 2009, www.nps.gov/civic/resources/CE_Manual.pdf (accessed November 17, 2014).

Neufeld, David. "Ethics in the Practice of Public History with Aboriginal Communities." *The Public Historian*, 28/1 (Winter 2006): 117–121.

Nickless, Karen and Huyck, Heather. "The First Step for Putting Women Back in History." *Preservation Nation Blog*, June 9, 2015, http://blog.preservationnation.org/2015/06/09/preservation-tips-and-tools-the-first-step-for-putting-women-back-in-history/#.VeTVo-dQjRL (accessed August 31, 2015).

Norris, Linda. "Do Museums Need Disaster Plans for People?" *The Uncataloged Museum*, July 17, 2014, http://uncatalogedmuseum.blogspot.com/2014/07/do-museums-need-disaster-plans-for.html (accessed August 29, 2015).

Oram, Alison. "Going on an Outing: The Historic House and Queer Public History." *Rethinking History*, 15/2 (2011): 189–207.

Paku, Rhonda. "Biculturalism at Te Papa Tongarewa." Museum of New Zealand, undated, www.magsq.com.au/_dbase_upl/RhondaPaku-09%20Summit.pdf (accessed August 29, 2015).

Peers, Laura. *Playing Ourselves: Interpreting Native Histories at Historic Reconstructions*, Lanham: AltaMira Press, 2007.

Peterson, Trudy Huskamp. *Final Acts: A Guide to Preserving the Records of Truth Commissions*, Baltimore: Johns Hopkins University Press, 2005.

Prison Memory Project. Website, undated, www.prisonpublicmemory.org/about/ (accessed November 13, 2014).

Prosalendis, Sandra, Marot, Jennifer, Soudien, Crain, Nagia, Anwah, and Rassool, Ciraj. "Recalling Community in Cape Town: Creating and Curating the District Six Museum." In *The Public History Reader*, edited by Hilda Kean and Paul Martin, London and New York: Routledge, 2013, 283–297.

Rand, Jacki Thompson. "Why I Can't Visit the National Museum of the American Indian: Reflections of an Accidental Privileged Insider, 1989–1994." *Common-Place*, 7/4 (July 2007), www.common-place.org/vol-07/no-04/rand/ (accessed August 31, 2015).

Regan, Paulette. *Unsettling the Settler Within: Indian Residential Schools, Truth Telling, and Reconciliation in Canada*, Vancouver: University of British Columbia Press, 2011.

Restitution Study Group. Website, homepage, undated, www.rsgincorp.com/ (accessed November 13, 2014).

Rizzo, Mary. "Finding the Roots of Civic Engagement in the Public Humanities." *Public History Commons*, July 21, 2014.

Rizzo, Mary and Swan, Martha. "Public History and Mass Incarceration: Interview with Martha Swan." *The Public Historian*, 36/1 (February 2014): 61–70.

Ševčenko, Liz and Russell-Ciardi, Maggie. "Sites of Conscience: Opening Historic Sites for Civic Dialogue." *The Public Historian*, 30 (Winter 2008): 9–15.

Spence, Marc David. *Dispossessing the Wilderness: Indian Removal and the Making of the National Parks*, Oxford: Oxford University Press, 2000.

STAM. *Sticking Around*, undated, www.blijvenplakkeningent.be/en (accessed August 31, 2015).

Stanton, Cathy. "Where is the Next Generation of Gender Studies in Public History?" *Public History Commons*, August 9, 2013, http://publichistorycommons.org/next-generation-of-gender-studies/#more-3561 (accessed November 18, 2014).

Stanton, Cathy. "Hardball History: On the Edge of Politics, Advocacy, and Activism." *Public History Commons*, March 25, 2015, http://publichistorycommons.org/hardball-history-stanton/#sthash.T18EK3jY.dpuf (accessed August 31, 2015).

Taparata, Evans. "GITMO in MSP." *Public History Commons*, July 4, 2014, http://publichistorycommons.org/gtmo-in-msp/#more-5309 (accessed August 31, 2015).

Thompson, Heather Ann. "Why Mass Incarceration Matters: Rethinking Crisis, Decline, and Transformation in Postwar American History." *The Journal of American History* (December 2010): 703–734.

Tyrrell, Ian. *Historians in Public: The Practice of American History, 1890–1970*, Chicago: University of Chicago Press, 2005.

United States Holocaust Memorial Museum. *Looted Art*, Washington, DC, undated, www.ushmm.org/research/research-in-collections/search-the-collections/bibliography/looted-art (accessed August 31, 2015).

University of Minnesota. "GITMO in MSP." 2014, http://gpmp.cla.umn.edu/web/gtmoinmsp.html (accessed August 31, 2015).

Wallace, Michael. *Mickey Mouse History: And Other Essays On American Memory*, Philadelphia: Temple University Press, 1996.

Weyeneth, Robert W. "The Power of Apology and the Process of Historical Reconciliation." *The Public Historian*, 23/3 (Summer 2001): 9–38.

13 Historians as Consultants and Advisors
Clients, Courtroom, and Public Policy

The professionalization of historical practices in the late 19th and early 20th centuries encouraged historians to look for scientific objectivity in their work. However, the search for objectivity did not stop pragmatic approaches. This materialized in what Benjamin Schambaugh – historian and first Superintendent of the State Historical Society of Iowa – called "applied history." In 1909, he stated:

> I do not know that the phrase "Applied History" is one that has thus far been employed by students of history and politics ... But I believe that the time has come when it can be used with both propriety and profit.
>
> (Conard 2002, 33)

Through the "pragmatic roots of public history," some historians reconsidered the strict opposition between objectivity and usability (Conard 2015). This trend was not at all limited to the United States. As Ann Rigney underlines in her work on *Historians and Social Values*, the pragmatic turn in theoretical reflection has "prepared the way for a reconsideration of the historian's social role." Many British historians, according to her, "rejected what they saw as a relativist free-for-fall claim in support of the unmitigated objectivity of the historian and the scientificity of history" (Rigney 2000, 8). In spite of a pragmatic turn, the usability of history remains a subject of controversy. The relations between historians and employers – and the pressure that historians can feel from clients – are perhaps the most visible subjects of tension. Among the different uses of history, this chapter focuses on three categories of historians: those who work under temporary contracts as consultants, those who are part of the staff and work as in-house advisors, and historians as policymakers.

Many different individuals, companies, or institutions may use historians. The term consultant therefore refers to a wide category of historians. Most consulting positions fall "into one of two categories, either a staff position within a firm or agency, or the role of independent contractor/consultant" (AHA undated). However, if the goals are essentially in-house, corporations and agencies can employ a permanent historian as advisor. For short-term projects, clients may hire independent historians, historians working for a consulting company, or historians who have an academic position (Ryant 1986, 36).[1]

The role of consultants and in-house advisors is as wide as the field of public history.[2] They can trace family history for a client, prepare a National Register nomination for a community, survey a site's historic resources for a construction company, process an archival collection for a corporation, or research an exhibit for a museum or court case (AHA undated). The American Historical Association's (AHA) review of historians as consultants and contractors gives a good overview of the different activities such as preservation (cultural resources management, nomination for historic preservation, Section 106), museums (conservation, exhibition, interpretation), archives (assessment, reorganization), media (film advisers), anniversaries, environmental issues (toxic wastes), and litigation (land issues).

These uses of history in public and private institutions have resulted in new debates among historians. Questions emerged in the 1980s to know "whether the professional ethics that govern academic scholars adequately guide adjudication of ethical situations in the public arena." In 1986, Ronald Tobey argued in *The Public Historian* that academic ethics were inadequate for public historians (1986, 21). While codes of ethics had already been established for oral history (1968) and for museums (1978), historical consultants approached the National Council on Public History (NCPH) in 1982 to design a new Code of Ethics.

For consultants and advisors, the main challenge has been the relations with their employers. In other words, to what extent do clients and employers control the production of historical narratives, and how historians can perform valid historical research when questions come from someone else? Questions such as "Who controls the product of a contract history? What are the duties of historians to their clients or agencies?" are often part of the discussions on consulting historians. Pressure from clients and employers may result in different misuses such as false analogies and distortion for political purposes or economic gain (Tobey 1986). Ethical issues also matter because historians working for corporations or as civil servants in federal agencies may have conflicting duties. In addition to their responsibility towards their employers (clients or federal agencies), professional historians have an additional responsibility to the public (Karamanski 1999, 130).

The relations with employers question the term public historian itself. Since most of the consultants work for clients, the public components of those historical activities are also debatable. In many aspects, the practices detailed below refer more to applied than public history. In order to work as consultants or advisors, historians need to know the specific jargon of entrepreneurship, legal process, and federal agencies. Specific skills – such as budget planning, accounting – and a basic knowledge of the legal process may be very useful.

Public Historians under Contract

Entrepreneurship and Corporate Historians

Entrepreneurial history is based on activities "which are organized for the express purpose of generating history as a marketable product" (Overbeck 1986, 440). Entrepreneurship is not only a practice but also a way of thinking (Bookspan 2006). Thinking in entrepreneurial terms implies, according to Philip Cantelon (founder of History Associates), "making the unusual connection, creating a great idea, and selling it to others," in other words, creating "a useable product" (2006, 387). In general, historians (and more broadly humanists) remain aside from entrepreneurialism (Clark 2012). Shelly Bookspan regrets that "After twenty-five or more years of public history education, practice, and scholarship, entrepreneurship generally remains unexplored territory in our literature" (2006, 67). Many historians have seen the production of usable history for clients as betraying the principles of the profession. For instance, in 1986 in *Presenting the Past: Essays on History and the Public*, Terence O'Donnell considered the activity of working for clients as "a heinous compromise" (O'Donnell 1986, 240–241).

However, historians' involvement in private corporations is not new. It developed with the corporations' wish to preserve their records and make them available for research

(Mooney 1986). Krupp Company (Germany) developed internal archives in 1905 with the help of historians (Mooney 1986, 427). In the United States, World War II is "a convenient demarcation point for the advancement of professional history in the private sector" (Conard 2002, 161). Historian William D. Overman became a permanent employee of Firestone Tire and Rubber Company in 1943 to "establish the first professionally staffed corporate archive in the United States" (Conard 2002, 161).[3]

The first companies of consulting historians in the United States emerged in the 1970s.[4] Historical Research Associates and The History Group, Inc. were created in 1974 and 1975 respectively. The first Directory of Historical Consultants, published in 1981, listed approximately 30 individuals or firms (Conard 2002, 169). The rise of the public history movement in the 1970s also included the business/corporate history field.[5] However, from the beginning "history-for-profit raised eyebrows in the historical profession" since, as Rebecca Conard underlines, it "challenged an implicit assumption, shared by many, that public history was somehow integrally linked to public service, public affairs, or public benefit" (2002, 169). The discussions underline that public history is not devoid of internal tensions and is constantly in redefinition.

Working Under Contract

Clients and Contracts

Consultants usually work under contract. Working for clients implies certain duties and certain skills. To work under contract, as independent historians or through a consulting company, historians need to find a specialty, or niche, to create a professional identity (Young 2012). Jannelle Warren-Findley suggests starting by making an inventory of one's personal assets, fields of expertise, and work experience (2006, 77–78). This inventory helps establish the sort of consultant historians want to be. Historians can then find a name for their consulting company and eventually register on the NCPH's consultants' lists.

Both as independent historian and as part of a consulting company, consultants should know how to run a business. As Darlene Roth – founder of The History Group, Inc. – explains, "You have to learn how to run a business, how to deal with 'LIFT': laws, insurance, finances, and taxes" (NCPH 2010). Consultants may need to be able to design business plans (start-up costs and how to cover them, target clients, services one can provide) (Warren-Findley 2006, 85). Consultants must be aware of the tax system and other legal responsibilities, and can contact an accountant and a lawyer.

As the AHA points out, "most consultants need to be familiar with the bidding process and the ability to accurately outline and propose a potential project" (AHA undated). Consultants must know how a contract is designed and where they can find clients (Cantelon 2006, 393–394). The relations with (possible) clients are critical. Historians should know about the clients and how they intend to use the historical research. As the NCPH's Code of Ethics states, "Public historians should be fully cognizant of the purpose or purposes for which their research is intended, recognizing that research-based decisions and actions may have long-term consequences" (NCPH 2007). Public historians must therefore assess the motives of prospective clients. As Alan Newel – founder of Historical Research Associates – points out, "The historian may differ politically or philosophically with a client on a specific issue and must decide whether this disagreement prevents him or her from accepting the work." For example, he explains how, in a specific case, Historical

Research Associates staff had long discussions to decide whether or not they would work for a company that was struggling with environmental issues (Newell 2006, 107). It should be clear that – although it is easier for consultants who have regular funding such as academics – consultants can refuse certain projects. Consulting historians should not take work they cannot complete, and should not be afraid "to recommend someone who has the skills for a job" (Anderson 2013). The NCPH's Code of Ethics stresses that "a public historian should not perform work if there is an actual, apparent, or reasonably foreseeable conflict of inter-est, or an appearance of impropriety, without full written disclosure to the affected client/s or employer/s" (NCPH 2007).

Historians and employers establish a contract from the beginning, before undertaking any historical research. Every step of the project must be studied, discussed, and agreed. A contract is both a limitation and a protection for historians. The purpose of the contract is to foresee and plan how to fix possible conflicting and challenging situations during the consulting job (PHAN 2008). For instance, the Australian Council of Professional Historians (ACPH) suggests to "include from the outset in any agreement a provision for dispute arbitration by an appropriate independent person or body with historical exper-tise" (PHAN 2008). The contracting relations imply certain practices and methodological consequences for historians.

Restriction

Consulting historians may have specific agendas. Indeed, the time structure and the unpre-dictability of assignments for consultants diverge from the traditional academic calendar (Warren-Findley 2006, 82–83). The clients can utterly design the calendar and deadlines. Clients usually need fast answers for problem-solving issues. Consultants may have to work under pressure with short-term deadlines. The ACPH stresses that "members should care-fully plan and adhere to a firm and achievable date for the completion of a project" (ACPH 2006).

Clients may not only design the agenda, but also the research questions. Adopted in 2007, the NCPH's Code of Ethics and Professional Conduct asserts that "a public historian should respect the decisions of a client or employer concerning the objectives and nature of the professional services to be performed unless such performance involves conduct which is illegal, immoral, or unethical" (NCPH 2007). Clients need historians for specific issues and can decide on the final product. While they work for clients, consultants remain professional historians, and this implies ethical restrictions. The NCPH's Code of Ethics underlines that "a public historian should maintain exclusive supervision over historical research studies and investigations" (NCPH 2007). The links between the duties towards clients and the validity of historical research are therefore the crux of the ethical tensions.

Historians can discuss with clients the shape of the product (Newell 2006, 109). As Jannelle Warren-Findley explains in her essay on consultants, there is usually no room in the final production for "the kind of 'on the one hand, on the other hand' argument that historians use to indicate the complexity of historical information" (2006, 84). In spite of this specificity, clients – individuals, corporations, or federal agencies – ask for valid historical research. As Roy Lopata argues about ethics and public history "a client ... is obviously interested in a real past, not fiction" (1990, 27). Indeed, invalid historical research would be easily criticized and would undermine the clients' public image. This is why Ryant argues that it is the role of the public historian to educate the business com-munity to the professional and ethical standards (1986, 37). Many clients may focus on the immediate and obvious present uses of the historical research, but historians can also point out "the value to the public" and explain to the clients how historical research can have broader and long-term impacts.

A major restriction for consulting historians can be about the final production. In *Ethics and Public History*, Donald Page addresses the right of the agency or employer to change the manuscript before publication and wonders whether an employer could "disallow the use of certain sources, expunge parts of the text, deny authorship, or refuse to publish it with or without changes?" (Page 1990, 65). This is particularly true for biographical or family history but can apply to any type of contract. For instance, Ruth Ann Overbeck explains that "the historian has an obligation to respect the client's wishes that the sensitive material remain secret, if that is the decision" (1986, 444). The NCPH's Code of Ethics agrees, and acknowledges "a public historian is obligated not to disclose information gained in a profes-sional relationship when the client or employer has requested such information to be held confidential" (NCPH 2007). The only exceptions come from legal restriction, for instance, "when disclosure would prevent a violation of law or prevent a substantial injustice to the public interest" (NCPH 2007).[6]

Clients may want to prohibit some aspects of the historical research because they do not fit the corporate, agency, or family images. In that case, Page explains "historians must decide if this is sufficient reason to warrant it not being published with their blessings" (1990, 68). It is important for consulting historians to make sure they have the right not to be associated with the final use of the product if they think it goes against the historical ethics. This is why historians can include the possibility to "withhold their names from publication" in their contract (Page 1990, 69). Another solution may be found in "the wording of the preface to explain the limitations, *i.e*, the degree to which the text has been censored" (Page 1990, 68).

Contracts for Historians' Benefit

Contracts are not at the unique detriment of historians. They may also protect consult-ants from un-ethical activities. The contract should protect the historian's credibility and reputation. Importantly, the contract should detail the access to materials, collections, and archives. From the beginning, it must be clear to the historian whether – and to what extent – (s)he would be able to present the findings with historical integrity. Disclosure must be discussed in the contract. The ACPH advises consultants to:

> do your best to inform the client(s) of probable consequences of the project ... signal any major problems or challenges in a project ... include from the outset in any agree-ment a provision for dispute arbitration by an appropriate independent person or body with historical expertise.
>
> (PHAN 2008)

Any access restriction should be notified in the contract in order for historians to judge the extent to which they would be allowed to perform valid historical research. The list of restrictions can also protect historians from further criticism. The publication of the restric-tion in the final product may explain why the final production ignores certain aspects of the past. It must be clear to the public – including peers – what the restrictions and roles of the historians were in the project.

Fees and Expenses

Historians under contract need to discuss fees and expenses. Consulting historians must know how much they would charge for their different activities. For instance, in a post about historians as consultants, Walter Woodward regrets the habit of not financially compensating historical advisors for film and documentaries (NCPH 2009). However, in order to avoid conflict of interests, the ACPH stresses that "Members should not accept compensation, financial or otherwise, from more than one party for services on the same project, unless the circumstances are fully disclosed and agreed to by all interested parties" (ACPH 2006).[7] Evaluating the right value for a consulting job is a hard task and historians, at least at the beginning, tend to undervalue their work. Public history students could, at one point in their training, design contracts with cost and salary.

Fee and charge are often secret issues. Consulting historians are reluctant to give accurate figures regarding how much they charge (Adamson 2012). In a very interesting post, Christopher Clark goes against the tide and details his own experience. He stresses "most independent consultants provide services on an hourly basis" (2012). The rate depends on several factors such as competitors and consulting experience. Consulting historians should be careful not to undervalue their expenses such as research, materials, office, utilities, travel, mailing, but also less obvious costs like health insurance and tax. There is here a huge difference between full-time consulting historians and others who perform this activity in addition to a salaried position (usually in academy) and who may charge lower hourly rates. Clark argues that "a ballpark figure for an experienced public history consultant would be $100 per hour" and that this number could vary according to the market and experience, down or up by 50 percent. As he argues, consulting is not charity (2012). In addition to Clark, the ACPH provides a more official scale of fees for professional historians with different levels according to experience and expertise in Australia (Professional Historians Australia 2014).

Historians in the Legal Process

A Variety of Issues

Some consulting historians work in a special environment: the legal process. However, few court cases encompass a historical perspective and few historians become involved in litigation. Although there have been old examples of historians involved in trials – the late 19th century Dreyfus Affair in France, for example – historians' involvement in the legal process arose only after World War II (Delafontaine 2015, 35–43; Petrovic 2009, 56–66). Historians offer their expertise to prosecution and defense in civil, criminal, and administrative proceedings (Kousser 1984).

In the United States as well as in Canada, Australia, and New Zealand, one of the main fields has been about historians involved when some indigenous tribes have sought compensation for past land takings (Newell 2004, 87). For instance, Arthur Ray undertook academic historical research on the Indians and the Canadian fur trade. Because of his research, Ray became an expert witness in the Canadian legal system, and has had a role in "intensifying struggles of Aboriginal people to use history to define and defend their Aboriginal and treaty rights in Canadian courts" (Ray 2011). In the United States, Delafontaine shows that 50 historians have witnessed in 314 tobacco litigation court cases from 1986 to 2014 (Delafontaine 2015). In Europe, examples of historians as expert witnesses are recent. In his analysis of expert historians in France and their changing roles in court, Olivier Dumoulin shows how the presence of expert historians during World War II criminals' – Maurice Papon and Klaus Barbi – trials was revolutionary (Dumoulin 2003; Golsan 2000). The role of expert historians in Europe developed since 1989 through trials and inquiries for historic crimes (Jones et al. 2007). In Northern Ireland, the Saville Tribunal offers another example of historians working in trials. The Tribunal was set up by the British government in 1998 to determine what happened on Bloody Sunday in Londonderry on January 30, 1972. The main role of the two historians was "to scrutinize public documents released in breach of the 30-year rule" (Tosh 2008, 108).

It is important for historians involved in the legal process to know about the field, to understand legal procedures, and to know what attorneys and judges expect from them. Ramses Delafontaine's recent book, *Historians as Expert Judicial Witnesses*, offers a broad view on the different historians' activities (2015). In particular, his third chapter discusses a step-by-step guide to the practice of expert witnessing (Delafontaine 2015, 67–105).

The Role of Historians as Expert Witnesses

There are three main sorts of activities for historians in the legal process. They can be permanent staff members of tribunals (Saville Tribunal in Northern Ireland or the Waitangi Tribunal in New Zealand), they can be hired as consultants by one side to undertake historical research and collect materials, or become expert witnesses. As consultant, the practice is close to traditional research activities, so historians need strong methodological skills. The research usually remains privately used by the clients. The role of expert witnesses is different.

The role of historians as expert witness deserves more detailed discussion due to the specificity of the tasks. The profile of these historians has been the subject of numerous studies (Wijffels 2001; Petrovic 2009). It is yet necessary to draw the profile of an expert witness. An expert witness testifies in court because he/she is an accredited expert on the issue at hand. Unlike consultants, expert witnesses are allowed to give their opinion in court based on their historical knowledge (Delafontaine 2015, 31). In the United States, as the 1975 Federal Rules of Evidence stress, a witness may be qualified as an expert by knowledge, skill, experience, training or education, and may testify in the form of opinion or otherwise.[8] The expert witness can, unlike other experts, "offer opinions, based on his expertise, on the ultimate questions before the court" (Newell 2004, 85). Unlike consultants whose work may only be used by clients, expert witnesses' work and opinion are open to consultation by adversaries (Martin 2002, 4). The role of the historian is "to present analyses of historical facts to help a judge or jury understand the technically complex historical context in which events took place, events that require scientific expertise to analyze theoretically" (Quivik 2004, 83). If consultants mostly need research skills, expert witnesses also need communication skills to testify (Martin 2002, 4).

Historians have testified in court as expert witnesses on various topics such as "school segregation, voting rights, employment discrimination, abortion policy, and even tobacco company liability" (Graham 1993, 17). Among those topics, litigation concerning the environment has increased since the 1980s and become a major field of expert witnessing in the United States. The 1980 Comprehensive Environmental Response, Compensation and Liability Act (CERCLA), the Superfunds Amendments and Reauthorization (SARA) in 1986, and the Natural Resource Damage litigation (Oil Pollution Act) in 1990 reinforced the need for expert witnesses in environmental cases (Newell 2004, 88). Cases deal

mostly with payment for pollution and environmental damages. Historians serve to identify historic uses of contaminated sites "in support or defense of a 'potentially responsible
party' (PRP)" (Newell 2004, 89). For example, Craig Colten explains that his role was
"to offer a historical perspective on industrial waste-management practices and capabili-
ties, the state of knowledge about the potential for groundwater contamination, and the
legal framework for addressing waste-disposal practices from the 1940s through the 1960s"
(Colten 2006, 111). The role of expert witnesses affects, therefore, historians' role and
practices.

Why Historians? What Sort of History?

Pressure and Ethical Works

Expert witnesses are presented – and paid – by the prosecution or/and the defense. So it is
important to understand the relations between historians and their clients and how history
is presented in court. The first step is for historians to discuss with attorneys about the legal
process, the need for historical account, and how the latter could be presented in court.
The main asset for historians is their capacity to offer broad presentations – situated within
the discourse shaped by other professionals – of specific cases (Colten 2006, 113). However
it is extremely important that even if clients asked historians to provide broad analysis,
the latter only give testimony in their area of expertise. If not, it could both undermine
their professional credibility, and offers court opponents counter-arguments based on the
lack of expertise (Jellison 1987, 16). In "Historians as Expert Witnesses: The View from
the Bench," John Neuenschwander presents views from judges who explain that the main
limits to historians' credibility in court are linked to improper areas of expertise and a lack
of access to primary materials (2002).

As for any consultants, historians in the legal process have particular relations with their
clients. However, the role and activities of historians as consultants and expert witnesses
vary. As consultants, historians are often asked by attorneys to provide an exhaustive
research and to present every useful source, even though those sources may go against their
cases. The reason is that attorneys do not want to be surprised in court by historical sources
provided by the opposite side (Martin 2002, 4). As expert witness, historians may feel more
pressure since they can testify in courts. As Colten argues:

> although the lawyers need, and call for, an impartial expert, their job is advocacy, and it
> is all too common in the midst of high-stakes litigation for them to desire their expert's
> testimony to be in perfect alignment with their position.
>
> (Colten 2006, 113)

Historians may, therefore, feel pressure to provide usable historical accounts that result in
distortion and other misuses. Although historians as expert witnesses have an obligation to
serve their clients, this should not lead to unethical production (Newell 2004, 86).

Evidence

The legal framework affects the historical production. Lawyers expect expert witnesses to
offer sound and reasonable opinions that are supported by evidence (Colten 2006, 111).

Indeed, lawyers and historians share a "same interest in evidence" (Martin 2002, 4). However, the use of historical research in court is more based on "facts" than interpretation (Tosh 2008, 107). This may be a challenge for historians who "are far more comfortable offering interpretations than they are rendering conclusive opinions" (Newell 2004, 85). Historical research produced for the legal process has to be useful, answer specific legal interrogations, and be based on legally framed evidence for which the context and interpretation are secondary. For instance, Giselle Byrnes was commissioned to write historical research in the legal process of the Treaty of Waitangi (New Zealand). She acknowledges that "without the resources to investigate fully not just what happened but why, it becomes too easy to paint a villains and victims scenario" (1998, 18). As Alan Newell underlines, "the challenge for the historian as expert witness is to present an opinion as succinctly and with as few qualifications as possible, while maintaining the nuance and uncertainty inherent in historical inquiry" (Newell 2004, 87). He adds that historians should predicate their testimony on documentary evidence rather than generalized theory, and to strive for synthesis (Newell 2004, 95).

One challenge for historians as expert witnesses is to know how to deal with exceptions. Historians usually add exceptions to their main arguments, using expressions such as "on the one hand, on the other hand." This is problematic while working with attorneys who need clear-cut and usable historical accounts. There are two main ways to deal with exceptions. In order to present a clear argument, historians may simply "avoid to the extent possible the exceptions and qualifications that are inevitable components of historical epistemology" (Newell 2004, 96). However, silencing facts may be counter-productive, even if they go against the client's side. The opposite side – and the judge – may consider that silence on exceptions shows an unethical historical research and undermines the historian's credibility. Historians can, therefore, also provide richer interpretations. In offering both supportive and apparently unsupportive documentation to the case, historians can "alert the court to the full range of historical interpretation, while lending support to the validity of (their) argument" (Newell 2004, 96).

Conflicts of Interest

Working in the legal process implies some precautions. Historians must avoid conflicts of interest, especially when court decisions may affect their own financial interest (Tobey 1986, 27). This is why historians hired by clients to testify in court should not be paid according to the result of the case. This could raise the pressure on historians to produce/distort historical account in favor of their clients – and to their own benefit. Brian Martin therefore encourages consultants and expert witnesses to have hourly rates and not financial gain based on the outcome of the case (2002, 6). Likewise, information about the historian could be publicly available. This would show that historians do not represent other private interests (Tobey 1986, 28). As with other consultants, historians as expert witnesses must also deal with some restrictions regarding the materials they can use for their research. Historians may indeed not be allowed to decide what sources they can use. This is problematic since an incomplete access can undermine their research and credibility. It is critical to discuss the access to sources in the contract and to make it clear in any published research.

Federal and Government Historians, Public Policy, and Policymaking

Federal and Government Historians

Typology

Historians in federal and government agencies are not usually considered as working under contract. As staff members, they may have different status such as in-house historians, archivists, but also policy advisors, or policymakers. As institutional historians, they are part of the structures and systems of the agencies. The wide range of federal and government historians prevents an exhaustive presentation.[9] The guide to historical programs in the federal government provides a useful overview of the role of federal historians in the United States (SHFG 1992). In an article in *Perspectives on History*, Victoria Harden offered a clear introduction on "What Do Federal Historians Do?" (1999). Federal historians can be civil servants or temporary contractors. As civil servants in the United States, they may work for the federal government as official agency historians in the executive branch or work for Congress or the Supreme Court. In the United States, federal history positions are classified under the "*GS-170 Historian*" job classification, but many other positions – curators, archivists, librarians, and records managers – are occupied by historians without this title.[10] In addition to those historians, Harden adds historians in the private sector "who contract with some federal agencies to undertake virtually all of the above activities" (1999).

Many historians have been part of military organizations (Kohn 1997; Stensvaag 1992; Pogue and Shulman 1993). The military historical offices of the federal government include the Army, Navy, Marine Corps, Air Force, and U.S. Coast Guard (Jones 2012, 35). In the United States, the roots of the relations between historians and the federal government date back at least to the 19th century. In 1863, Maj. Gen. Henry W. Halleck – commander of the Union Army – initiated a project to collect and publish Civil War military records (Reuss 1986b, 294). Later, the employment of historians was boosted by the two world wars. As Rebecca Conard explains, World War I transformed isolated military history initiatives "into a more serious effort to document various aspects of the war as it was taking place" (2002, 149–150). After 1945, the Historical Division of the War Department was "set to writing the official history of the army in World War II" and became the Office, Chief of Military History (OCMH) in 1950 (Conard 2002, 156). This example is not unique to the United States. In an article on government historians and public policy, Alix Green demonstrates how official war histories were the foundation for the British experiment for history in government (2015).

History

Although historians in the United States have been involved in federal agencies since the late 19th century, their number only increased in the 1930s during the New Deal, and above all after World War II. In 1942, Franklin D. Roosevelt "issued an executive order mandating that all government agencies collect records and write a history of their part in the war effort" (Jones 2012, 31). Similarly, in the United Kingdom, government departments created historical sections and a program of official histories right after World War II (Beck 2006b). Although some historians worked as political advisors in the 1960s – especially in Kennedy's administration – the overall number of federal historians in the United States later decreased (Jones 2012, 33; Armitage 2014). Like for public history, the context changed in the 1970s and 1980s. For instance, Raymond Smock became the first official historian of the House of Representatives in 1983. The job crisis in the 1970s forced historians to consider non-academic fields such as government agencies.

Concerns rose among federal historians regarding the need for an acknowledgment of their research (Hewlett 1999). Federal historian Jack Holl remembers that, in the late 1970s, he "did not believe that the professional concerns of federal historians could ever be satisfied in an organization (OAH) overwhelmingly dominated by academic historians who regarded our employment as 'alternative careers'" (Holl 1999, 50). As a consequence, the Society for History in the Federal Government (SHFG) was founded in 1979 and has provided organizational strength for historians often isolated from their colleagues. Published by the SHFG, *The Federalist* (a quarterly newsletter) and *Federal History* (an annual scholarly journal) give lots of information on SHFG activities, on federal historical offices, and topics of current interest. The SHFG also provides a useful list of internship opportunities in federal history offices that public historians can apply to, a listserv on H-Net (H–FedHist), and other resources such as a *Directory of Federal Historical Offices and Activities* about the various offices in all branches of government that perform history-related work.

The Role of Historians in Federal and Government Agencies

The contemporaneous creations of the NCPH and SHFG indicate some proximity, but the existence of the two institutions also shows some specificities. Some federal historians have, as members of the NCPH, "at times felt 'out on the edge' within the organization" (Morin 2015). It is important to detail the variety of roles for historians in federal and government agencies to understand those internal debates. The role of historians in military agencies may sometimes take place way beyond their agency office. The U.S. Army has sent in historians during operations in Iraq and Somalia. Historians have been doing research in Bosnia, Haiti, Kosovo, and other hot spots. However, most of the time, the historian's activity takes place in more traditional sites.

The role of historians in federal agencies is divided into different tasks. They may collect historical records, conduct historical research, or write official history related to their agency (U.S. Office of Personnel Management 1962). For example, the Air Force Historical Research Agency is the repository for Air Force historical documents and provides research facilities for professional military education students, the faculty, visiting scholars, and the general public. As noted by the SHFG's Principles and Standards, "A primary function of federal historians is to collect historical evidence relating to the history of their agencies" (SHFG undated). Historians may also have to assist the National Archives and Records Service to identify records of historical significance for eventual deposit (SHFG undated).

Historians act as internal memories in the different agencies. This is why oral history is so important for federal historians who may want to record civil servants' memories and first accounts. As Virginia Berridge explains about British agencies, "Civil servants rarely stayed in post for long and one adviser found himself the only source of institutional memory in being able to think back to the Thatcher market reforms in health" (2008, 519–520).

Historians may also be in charge of the official history of their agency. For instance, the U.S. Office of the Historian is "responsible, under law, for the preparation and publication of the official documentary history of U.S. foreign policy in the Foreign Relations of the United States series" (U.S. Department of State undated). The top priority of Smock when he was hired as official historian of the House of Representatives was to publish a new edition of the *Biographical Directory of the United States Congress* (Smock 1995, 53). Federal work can therefore produce a very good study of political history.[11]

Historians may also participate in broader projects. For instance, the NASA history program was established in 1959, not only to understand NASA's origins and development, but also to comprehend its present situation and help illuminate possible future direction (Launius 1999, 64).[12] Historians can be involved as advisors in regular events and policies that deal with historical issues. For instance, historian Kevin Whelan was hired by the Irish government from 1995 to 1998 to work as historical advisor during the commemorations of the Great Famine (1995) and 1798 Rebellion (1998). In addition to writing the prime minister's speeches, Whelan had an active role in the design of an official understanding of the past (Cauvin 2011). In the United States, for the bicentennial of the American Revolution, Smock participated in exhibits arranged by the Library of Congress and the National Portrait Gallery, contributed to Ken Burns's PBS film on the history of Congress, and to the issuance of bicentennial postage stamps and commemorative coins (Smock 1995, 53).

In 2012, the Canadian government organized commemorations for the War of 1812. Among various events, the government presented the War of 1812 National Recognition Ceremony (see Figure 13.1) "for 48 First Nations and Métis communities with a heritage link to the War of 1812." In Figure 13.1, the delegates from the Algonquins of Pikwàkanagàn

Figure 13.1 His Excellency the Right Honourable David Johnston (right), Governor General and Commander-in-Chief of Canada, and accompanied by the Right Honourable Stephen Harper (left), Prime Minister of Canada, presented delegates from the Algonquins of Pikwàkanagàn First Nation (center) with a Commemorative War of 1812 medal and banner. In the background, Jean-Pierre Morin, staff historian for the department of Aboriginal Affairs and Northern Development Canada. Credit: MCpl Dany Veillette, Rideau Hall. Courtesy of Her Majesty The Queen in Right of Canada represented by the Office of the Secretary to the Governor General, 2012.

receive the War of 1812 Medal and Banner from His Excellency the Right Honourable David Johnston (right), Governor General and Commander-in-Chief of Canada, accompanied by the Right Honourable Stephen Harper (left), Prime Minister of Canada.[13] Staff historian for the department of Aboriginal Affairs and Northern Development Canada, Jean-Pierre Morin stands in the background. He was one of the main organizers of the ceremony and worked as facilitator between native populations and the Canadian government. His work participated in the recognition of the plurality of voices and heritages associated with the War of 1812.

Finally, historians may have to deal with day-to-day requests from politicians, officers, researchers, journalists, and broader audiences. The U.S. Office of the Historian prepares "policy-supportive historical studies for Department principals and other agencies. These studies provide essential background information, evaluate how and why policies evolved, identify precedents, and derive lessons learned" (U.S. Department of State undated). This means that historians may be at the crossroads between government agencies and public actors. It also means that historians may have to deal with non-historical topics. In her course on history and public policy, Arnita Jones explores:

> the role of historians in the work of special commissions established to aid both government and their publics understand such extraordinary event as the 9/11 attacks on the United States or NATO's failure to prevent the massacre of thousands of civilians in Srebrenica.
>
> (2011, 2012, 39–40)

Historians are increasingly employed as consultants in bodies "established to understand or address a crisis, a problem, or a watershed event" (Jones 2012, 39).[14] These non-historical topics lead to an exploration of the role of historians in public policy at large.

Publication

Being a federal or government historian has certain implications. Historians working in federal agencies are public servants, so they are bound by codes of conduct regarding their comments and statements on current government policies. Harden explains that:

> federal historians, whether civil servants or contractors, do not speak or write from a personal viewpoint when acting in their official capacities on matters that have political consequence for their agencies. Their work, whether an exhibit, a book, an article, or a web site, is subject to review and approval by agency administrators.
>
> (Harden 1999)

As historian, this may result in tensions between the duties toward the employer and the historical validity of their research. As the SHFG's professional standards explain, "federal historians have a responsibility to serve their scholarly profession and the public as well as the federal agencies for which they work." However, "they should not be expected to bias their historical interpretations to accommodate current policy considerations" (SHFG undated). In his evaluation of the ethics for federal historians, Martin Reuss listed the main contested issues. He quoted the historians' denial of access to documents, the pressure to ignore certain topics or not to publish embarrassing aspects for the agency (1986a, 13). In 1999, Reuss was even more worried in listing "external threats to federal history."

He quoted the "highly visible and patently political motives" that "contributed to the Enola Gay debacle and the elimination of the House of Representatives historical office" (Reuss 1999, 135).[15]

On the one hand, government historians usually do not have major restrictions on accessing documents, as may face consultants or external historians. On the other hand, they may well face restrictions on the publication of specific findings or assessments deemed to be "too sensitive." The SHFG's professional standards assert that historians have a "responsibility as federal employees to accept limitations on their right to publish material or to make public statements when such information has not been reviewed for classified content or for data exempt from disclosure under the Freedom of Information Act" (SHFG undated). Historians' research may not be publicly available. For instance, Harden mentions historians in the Central Intelligence Agency (CIA) whose research based on classified sources "may not be made public and subject to open review of their peers until after they have retired" (Harden 1999). Official – through the agency – publications must meet specific internal requirements. Agreement can exist for conferences, papers, and projects in which historians are allowed to present their research while acknowledging that the views of the author are not specifically those of the department or agency.

Public Policy

Public Policy in Need of Historians

While working within political institutions, historians may take part in policy not directly linked to their main field of research. As Virginia Berridge remarked in her study of British public policy, relations between history (and historians) and public policy vary according to "factors like timing and national location" (2008, 511). In some countries, links exist between historians and public policy. For example, the History and Policy network was set up in the United Kingdom in 2002 by Cambridge historians Alastair Reid and Simon Szretzer in order to connect British historians with policymakers. Voices in Britain like John Tosh have argued that the time has come for "applied history" (2006). Not far away – on the other side of the Channel – French historians had very dissimilar views. In 2005, some French historians campaigned against certain uses of history by politicians (Stevens 2010, 120). In June 2005 a collective of historians created the Committee for Vigilance with regard to the Public Uses of History. Its manifesto denounced "the increasing intervention of political authorities and the media in historical questions which tends to impose value judgments to the detriment of critical analysis" (Stevens 2010, 122–123). These two examples illustrate the constant tensions between pragmatic historians who intend to participate in the public policy process and the risk of being instrumentalized for political purposes.

In the United States, public policy was, in the 1970s, the focus of several early public history programs (Jones 2012, 29). Robert Kelley, one of the founders of the public history movement, was enthusiastic about the links between historians and public policy. In 1989, he wrote:

> from the days of Thucydides historians have written narratives of the making and implementing of public policy. This has been, in fact, what most historians have primarily set out to achieve: the preparing of reliable descriptions of great public decisions and of the efforts made to put them into effect.
>
> (Kelley 1988, 35)

Likewise, Richard Neustadt and Ernest May published *Thinking in Time: The Uses of History for Decision-Makers* that has become one of the most comprehensive argumentations in favor of the use of historical analysis in policymaking (1986).

The term policy history reflects these links between history and policymaking (Zelizer 2000; Zelizer 2005). As the *Journal of Policy History* – the leading journal in the field – stresses, policy history is concerned with the application of historical perspectives to public policy studies. The field deals with the history of the formation of public policy, the historical changes and shifts in policymaking, and the historical study of their impact. However, historians do not only help understand public policy, they can also participate and become policymakers.

Certain issues such as history education and history curriculum reforms have obvious connection with historians (Symcox 2002). Historians may also be involved in other issues such as health, immigration, crime and poverty, urban life, or public and cultural institutions (Reverby 2011; Berridge 2003, 2008; Graham 1986). In urban policy, Stephen Grable's article "Applying Urban History to City Planning: A Case Study in Atlanta" is still an important contribution for policymaking (1979). Another example comes from Australia where historians have participated in the Royal Commission into Institutional Responses to Child Sexual Abuse, in particular through the "'Find & Connect' website which is designed for people seeing records about their time in Australian orphanages, children's homes and other institutions" (Anonymous Blog Post 2014).

The links between historians and public policy stem from a need for historical context in policymaking (Mock 1991). In a 2014 article in the *Guardian*, David Armitage (author with Jo Guldi of *The History Manifesto* that encourages the public role of historians) explained – as Kelley did 40 years before – that politicians need historians in the design of informed public policy (Armitage 2014). Going into more detail, Jennifer Stevens stresses that since policymakers and politicians "are constantly dealing with the past" when they debate and make important policy decisions, they should involve historians to "consider what has been tried and failed, and what options were overlooked and why" (2015).

History in Policymaking Rather Than History for Policymakers

As consultants or advisors, historians are not limited to give historical reports for policy makers. Historians can offer much more than simple usable accounts. Historians such as Alix Green in the United Kingdom argue for a history embedded in policymaking as an alternative to history presented to policymakers (2015). Green supports the argument that historians can "help interpret policymaking by adding a richer awareness of the complex rules that may be in play in particular contexts" (2015, 30). Historians have the advantage of studying processes and not only facts, so that they can provide understanding of the policy mechanism. Understanding not only policy issues but the complex historical policymaking mechanisms is the reason why Kelley encouraged the use of the historians' understanding of the dynamics in "considering contemporary urban policy or our failings in Vietnam" (1988, 38). Historians in policymaking can help other actors to think of history "not (or not just) as content, but rather as process, as an intellectual resource – a form of expertise – that can contribute to the formation of policy" (Green 2015, 31).

Gregory Papanikos, Director of Athens Institute for Education and Research, proposes a useful classification of the historian's activities in policymaking. He asserts that policymakers can benefit from history in at least three ways: identify the (historical) roots of an issue (problem); generate and process historical data in order to understand and interpret contemporary issues; and expand the set of ideas or use old ones in order to formulate new policies (Papanikos 2006, 2).

One step of the policymaking process is the identification of a policy problem. Historians are equipped to identify trends and transition points. Historians can try to explain why "certain approaches to an issue or options for its resolution were seen as possible, others never considered" (Green 2015, 30). Historians can also bring their methodological approach to identify the duration of the problem. With respect to policymaking, it allows for a better understanding of why a policy is required, and to help predict potential outcomes (Bartholomew 2014). Papanikos quotes youth unemployment in Greece as an example of a policy problem. He asserts that an a-historical approach based on statistical analysis could date the problem to the 1980s, but that a careful historical analysis "would reveal that this problem has a very deep root" but that "it did not show up in the official statistics because the solution was emigration" (Papanikos 2006). In consequence, the historical analysis would show that the true cause has been the inherent inability of Greece's economy to offer employment to all young people since World War II (Papanikos 2006).

In a recent report based on a series of seminars organized by the Arts and Humanities Research Council (AHRC), participants discuss the "Value of History in Policymaking."[16] They discussed how historical reinterpretations of Western policy toward Russia could help understand Russia's intervention in Ukraine (Haddon et al. 2015, 7). In a 2006 article, Beck details the role played by Rohan Butler – British Foreign Office historian – in the 1951–1954 Abadan crisis.[17] Beck asserts that Butler's historical analysis "fed into, guided, and influenced on-going discussions and reviews within Whitehall by juxtaposing the lessons of history, contemporary realities, and possible new directions for both foreign policy and methods" (Beck 2006a, 545). Historians can help policymaking be more efficient by identifying the historical roots of the problem. In doing so, historians may not only be advisors but can also participate in the decision-making process.

The second practice listed by Papanikos deals with historians who "generate and process historical data in order to understand and interpret contemporary issues." One British official acknowledges that quantitative work is easier to put in a submission and is seen as stronger support for a policy position (Haddon et al. 2015, 13). Historians involved in the analysis of public policy should, according to Papanikos, be familiar with cliometrics (analysis of historical data) and performing simulations (Davis and Engerman 2003). For instance, research on the future of pandemic flu has drawn on data from the 1918 flu epidemic and has used historical evidence in this way (Berridge 2008, 523–524).

The third way in which historians can participate in policymaking is by providing historical solutions for present policies. In 1988, Kelley was convinced that "we can develop an ordered, informed way of looking at, say, the American Revolution which we can also, at later points in the narrative, apply to subsequent crises and controversies" (1988, 39). According to Ruth Rennie's article on history and policymaking, it seems that French and English governments have established history offices within their individual ministries in order to investigate the historical analogy of old ideas to propose ideas of tackling a contemporary policy issue (1998). However, Papanikos warns that "policy-makers should be very careful when they attempt to present old (historical) ideas as new ones" (2006). Indeed, lessons from the past are attractive and powerful resources for policymakers, but the dangers – such as misuses, distortion, and instrumentalization – are at least as high as the possible benefits (Graham 1983; Berger 2007). Papanikos explains that what he calls "historical transplanting," in other words the lessons from the past, should respect two basic principles: the principle of historical analogy and the principle of spatial analogy. What worked in the past may not work in the present. Likewise, what worked in some countries may not work in others. The historical contextualization of the issue is critical. This is why Papanikos asserts that historians in public policy should help "avoid the mistake of violating the principles of historical and spatial analogy" (2006).

To conclude, historians who intend to become consultants should be prepared for the specific practices of their job. Public history students – especially if public funding keeps declining – should be prepared to consider working with clients and private actors. Some courses present the history of public policy. Others focus on the links between history and policymaking. In order to prepare historians to work as consultants, experts, or advisors, public history programs could offer training in business, administration, and consulting practices. Digital media fluency (HTML, publishing software, photo and video editing software) and communication tools (collaborative platforms, video conference tools) are more and more important to present the research in a clear and creative way (Shine 2012).

An interesting recent example is Robert Pomeroy's proposal for a course that links historical methodology to the variety of business procedures (2015). Pomeroy presents different ways to include the business "functional activities" – accounting, quantitative analysis, information management, marketing, and communications – into history training. In the program, he explains that a basic grasp of financial accounting (balance sheets, income and cash flow statements, audit, and other financial information), quantitative analysis (statistical theories, sampling, probability, ratio analysis, and cost–benefit analysis) is essential for students.[18]

In addition to practices, training should deal with ethics too. It is necessary that students face the difficult task of designing contracts to work for clients. Focus on ethics can also create bridges between traditional and public history courses. Analyzing the uses and misuses of history is an activity that every historian can share. The Major in Ethics, History, & Public Policy at Carnegie Mellon University offers an example. The program focuses "on the historical understanding of how modern-day problems have evolved, and the importance of developing clear criteria for ethical decision-making." The objective is to "apply the knowledge and skills ... to a contemporary policy problem" such as the effects of economic crises, climate change, or the health system (Carnegie Mellon University undated).

Since public history programs may not provide courses for every single practice, other projects and initiatives may be considered. Programs may establish good relationships with historical policy institutions through internships and other employment (Jones 2012, 29).[19] It is highly beneficial for historians who wish to pursue a career as consultants, experts, or advisors, to participate – as volunteers, interns, or fellows – in federal and/or for-profit companies. Independent consulting historians often work by themselves, so it is vital for them to build strong networks of colleagues, partners, and possible clients. Some historians may want to enter larger teams that pool different expertise. The Australian Council of Professional Historians Associations published in 2008 a Directory of Consultant Historians and Researchers with useful details on how to present oneself, especially regarding professional experience, skills and services offered, and research interests.

Regarding public history as a field, it could be useful to develop initiatives such as the AHRC seminars that have gathered both academics and policy officers. Institutes or units such as the History and Policy network in the UK could facilitate the interaction between history, public policy, the legal process, and other fields of historical uses.[20] The History and Policy website provides numerous resources such as policy papers, workshops, seminars, training – especially about Impact Skills for Historians, and information about consultation.

Notes

1 Incorporated company means "that each of the founders invested the same amount of money into the corporation and received an equal number of shares in return" (Cantelon 2006, 388).

2 See Cantelon for an overview of the variety of activities (2006).

3 Texaco; Ford Motor Company; Sears Roebuck; New York Life Insurance; Eli Lilly; Procter & Gamble; Coca-Cola; and Bank of America established archives during the 1940s and 1950s (Conard 2002, 162).

4 Although most of them are in North America, some consulting companies also emerged in Europe in the 1980s. For instance, Public Histoire was created in France in 1983 by Felix Torres, www.public-histoire.com/Public-Histoire (accessed May 3, 2015).

5 The1981 summer issue of *The Public Historian* was devoted to Business and History.

6 Public injustice may be very hard to defined, so the NCPH Code of Ethics adds that: "In such instances, a public historian must verify the facts and issues of the circumstance and, when practicable, make every reasonable effort to obtain separate opinions from other qualified professionals employed by the client or employer and every reasonable effort to obtain reconsideration from the client or employer" (NCPH 2007).

7 Researchers working for federal agencies "are similarly bound by the obligation to be free from financial interest in projects they are evaluating" (Tobey 1986, 22).

8 Federal Rules of Evidence, Article 701–706, see Cornell Legal Information Institute, www.law.cornell.edu/rules/fre/rule_701 (accessed May 4, 2015).

9 Despite their number, federal historians working in the National Park Service and in the different federal museums and cultural institutions will not be explored in this chapter.

10 See the interviews of federal historians: John Fox, historian, Federal Bureau of Investigation; Jeffrey G. Barlow, historian, U.S. Naval History and Heritage Command; Robert S. Arrighi, archivist/historian, NASA's Glenn Research Center; Richard Baker, Senate Historian, at http://shfg.org/shfg/programs/interviews/ (accessed May 10, 2015).

11 Victoria Harden quotes Donald Ritchie (Senate Historical Office) – Donald A. Ritchie, *Press Gallery: Congress and the Washington Correspondents* (Cambridge, MA: Harvard University Press, 1991) (Harden 1999).

12 The NASA History Program Office now offers a list of internships, historical references and collections, a listserv, and the list of different centers and historical offices. See also the various resources offered by NASA's historical program website, www.nasa.gov/hqpao/History/hist (accessed September 7, 2015). Historians can contact the U.S. Army's Center of Military History (CMH), consult the Army History journal, or access the different historical offices for more information.

13 These honorary titles were requested by the Canadian government to get permission to use the image.

14 The 9/11 Commission was established in November 2002 to investigate the facts and circumstances relating to the events of September 11, 2001 (Jones 2012, 40).

15 For the Enola Gay controversy, see Chapter 11.

16 The Making History Work initiative comprised a series of roundtable discussions organized by the Arts and Humanities Research Council's (AHRC's) Care for the Future: Thinking Forward Through the Past and Translating Cultures research themes and the Institute for Government. Arts & Humanities Research Council (AHRC), *Care for the Future: Thinking Forward Through the Past*, AHRC website, www.ahrc.ac.uk/research/fundedthemesandprogrammes/themes/careforthefuture/ (accessed September 7, 2015).

17 The crisis took place when Iran nationalized the assets of the Anglo-Iranian Oil Company.

18 Pomeroy also provides a very useful short bibliography on business and management, accounting and auditing, and quantitative literacy for such a course.

19 A good example is the Woodrow Wilson International Center for Scholars that connects scholars with policymakers through fellowships. See www.wilsoncenter.org/about-us (accessed May 5, 2015).

20 Another successful example is the Cambridge-based Centre for Science and Policy (CSAP). Centre for Science and Policy, www.csap.cam.ac.uk/about/ (accessed May 7, 2015).

Bibliography

Adamson, Michael R. "What it's Worth: Valuing and Pricing the Work of Historical Consultants." OAH and NCPH meeting, Milwaukee, April 19, 2012, http://ncph.org/cms/wp-content/uploads/Adamson.pdf (accessed May 13, 2015).

American Historical Association (AHA). "Historians as Consultants and Contractors." Undated, www.historians.org/jobs-and-professional-development/career-resources/careers-for-students-of-history/historians-as-consultants-and-contractors (accessed September 5, 2015).

Anderson, Pete. "Resources for the Consulting Historian." *History Applied*, April 22, 2013, www.historyapplied.com/2013/04/resources-for-consulting-historian.html (accessed September 10, 2015).

Anonymous Blog Post. "Big Questions in History: Historians and Public Policy." *Stumbling Through the Past*, July 16, 2014, https://stumblingpast.wordpress.com/2014/07/16/big-questions-historians-and-public-policy/ (accessed September 7, 2015).

Armitage, David. "Why Politicians Need Historians." *Guardian*, October 7, 2014.

Australian Council of Professional Historians. *Code of Ethics and Professional Standards for Professional Historians in Australia*, 2006, www.historians.org.au/acpha/bm~doc/code-2.pdf (accessed September 3, 2015).

Bartholomew, Richard. "Policy Impact Skills for Historians: Introduction to Public Policy Engagement." *History and Policy, Podcast. Public Policy Engagement Practice and Actors*, 2014, https://soundcloud.com/history-policy/richard-bartholomew-1/s-uNu7T?in=history-policy/sets/policy-impact-skills-for-2#t=3:57 (accessed September 5, 2015).

Beck, Peter. "The Lessons of Abadan and Suez for British Foreign Policymakers in the 1960s." *The Historical Journal*, 49/2 (2006a): 525–547.

Beck, Peter. *Using History, Making British Policy: The Treasury and the Foreign Office, 1950–76*, Basingstoke: Palgrave Macmillan, 2006b.

Berger, Stefan. "History and National Identity: Why They Should Remain Divorced." *History and Policy* (December 1, 2007), www.historyandpolicy.org/papers/policy-paper-66.html (accessed September 5, 2015).

Berridge, Virginia. "Queen Victoria's Cannabis Use: Or, How History Does and Does Not Get Used in Drug Policy Making." *Addiction Research and Theory*, 11/4 (August 2003): 213–215.

Berridge, Virginia. "History Matters? History's Role in Health Policy Making." *Medical History*, 52/03 (May 2008): 311–326.

Bookspan, Shelley. "Something Ventured, Many Things Gained: Reflections on Being a Historian-Entrepreneur." *The Public Historian*, 28 (Winter 2006): 67–74.

Brodsky, Stanley L. *The Expert Witness: More Maxims and Guidelines for Testifying in Court*, Washington, DC: American Psychological Association, 1999.

Byrnes, Giselle M. "Jackals of the Crown? Historians and the Treaty Claims Process in New Zealand." *The Public Historian*, 20/2 (Spring 1998): 9–23.

Cantelon, Philip L. "As a Business: Hired, Not Bought." In *Public History: Essays from the Field*, edited by James B. Gardner and Peter S. LaPaglia, Malabar: Krieger Publishing Company, 2006, 385–396.

Carnegie Mellon University. "The Major in Ethics, History, & Public Policy." Undated, www.cmu.edu/hss/ehpp/ (accessed September 7, 2015).

Cauvin, Thomas. "Quando è in gioco la Public History: musei, storici e riconciliazione politica nella Repubblica d'Irlanda." *Memoria e Ricerca*, 37 (2011): 53–71. English translation: www.fondazionecasadoriani.it/modules.php?name=MR&op=body&id=550 (accessed May 3, 2015).

Clark, Christopher S. "Mind in the Marketplace (Part 4): All about Money." *Public History Commons*, September 25, 2012, http://publichistorycommons.org/mind-in-the-marketplace-part-4-all-about-money/ (accessed February 2, 2015).

Cole, Elizabeth A. *Teaching the Violent Past: History Education and Reconciliation*, Lanham: Rowman & Littlefield, 2007.

Colten, Craig E. "The Historian's Responsibility in Litigation Support." *The Public Historian*, 28/1 (Winter 2006): 111–115.

Conard, Rebecca. *Benjamin Shambaugh and the Intellectual Foundations of Public History*, Iowa City: University of Iowa Press, 2002.

Conard, Rebecca. "The Pragmatic Roots of Public History Education in the United States." *The Public Historian*, 37/1 (February 2015): 105–120.

Davis, Lance and Engerman, Stanley. "History Lessons: Sanctions: Neither War nor Peace." *Journal of Economic Perspectives*, 17/2 (Spring 2003): 187–197.

Delafontaine, Ramses. *Historians as Expert Judicial Witnesses in Tobacco Litigation: A Controversial Legal Practice*, New York: Springer, 2015.

Dumoulin, Olivier. *Le rôle social de l'historien: de la chaire au prétoire*, Paris: Albin Michel, 2003.

Golsan, Richard. *Memory and Justice on Trial: The Papon Affair*, New York: Routledge, 2000.

Grable, Stephen W. "Applying Urban History to City Planning: A Case Study in Atlanta." *The Public Historian*, 1/4 (Summer 1979): 45–59.

Graham, Hugh Davis. "The Stunted Career of Policy History: A Critique and an Agenda." *The Public Historian*, 15/2 (Spring 1993): 15–37.

Graham, Otis L. Jr. "The Uses and Misuses of History: Roles in Policymaking." *The Public Historian*, 5 (Spring 1983): 5–19.

Graham, Otis L. Jr. "Uses and Misuses of History in the Debate over Immigration Reform." *The Public Historian* (Spring 1986): 41–64.

Green, Alix. "History as Expertise and the Influence of Political Culture on Advice for Policy Since Fulton." *Contemporary British History*, 29/1 (2015): 27–50.

Haddon, Catherine, Devanny, Joe, Forsdick, Charles, and Thompson, Andrew. *What Is the Value of History in Policymaking?* London: Institute for Government, January 2015, www.instituteforgovern ment.org.uk/publications/what-value-history-policymaking (accessed May 1, 2015).

Harden, Victoria A. "What Do Federal Historians Do?" *Perspectives on History* (May 1999), www. historians.org/publications-and-directories/perspectives-on-history/may-1999/what-do-federal-historians-do (accessed May 2, 2015).

Hewlett, Richard G. "The Washington Scene, 1977–1981." *The Public Historian*, 21/3 (Summer 1999): 39–42.

Holl, Jack M. "Getting on Track: Coupling the Society for History in the Federal Government to the Public History Train." *The Public Historian*, 21/3 (Summer 1999): 43–55.

Jellison, Katherine. "History in the Courtroom: The Sears Case in Perspective." *The Public Historian*, 9/4 (Autumn 1987): 9–19.

Jones, Arnita A. "History and Public Policy: Syllabus." 2011, www.american.edu/cas/history/pdf/ upload/History-and-Public-Policy.pdf (accessed September 7, 2015).

Jones, Arnita A. "The Promise of Policy History in the Public History Curriculum." *Federal History Journal*, 4 (2012): 28–42, http://shfg.org/shfg/wp-content/uploads/2012/12/3-Jones-final.pdf (accessed May 3, 2015).

Jones, Arnita A. and Rasmussen, Wayne D. "Wayne Rasmussen and the Development of Policy History at the United States Department of Agriculture." *The Public Historian*, 14 (Winter 1992): 11–29.

Jones, Harriet, Ostberg, Kjell, and Randeraad, Nico, eds. *Contemporary History on Trial: Europe Since 1989 and the Role of the Expert Historian*, Manchester: Manchester University Press, 2007.

Karamanski, Theodore J., ed. *Ethics and Public History: An Anthology*, Malabar: Robert E. Krieger Publishing Company, 1990.

Karamanski, Theodore J. "Reflections on Ethics and the Historical Profession." *The Public Historian*, 21/3 (Summer 1999): 127–133.

Kelley, Robert. "The Idea of Policy History." *The Public Historian*, 10/1 (Winter 1988): 35–39.

Kohn, Richard H. "The Practice of Military History in the U.S. Government: The Department of Defense." *The Journal of Military History*, 61/1 (January 1997): 121–147.

Kousser, J. Morgan. "Are Expert Witnesses Whores? Reflections on Objectivity in Scholarship and Expert Witnessing." *The Public Historian*, 6/1 (Winter 1984): 5–19.

Launius, Roger D. "NASA History and the Challenge of Keeping the Contemporary Past." *The Public Historian*, 21/3 (Summer 1999): 63–81.

Lopata, Roy H. "Ethics in Public History: Clio meets Ulasewicz." In *Ethics and Public History: An Anthology*, edited by Theodore J. Karamanski, Malabar: Robert E. Krieger Publishing Company, 1990, 25–34.

Martin, Brian. "Working with Lawyers: A Historian's Perspective." *The Organization of American Historians' Newsletter* (May 2002).

Mock, David B. *History and Public Policy*, Malabar: Krieger Publishing Company, 1991.

Mooney, Philip F. "The Practice of History in Corporate America: Business Archives in the United States." In *Public History: An Introduction*, edited by Barbara J. Howe and Emory L. Kamp, Malabar: Krieger Publishing Company, 1986, 427–439.

Morin, Jean-Pierre. "Government Historians and the NCPH." *Public History Commons*, May 22, 2015, http://publichistorycommons.org/government-historians-and-ncph/#sthash.1EURoDgI.dpuf (accessed June 1, 2015).

National Council on Public History. *Code of Ethics and Professional Conduct*, 2007, http://ncph.org/cms/about/bylaws-and-ethics/#Code%20of%20Ethics%20&%20Prof%20Conduct (accessed May 4, 2015).

National Council on Public History. "Working Group: Consultants." 2009, http://ncph.org/cms/wp-content/uploads/2009/11/Consultants-compilation3.pdf (accessed September 3, 2015).

National Council on Public History. "Forum on Consulting." *Public History News*, 30/4 (September 2010), http://ncph.org/cms/wp-content/uploads/2010/09/2010-September-Newsletter-Compressed.pdf (accessed September 13, 2015).

Neuenschwander, John. "Historians as Expert Witnesses: The View from the Bench." *The Organization of American Historians' Newsletter* (August 2002).

Neustadt, Richard E. and May, Ernest R. *Thinking in Time: The Uses of History for Decision-Makers*, New York: The Free Press, 1986.

Newell, Alan S. "Environmental Historian as Expert Witness: A Practical Evil." In *Public History and the Environment*, edited by Martin V. Melosi and Philip V. Scarpino, Malabar: Krieger Publishing, 2004, 85–105.

Newell, Alan S. "Personal and Professional Issues in Private Consulting." *The Public Historian*, 28/1 (Winter 2006): 107–110.

O'Donnell, Terence. "Pitfalls Along the Path of Public History." In *Presenting the Past: Essays on History and the Public*, edited by Susan Porter Benson, Stephen Brier, and Roy Rosenzweig, Philadelphia: Temple University Press, 1986, 239–244

Overbeck, Ruth Ann. "History as a Business." In *Public History: An Introduction*, edited by Barbara J. Howe and Emory L. Kamp, Malabar: Krieger Publishing Company, 1986, 440–454.

Page, Donald. "Ethics and the Publication of Commissioned History." In *Ethics and Public History: An Anthology*, edited by Theodore J. Karamanski, Malabar: Robert E. Krieger Publishing Company, 1990, 65–71.

Papanikos, Gregory T. "The Use of History as a Tool of Policy-Making." Opening Speech at the 4th International Conference on History, Athens, December 28–31, 2006, www.atiner.gr/docs/Paper25_History.doc (accessed May 2, 2015).

Petrovic, Vladimir. *Historians as Expert Witnesses in the Age of Extremes*, Budapest: Central European University, 2009, www.etd.ceu.hu/2009/hphpev01.pdf (accessed May 1, 2015).

Pogue, Forest C. and Shulman, Holly C. "Forrest C. Pogue and the Birth of Public History in the Army." *The Public Historian*, 15/1 (Winter 1993): 27–46.

Pomeroy, Robert. "Proposing a Business and History Program." *Public History Commons*, March 30, 2015, http://publichistorycommons.org/author/robert-pomeroy/ (accessed May 14, 2015).

Professional Historians' Association of New Zealand/Aotearoa. "Code of Practice." 2008, www.phanza.org.nz/content/code-practice (accessed September 9, 2015).

Professional Historians Australia. "Scale of Fees Recommended for the Engagement of Accredited Professional Historians in Australia." 2014, www.historians.org.au/acpha/bm~doc/feescale-2014-15.pdf (accessed September 3, 2015).

Quivik, Frederick. "Of Tailings, Superfund Litigation, and Historians as Experts: U.S. v. Asarco, et al. (The Bunker Hill Case in Idaho)." *The Public Historian*, 26/1 (Winter 2004): 81–104.

Ray, Arthur J. *Telling it to the Judge: Taking Native History to Court*, Montreal and Kingston: McGill-Queen's University Press, 2011.

Rennie, Ruth. "History and Policy-Making." *International Social Science Journal*, 50/156 (June 1998): 289–301.

Reuss, Martin. "Federal Historians: Ethics and Responsibility in the Bureaucracy." *The Public Historian*, 8/1 (Winter 1986a): 13–20.

Reuss, Martin. "Public History in the Federal Government." In *Public History: An Introduction*, edited by Barbara J. Howe and Emory L. Kamp, Malabar: Krieger Publishing Company, 1986b, 293–309.

Reuss, Martin. "Government and Professional Ethics: The Case of Federal Historians." *The Public Historian*, 21/3 (Summer 1999): 135–142.

Reverby, Susan M. "'Normal Exposure and Inoculation Syphilis: A PHS Tuskegee Doctor in Guatemala, 1946–1948." *Journal of Policy History*, 23/1 (2011): 6–28.

Rigney, Ann. "Introduction: Values, Responsibilities, History." In *Historians and Social Values*, edited by Ann Rigney and Joep Leerssen, Amsterdam: Amsterdam University Press, 2000, 7–18.

Ryant, Carl. "The Public Historian and Business History: A Question of Ethics." *The Public Historian*, 8/1 (Winter 1986): 31–38.

Shine, Greg. "Measuring Up: What Employers Look for in Historical Consultants." *Public History Commons*, December 14, 2012, http://publichistorycommons.org/measuring-up-part-2/#more-1737 (accessed May 21, 2015).

Smock, Raymond W. "Public History at the US House of Representatives." *The Public Historian*, 17/2 (Spring 1995): 49–57.

Society for History in the Federal Government (SHFG). "Principles and Standards for Federal Historical Programs." Undated, http://shfg.org/shfg/programs/professional-standards/ (accessed May 3, 2015).

Society for History in the Federal Government (SHFG). *Historical Programs in the Federal Government: A Guide*, Washington, DC, 1992, http://shfg.org/shfg/publications/directory-of-history-offices/ (accessed May 4, 2015).

Stensvaag, James T. "Searching for Congruence: Historians and Policymakers in the U.S. Army." *The Public Historian*, 14 (Winter 1992): 55–70.

Stevens, Jennifer. "Public History and Policy: A Synergy." *Public History Commons*, June 8, 2015, http://publichistorycommons.org/public-history-and-policy-a-synergy/ (accessed May 5, 2015).

Stevens, Mary. "Public Policy and the Public Historian: The Changing Place of Historians in Public Life in France and the UK." *The Public Historian*, 32/3 (Summer 2010): 120–138.

Stiller, Jesse. "Federal History Programs: Ensuring the Future." *The Public Historian*, 21/3 (Summer 1999): 83–89.

Symcox, Linda. *Whose History? The Struggle for National Standards in American Classrooms*, New York: Teachers College Press, 2002.

Tobey, Ronald C. "The Public Historian as Advocate: Is Special Attention to Professional Ethics Necessary?" *The Public Historian*, 8/1 (Winter 1986): 21–30.

Tosh, John. "In Defence of Applied History: The History and Policy Website." *History and Policy* (2006), www.historyandpolicy.org/papers/policy-paper-37.html (accessed May 13, 2015).

Tosh, John. *Why History Matters*, New York: Palgrave Macmillan, 2008.

Trask, David F. "Does Official History Have a Future?" *The Public Historian*, 11/2 (Spring 1989): 47–52.

Tyrrell, Ian. *Historians in Public: The Practice of American History, 1890–1970*, Chicago: University of Chicago Press, 2005.

U.S. Department of State. "About the Office of the Historian." Undated, https://history.state.gov/about (accessed September 9, 2015).

U.S. Office of Personnel Management. "Position Classification Standard for History Series, GS-0170."

1962, www.opm.gov/policy-data-oversight/classification-qualifications/classifying-general-schedule-positions/standards/0100/gs0170.pdf (accessed May 13, 2015).

Warren-Findley, Jannelle. "Contract Historians and Consultants." In *Public History: Essays from the Field*, edited by James B. Gardner and Peter S. LaPaglia, Malabar: Krieger Publishing Company, 2006, 75–86.

Wijffels, Alain. *History in Court: Historical Expertise and Methods in a Forensic Context*, Leiden: Ius Deco, 2001.

Young, Morgen. "Finding a Niche as a Public History Consultant: Advice from the Northwest History Network." *Public History Commons*, July 13, 2012, http://publichistorycommons.org/finding-a-niche-as-a-public-history-consultant/ (accessed May 13, 2015).

Zelizer, Julian E. "Clio's Lost Tribe: Public Policy History Since 1978." *Journal of Policy History*, 12/3 (2000): 369–394.

Zelizer, Julian E., ed. *New Directions in Policy History*, University Park: Pennsylvania State University Press, 2005.

Index

Page numbers in *italic* refer to figures.

Emmert, Thomas 244
emotions: artifacts and 40; collections 102; historians and 217–19, *218*; introduction 15–16; oral history 91, 95; participatory 143; radio programming 164, 167, 169; remembering slavery 156–7; writing skills 116–18
empowerment *see* social empowerment
encoding *see* text encoding
English National Trust 60
entertainment/reality TV 169–70
entrepreneurship and corporate historians 251–2
environments *see* immersive environments
ethics 21, 29, 43, 48, 251; *see also* Code of Ethics
Ethics and Public History (Karamanski) 230
ethnic minorities: civic engagement 241; collections 72, 78; exhibitions of 141; historic preservation and 63; interpretation 221; introduction 18; mainstream history 239; oral history 91; public history of 164; user profiles 37
European Historical Primary Sources (EHPS) 45
European University Institute (Italy) 45
everyday life history 97, *97–8*
everyday suffering 239–41
examination process 31–3
exhibit/exhibition: for children 144–5, 149, 152, 156; design and art 150, 154; ethnic minorities 141; public and exhibition design 152–4, *153*
exhibition strategy 151
Exhibit Labels (Serrell) 155
Experience Music Project 157
expert witness role 256–8

Facing History and Ourselves 244
Fagniez, Gustave 4
Falk, Candace 128
family history 1, 96, 98–9
Farmer-Paellmann, Deadria 243
fascist material culture 222
federal and government historians 259–63, *261*
Federal Writers' Project 90–1
fiction and public history 108–10, 119–20
Filene, Benjamin 142
film and documentary history 164–5
Finchum, Tanya 90
Firestone Farm 190
first-person interpretation 191–2, 195, 217
Flanders Field Museum (Belgium) 153
Fleming, McClung 40
Flickr Commons project 180
folklife 91
Foner, Eric 236
food 97, *97–8*, 170

Foote, Shelby 166
Ford, Henry 58–9, 189
Foster, Meg 178–9
Foundation Center 112
France 10, 14, 18, 170, 256
Frears, Stephen 165
Freeman, Michael 166
French National Library 44
Frisch, Michael 14, 216
Frischer, Bernard 197
fundraising and public history 111–12

games *see* video games and history
game shows 169
Gardner, Jim 14, 16, 216, 225
Gay, Enola 220
Genealogical Society of Utah 96
genealogy 96, 100
Geographic Information Systems (GIS) 42
George Mason University's History News Network 118
Germany 2, 200, 222–4, *223*
Getty Research Institute 234
Gilden Seavey, Nina 166
Gilliland, Anne 33
Glassberg, David 16, 56, 167, 217
GLBT Historical Society 238
Google Books 127
Gordon, Tammy 141
government historians *see* federal and government historians
Grandin, Greg 244
grant applications 111–12
graphic novels writing 121–2
grassroots activism 58–61, *59*
Green, Alix 11, 264
Greenfield Village 189
Grele, Ronald 2, 89
Gross, Jan 243
GTMO in MSP (Minneapolis-Saint Paul) 240
Guantánamo Public Memory Project (GPMP) 152–3, *153*, 240
Guide to the Study of Documentary Film (Freeman) 166

Halbwachs, Maurice 15
Haley, Alex 96
Halleck, Henry W. 6
Harden, Victoria 241
Harding, Samuel B. 5–6
Harper, Stephen 262
Harris, Donna 62
Hayden, Dolores 79
Hayward, Claire 122
Healing Through Remembering (HTR) 148, 245
Heppler, Jason 177